The New
CAMBRIDGE
English Course

TEACHER

2

MICHAEL SWAN
CATHERINE WALTER

CAMBRIDGE
UNIVERSITY PRESS

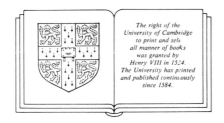

The right of the University of Cambridge to print and sell all manner of books was granted by Henry VIII in 1524. The University has printed and published continuously since 1584.

Published by the Press Syndicate of the University of Cambridge
The Pitt Building, Trumpington Street, Cambridge CB2 1RP
40 West 20th Street, New York, NY 10011–4211, USA
10 Stamford Road, Oakleigh, Victoria 3166, Australia

© Michael Swan and Catherine Walter 1990

First published 1990
Third printing 1992

Designed by Banks and Miles, London
Cover design by Michael Peters & Partners Limited, London
Typeset by Wyvern Typesetting, Bristol
Printed and bound by Mateu Cromo Artes Gráficas, S.A., Madrid

ISBN 0 521 37666 1 Teacher's Book 2

ISBN 0 521 37638 6 Student's Book 2

Student's Book 2 split edition:
ISBN 0 521 37643 2 Student's Book 2A
ISBN 0 521 37644 0 Student's Book 2B

ISBN 0 521 37650 5 Practice Book 2

Practice Book 2 split edition:
ISBN 0 521 37655 6 Practice Book 2A
ISBN 0 521 37656 4 Practice Book 2B

ISBN 0 521 37662 9 Practice Book 2 with Key

ISBN 0 521 37670 X Test Book 2

ISBN 0 521 37503 7 Class Cassette Set 2

ISBN 0 521 37507 X Student's Cassette Set 2

Student's Cassettes 2 split edition:
ISBN 0 521 38224 6 Student's Cassette 2A
ISBN 0 521 38225 4 Student's Cassette 2B

Authors' acknowledgements

We are grateful to all the people who have helped us with this book. Our thanks to:
- The many people whose ideas have influenced our work, including all the colleagues and students from whom we have learnt.
- Those institutions and teachers who were kind enough to comment on their use of *The Cambridge English Course*, and whose suggestions have done so much to shape this new version.
- The Cambridge University Press representatives and agents, for their valuable work in transmitting feedback from users of the original course.
- The people who agreed to talk within range of our microphones: Alwyn Anchors, Kara Anchors, Patrisha Anchors, Gladys Blissett, Ken Blissett, Dai Colven, Steve Dixon, Debra Freechild, Joanne Haycox, Lawrence Jones, Ellen Lessner, Marilyn Norvell, Ted Norvell, Rita Peake, Daniel Scharfe, Adele Stone, Richard Stone, Rufus Stone, Diana Thompson, June Walmsley, Mark Walter Swan, Adrian Webber, Susan Webber and Celia Wilson.
- Steve Hall of Bell Voice Recordings, and Jonathan Dykes and Robert Campbell of International House, Barcelona, and all the singers and musicians: for doing a wonderful job on the songs.
- Christine Lindop and Dominic Fisher, for providing a most valuable selection of additional reading material for the Practice Book.
- Paul Burlet, Catherine Favre, Tom Gaetjen, Desmond Nicholson of Cambridge University Press Spain, and Roy Rodwell of GEC-Marconi Limited, for their invaluable help with research.
- Peter Taylor of Taylor Riley Productions Limited, Peter and Diana Thompson and Andy Tayler of Studio AVP, and all the actors and actresses: they made recording sessions seem easy and created an excellent end product.
- Susan Sheppard, Sally Palmer-Smith, Marjorie Pereira, and Denise Quinton of Banks and Miles, for their creativity, skill and hard work in the design of the printed components of the course; and all the artists for their talent and their willingness to work to an exacting brief.
- Val Mercer, Lindsey Cunningham and Neil Howe of Michael Peters & Partners Limited for their excellent cover design.
- Eric Linsell and his colleagues at Progress Colour Limited, and all the staff at Wyvern Typesetting, for their care and attention to detail.
- Gill Clack Annie Cornford and Derek Mitchell for their careful and professional help with production.
- Cathy Hall of Cambridge University Press, for her dedication, skill and intelligence as our desk editor for the Student's Book.
- Mark Walter Swan, Helen Walter Swan, Inge Bullock, June Walmsley and Barbara Broad for their readiness to be of help at all stages of the project.
- Adrian du Plessis, Colin Hayes and Peter Donovan of Cambridge University Press, whose confidence and support have made the author-publisher relationship so unproblematic.
- And finally Desmond O'Sullivan of ELT Publishing Services: His skills in dealing with people and with print, as well as his devotion, patience, stamina and unfailing good humour, have made this course possible.

Contents

Authors' acknowledgements II

Map of Book 2 VI

Introduction: The nature and purpose of the course VIII

            The organisation of the course VIII

            Basic principles VIII

            Using the course IX

Lesson 1   May I introduce myself? 8

Lesson 2   Who's who? 10

Lesson 3   My mornings usually start fairly late 12

Lesson 4   How people live 14

Lesson 5   There's a strange light in the sky 16

Lesson 6   Things are changing 18

Summary A 20

Revision A 22

Test A 24

Lesson 7   A true story 26

Lesson 8   I was getting ready to come home 28

Lesson 9   People are different 30

Lesson 10 Things are different 32

Lesson 11 Stuff for cleaning windows 34

Lesson 12 I haven't got anything to wear 36

Summary B 38

Revision B 40

Test B 42

Lesson 13 Have you ever . . ? 44

Lesson 14 Things have changed 46

Lesson 15 What do you say when you . . . ? 48

Lesson 16 Here is the news 50

Lesson 17 USA holiday 52

Lesson 18 Knife-thrower's assistant wanted 54

Summary C 56

Revision C 58

Test C 60

Lesson 19 Their children will have blue eyes 62

Lesson 20 A matter of life and death 64

Lesson 21 If you see a black cat, ... 66

Lesson 22 We don't get on well 68

Lesson 23 If I were you, ... 70

Lesson 24 How about Thursday? 72

Summary D 74

Revision D 76

Test D 78

Lesson 25 From tree to paper 80

Lesson 26 Who? What? Where? 82

Lesson 27 Probability 84

Lesson 28 Somebody with blue eyes 86

Lesson 29 Things 88

Lesson 30 Self and others 90

Summary E 92

Revision E 94

Test E 96

Lesson 31 Before and after 98

Lesson 32 I hadn't seen her for a long time 100

Lesson 33 All right, I suppose so 102

Lesson 34 If he had been bad at maths, ... 104

Lesson 35 Travel 106

Lesson 36 Shall I open it for you? 108

Summary F 110

Revision F 112

Test F 114

Vocabulary index 116

Additional material 124

Tapescripts 127

Index (structures, notions, functions and situations) 130

Acknowledgements 135

Phonetic symbols; Irregular verbs 136

Map of Book 2

	Grammar	Phonology
	Students learn or revise these grammar points	**Students work on these aspects of pronunciation**
1 to 6	*Be*, *can* and *have got*; Simple Present and Present Progressive; comparison of adjectives; frequency adverbs and adverbials; word order (position of adverbs); structures with question-word as subject and object; linking words and expressions.	Polite intonation; strong, weak and contracted pronunciations; decoding rapid speech; /iː/ and /ɪ/; pronunciations of the letter *i*.
7 to 12	*Have got*; *do* as pro-verb; *can*; *could*; *had better*; *will*/*'ll* in offers and agreement; *shall* in offers; *should*; *would*; Simple Past and Past Progressive; irregular verbs; infinitives with and without *to*; comparison of adjectives; comparative structures; quantifiers; possessive pronouns; *when*- and *while*-clauses; *so*/*neither do I* etc.; ellipsis in speech.	Perceiving and pronouncing final consonants; pronunciations of *-ed*; decoding rapid speech; rhythm and stress; /eɪ/ and /e/; spellings of /eɪ/; pronunciations of the letter *a*; other spelling/pronunciation correspondences.
13 to 18	*Can* and *be able*; *may*; *must*; *will*; *used to*; Present Perfect Simple and Progressive; Present Perfect and Simple Past; Present Perfect and Present; non-progressive *be*, *know* and *have* in Present Perfect; *ever* and *just* with Present Perfect; *since* and *for*; quantifiers.	Linking; pronunciations of the letter *e* in stressed and unstressed prefixes; /ə/ in unstressed syllables; voiced and unvoiced *th* (/ð/ and /θ/).
19 to 24	*May*; *be able*; *should*; *have (got) to*; *will*; *would*; Present Progressive; future reference (*will*, *going to* and Present Progressive); reported statements and questions; infinitive after adjective; *if*-clauses (open and hypothetical); *If I were you . . .* ; *when*-clauses; *if* and *when*; punctuation of complex sentences; verbs with adverb particles; time prepositions; end-position of prepositions; verb + object + infinitive; demonstratives.	Decoding rapid speech; signalling a question by intonation; linking; stress and rhythm; developing fluency and confidence; consonant clusters; conversational pronunciation of *going to*, *want to* and *got to*; /əʊ/; 'dark *l*'; /ɪ/; /ɜː/, /eə/ and /ɪə/; spellings of /ɜː/.
25 to 30	*Can*; *could*; *do* as pro-verb; *might*; *must*; *should*; Present Simple and Progressive Passive; Past Simple Passive; reported statements and questions; *say* and *tell*; present and past participles; irregular verbs; reflexive/emphatic pronouns; *each other*; *somebody else*; relative pronouns and clauses; compound adjectives; zero article in generalisations; quantifiers (*both* and *neither*); word order (position of *both*, end-position of prepositions).	Decoding rapid speech; stress and rhythm; linking; initial clusters beginning with /s/; perceiving /ə/; /eɪ/; /h/; /θ/; /ɪ/; pronunciations of the letter *u*.
31 to 36	*Can*; emphatic *do*; *will*; *shall*; *must*; *would*; Past Perfect unfulfilled past conditions; phrasal verbs; question tags; imperatives; reported instructions; *before*, *after*, *as soon as* and *until*; *to* as pro-verb; verb + object + infinitive; place prepositions; *so* and *such*; *still*, *yet* and *already*; linking words and expressions; sequencing markers.	Intonation of question tags; strong and weak pronunciations; stress and rhythm; emphatic and contrastive stress; perceiving unstressed syllables; unstressed vowels in initial syllables; /ɒ/, /ɔː/ and /əʊ/ and their spellings; pronunciation of the letter *r*; words with misleading spellings.

Functions

Students learn how to

Greet; introduce; begin conversations with strangers; keep conversations going; agree and disagree; describe people and things; compare; ask for and give personal information; exchange opinions; construct continuous spoken and written text; ask about English.

Ask for things; ask for things when they don't know the words; use appropriate language in shops; react to information; express sympathy; make and reply to requests, offers and suggestions; agree and refuse to do things; borrow; lend; describe and compare people and things; ask about and express wishes; narrate; report; ask for clarification; manage conversation.

Give news; ask and talk about experience; make appointments; bargain; borrow and lend; ask for and give directions; make enquiries; make applications; thank; persuade; give polite refusals; telephone; ask about English; distinguish formal and informal language; use appropriate language in various common situations.

Advise; agree and disagree; persuade; show interest; make appointments; telephone; describe people; express feelings about people; discuss; predict; invite; make suggestions; make offers; agree to do things; report; give opinions.

Describe, compare and contrast people and things; describe processes; define; agree and disagree; ask for and give information; exchange opinions; express doubt and certainty; generalise; report; write a simple narrative; ask about English.

Make enquiries; offer; discuss; agree and disagree; ask for agreement; tell people to do things; make, grant and refuse requests; ask for and give directions; tell stories; report instructions; emphasize; express degrees of formality; construct continuous spoken and written text; use language appropriate to various situations.

Topics and notions

Students learn to talk about

Ability; change; habits and routines; events happening at the time of speaking; personal details; personality traits; frequency; parts and shapes; food; prices; economic and political development.

Time and place; quantity; things happening at the same time and in sequence; physical appearance; physical characteristics; differences and similarities; possession; routines; people's past lives; wishes; obligation; accidents; misfortune; speed and weight; shopping; clothes.

Ability; certainty and possibility; change; duration; quantity; sufficiency; excess; lack; experience; recent events; finished habits; economic and political development; travel; weather; prices; traffic; holidays; work; interviews; food and drink; places; personality.

Ability; arrangements; certainty, probability and possibility; conditions; feelings and emotions; remembering and forgetting; time relations; the future; plans; obligation; hope; quantity; intentions; likes and dislikes; personal and professional relationships; orientation in space; present/future events; geographic features; weather.

Materials and products; manufacturing and other processes; causes and origins; historical events; agents; certainty, probability and possibility; doubt; truth and lies; similarities and differences; ability; actions directed towards oneself; reciprocal action; self and others; present and past time relations; obligation; household chores.

Present, past and future time relations; place relations; conditions, including unfulfilled past conditions; obligation; parents and children; parties and entertaining; travel.

Skills

The Student's Book and Class Cassettes, together with the Practice Book, provide regular work on the basic 'four skills'. Special skills taught or practised at Level 2 include decoding rapid colloquial speech, reading and listening for specific information, writing simple connected prose (expository, descriptive, narrative, persuasive) and writing simple business letters.

Vocabulary

In addition to revising vocabulary taught at Level 1, students will learn 900 or more new words and expressions during their work on Level 2 of the course.

Introduction

The nature and purpose of the course

This is Level 2 of *The New Cambridge English Course,* a four-level course designed for people who are learning English for general practical or cultural purposes. The course generally presupposes a European-type educational background, but with some adaptation it can be used successfully with learners from other cultural environments. The course teaches British English, but illustrates other varieties as well.

The material at each level includes a Student's Book, a Teacher's Book and a set of Class Cassettes (for classwork); a Practice Book, with or without Key (for homework); two optional Student's Cassettes; and an optional Test Book for teachers. Split editions of the Student's Book, Practice Book and Student's Cassettes are also available.

Level 2 is for elementary and lower intermediate students. They will have had 75 to 100 hours' classwork before Level 2 and will be able to use English to achieve a certain number of simple practical aims. The book can be used to follow on from *The New Cambridge English Course 1* or any other beginners' course. There is systematic revision work for students who still have problems with basic structures.

Student's Book 2 contains 72 to 100 hours' classwork (depending on the students' mother tongue, the way their classes are organised, where they are studying, whether they use the Practice Book, how strong their motivation is, their previous learning experience of English, and various other factors). Used as suggested, the book will take students up to a point where they can understand and produce English well enough to handle a variety of everyday situations and topics with relative ease (around the level of the Council of Europe's 'Threshold' level).

The approach is different from that of most lower intermediate courses. Features which may be new to your students include:
– multi-syllabus course organisation
– wide variety of presentation methodology
– mixture of factual and fictional topics
– opportunities for student choice
– emphasis on systematic vocabulary learning
– regular pronunciation and spelling work
– some use of authentic listening material
– deliberate inclusion of some 'too difficult' material (see *Basic principles*)
– active and varied 'communicative' practice.
These points are dealt with in more detail in the following sections.

The organisation of the course

Level 2 of *The New Cambridge English Course* consists of six blocks of nine lessons. A lesson generally provides enough work for an hour and a half upwards (depending on the learners' speed, motivation and previous knowledge). The first six lessons of a block are topic- or function-based. Work on grammar, vocabulary, pronunciation, etc. leads up to communicative exchanges, dramatisations or writing exercises related to one or more of the themes in the block. The last three lessons in each block display, revise and test the language learnt in the previous six lessons.

Basic principles

The pedagogic design of *The New Cambridge English Course* reflects the following beliefs.

Respecting the learner
People generally learn languages best when their experience, knowledge of the world, interests and feelings are involved, and a course must allow students to 'be themselves' as fully as possible. But not everybody learns in the same way, and not everything can be taught in the same way. A course must provide fiction as well as fact; role play as well as real communication activities; personal as well as impersonal discussion topics; learner-centred as well as teacher-centred activities. Elementary course material should not be childish and patronising, and it is worth remembering that the best classroom humour generally comes from the students, not from the textbook.

The language: multi-syllabus course design
A complete English language course will incorporate at least eight main syllabuses:
– **Vocabulary**: students must acquire a 'core' vocabulary of the most common and useful words in the language, as well as learning more words of their own choice.
– **Grammar** basic structures must be learnt and revised.
– **Pronunciation** work is important for many students. Learners need to speak comprehensibly, and to understand people with different accents speaking in natural conditions (not just actors speaking standard English in recording studios).
– **Notions**: students must know how to refer to common concepts such as *sequence*, *contrast*, or *purpose*.
– **Functions**: learners must be able to do things such as *complaining, describing, suggesting*, or *asking for permission* in English.
– **Situations**: a course must teach the stereotyped expressions associated with situations like *shopping, making travel enquiries, booking hotel rooms, telephoning* etc.
– **Topics**: students need to learn the language used to talk about subjects of general interest. The coursebook should include some controversial and emotionally engaging material, rather than sticking to bland middle-of-the-road 'safe' topics.
– **Skills**: learners need systematic practice in both receptive and productive skills. Reading and listening work will include some authentic interviews and texts, as well as specially written material.

How important is grammar?
Obviously grammar is important, especially at the early stages of learning a language, but it can be overvalued at the expense of other areas such as skills development and vocabulary growth. (Vocabulary mistakes tend to outnumber grammar mistakes by more than three to one.) Students often feel that a lesson with no new grammar in 'doesn't teach anything'; they must learn not to judge their progress simply by the number of new structures taught.

'Learning' and 'acquisition'
Most people seem to learn a foreign language more effectively if it is 'tidied up' for them. This helps them to focus on high-priority language and to see the grammatical regularities.

However, learners also need to encounter a certain amount of 'untidy' natural language (even if this seems a bit too difficult for them). Without some unstructured input, people's unconscious mechanisms for acquiring languages may not operate effectively.

A course should cater for both these ways of approaching a language (sometimes called 'learning' and 'acquisition' respectively). The occasional use of unsimplified authentic materials may require a change in learner expectations: many students and teachers are used only to texts in which every new word and structure has to be explained and learnt.

Methodology

- **Communicative practice:** where possible, language practice should resemble real-life communication, with genuine exchanges of information and opinions. Pair and group work can greatly increase the quantity and quality of practice.
- **Input and output; creativity:** students generally learn what they use and forget what they don't use. At least some lessons should lead up to genuine conversations, role play or writing activities in which students use creatively what they have learnt. If they can use their new language to entertain, inform or amuse each other, so much the better.
- **Error** is a natural part of learning, and over-correction can destroy confidence. Some learners will need a high level of accuracy, but very few will ever be perfect. Students' achievement should not be measured negatively (by how far away they are from perfection), but positively (by how successfully they can use the language for their own purposes).
- **Regularity and variety** need to be carefully balanced. If all the lessons are constructed in the same way, a course is easy to use but monotonous. Variety makes lessons more interesting, but too much variety can make material more difficult for teachers to prepare and students to get used to.
- **Study and memorisation** are necessary, for most learners, for really thorough learning.
- **Learning and acquisition** should both be catered for. This will mean that students will sometimes focus intensively on language items, and sometimes do tasks involving 'untidy' texts where only a part of the material need be understood. Likewise, there will sometimes be 'preview' appearances (for instance in exercise rubrics) of language items that will be studied intensively somewhat later.
- **The mother tongue,** if it can be used, can help to make explanations faster and more precise. The same is true of bilingual dictionaries, and students should practise their use.

Knowing where you are

Students can easily get lost in the complicated landscape of language study. A course must supply some kind of 'map' of their language-learning, so that they can understand the purpose of each kind of activity, and can see how the various lessons add up to a coherent whole. Regular revision should be provided, helping students to place the language items they are learning into the context of what they already know.

Using the course

(Many teachers will of course know very well how to adapt the course to their students' needs. These suggestions are meant mainly for less experienced teachers who are unfamiliar with this approach.)

Preparation

You may need to prepare the first lessons carefully in advance, until everybody is used to the approach. Later, less work should be needed – the teachers' notes will guide you through each lesson.

Choice

You may not feel it necessary to do absolutely all the lessons in the book. (But if you drop a lesson, check that you don't 'lose' language material which is important for your students.)

Leave out exercises that cover points of language which your class don't need.

Don't do an exercise if you or your students really dislike it. (But don't leave out a strange-looking activity without giving it a try!)

Don't force a lesson on your students if it bores everybody; find another way to teach the material. But don't automatically drop a topic because it makes people angry – rage can get people talking!

Timing

Motivated students should average an hour and a half or more per lesson. (Some lessons will of course go more quickly or more slowly than others.) The book should take a minimum of 72 hours to complete (plus any time spent on tests, homework correction, etc.). If you don't have that much time, you will need to look through the book in advance and decide what to leave out.

Authentic recordings

The course contains some 'real-life' recordings of conversations, interviews and other material. These teach vocabulary, stimulate discussion, and train learners to understand natural speech (in a variety of accents). Students may not understand every word of what they hear. THIS DOES NOT MATTER! They need to experience some language which is beyond their present capacities – this happens in natural language learning all the time. (You can help by sometimes talking naturally in English about your interests, events in your life, etc.)

Discourage students from asking for complete transcriptions and explanations of long recordings – this is not usually an efficient use of time.

Vocabulary learning

Words and expressions to learn are listed at the end of each lesson. You may need to suggest techniques of learning this vocabulary. Some possible approaches are for students to:

- Copy new words with their translations in special notebooks. Cover the words and try to recall them from the translations.
- Note English-language explanations or examples of the use of new words. Write more examples.
- Keep 'vocabulary diaries', listing new words under subject/grammatical headings (e.g. 'verbs of movement'; 'professions'). Revise occasionally by trying to write from memory as many words as possible from each list.

Different people learn best in different ways – but for most students, some systematic vocabulary study is necessary.

You may want to point out to students that there is an alphabetical index of vocabulary at the back of their books (pages 116–123). This includes phonetic transcriptions; you may wish to introduce your students gradually to their use.

Consolidation sections

The last three lessons in each block of nine are used for summary, revision and testing. You may need to show students how to use the 'Summary' lessons. They should spend time, with you or on their own, looking at the material and studying the structures and vocabulary. Encourage them to look back at the previous lessons to see exactly how the new items are used.

The 'Revision' lessons revise the major items taught in the previous six numbered lessons, and in each Revision lesson there is an opportunity for extended speaking practice. Doing these exercises will help learning and build confidence. The 'Test' lesson which follows each Revision lesson covers the language from the previous six numbered lessons. It is meant to give students and teacher an idea of how well the material has been assimilated. Only use those parts of the test that cover material important to your students. If you wish to administer unseen tests as well, the Test Book provides a parallel test at the level of each consolidation section.

Practice Book

The Practice Book is an essential part of the course. It provides a choice of consolidation and revision exercises, together with regular work on reading and writing skills; it also includes activities using the Student's Cassettes. Together with the consolidation sections, the Practice Book ensures that students integrate current learning with areas previously covered and get sufficient opportunities for skills development. A 'with Key' version of the Practice Book contains answers to all the exercises, where appropriate, for learners wishing to do further homework on a self-study basis.

At the end of the Practice Book there is a series of reading texts on different topics, selected and adapted by Christine Lindop and Dominic Fisher. You can use these texts to supplement students' exposure to written English. They are grouped according to the blocks of lessons in the Student's Book, so that students should be able to handle either of the texts in the first section after completing Revision Lesson A in the Student's Book.

The Practice Book also includes a 'Mini-grammar': a concise summary of all the grammar points covered in Levels 1 and 2 of the course.

Student's Cassettes

The Student's Cassette set consists of a selection of material from Class Cassette set 2, including all the recordings for the optional listening exercises in the Practice Book as well as all the songs. Motivated learners who have the time can thus make active use of the Student's Cassettes at home.

Supplementing the course

The course is relatively complete, and it should not need much supplementation. But of course, the more extra reading, listening and speaking students can do – in or out of class – the better. A circulating class library of supplementary readers can be useful. *Something to Read 2* by Christine Lindop and Dominic Fisher (Cambridge University Press, 1989) has been written especially for students working with this course.

Learner expectations and learner resistance

Students have their own ideas about language learning. Up to a point, these must be respected – individuals have different learning strategies, and will not respond to methods which they distrust. However, learners sometimes resist important and useful activities which do not fit in with their preconceptions, and this can hinder progress. So you may have to spend time, early in the course, training students in new attitudes to language learning. Problems are especially likely to arise over questions of grammar and correction (students may want too much), over the use of authentic materials, and over exercises involving group work.

Comments

The New Cambridge English Course, as a completely revised edition of a very successful course series, has had the benefit of the best sort of piloting programme – thousands of teachers have used the original edition over several years, and their feedback has helped us to shape the present version. But improvements are always possible, and we would be delighted to hear from users. Letters can be sent to us c/o Cambridge University Press (ELT), The Edinburgh Building, Shaftesbury Road, Cambridge CB2 2RU, Great Britain.

Michael Swan   Catherine Walter   August 1989

1 <u>May I introduce myself?</u>

Lesson 1

Students learn the expressions used in introductions; they revise the language used for giving and eliciting personal information.
Phonology: intonation and rhythm.

Methodology and class dynamics

This lesson and the next one give students a chance to 'break the ice' and to get to know each other (and you). At the same time, you have the chance to watch a new class in action, and to see where their main strengths and weaknesses are. The class will start getting used (if they are not already) to the methods used in the course; it will help if you can explain the reasons for any exercises which students find unfamiliar or confusing. If students are not used to working in pairs or small groups, this kind of activity may need to be introduced gradually.

If the students know one another well, you will need to adapt some of the exercises (suggestions below).

Names

It is usually easier (and more friendly) to use first names, but note that students from certain cultures may find it strange or even offensive to use first names to strangers. Some students may find it particularly difficult to address a teacher in this way, because of the seeming lack of respect involved. You may wish to tell students about British and American attitudes in this area.

Note: revision

Structures: This lesson gives you an opportunity to see whether your students already have a good grasp of basic structures. Present tenses, and *be*, *have* and *can* will be revised in detail in the next five lessons.

Try to avoid correcting too much of the students' language in this lesson. The activities create a need for language, and encourage communication in English. If you overemphasize grammatical accuracy, this may make the students feel uncomfortable and hesitant to talk. You can make it clear that you are only going to correct mistakes that interfere with communication in this lesson, but that you will note other mistakes and deal with them in lessons to come.

Vocabulary: Important words taught in Level 1 of the *The New Cambridge English Course* have been listed along with new vocabulary under *Learn/revise* in the Student's Book.

Optional extra materials

Labels (see alternatives to Exercise 4).

If you are short of time

Drop Exercise 6.

Recordings

Recorded material is indicated in the Teacher's Book by one of two symbols. The dark symbol [▣] shows that the recording is essential to the exercise. The light symbol [▢] means that the exercise can be done without the use of the recording. Exercises using authentic recordings are marked [▣] Ⓐ.

If you fast forward in 'Play' mode, you will hear a signal at the end of each exercise on the recording which will help you find your place.

Test Book recordings

A recording for the Entry Test in the Test Book precedes this lesson on the Class Cassette.

1 Introductions

- Introduce yourself and find out the students' names.
- Then play the recording, while students listen with their books closed.
- See how many of the expressions they can remember.
- Play the recording again (books open this time).
- Explain any difficulties (for instance, the difference between *How do you do?* and *How are you?*). Practise the pronunciation of the sentences, paying special attention to intonation and rhythm.
- Get students to introduce themselves to their neighbours or (even better) to go round the class introducing themselves to several other people.
- Then get students to practise introducing people to each other (using the expressions they have learnt).
- If students already have some fluency, this can develop into a more general conversation involving questions about nationality, occupation and so on.
- Finish by making sure that students know *first name*, *Christian name* (if they are likely to be Christian), *surname*, *Mr, Mrs, Miss, Ms*.

Alternative to Exercise 1

- If your students already know each other well, this exercise can be done using false names.
- Ask students to get into groups of four or five. In each group, they should give each other new names.
- When they have done this, tell students to introduce themselves to people from other groups, and to introduce members of their groups to other people, using the expressions they have practised.

2 Making up questions

- Make sure students understand that they are preparing questions for real interview activities (Exercises 3 and 4). If they know each other well, they should avoid preparing questions to which they know the answers.
- Encourage students to use bilingual dictionaries, and to ask you and other students for help, using the expressions shown in the Student's Book. (Explain these and practise the pronunciation if necessary.)
- They can use the words and expressions in the box if they wish, but should not limit themselves to these.
- When each group has prepared at least ten questions (faster groups may prepare more), look over the questions to check that they are reasonably correct and comprehensible (see the note on revision above).

3 Interviewing the teacher

- Try to give the students some genuine and interesting personal information about yourself. This will encourage them to feel that English is a real vehicle of communication and not just a classroom subject.

4 Interviewing other students

- If possible, make sure students work with partners whom they don't know well. Each student in the pair should interview the other.
- Teach the expression *Sorry, I'd rather not answer that,* for use if somebody finds a question embarrassing.
- With fluent, confident students the exercise may go on for a long time; with a less experienced class it may last no more than two or three minutes.
- You may want to give some sort of 'change-over' signal at half-time.
- If you have an odd number of students, put three good speakers in one group.

Alternatives to Exercise 4

LABELS

- If your students have had few problems forming questions in Exercises 2 and 3, you could try this exercise: ask each student to take a label and write three words or expressions on it that tell about him- or herself: for example, *swimming, patient, guitar.*
- Students then walk round asking one another about the words on their labels.

SPIES

- You could use this exercise if students already know one another.
- Students work in small groups. Each group chooses one of their members to be a spy in a foreign country. They devise as complete a cover story as possible – false identity, life story, job, etc.
- Then each group 'captures' another group's spy and interrogates him or her. In answering questions, the spy must invent any answers that have not been planned. The interrogators try to catch the spy out in a contradiction.

5 Reporting

- Before starting the exercise, ask everybody to tell you something they have found out about their partner. This checks on the correct use of third-person forms.
- Then get pairs to move into groups of four (you may have one or two larger groups).
- Each student should tell the new people in the group about his or her partner.

6 Half and half dialogue

- Divide the class in two down the middle. Ask students on one side of the class to turn to page 124 in the back of their books, and the students on the other side of the class to turn to page 126 in the back of their books. If it is possible, push chairs or move students so that the two halves of the class are well separated from each other.
- Each student should take a clean piece of paper, and, working with a partner, invent the other half of the dialogue on the page you have indicated. Each person should write *only* the newly invented lines of the dialogue on his or her paper.
- Walk round to give help as needed. For example, if students are doing Student A you may need to point out that A's second line must contain some mention of A's sister and her relationship to B.
- When students have finished, ask them to close their books.
- Each student should take his or her new half-dialogue and find a partner from the other side of the room. They should combine their two half-dialogues.
- In some cases there may be a problem of the two dialogues' not fitting together exactly; walk round to help students make any necessary adjustments.
- Let them practise their half-dialogues; they may then want to perform their dialogues for other students, or change partners and make new dialogues.

Practice Book exercises

1. Gap-fill exercise practising introductions.
2. Matching questions and answers.
3. Writing questions for answers.
4. Vocabulary revision: names of days and months.
5. Student's Cassette exercise (Student's Book Exercise 1). Students listen and repeat, trying for good intonation.
6. Recreational reading. Encourage students to read the text once without looking up any more words than they absolutely need to in order to get the meaning of the text.

Introductions; exchanging personal information.

1 🔊 Introductions.
1. Close your books and listen to the conversations. Then open your books, listen again, and practise the sentences.
2. Introduce yourself to some other students. Find out their names and where they come from.
3. Then introduce some students to each other.

2 Work in groups. Write ten or more personal questions to ask people in the class. For example:

*Where do you live?   Who lives with you?   How old are you?
    Are you a patient person?*

You can use some of the words and expressions in the box, and you can ask the teacher for help, like this:

'How do you say marié?'   *'Married.'*
'What's the English for atletismo?'   *'Athletics.'*
'How do you pronounce archaeology?'
'How do you spell . . . ?'
'What does hobby *mean?'*
'Is this correct: " . . . "?'

any	brothers	can	do	English	father	How
How often	like	live	look	married	mother	music
nationality	old	piano	read	self-confident	shy	
sisters	spare time	sport	tall	What	Where	Why

3 Interview the teacher. Find out as much as possible about him/her.

4 Work in pairs. Interview your partner and find out as much as possible about him/her.

5 Work in groups of four. Tell the other students about your partner from Exercise 4.

6 Turn to the page your teacher tells you. Work in pairs to write ONLY the other half of the dialogue on another piece of paper. Then combine your half-dialogue with someone from the other side of the classroom.

Learn/revise: whereabouts; How do you do?; so much; mean (meant, meant); introduce; I'd like to introduce . . . ; May I introduce myself?; I'm glad to meet you; Nice to see you again; I didn't catch your name; What's the English for . . . ?; What does . . . mean?; How do you spell . . . ?; correct; nationality; piano; orange juice; self-confident; shy; married; spare time; as much as possible.

2 Who's who?

Be, can and have got; connecting expressions in conversation; descriptions; listening and speaking skills.

| Anna | Jake | Peter | Polly | Rob | Sally |

1 🔊 **Listen to the recordings and answer the questions.**

First recording
1. What is the man's name?
2. Which is his picture?
3. Who is the woman?

Second recording
4. Who is the first speaker?
5. Who is the other speaker?
6. Who are they talking about?
7. Which is his picture?

Third recording
8. Who is speaking?
9. Which is her picture?
10. Which is Sally's picture?

Fourth recording
11. Who is the first speaker?

2 **Look at these words and expressions. Can you remember which of them came in the recordings? Listen again and check.**

Look	even	perhaps	I do think
You're just too old	Well, yes, I know	perhaps not	maybe
Well, yes, OK	What's he like, then?	I don't know	maybe not
That's it	Well, you know	On the other hand	
So what?	I must say	though	
I don't agree	actually	still	

10

Lesson 2

Students work on linking words and expressions; they revise some elementary grammar, and practise listening and speaking skills in the context of descriptions.
Principal structures: *be, can* and *have got*; linking in conversation.
Phonology: strong, weak and contracted forms.

Language notes and possible problems

1. Grammar revision This lesson briefly revises the basic grammar of *be, can* and *have*. Most students should have mastered these structures already; people who have difficulty should study the grammar tables at the end of the lesson and do the appropriate Practice Book exercises.

2. *Have got* Some students may not realise that present-tense forms of *have* (when used to talk about possession, characteristics and relationships), are normally accompanied by *got* in informal British English. You may need to explain that *got* has no meaning of its own here, and that the two words *have got* mean the same as *have*. Students who find *have got* too complicated should just use *have* (but they may sound unnaturally formal in some contexts).

3. Discourse markers, fillers, etc. Spoken language typically contains a large number of words and expressions whose purpose is to show the relationships between utterances, to express the speaker's mood or reactions, to give the speaker time to think, to make what is said sound more or less definite, and so on. Exercises 2 and 3 draw students' attention to some common examples. Note that *actually* is a 'false friend' – similar words in most European languages mean 'at present'.

4. Weak forms If students can learn to pronounce unstressed syllables correctly, their English becomes much more natural and easier to understand. Exercise 4 contrasts unstressed and stressed pronunciations of *be, have* and *can*. Note that students from certain cultures may be unwilling to pronounce 'weak forms' because they may perceive them as careless and incorrect. It is important for such students to realise that it is actually incorrect to use a strong form when a weak form is appropriate.

1 Listening and identifying

● Play the four recordings right through without stopping.
● Then ask students to read through the questions, and to look at the names and pictures. Tell them that recordings are about four of the people illustrated (there are two names and two pictures too many).
● Play the first recording again, telling students to listen for the names. See if they can answer the first three questions.
● Carry on through the other recordings, stopping after each while students discuss their answers.
● At the end of the exercise, students may ask to be shown the complete text of the recordings. Explain that this is not necessary for the purposes of this exercise (listening for particular pieces of information), and that it would take up time which can be used better in other ways.

Answers to Exercise 1
1. Jake
2. B
3. Sally
4. Sally
5. Polly
6. Rob
7. F
8. Polly
9. C
10. E (If Polly is C, Sally must be A or E. But she's 20 years younger than Jake, so she can't be A.)
11. Jake

Tapescript for Exercise 1

SALLY: Look, Jake, you're just too old for me.
JAKE: No, I'm not.
SALLY: Yes, you are. You're 20 years older than me.
JAKE: Well, yes, OK, but so what? Age isn't important, Sally.
SALLY: Yes it is, Jake. You're boring. You can't dance, you don't like my friends, you've got no sense of humour, and you haven't got any hair. All you can do is talk about yourself and read books and listen to music. You haven't even got any money.
JAKE: Well, yes, I know, but money isn't everything.

SALLY: What's he like, then, Polly?
POLLY: Who, Rob? Well, you know, he's very good-looking.
SALLY: What, tall, dark and handsome?
POLLY: Well, not as tall as your Jake. But he's dark and handsome all right. He's got lovely brown eyes and a super smile. And he's got a great sense of humour. And he can dance all night. And he thinks I'm great.
SALLY: I must say you're lucky. I can't say the same about Jake. Rob's older than you, isn't he?
POLLY: No, actually, he isn't. We're the same age. Both 21 next summer.

POLLY: Perhaps my nose is too big. Do you think it is? No, perhaps not. I don't know. On the other hand, my hair's nice. Rob says he likes long fair hair. He's sweet. My eyes are a bit small, though. Still, they're pretty. And I know I've got really nice teeth. Look at that smile. I do think my nose is too big, though. Well, perhaps not. I don't know.

JAKE: I don't know what the problem is. I'm good-looking, I'm very intelligent, though I say it myself, I'm an interesting person, I've got a lot of experience of the world, I've got a good job, I can speak three languages. Why isn't she happy?
ROB: Well, perhaps you're too perfect. You're just too good for her.
JAKE: Yes, maybe you're right, Rob. Perhaps that's it.

2 Linking words and expressions

● Ask students to look through the list in groups. Each group should try to decide which of the words and expressions came in the recordings.
● Play the recordings again while they check their answers.
● Clear up any problems about particular words and expressions.

Answer to Exercise 2
All the expressions occur except *That's it, I don't agree* and *maybe not*.

10

3 More on linking words and expressions

- Divide the class into two; tell one half to work in small groups on John's part of the conversation while the others work on Mary's.
- Then ask for pairs of volunteers (one from each half) to try reading the whole conversation.
- Discuss the possible answers and clear up any problems.
- Ask students where it would be possible to put *on the other hand* (in gap 6), and *maybe* (in gaps 5 and 8).

Answers to Exercise 3
1. Look (*or* Actually)
2. just
3. So what
4. even
5. Perhaps
6. Still (*or* I don't know)
7. Actually (*or* Look *or* I don't know)
8. I do think (*or* perhaps)
9. I don't know
10. I don't know
11. though

4 Strong, weak and contracted pronunciations

- Ask students to try the sentences in each group.
- The first five groups practise the contrast between unstressed or contracted pronunciations of *are*, *has* and *can*, and stressed pronunciations of the same words.
- Help students to see when these words are stressed (for instance, at the end of a sentence or before *n't*).
- Pay special attention to the unstressed pronunciations, to the contractions *you're*, *we're* and *they're*, and to the vowel in *can't*. The recording can be used as a guide if you wish.
- Note that the American pronunciation of *can't* (/kænt/) is very different from the British pronunciation. You may like to point this out.
- The final group practises the difficult consonant cluster /znt/ in *isn't* and *hasn't*.

5 Students' conversations

- Go over the instructions and make sure students understand what they have to do.
- Tell them to decide whether they want to work alone or in pairs, and to make up their minds as quickly as possible what they want to talk about.
- Play the recordings for Exercise 1 again, to remind students of the kind of thing they should be aiming at.
- Then give them twenty minutes or so to prepare and practise their monologues or conversations. Go round helping as necessary. They should keep the language relatively simple, using *be*, *can*, *have got* and linking expressions as much as possible.
- Finally, let them give their 'performances' for the rest of the class.

Optional activities

- A fun way to practise *can* is to do a 'boasting and confessing' competition. Get students to prepare either a piece of boasting (in which they say they can do large numbers of clever things, not necessarily all true), or a confession, in which they say all the things they can't do. The class can vote for the best piece of boasting and the best confession.
- For more simple practice on *be* and *have got*, get students to prepare and give descriptions of other people in the class (or other well-known personalities) without giving the names. The class have to guess who is being described.
- Another approach is for students to talk about themselves, including one lie in what they say. The class have to spot the lie.

Practice Book exercises
1. Vocabulary revision: parts of the body.
2. Short answers with *be*, *have* and *can*.
3. Questions with *be*, *have got* and *can*.
4. Negative sentences with *have got*.
5. Fast reading practice.
6. Student's Cassette exercise (Student's Book Exercise 1). Students listen to the third recording (Polly's description of herself) and write it down.

Pair and group work

Many of the exercises in the course require students to work together in pairs or groups, or to move round the classroom talking to each other. Except in very small classes this is essential: it is the only way that students can get enough speaking practice to learn the language successfully. However, students may not be used to work of this kind, and you may need to introduce them to it gradually. With some classes (particularly with teenagers) it may be better to avoid full-scale walk-round exercises at the beginning. Instead, get students to talk to as many people as they can without moving from their seats.

In activities where more than one student is speaking at a time, teachers sometimes worry about the fact that they cannot listen to and correct everybody. This loss of control should not be seen as a problem. It is very important to do practice which bridges the gap between totally controlled exercises (where everything is checked) and real-life communication (where nothing is checked). In pair work and group work, you can supervise just as many people as you can in fully controlled exercises (i.e. one at a time); meanwhile, the people you are not supervising also get useful fluency practice. Even if some students take the opportunity to waste time or lapse into their own language, there will still be far more people practising English during group work than when students take turns to speak.

3 Read the conversation and put the expressions into the right places. (More than one answer is possible in some cases.)

> JOHN: actually; even; I don't know; just; look
> MARY: I do think; I don't know; perhaps; so what; still; though

JOHN: ......1......, Mary, the problem is, we're ......2...... too different.

MARY: OK, we're different. ......3......? People are different.

JOHN: Well, we don't have the same interests. We don't ......4...... like the same people.

MARY: ......5...... not. ......6......, we get on very well together most of the time.

JOHN: ......7......, Mary, I don't think we do.

MARY: Well, OK, John, maybe there are some problems. But ......8...... we should go on trying for a bit longer.

JOHN: ......9......, Mary. Do you think we're getting anywhere?

MARY: ......10...... either. Let's have one more try, ...11.......

JOHN: OK. One more try.

4 Pronunciation. Practise these sentences.

You're too old.
Maybe you're right.
Yes, you are.

We're the same age.
Yes, we are.

My eyes are a bit small.
They're pretty.
Yes, they are.

He's got a great sense
of humour.
Yes, he has.
You've got pretty eyes.
You haven't got any
money.

I can speak three
languages.
He can dance all night.
Yes, he can.
You can't dance.
I can't say the same.

No, he isn't.
Age isn't important.
Why isn't she happy?
He hasn't got any hair.
No, he hasn't.

5 Prepare a short conversation like one of the recordings in Exercise 1. Possibilities:
a. a conversation about another person
b. a row with another person
c. a conversation with yourself about somebody (or about yourself)
In the conversation, use *be, can, have got* and some of the expressions from Exercise 2. Practise the conversation and then let other students listen to it.

Be

I am (I'm)
you are (you're)
he/she/it is (he's/she's/it's)
we are (we're)
you are (you're)
they are (they're)

---

am I?
are you?
is he/she/it?
are we?
are you?
are they?

I am not (I'm not)
you are not (you're not / you aren't)
he/she/it is not (he's not *etc.* / she isn't *etc.*)
we are not (we're not / we aren't)
they are not (they're not / they aren't)

Can

I can swim (~~I can to swim~~)
he/she/it can swim (~~he/she/it cans . . . .~~)
etc.

Can you swim? (~~Do you can . . . .?~~)
etc.

I cannot (can't) swim
etc.

Have (got)

I have got (I've got)
you have got (you've got)
he/she/it has got (he's/she's/it's got)
we have got (we've got)
you have got (you've got)
they have got (they've got)

---

have I got?
have you got?
etc.

I have not (haven't) got
he/she/it has not (hasn't) got
etc.

Learn/revise: picture; get on (well) together (got, got); go on . . .ing (went, gone); pretty; first; second; third; fourth; look; just; well; too; even; actually; though; still; maybe; the same; a bit; most of the time; on the other hand; So what?; not . . . either.

3 My mornings usually start fairly late

Routines and habits; Simple Present tense; frequency
adverbs and adverbials.

1 How do they spend their weekends? Make sure you know
the words in the box. Then listen to the recording and write down four
things that Adele says she does and four things that Rufus says he does
at the weekend.

business   crossword puzzle   gardening   guests   housework
ice skating rink   ironing   lie in   meal   midday   necessary
newspapers   sleep in   stay in bed   washing   weather
youth club

2 How often? Look at the expressions in the box. Do any of them
mean the same? Copy the line, and put the expressions from the
box on the line between NEVER and ALWAYS.

almost always   hardly ever   normally   not very often
occasionally   often   quite often   sometimes   usually
very often

NEVER   ALWAYS
───
0   1   2   3   4   5   6   7   8   9   10

3 Rewrite the sentences, saying how often these things happen. Be sure
you put the frequency adverb before the main verb (but after *don't/doesn't*).

1. Adele's mornings start fairly late. (*usually*)
   Adele's mornings usually start
   fairly late.
2. Adele gets up early. (*not very often*)
   Adele doesn't very often get up early.
3. Rufus brings Adele a cup of tea in bed. (*usually*)
4. Adele does housework on Saturday. (*sometimes*)
5. Adele takes the dog for a walk. (*often*)
6. Adele reads the newspapers at some time during
   the weekend. (*always*)

7. Adele visits her elderly mother in Newbury.
   (*quite often*)
8. They have breakfast. (*not usually*)
9. They have Saturday lunch. (*not often*)
10. They have a heavy meal in the evening. (*hardly
    ever*)
11. Rufus does the crossword puzzle in the Saturday
    newspaper. (*normally*)
12. Rufus lies in on Sunday morning. (*almost
    always*)
13. They go out in the car on Sunday afternoons.
    (*quite often*)

12

━━ **Lesson 3** ━━

Students practise asking and talking about routines and habits.
Structures: Simple Present tense; frequency adverbs and adverbials with single word verbs.
Phonology: decoding rapid speech.

Language notes and possible problems

1. The use of frequency adverbs with single word verbs is the most common and important use of these adverbs. In this lesson only this case is treated; other uses will be dealt with later in the course.

2. Details of the use of frequency adverbs are quite complicated: for example, you can say *not often* or *not usually*; but *not occasionally* and *not sometimes* are unacceptable. (Note that * marks an unacceptable utterance.) In this lesson these problems are not dealt with explicitly, but of course you may want to discuss them if students' work in Exercises 5 and 6 produces errors in this area.

3. Timing This lesson may overrun in some classes, where enthusiasm for Exercises 5 and 6 is high. See suggestions in *If you are short of time*.

If you are short of time

Only use Rufus's speech for Exercise 1. Get students to do the second part of Exercise 6 individually for homework.

---

1 Presentation: listening

• Go over the words and expressions in the box with the students, and make sure they understand them all.
• Then tell them that they are going to hear a husband and wife talking about their weekend. Ask them to listen to the recording and try and note down four of the activities that Adele mentions and four of the activities that Rufus mentions.
• Play the recording one or more times, until most students are satisfied that they have done the task correctly.
• Go over the answers with them and explain any difficulties.
• It is best to resist any pressure from the students to study the recordings in great detail at this point; you may want to tell them that they will need to get used to listening for gist in English, without worrying about every word that is spoken.

Tapescript for Exercise 1: see page 127

2 Frequency adverbs

• Ask each student to copy the line from the book, with NEVER at one end and ALWAYS at the other.
• Get them to work individually or in small groups, using dictionaries and/or pooling their knowledge to put the expressions from the box on the line. Point out that some of the expressions may mean the same.
• Walk round while they are working; if they are using dictionaries, you can use the opportunity to observe the way students are working and give practical advice.
• When they have finished, put the line on the board and let them help you complete it.

Answers to Exercise 2

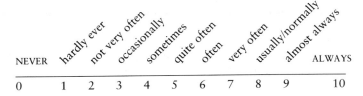

NEVER	hardly ever	not very often	occasionally	sometimes	quite often	often	very often	usually/normally	almost always	ALWAYS
0	1	2	3	4	5	6	7	8	9	10

3 Position of frequency adverbs

• Go over the examples with the students, pointing out where the frequency adverb comes in each kind of sentence.
• Let them work individually to rewrite the sentences, while you walk round to see that everyone has understood and to give any help that is needed.
• Let them compare answers in small groups before checking the answers with you.

Answers to Exercise 3

3. Rufus usually brings Adele a cup of tea in bed.
4. Adele sometimes does housework on Saturday.
5. Adele often takes the dog for a walk.
6. Adele always reads the newspapers at some time during the weekend.
7. Adele quite often visits her elderly mother in Newbury.
8. They don't usually have breakfast.
9. They don't often have Saturday lunch.
10. They hardly ever have a heavy meal in the evening.
11. Rufus normally does the crossword puzzle in the Saturday newspaper.
12. Rufus almost always lies in on Sunday morning.
13. They quite often go out in the car on Sunday afternoons.

4 How many words?

- This is an important exercise. It gives students practice in recognising and separating out common words pronounced naturally in rapid speech.
- The pronunciation of words (particularly unstressed words) often changes a good deal under the influence of the sounds that come before and after. Students who have learnt only the pronunciations that words have alone or in deliberate speech may have great trouble understanding them in natural conversation.
- Play the recording and ask students how many words they hear; then ask them if they can say what the words are.
- You will probably want to play the recording twice or more.

Answers to Exercise 4

1. I never have breakfast as such, but usually a couple of biscuits. (12)
2. I never have breakfast either. (5)
3. I'm retired, so I don't go to work. (10)
4. I never drink between meals, except when it's very hot. (11)
5. I usually have lunch about one. (6)
6. We then normally have our dinner at about eight or nine o'clock in the evening. (15)
7. I sometimes do the ironing while I'm watching TV. (10)

5 Survey (frequency adverbs and adverbials)

- Go over the examples with the students, making especially sure that they understand the meaning and the usage of the adverbials (*once / twice / three times a week* and *every . . . days/weeks* etc.).
- Get each student to choose a different question, and make sure he or she understands it. Students then go round asking their questions of as many people as possible. Ideally, they should get up and walk round the classroom; but if this is awkward, they can ask as many people as they can without moving from their seats.
- They should note the answers as they get them.

6 Reporting the survey

- Divide the class into groups of about eight to ten.
- Each group must pool the information its members gathered in Exercise 5.
- If you can, give each group a large (A2) piece of paper or a part of the board to work on. Each person can write his/her sentence down, and then the group can consult on the best way to combine the sentences into a paragraph.
- Otherwise, you may want students to dictate their sentences to the other members of the group, so everybody in the group has all the sentences in front of them to work with.
- They should decide on the best order to put the sentences in, and then work out whether they want to join some sentences with conjunctions or other linking devices.
- Walk round to give any practical help that is needed (e.g. giving the English word for a conjunction they want to use), but don't give advice on how they should order or construct their paragraph while they are working. You can work on English paragraph structure with them later if necessary, but it is best to let them organise their own thoughts now.
- Final products can be posted on a class notice board or photocopied for the whole class to see.

Practice Book exercises

1. Writing Simple Present forms.
2. Putting frequency adverbs in the right place in the sentence.
3. Writing sentences with frequency adverbials.
4. Reading (emphasis on guessing unknown words).
5. Extended writing on the students' weekend habits.
6. Student's Cassette exercise (Student's Book Exercise 1). Students use part of Rufus's monologue as a dictation.

4 How many words can you hear? What are they? (Contractions like *doesn't* count as two words.)

5 Survey of people's personal habits.
1. Make sure you know how to answer all the following questions in English. Use structures from the box.
2. Choose one of the questions (a different one from the other students), and go round the class. Note the answers.

> I sometimes/often/usually go dancing on Saturdays.
> I play tennis once / twice / three times a week.
> I go to the hairdresser every ten days / every week.

1. How often do you lie in bed after waking up?
2. What do you usually have for breakfast?
3. Do you usually get dressed before or after breakfast?
4. What do you usually wear in bed?
5. How often do you eat between meals?
6. Do you ever shut yourself in the bathroom to be alone?
7. How often do you talk to yourself?
8. How often do you daydream at work or school?
9. How often do you have arguments with other people in your head?
10. Are you usually more awake in the morning or in the evening?
11. How often do you sing in the bath or shower?
12. How often do you cook for yourself?
13. How often do you cook for other people?
14. How often do you go shopping?
15. How often do you eat in bed?
16. How often do you look in a mirror?
17. How do you usually travel to school or work?
18. Do you ever leave the telephone to ring without answering it?
19. How often do you go to the dentist?
20. How often do you go to the hairdresser?

6 Work in groups of eight to ten students. Your job is to write a portrait of the average student in your class.

1. Each member of the group contributes one sentence, from the work in Exercise 5. Examples:

'The average student in this class hardly ever cooks for himself/ herself.'
'He/She goes shopping for food once or twice a week.'

2. Combine your sentences into a paragraph. Example:

The average student in this class goes shopping for food once or twice a week, but hardly ever cooks for himself/herself . . .

Simple Present tense		
I start	do I start?	I do not (don't) start
you start	do you start?	you do not (don't) start
he/she/it starts	does he/she/it start?	he/she/it does not (doesn't) start
we start	do we start?	we do not (don't) start
you start	do you start?	you do not (don't) start
they start	do they start?	they do not (don't) start

Frequency adverbs

I **always** have coffee in the morning.
  (~~I have always coffee . . . .~~)
I **almost always** / **usually** / **normally** lie in on Sunday mornings.
I **very often** / **quite often** / **often** get dressed after breakfast.
I **sometimes/occasionally** have Sunday lunch.
We **hardly ever** / **never** have breakfast.
They **don't often** see their parents.

My brother goes shopping **once** / **twice** / **three times a week**.
I wash my hair **every day** / **every three days** / **every week**.

Learn/revise: business; gardening; housework; ironing; meal; newspaper; weather (*uncountable*); bath; shower; journey; dentist; hairdresser; lie (lay, lain); stay; bring (brought, brought); take (took, taken); get up (got, got); get dressed; go shopping (went, gone/been); shut (shut, shut); sleep (slept, slept); travel (travelled); necessary; heavy; short; early; in bed; awake; fairly; almost; always; usually; normally; (not) very often; quite often; sometimes; occasionally; hardly ever; never; away; between; during.

4 How people live

1 Separate the two mixed-up texts. Work in groups. Use dictionaries only if absolutely necessary.

AUSTRALIAN ABORIGINES
AMAZON INDIANS

The Karadjere people live in the desert of Western Australia,
These people live in the Amazon Basin, in Brazil,
where the climate is very hot.
where the climate is hot and wet:
It rains from January to March,
it rains for nine to ten months of the year.
and the rest of the year is dry.

They do not live in one place,
They live in villages;
but travel around on foot.
their houses are made of wood,
and the roofs are made of palm leaves.
They sleep in shelters made of dry tree branches.
Several families live in each house.
They travel by canoe.

Their food is fruit, nuts and kangaroo meat,
They eat fruit and vegetables, fish, and meat
    from animals and birds
and they eat fish in the wet season;
(for example monkeys, wild pigs, parrots).
they also make bread from grass seeds.
Water is often difficult to find.
The Karadjere like music, dancing and telling stories.
They like music, dancing and telling stories.
They do not wear many clothes.
They do not wear many clothes.

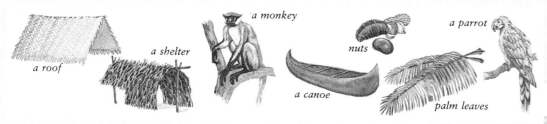

a roof   a shelter   a monkey   a canoe   nuts   a parrot   palm leaves

2 Pronunciation. Practise these words, and then read part of one of the texts aloud.

people   leaves   sleep   tree   each   meat
eat   season   seeds

live   in   Brazil   is   it   village   families
fish   pigs   difficult   music   dancing
telling   stories

a seal

14

Lesson 4

Students look at how sentences and texts are put together. They learn some facts about two unfamiliar cultures, and practise discussion and writing.
Structures: more revision of the Simple Present as used to refer to regular actions and events.
Phonology: /iː/ and /ɪ/.

Possible problem
Vocabulary The texts in Exercise 1 may contain a lot of words which the students do not know. It is important for them to realise that they do not need to understand every word in order to grasp the overall meaning of the texts and carry out the task. They should only learn those new words which are listed at the end of the lesson, or which they decide themselves they would like to know.

Optional extra materials
A copy of the text, cut into strips, for every four or five students (see Exercise 1).

1 Mixed-up texts

● You may like to start by pre-teaching *climate*, and asking students what they know (if anything) about the climate in Australia and the Amazon Basin.
● Start the exercise collectively. Write the two titles AUSTRALIAN ABORIGINES and AMAZON INDIANS on opposite sides of the board. Write the first fragment of the text under AUSTRALIAN ABORIGINES, the second under AMAZON INDIANS, and ask students where the next should go.
● Then get them to continue the exercise in groups, until they have written out the two texts separately. They should use dictionaries only for essential items.
● In order to do the exercise successfully, students need to pay attention to punctuation, capitalisation and the use of conjunctions.
● An alternative approach is to cut copies of the text into strips and give out a mixed-up set of strips to each group. This is more difficult for the students, as they have not only to separate the texts but also to arrange the fragments of each text in a logical order.
● When students are ready, discuss the answers and clear up any difficulties.

Answers to Exercise 1
(Slight variations are possible in the order of some of the clauses and sentences.)

AUSTRALIAN ABORIGINES
The Karadjere people live in the desert of Western Australia, where the climate is very hot. It rains from January to March, and the rest of the year is dry. They do not live in one place, but travel around on foot. They sleep in shelters made of dry tree branches. Their food is fruit, nuts and kangaroo meat, and they eat fish in the wet season; they also make bread from grass seeds. Water is often difficult to find. The Karadjere like music, dancing and telling stories. They do not wear many clothes.

AMAZON INDIANS
These people live in the Amazon Basin, in Brazil, where the climate is hot and wet: it rains for nine to ten months of the year. They live in villages; their houses are made of wood, and the roofs are made of palm leaves. Several families live in each house. They travel by canoe. They eat fruit and vegetables, fish, and meat from animals and birds (for example monkeys, wild pigs, parrots). They like music, dancing and telling stories. They do not wear many clothes.

2 Pronunciation: /iː/ and /ɪ/

● You will of course only need to do this exercise if your students have difficulty in distinguishing these two vowels.
● Note that /iː/ (the vowel in *eat*) is not only longer than /ɪ/ (the vowel in *it*); it is also pronounced with the tongue higher and further forward. Students who have difficulty pronouncing /ɪ/ may be helped by being told to relax their lips, tongue and jaw muscles, and to make the sound with as little energy as possible.
● When you have got students to practise the words (using the recording as a model if you wish), ask them each to practise and read a section (one or more sentences) of one of the texts. Each student's section should include at least one word that he or she finds difficult to pronounce.

14

3 Grammar revision: Simple Present questions

- Some students may still have difficulty in using *do* and *does* correctly, or in getting the right word order in questions with noun-phrase subjects. If your students don't have this kind of problem you can drop the exercise.
- It is probably best done by asking students to write at least some of the questions individually, so that you can check and see who is making mistakes.

Answers to Exercise 3

1. Where do Eskimos live?
2. Where does the President live?
3. What do cats usually eat?
4. What does Jane's cat eat?
5. When does it rain?
6. How do these people travel?
7. What do these people like?
8. What does the Prime Minister like?
9. What do the students usually wear?
10. What does Alice wear?

4 Guided composition

- This can be done as a class composition on the board, or as an individual exercise (perhaps for homework) as you prefer.
- The most important thing is that the students should use the first two texts to help them write the third. Most of the things they know about the Eskimos can be expressed using sentence-frames from Exercise 1 (*These people live . . .* ; *where the climate is . . .* ; *Their food is . . .* ; etc.).
- Help with vocabulary if necessary.
- Stress that students do not need to be experts on the Eskimos in order to do the exercise. The ordinary person's few odd bits of disorganised knowledge are quite enough. (But if they really know absolutely nothing, get them to write about some other remote tribe or social group that they know something about.)

5 Discussion

- This can be done as a brief follow-up to the reading and writing work. Again, no special knowledge is required.
- As students will probably imagine, most Eskimos today live in houses, travel by car and bus, and so on. (The large majority of Eskimos have never seen an igloo.)

Optional activity

- With a good class, you might get students (individually or in groups) to try writing pairs of mixed-up texts for the others to disentangle. These could be about the way of life either of particular groups of people, or of individuals known to the students.

Practice Book exercises

1. Grammar and vocabulary revision (names of countries; position of frequency adverbs).
2. Simple Present tense and third-person -*s*.
3. Word stress.
4. Students write about how they live.
5. Recreational reading.

Practice Book work

Students' progress through the course will depend very much on the amount of work they do outside the class. However successful the lessons appear to be, most students will forget much of what they have learnt unless they do more practice, revision and reading in their own time. Make sure that your students do regular work from the Practice Book. Most of this can be self-corrected with the answer key (if your students have the *with Key* edition), so Practice Book work need not involve a very heavy correction load for the teacher.

Note that the Practice Book provides a wide choice of work for different purposes, and it is not expected that students will do all the exercises. You will probably want to suggest something like two exercises for each lesson, though some students may need more.

3 Write questions. Example:

Eskimos eat . . .
What do Eskimos eat?

1. Eskimos live . . .
2. The President lives . . .
3. Cats usually eat . . .
4. Jane's cat eats . . .
5. It rains from . . . to . . .
6. These people travel by . . .
7. These people like . . .
8. The Prime Minister likes . . .
9. The students usually wear . . .
10. Alice wears . . .

4 What do you know about the Eskimos' traditional way of life?
Write what you know in a short text.

5 How do you think most Eskimos live today?

a kayak

a dog-sledge

an igloo

Learn/revise: Australia; Brazil; month; year; the rest; place; desert; village; wood; roof; tree; leaf (*plural* leaves); food; fish; meat; bread; vegetable; fruit (*uncountable*); animal; bird; family; clothes; wear (wore, worn); eat (ate, eaten); find (found, found); tell a story (told, told); made of; hot; wet; dry; several; each; around; on foot; also.

Lesson 5

Students learn to make commentaries.
Principal structure: revison of Present Progressive tense.
Phonology: /iː/ and /ɪ/.

Language notes and possible problems

1. Present Progressive (Present Continuous) This lesson revises the formation of the Present Progressive, and its use to say what is happening at the moment of speaking. Students may make mistakes with the word order of Present Progressive questions when the subject is a noun phrase (e.g. *What are doing the strange creatures?*). Exercise 4 gives work on this, as does the Practice Book; Revision Lesson A studies the Present Simple/Progressive contrast.

2. Commentaries Both present tenses are used in commentaries. The Progressive tends to be used for longer actions, and the Simple tense for actions which take less time to happen than to describe.

3. Pronunciation Exercise 5 is only necessary if students have a problem distinguishing between /iː/ (as in *eat*) and /ɪ/ (as in *it*).

Pronunciation work is useless unless it is followed up regularly. During the next few lessons, remind students of how /ɪ/ is pronounced, and pay a little extra attention to their pronunciation of words that contain this vowel (such as *if*).

The techniques used here can be adapted to practise any vowel or consonant contrast – just make your own list of 'minimal pairs' and proceed as in Exercise 5.

4. *Strange* Speakers of Romance languages may assume this word means *foreign*.

Optional extra materials
Cards for mime exercise (see Optional activities).

1 Finding differences
- Ask students to look at the first cartoon strip.
- Tell them that they will hear somebody talking about what is happening, but that he makes mistakes.
- Students do not have to understand every word, but they must find and note the differences.
- Play the recording without stopping; students should jot down quick notes of the differences.
- Play it again while students complete their notes.
- Let them discuss their answers together; tell them any points they haven't noticed.

Answers to Exercise 1
(The tapescript is on the next page.)
The score is *England 8, Spain 1.*
The flying saucer is *square.*
The door is in the *side* of the saucer.
The things have *four* arms and *four* eyes.
They are wearing *red* suits.
Two of them take hold of Evans, not one.
The thing is holding the gun in its top *right* hand.

2 Present Progressive forms
- The purpose of this exercise is to refresh students' memories of the Present Progressive tense.
- Ask for the first answer. If students have difficulty, write it on the board and remind them how the tense is formed (*I am* etc. + . . .*ing*).
- Get students to work out some of the other answers individually; then let them compare notes in groups before giving them the answers.
- Remind students that the Present Progressive can be used to talk about things that are going on around the moment of speaking, but not usually for permanent

states or repeated actions. The two present tenses will be contrasted in Revision Lesson A.

Answers to Exercise 2
1. 's (*or* is) looking
2. 's/is coming
3. 's/is opening
4. 's/is getting
5. 're/are wearing
6. 're/are walking
7. 's/is pulling
8. 's/is taking
9. 'm/am going
10. 's/is taking
11. 's/is pointing

3 Spelling of -ing forms
- Look through the examples, and find out whether students know the rules (*-e* is dropped before *-ing*; a single consonant after a single vowel at the end of a word is usually doubled before *-ing*; *ie* changes to *y*).
- Get students to write the answers and compare notes; discuss the answers and clear up any problems.

Answers to Exercise 3
looking, coming, landing, getting, wearing, walking, feeling, pulling, going, holding, pointing, dying, raining.

4 Present Progressive questions
- Ask students to write some answers individually, to make sure they all know the rule for word order.
- The rest of the exercise can be done by group or class discussion.

Answers to Exercise 4
1. Where is everybody looking?
2. Where is the machine landing?
3. Where is the door opening?
4. How many strange creatures are getting out?
5. What are the strange creatures wearing?
6. Where are the strange creatures walking?
7. Who is the commentator talking to?

5 Pronunciation: /iː/ and /ɪ/
- Play the first part of the recording (or say the words). Ask students whether they hear words from list A or list B, and tell them to write the words they think they hear.
- The words they actually hear are:

  eat green ship field it green sheep
  filled eat grin sheep filled

- Now get students to practise the words from lists A and B. Get them to work in pairs, 'testing' each other to see if one can identify the words that the other says.
- Then get them to practise the next two groups of words (*machine* etc.). (These are recorded.)
- Remember that the difference between /iː/ and /ɪ/ is not simply one of length – a long /ɪ/ doesn't sound like /iː/, and a short /iː/ is not at all the same as /ɪ/. /ɪ/ is pronounced with much less energy and muscle tension than /iː/.
- Finally, ask students if they can think of other words containing /iː/ or /ɪ/. You may like to mention three words pronounced with /ɪ/ that have misleading spellings: *women* (/ˈwɪmɪn/), *minute* (/ˈmɪnɪt/) and *business* (/ˈbɪznɪs/).

5 There's a strange light in the sky

Present Progressive; listening and speaking skills.

1 📼 Look at the pictures and listen to the commentary. There are some differences. What are they? (Useful words: *top*, *side*, *square*, *round*.)

2 How well can you remember the commentary? Complete the commentator's sentences.

1. 'Everybody .... up.'
2. 'The light .... from a strange machine.'
3. 'A door .... in the top.'
4. 'A strange thing .... out.'
5. 'They .... green suits.'
6. 'Now they .... across the field.'
7. 'He .... him over to the spaceship.'
8. 'He .... him inside.'
9. 'I .... down to have a word with our visitors.'
10. 'It .... out a gun.'
11. 'It .... it at me.'

3 Write the *-ing* forms. Examples:

work → working   take → taking
sit → sitting   wait → waiting
lie → lying

look   come   land   get   wear   walk
feel   pull   go   hold   point   die   rain

4 Make questions. Example:

light | where | come from?
——→ *Where is the light coming from?*

1. everybody | where | look?
2. machine | where | land?
3. door | where | open?
4. strange creatures | how many | get out?
5. strange creatures | what | wear?
6. strange creatures | where | walk?
7. commentator | who | talk to?

5 Pronunciation. Listen to the recording. Do you hear A or B? Practise the difference.

A: eat   green   sheep   field

B: it   grin   ship   filled

Now say these words:

machine   green   field   people   believe
dream

in   picture   listen   difference   is   coming
thing   him   ship   inside   visitor   think

16

6 Students' commentaries

- Tell students to look at the second set of pictures.
- Get them to say something about what is happening in each one. Make sure they use the Present Progressive tense.
- Then tell students to work in groups, preparing commentaries like the one in Exercise 1. They should incorporate some mistakes – if possible, mistakes that they hope the other students will not notice.
- Help with vocabulary if necessary.
- When students are ready, get one person from each group to read out the group's commentary, while the rest of the class listen *with their books closed*.
- The listeners must try to pick out the mistakes, relying on their memory of the cartoon strip.

Optional activity: 'Blind students'

- If you want more practice on the Present Progressive, it can be done as follows.
- Students sit in pairs, one facing the front and one with his/her back to you.
- Do a series of slow actions (for instance, stand up slowly, walk up and down, stop and look at one of the students, look out of the window, draw something on the board, . . .).
- The students who can see you have to tell their 'blind' partners what you are doing.
- If you wish, the 'blind' students can then practise past tenses by trying to remember what you did.

Optional activity: mime

- Prepare cards of two kinds.
- One set has the names of activities on the cards (e.g. *playing cards, singing, talking, shopping, watching football, playing football, taking a baby for a walk, waiting for somebody*).
- The other cards have one of these sentences:
  *It's raining.   It's snowing.   It's hailing.
  It's foggy.   It's windy.   The sun's shining.*
- Teach any words that students don't already know. Then divide the class into groups. Each group in turn takes two cards and has to mime the activity, while at the same time showing what the weather is like.
- The other students watch and try to guess. (For example: 'You're playing football. It's raining.')

Practice Book exercises

1. Students complete a text with appropriate Present Progressive verbs.
2. Students write a commentary.
3. Present Progressive questions.
4. Present Progressive negative forms.
5. Vocabulary revision: clothing.
6. Student's Cassette exercise (Student's Book Exercise 1). Students pick out and write phrases or sentences which do not correspond to the illustrations.

Tapescript for Exercise 1

. . . a beautiful afternoon here at Wembley, with the score at Spain 8, England 1. Campbell to Evans, to Murchison; Murchison on to Barker – and Gonzalez intercepts. Very good play there by Gonzalez, by Gonzalez . . . That's funny. There's a very strange light in the sky. A strange red light. Everybody's looking up. And I think – I think I can see – yes, the light's coming from a strange machine. Not an aeroplane – it's round, and very big – very big indeed. It's coming down very low now, and – yes – it's landing. This is amazing. Now a door's opening in the top, and a strange thing is getting out. And another. And another. Three strange things are getting out. They're wearing green suits, and they've got – just a moment – yes six arms and three eyes. Now they're walking across the field towards the centre. And now – one of them has taken hold of Evans, the England striker – yes, he's pulling him over to the spaceship. He's taking him inside. I must find out what's going on. I'm going down to have a word with our visitors.

. . . Excuse me, sir, er, madam, er, sir – I'm Brian Carter of BBC radio news. I wonder if I might ask you a few questions. Oh – it's taking out a gun. It's holding it up in its left hand – its top left hand – it's pointing it at me – Aaaaaaaaaaaaaargh!

Selective and global reading and listening

Not all spoken and written texts are meant to be studied in detail. Some texts are used just to present certain language points; the students' task is to extract particular pieces of information from the text, but not to study and understand every word. In other cases, students are required to grasp the main points of a text without worrying about details.

Students may have followed other courses in which nothing is presented without being immediately explained. So they may be uncomfortable if they leave a text without having studied every word in every line. It is important for them to realise that there are different ways of listening and reading for different purposes, and that it is not always necessary to understand everything in order to 'get the message'. Indeed, they must get used to coping with speech and writing in which not everything is clear – they will have to do this all the time in real-life use of English.

So if students ask you to spend an extra half hour or so 'going through' a text which is not meant to be studied in this way, it is probably best to refuse (telling the students why), unless you are very sure that the time could not be used more profitably for other purposes.

6 You are the commentator. The strange creatures have taken you away with Evans in the spaceship. You still have your portable radio transmitter, and you go on sending messages to Earth to tell people what is happening.
Look at the pictures below, and work with other students to prepare a commentary.
Make the commentary different from the pictures in four or five places.
Give your commentary, and see if the class can find the differences.

Present Progressive tense
I am (I'm) looking you are (you're) looking *etc.*
am I looking? is the commentator looking? ~~(is looking the commentator?)~~ *etc.*
I am (I'm) not looking you are not (aren't) looking *etc.*

Learn/revise: top; side; square; round; light; sky; in the sky; machine; thing; creature; door; suit; field; visitor; gun; message; Earth; difference; dream (dreamt, dreamt); hear (heard, heard); send (sent, sent); believe; land; open; happen; get out (got, got); go on . . .ing (went, gone); hold (held, held); strange; everybody; how many; across; over; inside.

6 Things are changing

Change; Present Progressive tense; comparatives and superlatives *get* + comparative.

1 What is happening to food prices in Fantasia? Look at the graph and make sentences.

| The price of |

| bananas |
| potatoes |
| bread |
| fish |
| sugar |
| chicken |

| is going up (is rising) |
| is going down (is falling) |

| fast. |
| slowly. |

FOOD PRICES IN FANTASIA

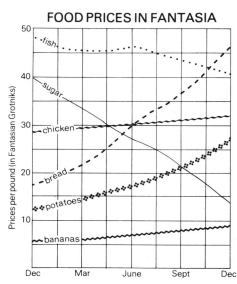

2 What is happening to prices in your country?

3 Listen to the figures and complete the table.

FANTASIA: SOME STATISTICS	100 YEARS AGO	50 YEARS AGO	NOW
Population	20m	35m	46m
Average number of children per family	4.5	3.6	2
Average July temperature	33°C		
Average January temperature			7°C
Average height (men)		1m 67	
Average height (women)		1m 62	
Length of working week	54hrs		
Paid holiday	–		
Average time taken for letter to travel 100km		2 days	
Size of Fantasian army	500,000		
Population of San Fantastico			3m
Percentage of population without homes			8%
Percentage of population unemployed		7%	

Lesson 6

Students learn to talk about change; they listen for specific information.
Structures: more work on Present Progressive; formation of comparative and superlative adjectives; *get* + comparative.
Phonology: pronunciations of the letter *i*.

Language notes

1. Changes   A common use of the Present Progressive is to talk about things that are changing. The verb *get* is often used in this context, generally followed by a comparative adjective.

2. Comparatives and superlatives   Note that the rules given (in the teaching notes for Exercise 5) are somewhat simplified; there are exceptions. For students who have trouble with this point, more practice in forming comparatives and superlatives is given in Practice Book Revision A.

If you are short of time

Get students to do Exercise 6 in writing for homework.

1   Interpreting the graph

- Ask students to look at the graph.
- Not everybody finds it easy to understand information presented in this way, and some students may need help (from you or from other students) to work it out.
- When they are ready, look at one of the lines (for instance, the one for the price of potatoes), and get the students to tell you what is happening to the price – is it going up or down, fast or slowly?
- Write on the board:
  The price of potatoes is going up fast.
- Teach *rise* and *fall* as alternatives to *go up* and *go down*.
- Get students to make more sentences about the graph.
- Let them compare notes to make sure they all interpret the information correctly.

2   Extension

- It should now be easy for students to make a few examples about real prices.
- Mention the possibility of saying, for instance, *Cigarettes are going up* instead of *The price of cigarettes is going up*.

3   Listening for information

- Go through the table of statistics with the students and explain any words and expressions that they don't know.
- To demonstrate the meaning of *average*, take the heights or ages of five students; add them and divide by five (do this on the board): explain that the result is the *average height* or *average age*.
- When everything is clear, play the recording and get the students to fill in the table. (If you don't want them to write in their books, get them to copy the table on a separate piece of paper first.)
- Note that the missing information is not always given in chronological order – students have to understand what they hear in order to do the exercise properly.
- Let students compare notes when they have finished; then go over the answers with them.

Tapescript for Exercise 3

- Fifty years ago the average July temperature was thirty-four degrees Centigrade. Now it is thirty-five degrees.
- Fifty years ago, the average temperature in January was eight degrees. A hundred years ago it was nine degrees.
- The average height of Fantasian men today is 1 metre 70. A hundred years ago it was 1 metre 65.
- A hundred years ago the average height of women was 1 metre 60. Now it is 1 metre 65.
- Fifty years ago, Fantasians worked forty-nine hours a week. Now they work forty-two hours.
- Fantasians have five weeks' paid holiday a year. Fifty years ago they only had two weeks.
- It takes a letter three days to travel a hundred kilometres in Fantasia. A hundred years ago it only took one day.
- Fifty years ago there were two hundred thousand men in the Fantasian army. Today there are fifty thousand.
- Fifty years ago, the population of San Fantastico, the Fantasian capital, was four million. A hundred years ago it was one million.
- Twenty-three per cent of the population had no homes a hundred years ago. Fifty years ago, the figure was seventeen per cent.
- Unemployment today is running at seventeen per cent of the working population. This is nearly as bad as the situation a hundred years ago, when unemployment was twenty per cent.

Answers to Exercise 3

FANTASIA: SOME STATISTICS	100 YEARS AGO	50 YEARS AGO	NOW
Population	20m	35m	46m
Average number of children per family	4.5	3.6	2
Average July temperature	33°C	34°C	35°C
Average January temperature	9°C	8°C	7°C
Average height (men)	1m 65	1m 67	1m 70
Average height (women)	1m 60	1m 62	1m 65
Length of working week	54 hrs	49 hrs	42 hrs
Paid holiday	–	2 wks	5 wks
Average time taken for letter to travel 100km	1 day	2 days	3 days
Size of Fantasian army	500,000	200,000	50,000
Population of San Fantastico	1m	4m	3m
Percentage of population without homes	23%	17%	8%
Percentage of population unemployed	20%	7%	17%

4 Pronunciations of the letter *i*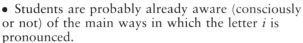

• Students are probably already aware (consciously or not) of the main ways in which the letter *i* is pronounced.
• This exercise will help them to see the rules more clearly.
• Practise the words in group 1 (using the recording if you wish). Make sure students say /ɪ/ and not /iː/.
• Then pronounce the words in group 2. Ask what makes these different (when *i* is followed by single consonant + *e* or *i*, or by *gh*, it is pronounced /aɪ/).
• Finally, practise the /ɜː/ sound in *thirty*, *first* and *shirt*. Ask when *i* is pronounced /ɜː/ (when it is followed by final *r* or *r* + consonant).
• Now get students to look at the words lettered (a) to (p), perhaps in groups. They should be able to pronounce all of the words correctly, even though they are not familiar with all of them.

Answers to Exercise 4

Group 1 (/ɪ/)	Group 2 (/aɪ/)	Group 3 (/ɜː/)
with	size	girl
fin	arriving	thirsty
fifty	tights	bird
	white	stir
	light	
	bright	
	slight	
	excite	
	ride	

5 Comparatives and superlatives

• Get students to work in groups of three or four. Ask them to look over the examples, and then try and write the comparative and superlative forms of the adjectives listed.
• If there are any difficulties, you may want to elicit or state the rules for comparison of adjectives:
– short (one-syllable) adjectives form comparatives and superlatives with *-er* and *-est* (or with *-r* and *-st* if they end in *e*).
– one-syllable adjectives ending in one vowel and one consonant double the consonant.
– long adjectives (with three or more syllables) form comparatives and superlatives with *more* and *most*.
– two-syllable words ending in *-y* have *-ier*, *-iest*.
– most other two-syllable words have *more*, *most*.
– *good* and *bad* are irregular.

Answers to Exercise 5

boring – more boring – most boring
clear – clearer – clearest
cold – colder – coldest
dangerous – more dangerous – most dangerous
dark – darker – darkest
expensive – more expensive – most expensive
fair – fairer – fairest
heavy – heavier – heaviest
hungry – hungrier – hungriest
large – larger – largest
late – later – latest
lazy – lazier – laziest
nice – nicer – nicest
quiet – quieter – quietest
rich – richer – richest
sleepy – sleepier – sleepiest
slim – slimmer – slimmest

6 How are things changing?

• Get students to look back at their completed tables.
• Go over the words in the exercise and explain any difficulties. Practise the pronunciation where necessary; students should make a special effort to pronounce words with *i* correctly.
• Do one or two of the examples together; then ask individuals for more.
• Get students to write one or two of the sentences.

7 Extension

• Students should be able to think of examples about the real world without too much difficulty.
• You may need to help with vocabulary.

Practice Book exercises

1. Students write true sentences about how they are changing.
2. Revision of vocabulary from the lesson.
3. Writing questions with *getting* + comparative and *going up/down*.
4. Vocabulary revision – various lexical fields.
5. Recreational reading.
6. Guided writing.

4 Pronunciation of the letter *i*. Say these words after the recording or after your teacher.

1. fish   chicken   million   big
2. price   time   rising   night   right
3. thirty   first   shirt

Now decide how to pronounce these words. Are they in group 1, 2 or 3? Check with your teacher or the recording. Can you write rules for the pronunciation of *i*?

a. girl	e. white	i. fin	m. slight
b. size	f. thirsty	j. bird	n. excite
c. arriving	g. light	k. stir	o. ride
d. tights	h. with	l. bright	p. fifty

5 Do you remember how to make comparative and superlative adjectives? Look at the examples:

old ⟶ *older* ⟶ *oldest*
cheap ⟶ *cheaper* ⟶ *cheapest*
fat ⟶ *fatter* ⟶ *fattest*
fine ⟶ *finer* ⟶ *finest*
happy ⟶ *happier* ⟶ *happiest*
interesting ⟶ **more interesting** ⟶ **most interesting**
good ⟶ **better** ⟶ **best**
bad ⟶ **worse** ⟶ **worst**

Now write the comparative and superlative forms of these adjectives:

boring   clear   cold   dangerous   dark
expensive   fair   heavy   hungry   large   late
lazy   nice   quiet   rich   sleepy   slim

6 How are things changing in Fantasia? Look at the table and make sentences.

| The population   The army   Holidays   The post |
| The housing problem   People   The climate |
| The working week   The unemployment problem |
| The population of San Fantastico   Families |

| is getting |
| are getting |

| bigger/smaller   faster/slower |
| longer/shorter   taller/shorter |
| warmer/colder   better/worse |

7 How are things changing in your country?

Learn/revise: banana; potato (*plural* potatoes); sugar; chicken; post; problem; unemployment; height; length; price; country; population; number; temperature; holiday; size; army; percentage; up; down; go up; go down; fall (fell, fallen); rise (rose, risen); change; get (= become) (got, got); average; cheap; clear; dangerous; hungry; large; lazy; rich; sleepy; better; worse; unemployed; fast (*adverb*); slowly; without.

Summary A

Be

I am (I'm)	
you are (you're)	
he/she/it is (he's/she's/it's)	
we are (we're)	
you are (you're)	
they are (they're)	

am I?
are you?
is he/she/it?
are we?
are you?
are they?

I am not (I'm not)
you are not (you're not / you aren't)
he/she/it is not (he's not etc. / she isn't etc.)
we are not (we're not / we aren't)
you are not (you're not / you aren't)
they are not (they're not / they aren't)

Can

I can swim (~~I can to swim~~)
he/she/it can swim (~~he/she/it cans . . .~~)
etc.

Can you swim? (~~Do you can . . . ?~~)
Can your brother swim?
(~~Can swim your brother?~~)
etc.

I cannot (can't) swim
etc.

Have got

I have got (I've got)
you have got (you've got)
he/she/it has got (he's/she's/it's got)
we have got (we've got)
you have got (you've got)
they have got (they've got)

have I got?
have you got?
Has your baby got blue eyes?
(~~Has got your baby blue eyes?~~)
etc.

I have not (haven't) got
he/she/it has not (hasn't) got
etc.

Simple Present tense

I work	do I work?
you work	do you work?
he/she/it works	does he/she/it work?
we work	Does your father work?
you work	(~~Does work your father?~~)
they work	do we work?
	do you work?
	do they work?

I do not (don't) work
you do not (don't) work
he/she/it does not (doesn't) work
we do not (don't) work
you do not (don't) work
they do not (don't) work

Spelling of third-person singular forms

stop $\longrightarrow$ stops	start $\longrightarrow$ starts
play $\longrightarrow$ plays	like $\longrightarrow$ likes
wish $\longrightarrow$ wishes	watch $\longrightarrow$ watches
miss $\longrightarrow$ misses	
try $\longrightarrow$ tries	study $\longrightarrow$ studies
go $\longrightarrow$ goes	do $\longrightarrow$ does

Present Progressive tense

I am (I'm) looking
you are (you're) looking
etc.

am I looking?
Is the commentator looking?
(~~Is looking the commentator?~~)
etc.

I am (I'm) not looking
you are not (aren't) looking
etc.

Spelling of -ing forms

MOST VERBS:	work $\rightarrow$ working
	wait $\rightarrow$ waiting
VERBS ENDING IN -e:	take $\rightarrow$ taking
	come $\rightarrow$ coming
VERBS ENDING IN ONE STRESSED VOWEL − ONE CONSONANT:	get $\longrightarrow$ getting
	sit $\longrightarrow$ sitting
VERBS ENDING IN -ie:	lie $\longrightarrow$ lying
	die $\longrightarrow$ dying

Talking about change

The price of bread is going up.
People are getting taller.

Summary A

Summary of language taught in Lessons 1–6.

This lesson displays most of the more important language points that students should have learnt or revised in the last six lessons. Spend a short time going over the material with the students, answering questions and clearing up any difficulties. Students may also need to spend time at home making sure everything is thoroughly learnt.

Practice Book exercises
1. Writing ordinal numbers.
2. Writing contractions.
3. Spelling third-person singular forms.
4. Puzzle pictures for practising Present Progressive.
5. Text completion as preparation for guided writing.
6. Guided writing.

Comparative and superlative adjectives

One-syllable adjectives

most adjectives: + -er, -est

old, older, oldest
cheap, cheaper, cheapest
young (/jʌŋ/), younger (/jʌŋgə(r)/), youngest (/jʌŋgɪst/)
long (/lɒŋ/), longer (/lɒŋgə(r)/), longest (/lɒŋgɪst/)

adjectives ending in -e: + -r, -st

fine, finer, finest

adjectives ending in one vowel + one consonant usually double the consonant

big, bigger, biggest

Longer adjectives

two-syllable adjectives ending in y ⟶ -ier, -iest

happy, happier, happiest

most other longer adjectives: more, most + adjective

boring, **more** boring, **most** boring
beautiful, **more** beautiful, **most** beautiful

Irregular adjectives

good, better, best
bad, worse, worst
far, farther, farthest

Frequency adverbs: how often?

I **always** have coffee for breakfast.
   (~~I have always coffee . . .~~)
I **usually** have toast and butter.
I **normally** lie in on Sunday mornings.
I **very often** go away at weekends.
I **often** go out in the evenings.
I **quite often** get dressed after breakfast.
I **sometimes** go to the cinema.
I **don't** stay at home **very often**.
I **occasionally** have Sunday lunch.
I **hardly ever** eat fish.
I **never** play golf.

How often do you go to Scotland?   **Every four weeks.**
Do you **ever** go to Ireland?   **About twice a year.**
I write home **once a week.**

Linking words and expressions

Look . . .
You're **just** too old.
Well, yes, OK.
So what?
You haven't **even** got any money.
Well, yes, I know.
What's he like, **then**?
Well, you know.
No, **actually**, he isn't.
perhaps/maybe
perhaps/maybe not
I don't know.
on the other hand
I do think my eyes are too small, **though**.
Still, they're pretty.

Introductions; meeting people

I'd like to introduce . . .
This is . . .
Do you know . . . ?
May I introduce myself? My name's . . .
Excuse me, aren't you . . . ?
I'm glad to meet you.
I'm sorry, I didn't catch your name.
How do you do?
Nice to see you again.
Where are you from?
Whereabouts in . . . ?

Getting help in class

How do you say . . . in English?
What's the English for . . . ?
How do you pronounce . . . ?
How do you spell . . . ?
What does . . . mean?
Is this correct: . . . ?

Revision A

Look at the exercises, decide which ones are useful to you, and do two or more.

VOCABULARY

1 Which word is different? Can you find a word or expression that names all the others? Example:

sofa   chair   table   wall   bed
'*Wall is different. The others are all furniture.*'

1. tea   coffee   bread   milk
2. kitchen   bathroom   bedroom   garage
3. green   big   blue   red
4. fair   red   green   grey   dark
5. water   meat   bread   fish
6. car   sheep   train   bicycle
7. Monday   Thursday   Sunday   Tuesday
8. July   Christmas   March   January
9. book   letter   TV   newspaper
10. uncle   friend   sister   mother

2 Now listen to the recording of a little boy doing the same kind of exercise. Which word does he choose each time, and what is his reason?

1. horse   dog   book   cat
2. fish   lamb   beef   pork
3. apple   orange   pear   banana
4. knife   fork   cup   spoon
5. run   walk   chair   jump
6. TV   grass   flower   tree
7. shout   cry   laugh   sing
8. Mummy   Daddy   Mark   Granny

GRAMMAR

1 Look at the table and examples and choose the best rules for each tense.

PRESENT PROGRESSIVE TENSE	SIMPLE PRESENT TENSE
I am working, you are working *etc.* am I working? *etc.* I am not working *etc.*	I work, you work, he/she works *etc.* do I/you work?, does he/she work? *etc.* I/you do not work, he/she does not work *etc.*
'Are you free now?' 'Sorry, I'm **studying**.' Look – Helen's **wearing** a lovely dress. The light **is coming** from a strange machine. 'What **are** you **eating**?' 'A cheese sandwich.' The world's climate **is getting** warmer. I'm not **working** next Saturday.	I always **study** from five to seven o'clock. Helen often **wears** red. Light and heat **come** from the sun. They **eat** fish in the wet season. The weather usually **gets** warmer in April. I never **work** on Saturdays.

Rules
We use the Present Progressive to talk about:
1. ....
2. ....
3. ....

Rules
We use the Simple Present to talk about:
1. ....
2. ....

    A things that are happening now, these days
    B things that are always true
    C things that happen often, usually, always, never *etc.*
    D things that are changing
    E plans for the future

Revision A

Students and teacher choose vocabulary, grammar, listening and speaking activities.
Principal structures: revision of the contrast between the two present tenses.

Language notes and possible problems

1. Grammatical explanations Students (and teachers) vary widely in their reactions to explicit grammatical information. The tense usage dealt with here is difficult, and knowledge of the rules will serve as a valuable support to many students. It will not, however, necessarily stop them making mistakes.

2. Choice There is a lot of material in this lesson, and you will probably not want or need to do all of it. You might get students to vote for the exercises they feel are most valuable.

3. _Who_ When _who_ is the subject of a question the verb has an affirmative form (subject + verb); when _who_ is the object the verb form is interrogative (auxiliary + subject). Grammar Exercise 3 helps to remind students of this. Note that in modern English (especially in informal usage) _whom_ is rarely used; _who_ functions as both subject and object.

VOCABULARY

1 Which word is different?

- Students can do this by group discussion, or try it individually before comparing notes.
- You will need to help them to find some of the 'superordinate' words.
- Students may well find other plausible answers besides the ones given below.

Answers to Exercise 1
1. _Bread_ is different (the others are all _drinks_)
2. _garage_ (_rooms_)
3. _big_ (_colours_)
4. _green_ (_hair colours_)
5. _water_ (_food_)
6. _sheep_ (_vehicles / means of transport_)
7. _Sunday_ (_weekdays_)
8. _Christmas_ (_months_)
9. _TV_ (_things you can read_)
10. _friend_ (_relations/family_)

2 Authentic listening

- Students listen to an English three-year-old doing a 'which word is different' exercise.
- The first time you play the recording, ask the students to listen only for the word the child chooses in each case.
- Then play the recording again one or more times, pausing after each answer, and ask students to see if they can understand the reasons the child gives. They will probably need some help.

Answers to Exercise 2
1. _Book_ 'because it's something to read in'.
2. _Fish_ 'because it lives underwater'.
3. _Banana_ 'because I can't eat it'. (The child is allergic to bananas.)
4. _Cup_ 'because you drink out of it'.
5. _Chair_ 'because it's something to sit on'.
6. _Tree_, _grass_ and _flower_ 'because sometimes you can climb on a tree, and you can smell the flowers sometimes, and you can walk on grass'.
7. _Sing_ 'because it's something that you enjoy'.
8. 'None of them are different; they're just all people.'

GRAMMAR

1 Contrasting the present tenses

- Give students plenty of time to look at the table and study the examples.
- Go through the five rules with them and help them to understand them. Ask them to decide which three rules are for the Present Progressive and which two are for the Simple Present.
- Let them discuss this in groups before you give them the answers (Present Progressive: A, D and E; Simple Present: B and C).

2 Discrimination test

- Ask for written answers to some of the questions to check that everybody understands the point.
- Discuss the reasons for the tense choices.

Answers to Exercise 2
1. smokes
2. are (you) looking
3. 's raining / is raining
4. go
5. Do (you) go
6. Do (you) spell
7. are (you) thinking
8. Do (you) like; hate
9. 'm working / am working
10. 's playing / is playing
11. boils
12. are(n't) watching
13. are going
14. is getting

3 Who loves who?

- Questions with _wh_-subjects are difficult.
- Tell students to look at the illustration and answer the questions as fast as they can. (Give a five-minute time limit, or organise the exercise as a contest.)

Answers to Exercise 3
1. Eric   2. Philip   3. Alice   4. nobody
5. Philip and Alice   6. nobody   7. Eric and Philip
8. Philip   9. Alice   10. nobody   11. He likes him
12. No   13. No

Grammar Exercises 2 and 3: see page 22 for instructions

LISTENING

1 Identifying the speakers

• Tell students to look at the illustration while you play the recording.
• Tell them to decide who is speaking in each section.
• Play the recording a second time if necessary.

Answers to Exercise 1
1. Alice 2. Janet 3. Eric 4. Philip and Alice

Tapescript for Exercise 1: see page 127

2 Imagining or miming a story

• Tell students that they will hear a story told in the present tense, beginning 'You are walking'.
• Shy students or adolescents can listen with eyes closed, imagining everything as vividly as possible.
• More confident and/or serious students can mime the story. You will need space for everybody to move around. Failing this, the mime can be done by three or four volunteers in front of the class.
• Tell them to listen and to do or mime the actions.
• Before starting, teach *beach*, *hot*, *stone*, *smile*.
• For a more structured task, ask students to listen twice and note all the *changes* in the story. (For instance, you are walking and then you stop; you are tired, but after standing in the sea you feel better.)

Tapescript for Exercise 2: see page 127

3 Song: *You're Perfect*

• Play the song once through for the students and ask them to tell you any words that they remember.
• Then tell them that you are going to play the song again, and they must try to write down all the verbs that they hear.
• They may want you to play the recording twice or more until they are satisfied with their answers.
• When they are ready, get them to turn to page 124 in their books, where the complete lyrics are printed, to check their answers.

SPEAKING

1 Descriptions: observation game
• Go over the examples with the students. Make sure they understand the reason for the Present Progressive in *She is wearing . . .* , and the use of *got* with *have*.
• Demonstrate with a volunteer. Then get students to do the exercise in pairs, in turn, or simultaneously ('*You're wearing . . .* ').
• (This exercise, and the following alternative, are adapted from *Drama Techniques in Language Learning* by Maley and Duff, Cambridge University Press.)

Alternative to Exercise 1
• Two teams of 6–8 students stand facing each other about ten feet apart. They have three minutes to observe and memorise the opposite team without speaking — clothes, appearance and position.
• Separate the teams. If possible, put one outside the classroom. One person in each team acts as secretary, and writes down everything the team can remember.
• Tell people to alter their appearance as much as possible, exchanging glasses, jewellery and clothing.
• Teams come back and line up opposite each other again, but *in a different order*.
• Students now speak in turn. Each student tries to get one thing put right. He/She might say, for instance: '*Juan, go and stand next to Fritz. Alice, that's Rosita's watch. Yasuko, where's your scarf? Brigitte, you've got Olga's shoes on.*'
• Put a few examples on the board (using these structures) to help students make their sentences.
• If possible, students should get the opposite team back in the original order, dressed as before.

2 Describing other people
• Get students to prepare a description of somebody else. They must not show who they are thinking about.
• Then get them to give their descriptions. The other students must try to guess who is being described.
• This can also be done as a written exercise, with descriptions put up for everybody to read.

3 'Twenty questions'
• Before starting, make sure students understand that an 'animal' object is one of animal origin (e.g. a woollen sweater), a 'vegetable' one is made of plant products, and so on.
• Think of an object yourself and get the class to ask questions that can be answered '*Yes*' or '*No*'.
• When they have discovered your object (or asked twenty questions without doing so), get a volunteer to think of another object and play again.
• Then let the class continue in groups.

Practice Book exercises
1. Distinguishing *be* and *have*.
2. *Somebody/-thing/-where*, *everybody/-thing/-where*, etc.
3. Simple Present and Present Progressive.
4. Student's Cassette exercise (Student's Book Listening Exercise 2). Students listen to the story and answer questions.
5. Reading comprehension practice.
6. Crossword.

Additional reading
Note that students have now reached a level where they should be able to cope comfortably with the texts in Section A of *Additional reading* in the Practice Book (page 108). You can set some of the readings for homework or just suggest that students read any of the texts that interest them when they have the time.

Student expectations: choice
In the revision lessons, and some others, a choice of activities is offered. Some students may be worried by this, feeling that they ought to do everything in the book, and fearing that if they leave something out their learning will not be complete. Help them to understand that language learning doesn't work like this. The list of things that can be learnt and activities that can be done is almost infinite; students are most likely to reach the level they want if they, the teacher and the course all co-operate to achieve the selection that best corresponds to their needs.

For this reason, it is important not to follow the course too slavishly. Teachers should not hesitate to drop or modify exercises and lessons that don't suit their students' purposes (and of course to supplement the course in cases where it does not fully meet the students' needs).

If time is short, remember that it is better to do part of the course thoroughly than to rush through the whole of it without giving students time to use and assimilate what they have learnt.

2 Put in the correct verb forms.

1. He .... twenty cigarettes a day. (smoke)
2. What .... you .... at? (look)
3. Look! It .... (rain)
4. I .... dancing every Friday night. (go)
5. '............... you often .... abroad?' 'Four or five times a year.' (go)
6. .... you .... your name with one *n* or two? (spell)
7. 'What .... you .... about?' 'I'm not going to tell you.' (think)
8. '............... you .... tea?' 'No, I .... it.' (like; hate)
9. 'Can you come and see me tomorrow?' 'Sorry, I ....' (work)
10. 'Is John here?' 'No, he .... football.' (play)
11. Water .... at 100° Celsius. (boil)
12. Can I turn off the TV? You ....n't .... it. (watch)
13. Prices .... up very fast these days. (go)
14. I feel my English .... better very slowly. (get)

3 Who loves who? Look at the picture and answer the questions as fast as you can.

1. Who does Janet love?
2. Who loves Janet?
3. Who does Eric love?
4. Who likes Eric?
5. Who dislikes Eric?
6. Who does Eric dislike?
7. Who loves Alice?
8. Who does Alice love?
9. Who does Janet hate?
10. Who hates Janet?
11. How does Eric feel about Philip?
12. Does Philip feel the same about him?
13. Do Philip and Janet love each other?

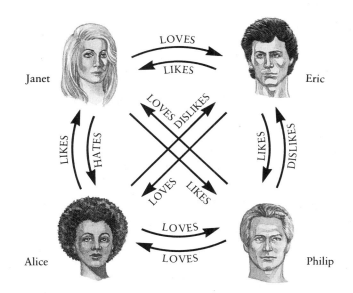

LISTENING

1 Listen to the recording and look at the illustration to Grammar Exercise 3. You will hear Philip, Eric, Alice and Janet (not in that order). Can you decide who you are listening to each time?

2 [cassette] Listen to the story and imagine or mime the actions.

3 [cassette] Listen to the song and try to write the verbs. Check your answers on page 124.

SPEAKING

1 Work in pairs. Look at your partner carefully for one minute. Then close your eyes (or turn your back) and say what he or she looks like, and what he or she is wearing. Examples:

'He's got dark brown hair.'
'She's wearing a light green blouse and black trousers.'

2 Describe a person in the class. The other students must decide who it is.

3 'Twenty questions'. Think of an object. Tell the other students whether it is animal, vegetable or mineral. They must find out what it is; they can ask twenty questions, but you can only answer *Yes* or *No*. Possible questions:

Can you eat it?
Is it useful?
Is it hard/soft/heavy/light?
Is it bigger than a . . . ?
Can you find it in a house/shop/car/. . . ?
Is it made of wood/metal/glass/. . . ?
Have you got one of these?
Is there one in this room?

Test A

LISTENING

1 Read the questions below. Then write the numbers 1 to 5 on your paper. Listen to the recording: you will hear five answers (a, b, c, d and e). Write the letter of each answer next to the number of the question the woman is answering.

1. What time do you usually get up?
2. How do you get to work?
3. How often do you stop during the day to have a hot drink?
4. What time do you have your meals?
5. What do you usually do in the evenings?

GRAMMAR

1 Write questions, using the correct forms of *be*, *have got*, *can* or *do*. Examples:

those children hungry

Are those children hungry?

your sister a car

Has your sister got a car?

1. your father live near here
2. how many languages you speak
3. Ann and Peter enough money
4. the baby walk
5. the children thirsty
6. this train go to Birmingham
7. why everybody looking at me

2 Write the third-person singular forms. Example:

stand *stands*

carry   come   die   get   go   pass   say
sit   stop   take   wait   wash

3 Write the *-ing* forms. Example:

play *playing*

get   hope   lie   live   put   run   start
stop   try   wait

4 Write the comparatives and superlatives. Example:

old *older oldest*

bad   cheap   easy   fat   good   heavy   hot
interesting   late   nice   tiring   young

5 Look at the table and write six or more sentences about how things are changing.
Example: *More people are going on holiday abroad.*

	20 YEARS AGO	10 YEARS AGO	NOW
Population	30m	52m	67m
Percentage unemployed	14%	16%	23%
Average income of richest 10%	£20,000	£31,000	£45,000
Average income of poorest 10%	£1,200	£1,100	£1,000
Percentage of population learning a foreign language	3%	12.5%	22%
Percentage of population who go on holiday abroad	2%	17%	35%
Average July temperature	27°	27.4°	28.2°
Average December temperature	3.3°	2.8°	2.1°
Price of small family car	£850	£2,500	£6,700
Price of apples per kilo	32p	32p	32p
Weekly rent for a 2-room flat	£5	£40	£100

The purpose of the test

This test covers material from Lessons 1–6. It is not of course necessary to do all of the sections, and teachers should select according to their students' needs. Teachers who do not feel the test will be useful should simply drop it altogether.

If possible, try to make the students feel that they are 'testing themselves', rather than 'being tested'. It is not intended that students should 'pass' or 'fail' the test, and it is not particularly useful to give marks. (If the school or education system requires that this be done, you will need to work out a simple marking scheme.) But students should of course be told whether you feel their performance is satisfactory. In principle, students who have worked systematically through Lessons 1–6 ought to get most answers right.

Administration

The test can be administered in various ways, depending on how strictly you want to control students' performance; whether you want to collect the answers and mark them, or allow the students to correct them in class; and so on.

The 'speaking' section will need to be done in pairs, with students interrupting their work on the other sections to come and do their interviews in front of you.

If you do not collect students' scripts, correction of most parts of the test can be done by class discussion when everybody has finished.

Notes, tapescript and answers are given below.

LISTENING

Matching questions and answers

Play the recording right through once while the students listen. Then play it again, pausing after each section so that they can write their answers.

Answers to Listening Test 1

1d; 2b; 3e; 4a; 5c.

Tapescript for Listening Test 1

a. I have lunch at one o'clock, because that's when we er, break for lunch at work, between one and two. Erm, we then normally have our dinner erm, at about eight or nine o'clock in the evening.

b. By car.

c. Most evenings I don't get home until nine o'clock, er, so there isn't very much left of the evening to do anything with – apart from maybe water the garden in this hot weather. Erm, but on Saturday evenings we like to go out together for a meal, 'cause it seems to be the only time we can sit and talk to each other. And nothing else very exciting, really.

d. As late as possible, but usually eight-thirty.

e. I drink all day long, because we have a coffee machine at work, and I don't have to make it myself.

GRAMMAR

1   1. Does your father live near here?
    2. How many languages can/do you speak?
    3. Have Ann and Peter got enough money?
    4. Can/Does the baby walk?
    5. Are the children thirsty?
    6. Does this train go to Birmingham?
    7. Why is everybody looking at me?

2   carries; comes; dies; gets; goes; passes; says; sits; stops; takes; waits; washes.

3   getting; hoping; lying; living; putting; running; starting; stopping; trying; waiting.

4   worse, worst
    cheaper, cheapest
    easier, easiest
    fatter, fattest
    better, best
    heavier, heaviest
    hotter, hottest
    more interesting, most interesting
    later, latest
    nicer, nicest
    more tiring, most tiring
    younger, youngest

5   (Various possible answers. Examples:)
    The population is getting bigger.
    The percentage of unemployed is rising.
    The rich are getting richer.
    More people are learning foreign languages.
    July is getting hotter.
    The price of cars is going up.

6
1. for
2. 're getting
3. 'm having
4. 's getting
5. goes
6. 's doing
7. than
8. wants
9. 's staying
10. don't like
11. know
12. talks
13. makes
14. 'm coming
15. come

VOCABULARY

1 interesting; expensive; hot/warm; fair/light; slim/thin; unhappy; early; young/new; poor; big/large.

2
1. o'clock
2. house
3. meat
4. plate

3 first; third; fifth; twentieth; (one/a) hundredth.

LANGUAGE IN USE

1
1. Look
2. just
3. why not
4. So what
5. even
6. Maybe
7. though
8. Well
9. Still

2
1. How do you spell . . . ?
2. How do you pronounce/say . . . ?
3. What does . . . mean?

PRONUNCIATION

1
1. home (*with* /əʊ/; *the others have* /ʌ/)
2. food (*with* /uː/; *the others have* /ʊ/)
3. word (*with* /ɜː/; *the others have* /ɔː/)
4. bread (*with* /e/; *the others have* /iː/)
5. how (*with* /aʊ/; *the others have* /əʊ/)
6. clear (*with* /ɪə/; *the others have* /eə/)
7. there (*with* /eə/; *the others have* /ɪə/)

2 across; actually; **always**; animal; be**lieve**; **confident**; correct; **dangerous**; **difference**; even; **everybody**; ex**pensive**; introduce; ma**chine**; maybe; **message**; nationality; piano; **picture**; **possible**; **several**; travel; usually; **village**; visitor.

WRITING

When correcting this, it is best to judge students mainly on their ability to communicate successfully, using appropriate vocabulary and structures. Excessive emphasis on minor errors of grammar and spelling can damage students' confidence.

SPEAKING

Go over the instructions with the whole class and make sure they understand what they have to do. Then test the students in pairs. Give each pair the same amount of time (say, five minutes); make sure one of the pair doesn't dominate the conversation too much, but otherwise try not to interfere. If you are giving marks, take into account not only correctness but also success in communicating, fluency, breadth of knowledge, appropriacy and variety of language.

Test Book recordings
A recording for Test 1 in the Test Book follows this lesson on the Class Cassette.

6 Read this and write down the missing words.

14 Peace Avenue
Saunton
Tuesday

Dear Tony,

Thanks a lot ......1...... your letter. I was sorry to hear you'd been ill, and I hope you ......2...... (get / 're getting) better now. We're OK. Ann's very well; I ......3...... (have / 'm having) a bit of trouble with my leg these days, but nothing serious.

The kids are in good shape. Jane's growing up fast, and I must say she ......4...... (gets / 's getting) very pretty. She ......5...... (goes / 's going) out almost every night – with a different boyfriend each time, as far as I can see. Billy ......6...... (does / 's doing) well at school now – much better ......7...... last year – and I think he should be OK in his exams. He ......8...... (wants / 's wanting) to get into university to do agriculture. We'll see.

Ann's mum ......9...... (stays / 's staying) with us for a week. She and I ......10...... (don't like / aren't liking) each other much, as you ......11...... (know / 're knowing), but we haven't had any trouble so far. She ......12...... (talks / 's talking) about people behind their backs all the time, which ......13...... (makes / is making) me pretty angry, but there isn't much I can do about it.

What are your plans? I ......14...... (come / 'm coming) to Ireland on business in July. Any chance of seeing you? If not, let's make it in the autumn. I ......15...... (come / 'm coming) over about six times a year, so it shouldn't be too difficult to fix something.

All the best. Don't work too hard, and keep smiling.

Yours,

Mike

VOCABULARY

1 What are the opposites? Example:

fast _slow_

boring   cheap   cold   dark   fat
happy   late   old   rich   small

2 Which word is different? Example:

car   bicycle   bus   horse

horse

1. month   year   o'clock   day
2. village   house   town   city
3. wood   glass   paper   meat
4. plate   bread   fish   meat

3 Write these in words.

1st   3rd   5th   20th   100th

LANGUAGE IN USE

1 Use the expressions from the box (once each) to complete the following conversation.

even	just	look	maybe	so what	still
though	well	why not			

'......1......, Andy, we ......2...... can't go on like this.'
'I don't see ......3......'
'We haven't got enough money.'
'......4......?'
'Don't you understand? We haven't ......5...... got enough to buy food.'
'That's all right. You eat too much anyway.'
'......6...... . We do need to eat, ...7......'
'......8......, yes, I know. ......9......, we can buy cheaper food, can't we?'
'Andy. We haven't got enough to buy cheap food. I can't feed both of us. You'll have to get a job.'
'Never.'

2 What would you say to your teacher to find out 1) the spelling; 2) the pronunciation; 3) the meaning of a difficult word?

PRONUNCIATION

1 Which word is different?

1. month   much   come   home
2. wood   look   foot   food
3. word   door   fall   fourth
4. meat   bread   each   dream
5. post   though   how   clothes
6. clear   fair   wear   square
7. we're   here   hear   there

2 Which syllable is stressed?

across; actually; always; animal; believe; confident; correct; dangerous; difference; even; everybody; expensive; introduce; machine; maybe; message; nationality; piano; picture; possible; several; travel; usually; village; visitor.

WRITING

1 Write a description of yourself or somebody else. (About 100–150 words.)

SPEAKING

1 Interview another student. Find out as much as you can about his/her family, or home, or interests.

7 A true story

1 Find these words and expressions in the story and then look them up in your dictionary. There is more than one translation for each word. Copy the definition that fits the word in the story best.

1. strapped (line 7)
2. broke (line 9)
3. badly (line 15)
4. bite (line 25)
5. seat (line 27)
6. body (line 28)

ESCAPE FROM THE JUNGLE (This is a true story.)

On Christmas Eve 1971 Juliana Koepke, a seventeen-year-old German girl, _____ Lima by air with her mother. They _____ on their way to Pucallpa, another town in Peru, to spend Christmas with
5 Juliana's father. Forty-five minutes later the plane _____ up in a storm, and Juliana _____ 3,000 metres, strapped in her seat. She was not killed when the seat _____ the ground (perhaps because trees broke her fall), but she _____ all night unconscious.
10 The next morning Juliana _____ for pieces of the plane, and _____ for her mother. Nobody answered, and she _____ nothing except a small plastic bag of sweets.
 Juliana's collar bone was broken, one knee was
15 badly hurt and she had deep cuts on her arms and legs. She had no shoes; her glasses were broken (so she could not _____ snakes or spiders, for example); and she was wearing only a very short dress, which was badly torn. But she decided to try
20 to _____ out of the jungle, because she _____ that if she stayed there she would die.
 So Juliana _____ to walk. She did not _____ anything to eat, and as the days went by she got weaker and weaker. She was also in bad trouble from
25 insect bites. She _____ helicopters, but could not see them above the trees, and of course they could not see her. One day she _____ three seats and _____ that they had dead bodies in them, but she did not recognise the people.
30 After four days she _____ to a river. She saw caimans and piranhas, but she _____ that they do not usually attack people. So Juliana walked and _____ down the river for another five days. At last she _____ to a hut. Nobody was there, but the next
35 afternoon, four men arrived. They _____ her to a doctor in the next village.
 Juliana _____ afterwards that there were at least three other people who were not killed in the crash. But she was the only one who _____ out of the
40 jungle. It took her ten days.

2 Now read the whole text and fill in the gaps with words from the boxes.

Put the correct forms of these verbs into the gaps marked ▆▆▆ .

be   break   call   fall   find   hit
leave   lie   look

Put the correct forms of these verbs into the gaps marked ▆▆ .

find   find   get   hear   know   see
see   start

Put the correct forms of these verbs into the gaps marked ▆▆▆ .

come   come   get   know   learn
swim   take

---

collar bone

snake

spider

jungle

helicopter

caiman

piranha

hut

Lesson 7

Students **work** on the language of past narrative.
Principal structures: revision of regular and irregular past verb forms.
Phonology: perceiving final consonants.

Language notes and possible problems
1. Dictionaries will be needed for Exercise 1. Students should bring their own bilingual dictionaries to class.
2. Irregular verbs In this lesson, students concentrate on revising irregular past tenses. Past participles will be revised later. (There is also frequent revision of irregular verbs in the Practice Book.)
3. Simple Past tense forms A common mistake is to use the Past tense instead of the infinitive after *did*. (For example *She did not saw; *Did you saw?*) Exercise 3 deals with this, and there is further work on the point in the Practice Book, if this is needed.
4. Spelling of regular Simple Past verbs is not focused on in this lesson. If you think your students may have difficulties in this area, ask them to do Exercise 4 in the Practice Book; you may then have to do more remedial work with them. This point will be revised again in Revision B.
5. Pronunciation of -ed If your students are aiming at a very good level of pronunciation, you may wish to work on the different pronunciations of the past ending *-ed*:
a. after a voiced sound: /d/ (e.g. *called*)
b. after an unvoiced sound: /t/ (e.g. *looked*)
c. after /t/ or /d/: /ɪd/ (e.g. *started*)
6. Pronunciation: final consonants Some students have difficulty distinguishing final consonants and consonant clusters (particularly if their language has a simpler syllable structure than English). This can lead to grammar problems, since they may not hear the difference between, for example, *stop*, *stops* and *stopped*. Exercise 5 will help with this.
7. Level This is a more difficult lesson than the previous ones. The text work is quite demanding, and weak students may not be able to get through all of it. Note, however, that there is no need for students to understand every word of the text.

If you are short of time
You may want to drop Exercise 1 if you are working with a multilingual class. You can leave some of Exercise 2 for homework, or drop Exercise 6. Drop Exercise 5 if the point is not difficult for your students.

---

1 Dictionary work
• Before you begin, you may want to discuss dictionary organisation and use with your students. Mention that one word can have several meanings, and using the dictionary efficiently means choosing the best meaning.
• Do the first word with the students: ask them to find the word in their dictionaries; then ask them to find the word in the text and read the sentence it appears in. Students then must decide which of the meanings of *strap* in their dictionary fits the word in the text.
• If students are familiar with the names of parts of speech (either in their own language or in English), you may want to point out how they can use the part-of-speech indications in the dictionary to help them find the right meaning.
• Get students to work on the other words individually, then compare notes in small groups before checking with you.
• If you are teaching a multilingual class, and you feel that students will be disoriented by an exercise that you cannot check, you may want to drop this exercise. But if you feel that you can give them a general introduction

and then let them do the exercise to their own satisfaction, it will provide them with useful learning of skills that can help them become more autonomous.

2 The text; irregular verbs
• Give students a few minutes to read over the text and look at the illustrations.
• Let them use dictionaries, or ask about difficult words, within reason, but encourage them to guess the meanings of new words from the context and the illustrations.
• Then get them to do the first part of the exercise. They should write down in order the verb forms which belong in the gaps coloured red.
• Remind them that there is an irregular verb list in the back of the Student's Book.
• When students are ready, let them compare notes in pairs or groups, and then check the answers with them.
• The second and third parts of the exercise can be done in the same way, or (for the sake of variety) by whole-class discussion.
• If time is short, leave some of this for homework.

Answers to Exercise 2
1. left; were; broke; fell; hit; lay; looked; called; found.
2. see; get; knew; started; find; heard; found; saw.
3. came; knew; swam; came; took; learnt (*or* learned); got.

26

3 Grammar: past tenses

- The purpose of this exercise is simply to ensure that students have no trouble making past tense questions.
- It is probably best to ask students to write the answers individually, so that you can spot anybody who has a problem.

Answers to Exercise 3
1. leave 2. left 3. fall 4. fell 5. look 6. looked

4 Students' questions

- Give students a few minutes to prepare their questions. Go round helping where necessary, and check that there are no serious mistakes.
- Before students start asking their questions, practise the 'first aid' sentences illustrated ('*Sorry, could you say that again?*' etc.).

5 Pronunciation

- Tell students to write down the words.
- Then play the recording, pausing after each sentence so that students can circle the word(s) they think they hear.
- Let them compare notes and then check their answers.

Tapescript and answers to Exercise 5
1. She *worked* in a dress shop.
2. It *rained* almost every day.
3. It's *starting* early.
4. *There's* something wrong with it.
5. It *smelt* strange.
6. It *stops* quite often.
7. *There was* no sound.
8. We *tried* to help them.
9. She *puts* food out for the birds.
10. My car's *using* a lot of oil.

6 Conversation

- Before starting the exercise, ask students to think for a minute or two, to try to remember a bad day in their lives.
- Go over the 'reaction' expressions with them to make sure they understand them. (Students may need to be told that the *dear* in '*Oh dear!*' is not a term of affection; '*Oh dear!*' is just a stereotyped expression of surprise and/or regret.)
- When the students are ready, get them to work in groups and tell each other about the experience they have thought of.
- You may like to start the ball rolling by telling them a very simple story about an experience of your own.
- This is a fluency exercise, so it is best to let students talk freely without correcting them. If you join one of the groups, choose a confident group which will not be intimidated by your presence.

Practice Book exercises
1. Reading a text and filling in (a) past tense verb forms and (b) discourse markers (conjunctions etc.).
2. Completing a conversation with past tense verb forms (including questions and negatives).
3. Writing negative past tense sentences.
4. Writing regular past tense forms.
5. Students write five things that they did not do yesterday.
6. Student's Cassette exercise (Student's Book Exercise 5). Students listen to the sentences and try to write them down.

Dictionary use

A bilingual dictionary is a very useful learning aid, particularly when used under a teacher's supervision. Students need bilingual dictionaries for some exercises in the course, and for autonomous work outside the classroom. They should buy good-sized dictionaries (not pocket editions): suggest titles if you can. To begin with, students may need help to make the best use of their dictionaries. Show how the entries are organised and what kinds of information they can provide. Make sure students understand that words have different translations in different contexts, and that one can only discover meanings with a dictionary by learning to select the appropriate translation from among the several that are offered.

English-only dictionaries can also be useful, especially at higher levels. Good simple dictionaries include the *Longman Active Study Dictionary* and the *Oxford Elementary Learner's Dictionary*; more advanced students could use the *Collins Cobuild English Language Dictionary*, the *Longman Dictionary of Contemporary English* or the *Oxford Advanced Learner's Dictionary*.

3 Choose the correct forms.

1. How did Juliana *leave/left* Lima?
2. She *leave/left* by air.
3. How far did Juliana *fall/fell*?
4. She *fall/fell* 3,000 metres.
5. What did Juliana *look/looked* for?
6. She *look/looked* for pieces of the plane.

4 Prepare five questions about the text. Example:

'When did Juliana leave Lima?'

When you are ready, work with another student. Close your books. Ask your questions, and answer your partner's. If you have problems understanding each other use these sentences to help you:

'Sorry, could you say that again?'
'I'm sorry, I don't understand.'
'What do you mean?'
'Please speak more slowly.'

If you can't answer a question, say:

'Sorry, I don't know.'
'I'm afraid I can't remember.'

5 🔊 **Pronunciation. Copy these words. Then listen to the recording and circle the words you hear.**

1. works / worked
2. rains / rained
3. starting / started
4. There's / There was
5. smells / smelt
6. stops / stopped
7. There's / There was
8. try / tried
9. puts / put
10. using / uses

6 Work in groups of five or six. Tell other students about a bad day in your life. You can react to other students' stories, too. Examples:

'Oh dear!'   *'That's awful!'*
'Poor you!'   *'How terrible!'*

Simple Past tense	
I left	did I leave?
you left	did you leave?
he/she/it left	*etc.*
we left	
you left	I did not (didn't) leave
they left	you did not (didn't) leave
	etc.

Learn/revise: Christmas (Eve); bag; dress; glasses; knee; town; crash; plane; helicopter; river; leave (left, left); look for; answer; spend (spent, spent); tear (tore, torn); hurt (hurt, hurt); kill; die; swim (swam, swum); arrive; hit (hit, hit); recognise; break (broke, broken); decide; learn (learnt, learnt); true; deep; dead; next; nobody; above; except; out of; afterwards; at least; for example; Sorry, could you say that again?; I'm sorry, I don't understand; What do you mean?; Sorry, I don't know; I'm afraid I can't remember; Please speak more slowly.

8 I was getting ready to come home...

Past Progressive tense; talking about the past; leaving
words out in speech; keeping a conversation going.

1 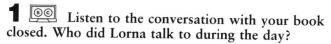 Listen to the conversation with your book
closed. Who did Lorna talk to during the day?

GEORGE: Hello, darling. Did you have a good day?
LORNA: Not bad. The usual sort of thing. Meetings, phone
calls, letters. You know.
GEORGE: Did you see anybody interesting?
LORNA: Well, Chris came into the office this morning. We
had a long talk.
GEORGE: Oh, yes? What about?
LORNA: Oh, this and that. Things. You know.
GEORGE: I see.
LORNA: And then Janet turned up. As usual. Just when I
was trying to finish some work.
GEORGE: So what did you do?
LORNA: Had lunch with her.
GEORGE: Where did you go? Somewhere nice?
LORNA: No. Just the pub round the corner. A pie and a
pint, you know. Then in the afternoon there was a
budget meeting. It went on for hours.
GEORGE: Sounds like a boring day. Did anything interesting
happen?
LORNA: Don't think so, not really. Can't remember. Oh, yes,
one thing. Something rather strange.
GEORGE: What?
LORNA: Well, it was this evening. I was getting ready to
come home. And the phone rang. So I picked it up.
And there was this man.
GEORGE: Who?
LORNA: Well, I don't know. He wouldn't say who he was.
But he asked me to have lunch with him tomorrow.
GEORGE: What?
LORNA: Yes. He said he wanted to talk to me. About
something very important.
GEORGE: So what did you say?
LORNA: Well, I said yes, of course. How was your day?

2 Look at this sentence:

Had lunch with her.

Lorna leaves out the pronoun *I.* Can you find any
more sentences where Lorna leaves out words?

3 Now listen again to George's side of the
conversation with your book closed. Can you
remember the beginnings of Lorna's answers?

4 Pronunciation: the letter *a.* Can you pronounce
these words?

1. bad   had   happen   rang   man   (/æ/)
2. darling   afternoon   rather   ask   glass   (/ɑ:/)
3. came   strange   day   say   train   (/eɪ/)
4. call   talk   saw   (/ɔ:/)

Put these words in group 1, 2, 3 or 4.

wait   hate   hard   glass   start   law   car
bath   late   ball   black   make   paid   arm
rain   fall   hat   part   happy   half   past
awful   may   all   stand   walk

Special pronunciations:

what   wasn't   want   watch   swan   (/ɒ/)
many   any   again   says   said   ate   (/e/)
about   America   England   umbrella   (/ə/)

28

Lesson 8

Students learn more about expressing past time relations; they learn ways of keeping a conversation going.
Structures: Past Progressive tense; *when-* and *while-*clauses; introduction to ellipsis.
Phonology: pronunciations of the letter *a*.

Language notes and possible problems

1. Past Progressive tense The Past Progressive (or 'Past Continuous') is often used to show the 'background' for past events – to say what was going on at the time when something happened. The Past Progressive is used for the longer 'background' action; the Simple Past is used for the shorter action which came in the middle, or interrupted what was going on. (See diagram in Student's Book Exercise 5.)

2. Conjunctions *When* and *while* are often used in sentences with the Past Progressive. Note that the *when/while*-clause can come either at the beginning or at the end of the sentence.

> I found some old letters **when/while I was cleaning up the attic**.
> **When/While I was cleaning up the attic**, I found some old letters.

For the moment, students should learn that *when* can introduce either a Simple Past or a Past Progressive, but *while* can only be used with a Past Progressive.

> They met **when** she was studying in Berlin.
> **When** they met, she was studying in Berlin.
> They met **while** she was studying in Berlin.

The rules determining the exact choice of structure and conjunction are complex, and it is not necessary for students to learn them at this stage.

3. Conversational syntax The dialogue contains some examples of structures which are more common in speech than in writing.

a. Ellipsis Subject pronouns are often left out in speech when they can be understood from the context. Examples: *Had lunch with her. Sounds like a boring day. Can't remember.*

b. Separation of clauses In writing, it is unusual to separate subordinate or coordinate clauses from the rest of the sentence they belong to. In speech, this often happens. Examples: *And there was this man. But he asked me to have lunch . . . Just when I was trying to finish some work.*

4. *Somebody, anybody* etc. You may wish to remind students of the difference between *somebody* and *anybody*, *something* and *anything*. Note also the structure *somebody interesting*; *something important*: this may be difficult for some students.

5. *Have* You may wish to point out the uses of *have* in the dialogue (*have a good day, have a talk, have lunch*).

6. Reported speech Reported speech is previewed here. It will be studied systematically later in the course.

If you are short of time

Drop Exercises 2 and 3 (but look over the text of the dialogue before doing Exercise 4).

1 Presentation

• Play the conversation while students listen with their books closed. Stop the recording before Lorna's last answer and see if students can guess what she says.
• Ask if students can remember the people Lorna talked to (Chris, Janet, people at a meeting, a man on the phone). See what else they can remember.
• Play the conversation again while students follow in their books.
• Explain any points which are preventing students from understanding the gist of the conversation. It is not necessary to deal with every point in the dialogue unless you particularly want to.
• Deal with any of the points from the *Language notes* that you think will be useful to your students.

2 Ellipsis

• Students do not need to be able to make sentences like these, but they should be familiar with the structure so that they can understand them easily.
• Other examples: *Sounds like a boring day; Don't think so; Can't remember.*

3 Recall and choice

• Tell students to close their books again.
• Play the conversation in Exercise 1 once more, stopping before Lorna's answers. See how well the students can predict what she is going to say.
• Then ask each student to choose three expressions from the dialogue to write down and learn.

4 Pronunciation

• This exercise helps students to see which vowel sounds are usually represented by the letter *a*, and what kinds of words have which vowel sounds (in standard southern British English).
• See if students can remember how to pronounce the words in the four groups.
• Help them to see the patterns (/ɑ:/ before *r* and often before *f*, *th* and *s*; /eɪ/ in the combinations *ai* and *ay*, and also before *consonant + e*; /ɔ:/ in *all*, *alk* and *aw*; /æ/ in most other cases).
• Get students to apply these rules by sorting out the list of words and putting them into the right groups.
• Then look over the 'special pronunciations'.
• The pronunciation rules given here have exceptions, of course. Note also that they are only valid for standard southern British English. Many educated speakers from other parts of Britain use /æ/, not /ɑ:/, in *after*, *rather*, *ask*, *glass*, *bath*, *half*, *past* and similar words. This also happens in American English.
• The exercise is recorded in a standard southern British, a northern English and an American version, for purposes of comparison.

Answers to Exercise 4
(Standard southern British pronunciation)

Group 1 (/æ/)	Group 2 (/ɑ:/)	Group 3 (/eɪ/)	Group 4 (/ɔ:/)
black	hard	wait	law
hat	glass	hate	ball
happy	start	late	fall
stand	car	make	awful
	bath	paid	all
	arm	rain	walk
	part	may	
	half		
	past		

28

5 Use of tenses

- Talk the students through the diagram. (See *Language notes* for a simple version of the rule.)
- The exercise can be done by class discussion, but you may like to ask students to do the last few questions individually, to make sure that everybody has grasped the point.
- There is further work on this point in the Practice Book.

Answers to Exercise 5
1. arrived 2. was having 3. was studying 4. was raining
5. was making 6. broke 7. saw 8. found
9. happened; were driving 10. lost; was travelling
11. saw; was sitting 12. went out; were having
13. was getting off; dropped

6 Preparation for improvisation

- Explain that students have to take on an imaginary personality for the purposes of this exercise.
- Get them to spend ten minutes deciding what their occupations are and how they spent their day.
- Go round helping where necessary.

7 Improvisation

- Ask students to get into pairs.
- First of all, they should decide what their relationship is (flatmates, husband and wife, . . .).
- Then ask two good students to begin. They should imagine that one of them is coming home after work (the other has already arrived home).
- They must improvise a conversation in which they exchange all the information they have prepared.
- Make sure they use the Simple Past and Past Progressive tenses where appropriate, as well as plenty of words and expressions from the dialogue.
- When they have finished, ask everybody to start improvising in pairs. They should go through the conversation several times until they are fluent.
- If there is time, ask some of the pairs to perform their improvisations for the class, or for other pairs or groups. You may like to tape-record or video-record the performances.

Optional activity: 'Talk yourself out of this'
- A woman rang her husband at the office, and was told he was in an important meeting.
- So she switched on the TV to watch the Wimbledon tennis finals.
- During the match, the camera showed a close-up of the crowd. There was her husband, sitting watching the match and talking to a beautiful woman.
- When he came home, she asked him for an explanation.
- Students should work in groups. Their task is to decide what the husband said.
- (*Note*: If you or your students feel the situation is too much of a cliché, you can reverse the sex-roles, making it a man who rings his wife at the office, etc.)

Optional activity: personalisation
- Put students in groups of four or so.
- Give them a minute or two to choose a subject from this list to talk about: what you did yesterday; your last holiday; a journey that you made once; your earliest memory. Help with vocabulary if necessary.
- Then tell them to start talking.
- If necessary, remind them not to use the Present Perfect for past narrative.
- When everybody has spoken, ask each group to choose *one* of the narratives for the whole class to hear.

Optional activity: remembering two accounts
- Ask two students to prepare accounts of what they did yesterday.
- They should make their accounts as similar as possible (for instance, by both saying what they had for breakfast, what they listened to on the radio, . . .).
- They give their accounts to the class in turn.
- Then the other students see if they can recall both accounts without getting mixed up.

Optional activity: 'Who is lying?'
- Two students prepare accounts of what they did yesterday: one true, the other completely untrue.
- They tell their stories in turn, making them sound equally plausible. The class decide who is lying.

Practice Book exercises
1. Completing a dialogue with words and expressions from the lesson.
2. Choosing the right tense (Simple Past or Past Progressive).
3. Revision of prepositions.
4. Revision of telling the time.
5. Punctuation and capitalisation.
6. Student's Cassette exercise (Student's Book Exercise 1, first part of the conversation). Students listen and try to write down at least ten words containing the letter *a*.

Correctness and correction
Fluency practice activities (like Exercise 7 and the Optional activities in this lesson) work best if the students are allowed to talk without being corrected. Mistakes which seriously impede communication are worth dealing with on the spot, but anything else should be noted for attention later or ignored. Teachers sometimes feel (and students may encourage them to feel) that they are not doing their jobs unless they correct every mistake. This is quite unrealistic: casual correction has very little effect on students' accuracy, and too much correction can have a disastrous effect on learners' confidence. During fluency practice activities, it is much more constructive to pick out a limited number of high-priority errors to be dealt with by systematic work at another time.

5 Grammar: Simple Past and Past Progressive. Study the examples:

Just when I **was trying** to finish some work
———————×———————
Janet
turned up.

I **was getting** ready to come home
———————×———————
and the
phone **rang**.

The TV
broke down
———————×———————
while we **were watching** the news.

Now put the correct verb forms into the sentences.

1. Andrew .... when I was getting ready to go out. (*arrive*)
2. The phone rang while I .... a bath. (*have*)
3. I first met my wife when I .... in Berlin. (*study*)
4. When I looked out of the window it .... (*rain*)
5. I stopped because the car .... a funny noise. (*make*)
6. My brother .... his leg while he was skiing last week. (*break*)
7. Where were you going when I .... you yesterday? (*see*)
8. When I was cleaning the house I .... some old love letters. (*find*)
9. The accident .... while we .... into Copenhagen. (*happen*; *drive*)
10. I .... all my money when I .... from Istanbul to Athens. (*lose*; *travel*)
11. When I .... her she .... reading. (*see*; *sit*)
12. The lights all .... while we .... supper. (*go out*; *have*)
13. When I .... the train, I .... my ticket onto the railway line. (*get off*; *drop*)

6 Imagine that it is six o'clock in the evening. You have just arrived home after an interesting day. What did you do? Make up answers to the following questions (ask the teacher for help if necessary).

What is your job?
How did you spend the morning?
Where did you have lunch? What did you have?
How did you spend the afternoon?
What places did you go to? Why?
You saw somebody interesting during the day. Who? When did you meet? ('*When I was . . .ing.*') What did you talk about? What did you do together?
Something interesting or strange happened during the day. What? When did it happen? ('*When I was . . .ing.*')

7 Work in pairs. You and your partner are members of the same family, or husband and wife, or flatmates or room-mates in college. Talk about how you both spent your day (using the ideas from Exercise 6). Useful expressions:

Did you have a good day?
Did you see anybody interesting?
What about?
You know.
I see.
as usual
So what did you do?
Where did you go?
What did you say?
What happened then?
Did anything interesting happen?
Not really
(It) sounds like a boring/interesting day.

Past Progressive tense		
I was trying	was I trying?	I was not (wasn't) trying
you were trying	were you trying?	you were not (weren't) trying
he/she/it was trying	was he trying? *etc.*	he was not (wasn't) trying *etc.*
we were trying	were we trying?	we were not (weren't) trying
you were trying	were you trying?	you were not (weren't) trying
they were trying	were they trying?	they were not (weren't) trying

Learn/revise: darling; sort; meeting; talk (*noun*); phone call; office; pub; turn up; try; finish; get ready (got, got); ring (rang, rung); pick up; lose (lost, lost); usual; interesting; boring; together; (come/go) home; this morning; rather; anybody; anything; something; somewhere; just; when; into; onto; I see; as usual; round the corner; not really; of course; sound like.

29

9 People are different

Comparisons: *-er than, as . . . as; less than; so am I, neither do you* etc.

Clouet: François I, King of France

Dürer: Self-portrait

1 Look at the two pictures. Can you find three ways in which the two people are alike, and three ways in which they are different?

2 Look at these ways of comparing.

[+] happier than / more expensive than

[=] as happy/expensive as

[−] not as happy/expensive as
less happy/expensive than

Now look at the pictures of Dürer and the king and complete the sentences.

1. .... fairer than ....
2. .... look more expensive ....
3. The king's nose ....
4. Dürer was probably as tall .... the king.
5. Do you think the king could paint .... well .... Dürer?
6. .... doesn't look as happy as ....
7. .... isn't as long ....
8. Dürer's clothes .... heavy ....
9. .... looks less worried than ....
10. .... less happy ....

3 How are they alike? Complete the sentences, looking at the panel on the opposite page if you have problems.

1. Dürer has got a beard, and so .... the king.
2. Dürer hasn't got ear-rings on, and neither .... the king.
3. Dürer is in a room, and .... the king.
4. Dürer isn't laughing, and .... the king.
5. Dürer's clothes look expensive, and .... the king's.
6. Dürer doesn't look unhappy, and .... the king.
7. Dürer died in the sixteenth century, and .... the king.
8. Dürer didn't go to Italy before the year 1480, and .... the king.
9. Dürer could speak Latin, and .... the king.
10. Dürer couldn't speak Chinese, and .... the king.

Students practise talking about similarities and differences; they write a short text.
Principal structures: comparatives with *than*; (*not*) *as . . . as*; *so am I* etc.

Language notes and possible problems

1. As and *than* Some students may confuse these words. When you have explained their usage, the students should do Exercise 2 in the Practice Book.

2. *So/Neither am I* etc. may present problems for some students, who will need to practise putting the correct verb forms after these words. Extra practice is given in Exercise 1 in the Practice Book.

If you are short of time

The writing portion of Exercise 6 can be done for homework; if time constraints are serious, Exercise 4 can be dropped.

1 Warm-up exercise

● Get students to look at the pictures and say a few things about the similarities and differences between them.

2 Differences: three ways of comparing

● Look through the examples; make sure students understand the meaning and use of the various structures.
● Then ask students to work individually for a few minutes trying to complete the sentences. Walk round while they are working to give any help that is needed.
● Let students compare notes and then discuss the various possible answers.

Possible answers to Exercise 2
1. Dürer is fairer than the king.
2. The king's clothes look more expensive than Dürer's.
3. The king's nose is longer than Dürer's.
4. Dürer was probably as tall as the king.
5. Do you think the king could paint as well as Dürer?
6. Dürer doesn't look as happy as the king.
7. The king's hair isn't as long as Dürer's.
8. Dürer's clothes aren't as heavy as the king's.
9. The king looks less worried than Dürer.
10. Dürer looks less happy than the king.

3 Similarities: *so am I* etc.

● The forms covered in this exercise should be familiar to most students at this level.
● Ask your students to work individually for a few minutes trying to complete the sentences. Point out that they can look at the table at the end of the lesson if they need help.
● Walk round while they are working to take note of difficulties and give any help that is needed.
● Let them compare answers in small groups before you go over the answers with the class as a whole.
● Encourage the students to ask questions if there are any points that they do not understand.

Answers to Exercise 3
1. Dürer has got a beard, and so *has* the king.
2. Dürer hasn't got ear-rings on, and neither *has* the king.
3. Dürer is in a room, and *so is* the king.
4. Dürer isn't laughing, and *neither is* the king.
5. Dürer's clothes look expensive, and *so do* the king's.
6. Dürer doesn't look unhappy, and *neither does* the king.
7. Dürer died in the sixteenth century, and *so did* the king.
8. Dürer didn't go to Italy before the year 1480, and *neither did* the king.
9. Dürer could speak Latin, and *so could* the king.
10. Dürer couldn't speak Chinese, and *neither could* the king.

4 Practising comparisons

- Students should work in pairs, each student looking at a different picture. They must try to find out by talking only (*not* by looking at each other's pictures) as many differences as they can between the two pictures.
- Get one member of each pair to turn to page 124 in the back of the book, and the other member of the pair to turn to page 126. Remind them that they must not look at each other's pictures.
- If your students are competitive, you can give a small prize for the pair that finds the most differences.
- Walk round while they are working to give any help that is needed.
- Discourage them from writing complete sentences during this exercise; they will have an opportunity to write in Exercise 6, and writing now will take up too much time.
- When they have finished, see how many differences the whole class can tell you about.

5 Personalisation: talking about differences

- Put the students into pairs again; for variety's sake, you may want them to have different partners from the ones they had in Exercise 4.
- Get them to find out as many similarities and differences as they can between themselves: in appearance, interests, families, etc. They should take notes during this process, but not write anything out in sentences. Give them an appropriate time limit.

6 Writing about differences

- When the time limit is reached, students should work individually to write a text based on the frame in the book. They should *not* mention their names. Encourage them to use structures from the lesson.
- Give any help that is needed.
- When they have finished, collect the papers and number them. If you do not think students will recognise one another's handwriting, you can post the papers on a board or put them on a large table: students read and try to guess who each text is about.
- Alternatively, you can read out as many texts as you have time for, and students can try to guess who they are about.

Practice Book exercises

1. Choosing the correct verb forms with *so* and *neither*.
2. Completing sentences with *as* and *than*.
3. Blank-filling based on the Jeanne and Elizabeth pictures, using important words from the lesson.
4. Blank-fill model text (see Exercise 5) about two people.
5. Writing a comparison of two people from notes.
6. A choice of topics for writing comparisons.

4 Work with a partner. Turn to the page your teacher tells you. DON'T show your picture to your partner; just talk to him or her. How are the two pictures alike? How are they different? Try to use structures and expressions from Exercises 2 and 3.

5 Find another partner. Discuss how you are alike and how you are different: talk about appearances, interests, families, etc. Use structures and expressions from Exercises 2 and 3. Other useful structures:

Both/Neither of us . . .
the same as
the same colour/size/etc. as
different from
I'm . . . , but she isn't.
She's got . . . , but I haven't.

6 Now each of you should write two paragraphs comparing yourselves. Don't mention your names. Use this frame:

This person and I have got several things in common. For instance, . . . and . . . She/He . . . , and . . .

On the other hand, we are quite different from each other in some ways . . .

When you have finished, give your comparisons to the teacher. Try and guess which pairs have written which comparisons.

So am I etc.

'I **am** . . .'	'So **am** I.' / 'I'm **not**.'
'I **was** . . .'	'So **was** I.' / 'I **was**n't.'
'I **have** got . . .'	'So **have** I.' / 'I **have**n't.'
'He **can** . . .'	'So **can** she.' / 'She **can**'t.'
'I **live** . . .'	'So **do** I.' / 'I **do**n't.'
'She **likes** . . .'	'So **do** I.' / 'I **do**n't.'
'I **saw** . . .'	'So **did** I.' / 'I **did**n't.'

Dürer **is** wearing a hat, and so **is** the king.

'I'm **not** . . .'	'Neither **am** I.' / 'I **am**.'
'She **can**'t . . .'	'Neither **can** he.' / 'He **can**.'
'He **doesn**'t . . .'	'Neither **do** I.' / 'I **do**.'
'They **don**'t . . .'	'Neither **do** we.' / 'We **do**.'

The king **isn**'t smiling, and neither **is** Dürer.

As and *than*

(not) as . . . **as**	. . .er **than**
the same **as**	more . . . **than**
different **from**	less . . . **than**

Learn/revise: beard; ear-ring; king; room; nose; century; Chinese; way; in some ways; laugh; look; compare; speak (Chinese *etc.*) (spoke, spoken); expensive; happy; unhappy; fair; tall; long; worried; alike; probably; both; neither; several; than; as; more; less; but; the same as; (quite) different (from); on the other hand.

10 Things are different

More comparisons; *as* and *than*; *much* and *far* with comparative adjectives; quantifiers *more*, *the most* and *the fewest*.

1 📼 Copy the table. Then listen and fill in the gaps.

VEHICLE	A	B	C	D	E	F
Number of wheels	4					
How many people does it carry?						1
Top speed (in kph)						
Weight (in kilos)						
Price (in pounds)						

2 What are A, B, C, D, E and F? Look at the pictures and choose the correct vehicles.

plane

ship

tank

lorry

train

bicycle

motorbike

pram

32

Lesson 10

Students practise talking about similarities and differences between things.
Principal structures: revision of comparative and superlative adjectives; modification of comparatives; sentence structures used in comparisons; *as* and *than*; quantifiers *the most* and *the fewest*.
Phonology: decoding rapid speech.

Language notes and possible problems
1. *As* and *than* More practice for students who confuse these words is given in Exercise 1 in the Practice Book.
2. Modification of comparatives Make sure students realise that *very* cannot be used to modify comparatives. Exercise 5 has examples of *much* and *far* with comparatives.

If you are short of time
Exercise 7 can be dropped.

1 Listening for specific information

- This exercise helps students to realise that they do not need to understand every word they hear in order to interpret a spoken message.
- Go over the table with them, making sure they understand the various questions.
- Tell them to copy the table.
- Play the recording, pausing at suitable moments (but not after every sentence) while students fill in the answers.
- You will probably want to play each section more than once, but don't make it too easy – the purpose of the exercise is to accustom students to real-life listening.
- When they have completed the table as well as they can, let them compare notes in groups and then complete the table on the blackboard.
- Don't tell the students every word that was said – this is not the point of the exercise.
- You may want to follow up with further practice in understanding numbers, if students have found this difficult.

Answers to Exercise 1

VEHICLE	A	B	C	D	E	F
Number of wheels	4	4	2	6	10	2
How many people does it carry?	1–2	4	1–2	72	100	1
Top speed (in kph)	6	160	240	110	2,160	25
Weight (in kilos)	15	695	203	9,000	175,000	13.5
Price (in pounds)	185	7,000	4,893	91,000	?	195

2 Drawing conclusions
- Students shouldn't find it too difficult to guess what the vehicles are.
- A is a pram, B is a car, C is a motorbike, D is a double-decker bus, E is a supersonic airliner (Concorde), and F is a bicycle.
- Some of the data given are of course approximate (a bicycle doesn't really have a maximum speed, for instance). If students want to argue about the accuracy of the answers given, so much the better (provided they argue in English).

Tapescript for Exercise 1

A. It's got four wheels, and usually carries one person, but it can carry two. Its top speed is around six kilometres an hour, and it weighs about 15 kilos. It costs £185.

B. This vehicle costs about £7,000. It can go at up to 160kph, and can carry four people in comfort. It weighs 695 kilos when it's empty. There are four wheels.

C. These two-wheeled vehicles are very popular with teenagers. They are fast, but much less safe than vehicles A or B. This model has a maximum speed of 240kph, and weighs 203 kilos. It can carry one or two people, and costs £4,893.

D. This vehicle, which costs £91,000, is commonly used for public transport. It has two decks, or floors, and can carry 72 people when full. Its maximum speed is 110 kilometres an hour, but it doesn't usually go faster than 80. It has six wheels, and weighs 9,000 kilos.

E. This vehicle was built by two countries working in collaboration. It travels at 2,160kph – faster than sound – carrying a maximum load of 100 people. When it is fully loaded with passengers and fuel, it weighs 175,000 kilograms. It has ten wheels. Each of these vehicles cost hundreds of millions of pounds to produce – it's impossible to say exactly how much.

F. 'How many wheels?'
'Two.'
'What does it weigh?'
'Thirteen and a half kilos.'
'How much does it cost?'
'£195.'
'How many people can it carry?'
'Just one.'
'Top speed?'
'It depends. For most people, perhaps about 25kph.'

32

3 Superlatives: *most* and *fewest*

- This exercise gives practice in using superlatives, and introduces *most* and *fewest* as quantifiers.
- Students can work individually and then compare notes.
- (If they get stuck on 8, point out that the sentences come in pairs of opposites.)
- Make sure they don't forget the definite article.
- If necessary, remind students of the difference between comparatives and superlatives.

Answers to Exercise 3
3. E (a plane) can carry the most people.
4. F (a bicycle) can carry the fewest people.
5. E is the fastest.
6. A (a pram) is the slowest.
7. F is the lightest.
8. E is the heaviest.
9. E is the most expensive.
10. A is the cheapest.

4 How many words?

- This is an important exercise. It gives students practice in recognising and separating out common words pronounced naturally in rapid speech.
- The pronunciation of words (particularly unstressed words) often changes a good deal under the influence of the sounds that come before and after. Students who have learnt only the pronunciations that words have alone or in deliberate speech may have great trouble understanding them in natural conversation.
- In this exercise, the focus is on the unstressed pronunciations of *as* (/əz/) and *than* (/ðən/).
- Ask students first of all just to say how many words they hear, and then to try to decide what they are.

Tapescript and answers to Exercise 4
1. Today's not as cold as yesterday. (7)
2. She's older than he is. (6)
3. You're different from your photo. (6)
4. She goes to the same school as my brother. (9)
5. She's not nearly as tall as me. (8)
6. She's the nicest of the three girls. (8)
7. Her eyes are the same colour as yours. (8)
8. Both of us like dancing. (5)
9. Your house is much nicer than mine. (7)
10. There are a lot of words in this sentence. (9)

5 Comparatives in sentences

- Run over the list of structures and make sure students understand them all.
- The exercise can be done in pairs, in groups or as a whole-class activity.
- With a quick class it can be done orally without preparation, with students spontaneously saying their sentences as they work them out.
- A slower class may need time to prepare sentences.

6 Survey: preferences

- Begin by demonstrating. Choose one of the groups of things and ask several students which of the things in the group they would prefer to have.
- If possible, get them to say why. Encourage the use of comparatives and superlatives.
- Then each student should choose one of the groups, and walk round the class asking about people's preferences.
- They should note the answers and the reasons given.
- (If it is not feasible for students to walk round, tell them to ask as many people as they can without moving from their places.)

7 Reporting the survey

- Students can report either to the whole class or to groups, as you prefer.

Practice Book exercises
1. Choosing *as* or *than*.
2. Comparing pairs of things and people.
3. Spotting the differences between two pictures.
4. Choosing comparatives and superlatives.
5. Recreational reading: *Strange but true!*
6. Student's Cassette exercise (Student's Book Exercise 1, parts A and B). Students listen and try to write down as much as they can.

Rhythm, stress and comprehension
English is 'stress-timed'. Stresed syllables are slower and clearer than unstressed syllables; they come at roughly equal intervals. Unstressed syllables tend to be fitted in quickly so as not to interrupt the rhythm. (*There was a man in the garden*, with eight syllables and two stresses, doesn't take much longer to say than *back door*, with two syllables and two stresses.)

Speakers of 'syllable-timed' languages need a lot of practice in this area if they are to speak naturally enough to be easily understood. And they may have great difficulty in understanding English speech because they don't perceive unstressed syllables. (*There was a man in the garden* may simply be heard as *Bzzz man bzzz garden*.) Activities like Exercise 4 in this lesson are particularly important for such students.

3 Complete these sentences.

1. E has got ....*the most*.... wheels.
2. C and F have got ....*the fewest*.... wheels.
3. E can carry .... people.
4. F can carry .... people.
5. .... is the fastest.
6. A is the ....
7. .... is the lightest.
8. E ....
9. E .... expensive.
10. .... cheapest.

4 Listen to the recording. How many words do you hear in each sentence? (Contractions like *she's* count as two words.)

5 Look at the table and make some sentences (some true, some false). Ask other students if they are true or false. Use these structures:

. . . has got more wheels than . . .
. . . hasn't got as many wheels as . . .
. . . can carry (far) more people than . . .
. . . can't carry (nearly) as many people as . . .
. . . is (much) faster/heavier than . . .
. . . costs (much) more than . . .
. . . doesn't cost (nearly) as much as . . .
    (OR: . . . costs much less than . . .)
. . . has got the most/fewest . . .
. . . can carry the most/fewest . . .
. . . is the fastest/slowest/heaviest/*etc.*

6 Choose one of these groups of things. Ask other students which of the things in the group they would most like to have, and why. Ask as many people as possible, and write down the answers.

1. a dog   a cat   a horse   a bird
2. a Rolls-Royce   a Citroen 2CV   a motorbike
   a bicycle
3. a piano   a guitar   a violin   a trumpet
4. a holiday in the mountains / by the sea /
   in London / in San Francisco
5. a flat   a cottage   a big house
6. more money   more intelligence   more friends
   more free time

7 Tell the class what you found out in Exercise 6. Example:

'*I asked about Group 1. Most people would prefer a bird, because it doesn't eat as much as the others.*' (OR: '*. . . it eats less than the others.*')

Structures	
(far/much) more than	more wheels than
(far/much) less than	not as many wheels as
(not) as much as	the fastest
the most wheels	the most expensive
the fewest wheels	a lot more
	a lot faster

Learn/revise: wheel; ship; plane; car; bus; lorry; pram; train; motorbike; bicycle; horse; bird; dog; cat; guitar; flat; intelligence; free time; top speed; weight; kilo; kph (= kilometres per hour); pound; the mountains; the sea; carry; cost (cost, cost); fast; light; the most; the fewest; (not) nearly; true; false; far/much/a lot + *comparative*.

bus

car

33

11 Stuff for cleaning windows

Shopping; asking for something when you don't know the word.

1 Vocabulary. Do you know where you buy these things? Example:

'You buy sugar at a grocer's or at a supermarket.'

meat   bread   vegetables   sugar
shoes   soap   books   clothes
writing paper   petrol   stamps
aspirins   films

2 Look at the conversations and try to fill in some of the gaps. Then listen to the recording and write the complete conversations.

1. 'Good afternoon.'
   'Hello. .... a shampoo for dry hair.'
   'Large, medium or ....?'
   '............... the small bottle?'
   '76p.'
   '............... two bottles, please.'

2. '...............?'
   'Yes, ...'

3. 'Can I help you?'
   '............... I'm being served.'

4. '...............?'
   '............... a child's tricycle.'
   'Yes. .... the child?'

5. '............... a pint of milk, please?'
   'Yes, of course. ....?'
   'No, ..., thanks. ....?'
   '24p.'

6. 'Hello, Sid. .... any flashbulbs?'
   'I'm afraid not, Fred. .... some in next week. Can you look in on Monday?'
   '............... be away on Monday, but I'll call in on Tuesday.'
   'OK. ....'
   'Bye, Sid.'

7. '............... a dishwasher.'
   '............... make?'
   '............... Kleenwash XJ126?'
   'Yes, we have. It's a very good machine.'
   '............... guarantee?'
   'Five years, madam.'
   '............... deliver?'
   'Yes, we do, sir. Up to twenty miles.'
   'How much is it?'
   '..............., plus VAT.'

3 🔊 Rhythm and stress. Say these expressions.

Good af**ter**noon.
I'm being **served**.
a **pint** of **milk**
a **child's** tricycle
Yes, we **have**.
Yes, of **course**.
Here you **are**.
I'm a**fraid** not.
the **small bottle**
How **much** is the **small bottle**?
How **much** is it?
How **old** is the **child**?
It's a **very good** ma**chine**.

4 Work with a partner and practise one or more of the conversations from Exercise 2.

Lesson 11

Students **revise** and extend their knowledge of the language of shopping; they learn ways of asking for something without knowing the exact word.
Principal structures: *at a grocer's/butcher's; a thing with a hole/handle; a thing / some stuff for . . .ing.*
Phonology: rhythm and stress.

Note: timing
This lesson includes a dramatisation activity (Exercise 6); you will need to allow extra time on top of the normal lesson period.

Optional extra materials
A set of pictures for practising 'paraphrase strategies' (see instructions to Exercise 5).

If you are short of time
Drop Exercise 6.

1 Vocabulary revision and extension
- Work with books closed, so that students can't consult the list at the end of the lesson.
- Put the list of words on the board, and check that the students know them all.
- Practise the pronunciation; make sure students only put three syllables in *vegetables* (/'vedʒ·tə·blz/).
- Divide the class into groups; let them pool their knowledge to decide where each of the things is bought. (They can use dictionaries.)
- Supply any words that students cannot work out for themselves. Make sure they learn the normal modern English terms; dictionaries sometimes contain out-of-date words such as *shoemaker*.
- *Library* is a 'false friend' – in some European languages, a similar word means *bookshop*.
- An appropriate set of answers might be:
  meat: butcher's
  bread: baker's
  vegetables: greengrocer's
  sugar: grocer's
  shoes: shoe shop
  soap: chemist's
  books: bookshop
  clothes: clothes/dress shop
  writing paper: stationer's
  petrol: petrol station / filling station / garage
  stamps: post office
  aspirins: chemist's
  films: chemist's
- Of course, many things can also be bought in supermarkets or department stores.

2 Shop conversations
- This exercise has two purposes: to practise some of the expressions used in shopping, and to train students in understanding natural speech.
- You may not want to use all the conversations.
- Put students into groups of two or three; get them to try to fill in the gaps in the first conversation.
- When they can't do any more, play the recording.
- If they still cannot fill in everything, play the recording again one or more times, with a pause after each sentence. But don't make the exercise too easy: the purpose is to 'stretch' students' listening ability so that they get used to natural speech.

- Let them compare notes; then replay the conversation while you give them the answers.
- Deal with the other conversations in the same way.
- This may be a good opportunity to revise the difference between *some* and *any*.
- You may also need to explain the meaning of *VAT* (= 'Value Added Tax').

Tapescript and answers to Exercise 2
1. 'Good afternoon.'
   'Hello. *I'd like* a shampoo for dry hair.'
   'Large, medium or *small?*'
   '*How much is* the small bottle?'
   '76p.'
   '*I'll take* two bottles, please.'
2. '*Can I look round?*'
   'Yes, *of course.*'
3. 'Can I help you?'
   '*It's all right, thanks.* I'm being served.'
4. '*Can I help you?*'
   '*I'm looking for* a child's tricycle.'
   'Yes. *How old is* the child?'
5. '*Could I have* a pint of milk, please?'
   'Yes, of course. *Here you are. Anything else?*'
   'No, *that's all*, thanks. *How much is that?*'
   '24p.'
6. 'Hello, Sid. *Have you got* any flashbulbs?'
   'I'm afraid not, Fred. *We'll have* some in next week. Can you look in on Monday?'
   '*I'm going to* be away on Monday, but I'll call in on Tuesday.'
   'OK. *See you then.*'
   'Bye, Sid.'
7. '*We're looking for* a dishwasher.'
   'Yes. *What* make?'
   '*Have you got a* Kleenwash XJ126?'
   'Yes, we have. It's a very good machine.'
   '*How long is the* guarantee?'
   'Five years, madam.'
   '*And do you* deliver?'
   'Yes, we do, sir. Up to twenty miles.'
   'How much is it?'
   '*Two hundred and forty pounds*, plus VAT.'

3 Rhythm and stress
- These or similar expressions will be needed in Exercise 4; students should make sure that they can pronounce them with a good rhythm and stress.
- Practise the 'weak' pronunciation of *of* (/əv/) in *a pint of milk* and *Yes, of course.*

4 Dialogue practice
- Choose one or two of the dialogues from Exercise 2 for intensive practice.
- Go through the conversations again with the recording, explaining any difficult expressions and practising the pronunciation.
- Don't insist on students' pronouncing the sentences as fast as the speakers on the recording. They should learn to *understand* a fast colloquial pronunciation, but at this stage they should be satisfied if they can *speak* slowly and clearly with a good natural rhythm.
- Let them practise the dialogues in pairs; encourage them to learn them by heart if they can do this easily.

5 Paraphrase strategies

• The purpose of this lesson is *not* to teach vocabulary, but to help students to ask for things when they do not know the exact word for what they want.
• Look through the lists of 'useful words' and 'useful structures'. Make sure students understand these, and that they realise that *thing* is a 'blanket' term for countable nouns, while *stuff* replaces uncountables.
• (*Stuff* is a little slangy, and it may be better to use a more specific term such as *liquid*, *powder* etc. where possible.)
• When students have practised the words and expressions a little (pay attention to the pronunciation of *thing*), look through the example.
• Check whether students know common request structures (*I'd like . . . ; Could I have . . . ?; I'm looking for . . .*). Write them on the board.
• Then get individual students to try to ask the class for things whose names they don't know, using the expressions they have just learnt. (They can do this in groups if the class is large.)
• They can of course use any other ways of conveying meaning that they like, including mime, but they should include *some* language!
• The illustrations in the Student's Book can be used for this exercise, but it is even better if you prepare a set of pictures in advance (perhaps cut from magazines), and give them to individuals *without letting the others see them.*
• When a student asks for something, the rest of the class or group can try to draw the product or object he/she is describing, or name it in the mother tongue.
• After the exercise, students may want to know the names of some of the objects and substances they have been talking about. Try to persuade them not to spend too much time on learning these – they are not all very important words, and the purpose of the lesson is not to teach new vocabulary.
• The objects illustrated are: bubble-bath mixture, a foot pump, an alarm clock, washing powder, a bandage, crampons, a shopping bag, furniture polish, glue, a drill, a cardboard box, a wallet, a vacuum cleaner (hoover), a stapler, a nail brush, coloured ribbon, a hole punch, window-cleaning liquid.

6 Dramatisation

• This exercise will take up a good deal of time, and it will probably be necessary to allocate an extra period of 45–60 minutes.
• If time is short, you may prefer to drop the exercise, but if it is done it will prove to be a very effective aid to learning.
• The activity is relatively flexible as regards level. Weak students can prepare simple conversations with just one or two exchanges, while better students can work in groups of three or four to produce more elaborate sketches.
• You may wish to record the final sketches or film them on video: this can serve as a powerful incentive to students to practise what they have prepared.
• Give the groups a fair amount of time to prepare and practise their dramatisations, but set a time-limit of, say, 25–35 minutes.
• Students may want to write everything down; encourage them to work from brief notes or from memory if possible. Conversations that have been completely scripted usually sound unnatural.
• Don't let the students produce complicated material full of 'translationese': they should base what they say mainly on what they have learnt in the lesson.
• When all groups have prepared and practised their sketches, turn one end of the room into a 'shop'; let each group perform its sketch for the others.
• Start with a group that is likely to produce a successful performance, but don't take the best group first – this can discourage the others.
• Shy students will need to be pushed a bit, but are likely to enjoy the activity once they get going.

Practice Book exercises
1. Revision of expressions used in shopping.
2. Matching objects and their definitions.
3. Writing descriptions.
4. Learning new vocabulary.
5. Reading skills.
6. Student's Cassette exercise (Student's Book Exercise 3). Practising rhythm and stress.

Students' expectations: grammar
Students who are used to grammar-based courses may feel that a lesson with no new grammar 'doesn't teach anything'. Help them to see that they must not judge their progress simply by the number of new structures learnt. Grammar, though important, is only one of the many things which have to be learnt. Skills development and vocabulary, for example, are also vital. (Vocabulary mistakes tend to outnumber grammar mistakes by more than three to one.)

5 Here are some ways to ask for something when you don't know the word.

> **Useful words:**
>
> | a thing | stuff | square |
> |---------|---------|---------|
> | a machine | liquid | round |
> | a tool | powder | |
> | | material | |
>
> **Useful structures:**
>
> a thing **with** a hole / **with** a handle
>
> a machine **for making** holes
> a tool **for cutting** wood
> a thing **for putting** pieces of paper together
>
> some material **for making** curtains
> some liquid **for cleaning** windows
> some powder **for washing** clothes
> some stuff **for killing** insects

Example:

A: Excuse me. I don't speak English very well. What do you call the round glass in a camera?
B: The lens.
A: The lens. OK. I need some material for cleaning the lens.
B: A lens cleaner. Yes, we have . . .

Now look at the pictures and ask for one of the things.

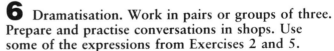

6 Dramatisation. Work in pairs or groups of three. Prepare and practise conversations in shops. Use some of the expressions from Exercises 2 and 5.

> **Learn/revise:** soap; writing paper; stamp; aspirin; film (*for a camera*); petrol; bookshop; grocer('s); greengrocer('s); butcher('s); baker('s); chemist('s); stationer('s); newsagent('s); shoe shop; clothes shop; petrol station; post office; supermarket; tool; stuff; liquid; powder; material; piece; hole; handle; make (*noun*); camera; bottle; milk; clean; cut (cut, cut); put (put, put); medium; away; Can I look round?; I'm being served; I'm looking for . . . ; That's all; I'm afraid not; Anything else?; What do you call . . . ?

12 I haven't got anything to wear

Suggestions, requests and offers; modal verbs; infinitives with and without *to*; possessive pronouns.

1 Read the conversation. The word *to* should go in some of the numbered gaps. Which ones?

JAN: Hello, Kate. What's the matter?

KATE: Hello, Jan. Oh dear. I'm going out with Tony tonight, and I haven't got anything ......1...... wear.

JAN: What about your blue dress? That's lovely.

KATE: That old thing? No. It makes me ......2...... look like a sack of potatoes.

JAN: Well, why don't you ......3...... borrow something of mine?

KATE: Could I really ......4......?

JAN: Yes, of course. Would you like ......5......?

KATE: Well, I'd love ......6....... If you really don't ......7...... mind.

JAN: What about that green silk thing?

KATE: Green silk?

JAN: Yes, you know. The dress I wore to Andy's birthday party.

KATE: Oh, yes. I remember.

JAN: You'd ......8...... look great in that.

KATE: Oooh!

JAN: And I'll ......9...... lend you my new shoes to go with it.

KATE: My feet are bigger than yours.

JAN: I don't ......10...... think they are, Kate. Anyway, try the shoes and see. What about a jacket? Have you got one that will ......11...... do?

KATE: Not really.

JAN: Well, have one of mine.

KATE: Oh, Jan. I feel bad, borrowing all your things.

JAN: That's all right. What are friends for? I'll ......12...... borrow something of yours one of these days.

KATE: Well, thanks a million, Jan. I'd better ......13...... get moving. Tony's coming in half an hour.

JAN: OK. Wait a second. I'll ......14...... go and get the dress. Shall I ......15...... iron it for you?

KATE: Oh, Jan, . . .

2 🔊 Read the conversation again and then listen to the recording. How many differences can you find?

3 Pronunciation and ear training.
1. Can you pronounce these words correctly? *Kate, wait, great, make, day, potatoes, anyway*. If you have difficulty, do part 2 of this exercise.
2. Which words do you hear?

A	B	A	B
sale	sell	paper	pepper
late	let	pain	pen
gate	get	whale	well
main	men	wait	wet

Now pronounce some of the words yourself. Ask other students which words they think you are saying.

4 Pronunciation and spelling. Say these words.

1. Kate   change   table   strange   make
2. day   way   play
3. wait   chain   fail
4. station   pronunciation

Can you think of any more words to put into groups 1, 2, 3 and 4?

36

Lesson 12

Students learn more about making and replying to suggestions, requests and offers.
Principal structures: modal verbs (*can, could, shall, will, would*); *had better*; infinitive with and without *to*; possessive pronouns.
Phonology: /eɪ/ and /e/; spellings of /eɪ/.

Language notes and possible problems

1. Infinitives Some students may tend to use the *to*-infinitive after *can, could* and other modal verbs. (For example: **Can I to help you?*)

2. Possessive pronouns Some students may find it difficult to see the difference between the pronouns *mine, yours* etc. and the determiners (often misleadingly called 'possessive adjectives') *my, your* etc. *Mine* and *yours* occur in Exercise 1; you may like to give a brief explanation.

3. Vocabulary load The dialogue in Exercise 1 contains a large number of useful idiomatic expressions and conversational structures. If many of these are new to the students, tell them just to choose a selection to learn rather than trying to memorise everything.

If you are short of time

Drop Exercises 3 and 4 if these are not essential for your students.

---

1 Infinitive with and without *to*

• Give students time to look through the conversation and get a general idea of its meaning. Don't discuss points of detail at this stage.
• Then get students to work in groups trying to decide whether or not *to* is used in each case. (Use *to* in gaps 1, 5 and 6.)
• Discuss the answers, and see if students can work out some of the rules:
– *to* is not used after modal verbs such as *will, shall, 'll, would, could* (and *had better*)
– *to* is not used after the auxiliary *do*
– *to* is not used in the structure *make somebody do something*
– *to* is used after (*would*) *like* and *love*
– *to* is used in the structure *something to wear/drink/eat/*etc., and similar structures with *anything, nothing* etc.
– *to* is used in most other cases.

2 Finding differences

• Give students a few minutes to read through the dialogue again. Explain important new words, but don't spend a lot of time on vocabulary at this stage.
• Tell students to close their books. Play the recording right through and ask students what differences they noticed.
• Let them listen again with their books open, and see if they can find some more differences.
• This can be done as a group task if you like.
• When the task is completed, you may want to spend a little more time on the text, pointing out useful words and structures. Note particularly:
– ways of making suggestions (*What about . . . ?*; *Why don't you . . . ?*)
– the use of *to* instead of repeating a whole infinitive (*Would you like to?*; *I'd love to.*)
– possessive pronouns.

Tapescript and answers to Exercise 2
(Items which are different are in italics.)

ANN: Hello, Kate. What's the matter?
KATE: Hello, *Ann*. Oh dear. I'm going out with *Tom this evening*, and I haven't got anything to wear.
ANN: What about your *red* dress? That's lovely.
KATE: That old thing? No. It makes me look like a sack of potatoes.
ANN: Well, why don't you *wear* something of mine?
KATE: Could I really?
ANN: Yes, of course. Would you like to?
KATE: Well, I'd love to. If you really don't mind.
ANN: What about that *blue* silk thing?
KATE: *Blue* silk?
ANN: Yes, you know. The dress I wore to Andy's *Christmas* party.
KATE: Oh, yes. I remember.
ANN: You'd look great in that.
KATE: *You're right. I would.*
ANN: And I'll lend you my new shoes to go with it.
KATE: My feet are *smaller* than yours.
ANN: I don't think they are, Kate. Anyway, try the shoes and see. What about a *belt*? Have you got one that will do?
KATE: Not really.
ANN: Well, have one of mine.
KATE: Oh, *Ann*. I feel bad, *taking* all your things.
ANN: That's all right. *We're friends, aren't we?* I'll borrow something of yours one of these days.
KATE: Well, thanks a *lot, Ann*. I'd better get moving. *Tom's* coming in *twenty minutes*.
ANN: OK. Wait a *minute*. I'll go and get the dress. Shall I iron it for you?
KATE: Oh, *Ann*, . . .

3 Pronunciation: /eɪ/ and /e/

• Students who do not have the sound /eɪ/ in their own language may pronounce it as a monophthong, so that, for example, *paper* sounds like *pepper*.
• Demonstrate the pronunciation of the word pairs and then play the recording, stopping so that students can decide whether words are in list A or list B.
• Repeat the exercise if necessary until students are clear about the difference between the two sounds.

The words recorded are: *sale; let; get; main; pepper; pen; whale; wet.*

• When students can hear the difference, get them to practise saying /eɪ/, first of all alone, and then at the ends of words like *say, may, way*.
• At the beginning of the vowel, the mouth should be relatively open, with the teeth far enough apart for one to be able to get one's little finger between them. During the vowel, the mouth closes and the tongue moves up to the position for /iː/.
• Finally, ask students to choose words from the two lists and say them. Other students must decide whether the words are from list A or list B.

4 Spellings of /eɪ/

• Point out that the four groups of words show typical spellings of the sound /eɪ/: *a* + consonant(s) + *e*; *ay*; *ai*; and in the ending *-ation*.
• Practise pronouncing them (using the recording if you wish).
• Then ask students if they can add more words to any of the groups.

---

5 Requests and offers

• This exercise revises common ways of making and replying to requests and offers, and also presents a number of useful conversational expressions.

• Note particularly the use of *can* and the more polite form *could* in requests; the use of *Shall I . . . ?* in offers, and the use of *I'll* when volunteering to do something.

• Make sure that students understand clearly the difference between *lend* and *borrow*.

• Give students a few minutes to try to match up the items on their own, and then let them continue in groups. Help with vocabulary if necessary.

Answers to Exercise 5
(Alternative answers are possible to some questions.)
1b; 2e; 3g; 4i; 5a; 6l; 7c; 8f; 9j; 10d; 11k; 12h.

6 Borrowing

• Give students a minute or two to prepare their requests, and then ask them to borrow things from as many people as possible.

• Encourage them to ask and answer in different ways, so that they practise as much of the new language as they can.

• At the end of the exercise, you can take the opportunity to practise the expression *give something back*.

7 Writing notes

• While students write their notes, you may like to walk round helping and checking that they are not making serious mistakes (but don't over-correct).

• When notes are ready, you can act as postman.

Practice Book exercises
1. Revision of vocabulary from the lesson.
2. Spelling: double letters.
3. Infinitive with and without *to*.
4. Preparation for guided writing: completing a story.
5. Guided writing.
6. Student's Cassette exercise (Student's Book Exercise 2). Students listen to part of the conversation and try to write down what they hear.

Supplementation

For most students, the course should need little supplementation (though specific nationalities may need some extra work on particular grammar or pronunciation problems). However, no coursebook can give learners enough exposure to the spoken and written language, and students will only learn English successfully if they do supplementary listening and reading.

A good way to give a class extra listening practice is to chat to them casually, for a couple of minutes in every lesson or so, about anything that comes into your head – your childhood, your family and friends, your education, what you did yesterday, or anything else you feel like talking about. There is no need to make this an 'exercise' with comprehension questions; what you say will be interesting enough in itself to make students concentrate.

As regards reading, a good approach is to provide a circulating class library of supplementary readers at the right level. You will need one copy each of as many different titles as you have students. The books should preferably be chosen mainly for their interest rather than for their cultural value. Again, this activity should be as undemanding as possible – only give questions or tasks if students really need them.

5 Match the questions and answers.

1. Can you lend me some stamps?
2. Excuse me. Have you got the time?
3. Can I borrow your pen?
4. Could you help me for a few minutes?
5. Have you got a light?
6. Shall I post these letters for you?
7. Could I borrow your bicycle for half an hour?
8. Have you got change for £1?
9. Could I use your phone?
10. Would you like to play tennis this evening?
11. Excuse me. Can you tell me the way to the station?
12. I'll give you a hand with the cooking, shall I?

a. Sorry, I don't smoke.
b. I think so. How many do you need?
c. Sorry, I'm afraid I'm using it.
d. Sorry, I'm not free. My son's coming round.
e. Just after half past three.
f. Perhaps – I'll have a look. Yes, here you are.
g. OK. Can you put it back on my desk when you've finished with it?
h. That's very kind of you. Could you do the potatoes?
i. Well, I'm in a bit of a hurry.
j. Of course. It's over there on the table.
k. Sorry, I'm a stranger here myself.
l. Yes, please, if you don't mind.

6 Ask other students if you can borrow things from them. Use questions and answers from Exercise 5.

7 Write two or more notes to other students. In your notes, you must ask somebody for something, offer something to somebody, or offer to do something for somebody. Answer the notes that you get. Use words and expressions from Exercises 1 and 5.

> Dear Anne,
> Could I borrow your bike this evening?
> Yours,
> Patricia

> Dear Pat,
> Of course you can. I'll give it to you after the lesson.
> Anne

> Dear Tony,
> Shall I drive you to the airport on Saturday?
> love,
> Alice

> Dear Alice,
> Thank you very much. That's very kind of you. My plane's at 11.30.
> Love T

Learn/revise: dress; jacket; foot (*plural* feet); borrow something from somebody; lend something to somebody / somebody something (lent, lent); try; feel (felt, felt); look like; look (great *etc.*); need; go out with somebody; have a look; lovely; in a hurry; half an hour; anyway; What's the matter?; Oh, dear; What about . . . ?; of course; I'd love to; I think so; if you don't mind; one of these days; I had (I'd) better . . . ; Wait a second; Shall I . . . ?; Have you got the time?; Have you got a light?; change for £1; Can you tell me the way to . . . ?; I'm a stranger here myself; That's very kind of you.

Possessive pronouns: mine; yours; his; hers; ours; theirs.

Modal verbs (+ infinitive without *to*): will; would; shall; should; can; could; had better.

Summary B

Simple Past tense

I left you left he/she/it left we left you left they left	did I leave? did you leave? *etc.*	I did not (didn't) leave you did not (didn't) leave *etc.*

Spelling of regular pasts

MOST REGULAR VERBS:	work ⟶ worked start ⟶ started wait ⟶ waited play ⟶ played
VERBS ENDING IN *-e*:	hate ⟶ hated like ⟶ liked
VERBS ENDING IN ONE STRESSED VOWEL + ONE CONSONANT:	stop ⟶ stopped plan ⟶ planned fit ⟶ fitted
VERBS ENDING IN CONSONANT + *-y*.	study ⟶ studied try ⟶ tried

Pronunciation of regular pasts

1. /d/ after vowels and voiced sounds (/b/, /g/, /v/, /ð/, /l/, /z/, /ʒ/, /dʒ/, /m/, /n/, /ŋ/)

   agreed /əˈgriːd/   played /pleɪd/   lived /lɪvd/
   pulled /pʊld/   used /juːzd/

2. /t/ after /p/, /k/, /f/, /θ/, /s/, /ʃ/, /tʃ/

   stopped /stɒpt/   worked /wɜːkt/   watched /wɒtʃt/

3. /ɪd/ after /t/ and /d/

   started /ˈstɑːtɪd/   decided /dɪˈsaɪdɪd/

Past Progressive tense

I was trying you were trying he/she/it was trying we were trying you were trying they were trying	was I trying? were you trying? *etc.*	I was not (wasn't) trying you were not (weren't) trying *etc.* .

Using the Past Progressive

We use the Past Progressive for 'background' events — to say what was going on at the time when something happened. We use the Past Progressive for the longer event and the Simple Past for the shorter event which came in the middle, or interrupted what was going on.

Just when I **was trying** to finish some work
———————×———————
Janet
turned up.

The TV
broke down
———————×———————
while we **were watching** the news.

I **was getting** ready to come home
———————×———————
and the
phone **rang**.

What **were** you **doing**
———————×———————
at 7.15
last night?

So am I, neither am I etc.

'I am . . .'   'So **am** I.' / 'I'm not.'
'I was . . .'   'So **was** I.' / 'I **wasn't**.'
'I have got . . .' 'So **have** I.' / 'I **haven't**.'
'He **can** . . .'   'So **can** she.' / 'She **can't**.'
'She **likes** . . .' 'So **do** I.' / 'I **don't**.'
'I **saw** . . .'   'So **did** I.' / 'I **didn't**.'

'I'm not . . .'   'Neither **am** I.' / 'I **am**.'
'She **can't** . . .' 'Neither **can** he.' / 'He **can**.'
'He **doesn't** . . .' 'Neither **do** I.' / 'I **do**.'
'They **don't** . . .' 'Neither **do** we.' / 'We **do**.'

Summary B

Summary of language taught in Lessons 7–12.

This lesson displays most of the more important language points that students should have learnt or revised in the last six lessons. Spend a short time going over the material with the students, answering questions and clearing up any difficulties. Students may also need to spend time at home making sure everything is thoroughly learnt.

Practice Book exercises
1. Revision of miscellaneous points of grammar.
2. Possessive determiners and pronouns.
3. *Have* and *have got*.
4. Writing a story with prescribed vocabulary.
5. Reading: a poem.
6. Crossword.

Some uses of the infinitive with *to*

– after *something, anything* etc.

> I haven't got **anything to wear.**
> Would you like **something to drink?**

– after *would like/love*

> **Would** you **like to come** to a party?
> I'd **love to.**

– after many other verbs

> I don't **want to go** to work.
> I **hope to see** you soon.
> Let's **try to understand** each other.

Some uses of the infinitive without *to*

– after modal verbs

> **Can/Could** you **lend** me some stamps?
> (~~Can/Could you to lend . . .~~)
> I'll **give** you a hand with the cooking.
> Shall I **post** these letters for you?
> **Would** you **like** a game of tennis?

– after *had better*

> I'd **better get** moving.

– after *make* + object

> It **makes me look** like a sack of potatoes.

– after *do*

> Why **don't** you **borrow** something of mine?
> If you **don't mind.**

Possessive determiners and pronouns

DETERMINER	PRONOUN
my	mine
your	yours
his	his
her	hers
its	–
our	ours
your	yours
their	theirs

> That's **my** book.   It's **mine.**
> This is **her** car.   It's **hers.**
> 'Whose is that house?'   'It's **ours.**'
> Why don't you borrow something of **mine?**
> **My** feet are bigger than **yours.**

More, most and *fewest*

> A plane has got **more wheels than** a pram.
> A plane can carry **the most** people.
> A bike can carry **the fewest** people.

(*Not*) as . . . as . . .

> Dürer doesn't look **as** happy **as** the king.
> My sister's nearly **as** tall **as** me.

(*Not*) as much/many as . . .

> She's got **as much** money as me.
> A car hasn't got **as many** wheels as a lorry.
> A bicycle doesn't cost **as much as** a motorbike.

Less . . . than

> Dürer looks **less** happy **than** the king.
> A motorbike costs **less than** a car.

As and *than*

(not) as . . . **as**	-er **than**
the same . . . **as**	more . . . **than**
as . . . **as**	less . . . **than**

NOTE: different **from** (~~different than~~)

Modification of comparatives

> A plane is **much faster** than a train.
> A bus can carry **far more** people than a car.
> A car costs **much less** than a plane.

Superlatives

> A plane is **the fastest.**
> A plane can carry **the most** people.

Something strange etc.

> **Something very strange** happened.
> anything/somebody/somewhere nice/important *etc.*

Leaving out words in conversation

> 'What did you do?'   '(I) had lunch with her.'
> (It) sounds like a boring day.
> 'Did anything interesting happen?'   '(I) don't think
>   so. (I) can't remember.'

Asking for things when you don't know the words

> a thing **with** a hole / **with** a handle

> a machine **for making** holes
> a tool **for cutting** wood

> some material **for making** curtains
> some liquid **for cleaning** windows
> some powder **for washing** clothes
> some stuff **for killing** insects

Suggestions, offers and requests

> **What about** your blue dress?
> **Why don't you** borrow something of mine?
> I'll lend you my new shoes.
> 'Shall I iron it for you?'   'If you really don't mind.'
> '**Would you like to** play tennis this evening?'   'I'd
>   love to.'
> **Can you / Could you** help me for a few minutes?

Revision B

Look at the exercises, decide which ones are useful to you, and do two or more.

GRAMMAR

1 Put in the correct past verb forms.

1. Your letter .... just when I .... to you. (*arrive; write*)
2. Susan .... while I .... breakfast. (*telephone; have*)
3. I first .... Harry when we .... at the bank. (*meet; work*)
4. It .... when I .... this morning. (*snow; get up*)
5. While she .... about her problems I .... to sleep. (*talk; go*)
6. I .... my knee while I .... football. (*hurt; play*)
7. I .... my coat because it .... (*take; rain*)
8. While I .... through my papers I .... a lot of unpaid bills. (*look; find*)
9. We .... trouble with the car when we .... through London. (*have; drive*)
10. I would like to know why you .... out of the room while I .... to you. (*walk; talk*)
11. I .... off the TV because smoke .... out of the back. (*switch; come*)
12. While I .... dinner with Alice she .... me that she wanted to change her job. (*have; tell*)

2 Choose the correct tense (simple or progressive).

1. 'Could I speak to Linda?' 'I'm afraid she *puts / 's putting* the baby to bed. Could you ring back in about half an hour?'
2. I first met my wife when I *worked / was working* in Detroit.
3. How often *do you see / are you seeing* your parents?
4. My father *worked / was working* for a long time in Nigeria when he was younger.
5. *Do you know / Are you knowing* my friend Alex Carter?
6. 'Would you like a cigarette?' 'No thanks. I *don't smoke / 'm not smoking*.'
7. 'What *do you do / are you doing*?' 'I *try / 'm trying* to mend my bicycle. Would you like to help?'
8. 'What *do you do / are you doing*?' 'I'm a chemical engineer.'
9. 'I called at your house yesterday evening, but you weren't there. What *did you do / were you doing*?' 'I was at a party.'
10. 'What *did you do / were you doing* after the party?' 'I went straight home.'

LISTENING

1 🔲 True or false? Listen to Marilyn and Pat, and write *T* or *F* for each sentence.

1. Marilyn's cousin has got a large nose.
2. Marilyn and her cousin are both short.
3. Marilyn has got the same temperament as her cousin.
4. Pat looks the same as her mother.
5. Pat and her mother are both short, but Pat's quite a bit shorter.
6. Pat has got the same temperament as her mother.

2 🔲 Try to fill in the missing words. Then listen to the song and see if you were right.

A BIGGER HEART

His arms are stronger than mine
His legs are .... than mine
His car's always cleaner
And his grass is always ....

But my heart is .... than his
And my love for you is stronger than his.

His shirts are .... than mine
His soufflés are lighter than mine
His video is ....
And his faults are fewer

But my heart is .... than his
And my love for you is stronger than his.

He's more ...., much more elegant
More charming and polite than me
He's more responsible, much more dependable
He's everything I long to be.

His office is .... than mine
His martinis are drier than mine
His roses are ....
And his overdraft is smaller

But my heart is .... than his
And my love for you is stronger than his.

Revision B

Students and teacher choose grammar, listening, speaking, writing and pronunciation activities.
Principal structures: Simple and Progressive Past tenses; comparison structures.

Note

There is a lot of material in this lesson, and you will probably not want or need to do all of it. You might get students to vote for the exercises they feel are most valuable.

GRAMMAR

1 Simple Past and Past Progressive
• Students who have worked through Lesson 8 and Summary B should have little difficulty with this exercise.
• You may like to have the class do part of it in writing, so that you can see if any individuals are still having trouble.

Answers to Exercise 1
1. arrived; was writing
2. telephoned; was having
3. met; were working
4. was snowing; got up
5. was talking; went
6. hurt; was playing
7. took; was raining
8. was looking; found
9. had; were driving
10. walked; was talking
11. switched; was coming
12. was talking; told

2 Simple and progressive tenses
• This can be done in the same way as Exercise 1.

Answers to Exercise 2
1. 's putting
2. was working
3. do you see
4. worked
5. Do you know
6. don't smoke
7. are you doing; 'm trying
8. do you do
9. were you doing
10. did you do

LISTENING

1 Authentic listening: comparisons
• Look over the sentences with the students, and make sure that they understand all the words.
• Each student should write the numbers 1 to 6 on a piece of paper.
• Play the recording while they work individually to write *T* for the true sentences and *F* for the false sentences.
• The students may want you to play the recording two or three times.
• Go over the answers with them; it may be useful to play the recording again, pausing after each answer.

Answers and tapescript for Exercise 1

1T, 2F, 3T, 4T, 5F, 6F

MARILYN:
I have no brothers and sisters for any comparisons. Erm, and the only person in my family that I resemble is a cousin who is also an only child. Erm, we're both fairly angular, with large noses, and tall, and er, we, we both have the same temperament, which is rather loud.

PAT:
I suppose I resemble my mum most. Erm, she's a bit shorter than me. She looks the same; well, I look the same as her. Erm, she's quite a bit shorter. Erm, she has a, rather a different temperament to me; she, erm, moans a lot, or nags a lot, certainly with my dad, but, erm, whereas I'm much more easygoing.

2 Song: *A Bigger Heart*
• Let students look over the text.
• Get them to guess at the missing words, individually at first and then in groups. If necessary, point out that rhyme is a clue.
• When they are ready, play the song.

Answers to Exercise 2

His arms are stronger than mine
His legs are *longer* than mine
His car's always cleaner
And his grass is always *greener*

But my heart is *bigger* than his
And my love for you is stronger than his.

His shirts are *whiter* than mine
His soufflés are lighter than mine
His video is *newer*
And his faults are fewer

But my heart is *bigger* than his
And my love for you is stronger than his.

He's more *intelligent*, much more elegant
More charming and polite than me
He's more responsible, much more dependable
He's everything I long to be.

His office is *higher* than mine
His martinis are drier than mine
His roses are *taller*
And his overdraft is smaller

But my heart is *bigger* than his
And my love for you is stronger than his.

40

SPEAKING

1 Students' dialogues: borrowing and lending
- After looking over the Lesson 12 material, students should prepare their conversations in pairs.
- These should not be too long — just enough to include a reasonable number of the new expressions.
- Listen to the conversations and make high-priority corrections before students perform for the class.

Note: interviews
- The next two exercises are best done on two separate occasions.
- You will need to arrange for two or more English-speaking visitors to come to the class.
- Organise several groups of students, each with a set of questions prepared, and as many visitors as groups, so that they can rotate. Choose visitors who won't mind being asked personal questions.
- Alternatively, try to arrange for students to interview English-speaking people outside the school. (If they are studying in an English-speaking country, they will be able to organise this for themselves.)
- If you can't get hold of outside English-speakers, use other English teachers from your school — preferably teachers that the students don't know well.

2 Preparing for interviews
- Get students to work in groups of about four.
- Tell them to prepare interesting questions to which they really want to know the answers. They shouldn't be afraid to ask personal questions.
- Encourage students to use vocabulary and structures from Lessons 7–12, and to make 'follow-up' questions.
- Each student should copy all the group's questions.
- Different groups can ask about different topics — for instance, one group can ask about people's childhood, another about likes and dislikes, etc.

3 Interviews
- Introduce your visitors to the students and then get them to spend about ten minutes with each group.
- Students should take turns to ask questions, while one student acts as secretary and notes the answers.

WRITING

1 Comparing visitors
- This can be an individual or class composition.
- Students should choose two visitors and write a comparison, covering as many points as possible.
- You may need to help with 'structuring' expressions like *on the other hand*, *however* and so on.

2 Completing a text
- Let students decide whether they want to work alone or with someone else.
- The exercise may start slowly while students search for ideas, but once they've found a way of starting they should manage it without too much difficulty.
- If anybody really has trouble finding an idea, suggest one of the following beginnings:

In September 1990, Ann Blake went to university / got married / left school / left home / went to live in Canada / got a job in a zoo / started teaching / became a racing driver.

- Students can read their finished stories to each other or put them up on the class notice board.
- Finally, in class or for homework, get students to write a similar but personalised text.

PRONUNCIATION

1 Rhythm and stress

- Practise the examples with the students, using the recording as a guide if you wish.
- Let them discuss the other expressions in groups.
- When they have drawn the rhythm patterns, play the recording or read out the expressions, letting students change their answers if they want to.
- Then go over the answers.

Answers to Exercise 1
(The phrases can of course all be stressed in various ways, depending on context and exact meaning. The following are normal neutral versions.)

I'd better stop.　　　　less than an hour

if you don't mind.　　　What did you do?

Whose is that house?　　I don't think so.

It's mine.　　　　　　　I can't remember.

She's taller than me.　　a thing with a handle

He's as old as me.

2 Vowels

- This can be done by group discussion.
- When students are ready, say the words or play the recording, letting students change their answers if they want to.
- Practise any especially difficult words.

Answers to Exercise 2
1. All /e/ except *break* (/eɪ/).
2. All /ʌ/ except *over* (/əʊ/).
3. All /ɔː/.
4. All /aɪ/.
5. All /ɜː/ except *beard* (/ɪə/).
6. All /ʊ/ except *shoe* (/uː/).
7. All /əʊ/.
8. All /ɑː/ except *false* (/ɔː/).

Practice Book exercises
1. Vocabulary revision: lexical sets.
2. Grammar revision: *a*, *some* and *one*.
3. Word stress.
4. Translation of material from Lesson 12.
5. Student's Cassette exercise (Student's Book Listening Exercise 1). Students use Marilyn's speech as a dictation.
6. Writing: comparisons between people.

Additional reading
Note that students have now reached a level where they should be able to cope comfortably with the texts in Sections A and B of *Additional reading* in the Practice Book (pages 108 and 109). You can set some of the readings for homework or just suggest that students read any of the texts that interest them when they have the time.

SPEAKING

1 Look again at Lesson 12, Exercises 1 and 5. Then work in pairs and prepare a short conversation. You are two presidents, two generals, two film stars, two pop singers, two Mafia bosses, two doctors, two students, two housewives, two cats, or two . . . (you decide). Perform your conversation for the class. They must decide who you are. Useful expressions:

What's the matter?
I'm . . .ing (. . .), and I haven't got anything to . . . / any . . . / enough . . .
Could I borrow . . . ?
I'll lend you . . .
What about . . . ?
Why don't you . . . ?
If you really don't mind, . . .
Sorry, I'm afraid I'm using it.
Of course. It's over there . . .

WRITING

1 Write a comparison between two of the people you interviewed in Speaking Exercise 3.

2 Complete the text. (You can make some small changes if you want to.) Read your text to the class. Then write a similar text about yourself or somebody you know well.

In September 19......., Ann Blake .... At first, she felt .... She ...., and life was .... She went to ...., she ...., and she .... lots of ....
   But then things changed. One day, while she was ...., she met .... As soon as she ...., she knew that .... was a strange person: ...., ... and ...., and Ann ....
   Both of them .... But Ann .... She .... She couldn't ...., and she spent all her time .... Finally, she decided to ...., and a few days later she ....

   ....

   ....

2 Prepare questions for an interview with an English-speaking stranger. You must find out as much as possible about him/her, including details of his/her childhood, education, family, work, interests. Prepare 'follow-up questions' for some of your questions. Examples:

'Do you like sport?' 'Yes, I do.' 'Which sports?'
'Where did you live when you were a child?'
   'In Belfast.' 'Did you like it?'

3 Working in groups, interview English-speaking visitors to your class.

PRONUNCIATION

1 Rhythm and stress. Practise the examples. Then try to draw the rhythm patterns for the other expressions.

□ □ □ □□
What were you doing?

□ □□
I'd love to.

□ □ □ □□
I don't want to go.

I'd better stop.
if you don't mind
Whose is that house?
It's mine.
She's taller than me.
He's as old as me.
less than an hour
What did you do?
I don't think so.
I can't remember.
a thing with a handle

2 In which groups do all the words have the same vowel? In the other groups, one word has a different vowel from the others. Which word is different?

1. heavy   dress   dead   break
2. glove   lovely   over   above
3. sort   talk   horse   yours
4. eye   die   try   mine
5. bird   beard   learn   turn
6. book   look   shoe   would
7. phone   clothes   soap   don't
8. false   laugh   glasses   after

Test B

LISTENING

1 **Listen to Alwyn's story and answer the questions.**

1. When the story began, was he going to see his friends or going home?
2. Was it early or late?
3. How far from his house was he when he saw the lights?
4. How big was the flying saucer (. . . *yards across*)?
5. Did the saucer move?
6. When he got home, did his father believe him?

flying saucer

pedalling

GRAMMAR

1 **Give the Simple Past of these verbs.**

go *went* break call come drink eat
fall find get hear hit know learn
leave lie look make meet read see
start swim take write

2 **Put each verb into the correct past form.**

1. I (*hurt*) my foot when I (*get*) out of the bath.
2. When I (*see*) John he (*walk*) down the road.
3. It (*rain*) when I (*get up*) this morning.
4. While Ann (*talk*) I (*have*) a wonderful idea.
5. I (*go*) to sleep while I (*watch*) TV.

3 **Complete the groups of sentences. Example:**

AFFIRMATIVE ('Yes'): *She arrived late.*

INTERROGATIVE ('?'): *Did she arrive late?*

NEGATIVE ('No'): *She didn't arrive late.*

1. AFF: It rained last night.
   INT: ....
   NEG: ....
2. AFF: ....
   INT: Did Ann telephone yesterday?
   NEG: ....

3. AFF: ....
   INT: ....
   NEG: Mr Ellis didn't know what to do.
4. AFF: The bus was late.
   INT: ....
   NEG: ....

4 **Write 'follow-up' questions. Examples:**

'I'm getting a new job.' *'Oh, yes? What are you going to do?'*
'I don't like pop music.' *'Do you like jazz?'*

1. My brother had a car crash last week.
2. Peter and Ann have just had a baby.
3. I play tennis twice a week.
4. I left school when I was fourteen.
5. I don't read newspapers.

5 **Put in *to* if necessary. Example:**

Would you ......—...... like ...*to*... dance?

1. I haven't got anything .... read.
2. You'd better .... go now.
3. I don't want .... go home.
4. Can you .... lend me £5?
5. I hope .... hear from you soon.
6. Please try .... understand.
7. Could I .... use your phone?
8. Would you like .... play tennis tomorrow?
9. That hat makes him .... look funny.
10. Why don't you .... go home?

6 **Complete the table.**

I	me	my	mine
you	....	....	....
he	him	....	....
she	....	her	....
it	....	....	—
we	....	....	....
you	....	....	....
they	....	....	....

7 **Put in a suitable word.**

1. I usually get up .... eight o'clock.
2. Come back again .... Tuesday.
3. I'm not free now — can you come back again .... ten minutes?
4. 'I've brought some flowers .... you.' 'Oh, thank you.'
5. 'How long are you going to stay here?' '............... March.'
6. I don't think she's as intelligent .... her sister.
7. It's impossible to travel faster .... light.
8. English food is very different .... French food.
9. 'Where's the meeting?' 'The same place .... last week.'
10. 'I didn't like the film much.' 'Neither .... I.'

Test B

Students do a simple revision test.

The purpose of the test

This test covers material from Lessons 7–12. It is not of
course necessary to do all of the sections, and teachers
should select according to their students' needs. Teachers
who do not feel the test will be useful should simply drop
it altogether.

If possible, try to make the students feel that they are
'testing themselves', rather than 'being tested'. It is not
intended that students should 'pass' or 'fail' the test, and it
is not particularly useful to give marks. (If the school or
education system requires that this be done, you will need
to work out a simple marking scheme.) But students should
of course be told whether you feel their performance is
satisfactory. In principle, students who have worked
systematically through Lessons 7–12 ought to get most
answers right.

Administration

The test can be administered in various ways, depending
on how strictly you want to control students' performance;
whether you want to collect the answers and mark them,
or allow the students to correct them in class; and so on.

The 'speaking' test will need to be done individually, with
students interrupting their work on the other parts of the
test to come and talk to you.

If you do not collect students' scripts, correction can be
done by class discussion when everybody has finished.

Notes, tapescript and answers are given below.

LISTENING

Listening for information

- Point out the illustrations of the young man pedalling
and the flying saucer.
- Tell the students to read the questions.
- Then play the recording through once without
stopping while students try to answer the questions.
- Give them a couple of minutes to look over the
questions and their answers, and then play the recording
again without stopping.
- If you feel that many of the students are still having
difficulty, you can play the recording a third time.

Answers to Listening Test 1

1. going home
2. (relatively) late
3. about half a mile
4. about fifty yards across
5. yes
6. no

Tapescript for Listening Test 1

This-, this was in my ear-, early teens, actually, and, and
I was pedalling home erm, after, you know, being with
my friends, and it was relatively late, and er, I was
about half a mile away from my house when I became
aware of er, very bright flashing lights above my head.
And er, as, I looked up and there was erm, what I can
only describe as a saucer-shaped object. Very large, in
fact, about fifty yards across, er, with multicoloured
lights all the way round that were flashing, er,
alternating in the flashing. And as, as I pedalled home, it
stayed above my head, and I pedalled home as, well,
obviously, as you can imagine, relatively fast, and er, I
shot into the house, and you, got hold of my father, and
said, 'You'll never believe this: I've just come up the
road, and a flying saucer's followed me all the way
home.' And he said, 'You're quite right, you little
bastard.' (*Sound of a smack*) 'Get to bed.' (*General
laughter*)

GRAMMAR

1 broke   called   came   drank   ate   fell
found   got   heard   hit   knew   learnt
left   lay   looked   made   met   read
saw   started   swam   took   wrote

2   1. hurt; was getting   4. were talking; had
2. saw; was walking   5. went; was watching
3. was raining; got up

3   1. Did it rain last night?
It did not (didn't) rain last night.
2. Ann telephoned yesterday.
Ann did not (didn't) telephone yesterday.
3. Mr Ellis knew what to do.
Did Mr Ellis know what to do?
4. Was the bus late?
The bus was not (wasn't) late.

4   (Various possible answers.)

5   1. I haven't got anything *to* read.
2. You'd better go now.
3. I don't want *to* go home.
4. Can you lend me £5?
5. I hope *to* hear from you soon.
6. Please try *to* understand.
7. Could I use your phone?
8. Would you like *to* play tennis tomorrow?
9. That hat makes him look funny.
10. Why don't you go home?

6

I	me	my	mine
you	*you*	*your*	*yours*
he	him	*his*	*his*
she	*her*	her	*hers*
it	*it*	*its*	–
we	*us*	*our*	*ours*
you	*you*	*your*	*yours*
they	*them*	*their*	*theirs*

7   1. I usually get up *at* eight o'clock.
2. Come back again *on* Tuesday.
3. I'm not free now – can you come back again *in*
ten minutes?
4. 'I've brought some flowers *for* you.'   'Oh,
thank you.'
5. 'How long are you going to stay here?'
'*Until/Till* March.'
6. I don't think she's as intelligent *as* her sister.
7. It's impossible to travel faster *than* light.
8. English food is very different *from* French food.
9. 'Where's the meeting?'   'The same place *as* last
week.'
10. 'I didn't like the film much.'   'Neither *did* I.'

VOCABULARY

1 (Various possible answers.)

2 (Various possible answers.)

3 warm/hot; cheap; dark; unhappy;
cold; boring; young/new; fat; false/untrue; black.

LANGUAGE IN USE

1 (Various possible answers.)

2 (Various possible answers.)

PRONUNCIATION

1 anyway; arrive; aspirin; Chinese; difference;
expensive; material; recognise; something;
usual.

2 1. here
2. ear
3. coat
4. shoe
5. want

SPEAKING

Go over the instructions with the whole class and make sure they understand what they have to do. Then test the students one by one. In the picture story, tell students to use past tenses. In the conversation, don't give students too much information at a time – make them ask plenty of questions.

WRITING

When correcting this, it is best to judge students mainly on their ability to communicate successfully, using appropriate vocabulary and structures. Excessive emphasis on minor errors of grammar and spelling can damage students' confidence.

Test Book recordings
A recording for Test 2 in the Test Book follows this lesson on the Class Cassette.

VOCABULARY

1 How many words can you add in each group?

Shops: chemist's, . . .
Vehicles: car, . . .
Jobs: shop assistant, . . .
Food: meat, potato, . . .
Parts of the body: arm, . . .
Animals: cat, . . .

2 Write the names of twenty things that you could buy in a supermarket.

3 Give the opposites. Example:

big _small_ cold expensive fair happy hot interesting old thin true white

LANGUAGE IN USE

1 Write three possible answers for each question. Example:

'Have you got a light?' *'Of course. Here you are.'* / *'I'm afraid I haven't.'* / *'Sorry. I don't smoke.'*

1. Can you lend me some stamps?
2. Could you help me for a few minutes?
3. Shall I post these letters for you?
4. Could I borrow your bicycle for half an hour?
5. Would you like to play football this afternoon?

2 Write a question for each answer.

1. Sorry, I'm afraid I'm using it.
2. That's very kind of you.
3. Of course. It's in the kitchen.
4. Yes, please, if you don't mind.
5. Sorry, I'm a stranger here myself.

PRONUNCIATION

1 Write these words and underline the stressed syllables. Example: a_bove_

anyway arrive aspirin Chinese difference expensive material recognise something usual

2 One word in each group has a different vowel. Which is it? Example:

cat bag (late) ran

1. here where hair wear
2. there their they're ear
3. coat talk horse sort
4. took book shoe would
5. don't want won't know

SPEAKING

1 Look at the pictures and tell the teacher the story.

2 Ask the teacher about his/her school, how he/she liked it, what he/she did there, *etc.* Find out as much as you can.

WRITING

1 Write the picture story.

13 Have you ever . . . ?

Present Perfect tense; talking about experience.

1 Here are some questions. Make sure you understand them. Then listen to the answers: which question goes with which answer(s)?

1. Have you ever been to a big carnival that you enjoyed?
2. Have you ever done anything surprising?
3. Have you ever been on a boat trip that you enjoyed?
4. Have you ever tried hard to do something and failed?
5. Have you ever been on a nature reserve that you liked?

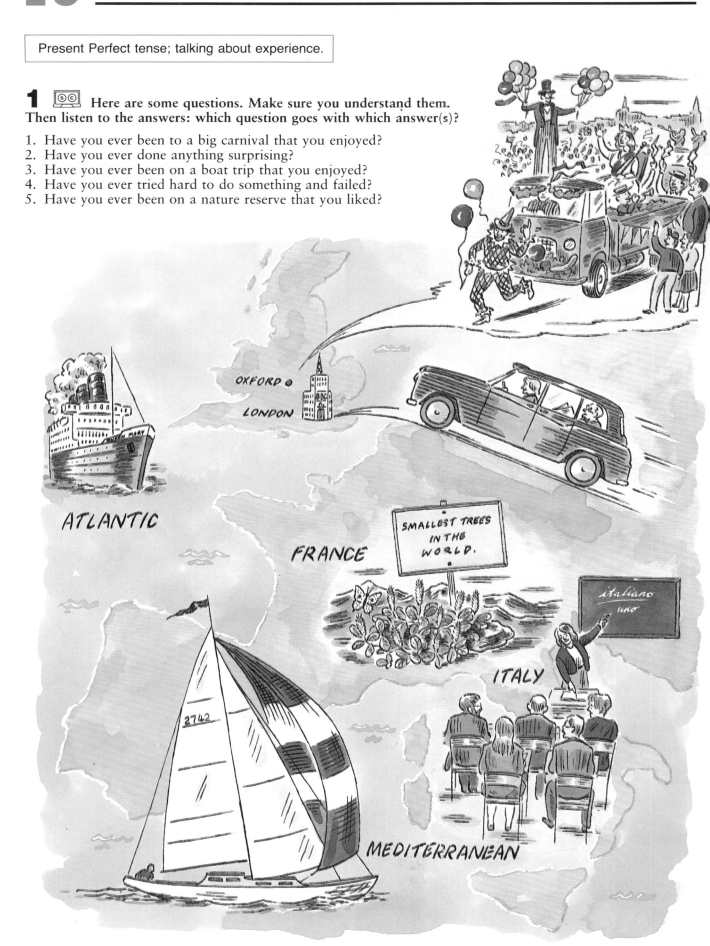

Lesson 13

Students practise ways of talking about people's experience.
Principal structures: revision of (Simple) Present Perfect tense; Present Perfect with *ever*; *I've been to . . .*

Language notes and possible problems

1. Level and workload   Lessons 13–18 include a good deal of work on the use of the Present Perfect tense. This is a difficult topic, and some of these lessons will therefore be a little harder and fuller than average.

2. Present Perfect tense   The rules for the use of the Present Perfect are complicated. Here, students revise the use of the Present Perfect Simple for **finished actions** in **unfinished time periods**: 'time up to now'. Example: *I've eaten snails twice (in my life)*. At the same time, students are reminded that they cannot use the Present Perfect tense with adverbs or other expressions which refer to a **finished** time period. Look out for mistakes like **I have had a car accident last year* – some western European languages have a tense which is constructed like the English Present Perfect but often used like the English Simple Past.

The Present Perfect Progressive, and some other uses of the simple tense, are studied in the next few lessons.

3. Past participles   Some students may be unclear about the difference between Simple Past forms and past participles. You may need to explain this.

---

1 Listening: *Have you ever . . . ?*

● Give students a few minutes to look over the questions and make sure they understand. They can use dictionaries and/or ask you about unfamiliar words.
● Tell them that they must listen and try to decide which question goes with which answer. One question has two answers.
● Stress that they do not need to understand everything the speakers are saying.
● Play the recording, two or three times if necessary, until students feel confident that they have matched questions and answers. Then go over the answers with them.
● You may want to play the recording again, pausing it to point out the words that give away the answers.

Answers to Exercise 1
1. c
2. f
3. a and d
4. b
5. e

Tapescript for Exercise 1
a. Yes, I took a middling-long trip on a sailboat in the Mediterranean once, and it really made me feel I'd, I'd love to go sailing properly again sometime.
b. I've always wanted to speak Italian, and I've tried year after year after year to teach myself to speak Italian with every book under the sun, even going to evening classes, and I've realised I must be too stupid.
c. Yes. St Giles' Fair in Oxford, which er, is only there for two nights in each year, erm, and fills the whole street with noise and excitement and colour, and stops all the traffic, which is wonderful.
d. I sailed across the Atlantic twice on the old Queen Mary and the Queen Elizabeth, in opposite directions of course. Erm, it would never be repeated, but I enjoyed that.
e. Well, I went to a national park in France in the mountains, and we saw, we saw the smallest trees in the world, which are about three centimetres high and, I thought they were lovely.
f. I drove a taxi to London, to the BBC, with an important personage on board, and managed to get there and back without bumping into anything.

2 'Have you ever . . . ?'

- Look at the example question with the students. Make sure they understand the meaning of *ever* with the Present Perfect (= 'at any time in one's life').
- Go over the answers and explain any difficulties.
- Point out that the answer *Yes, I ate some last summer* is in the Simple Past tense because there is an adverbial of finished time (*last summer*).
- Ask students if they can think of other examples of this sort of adverbial.
- Get a few students to ask others if they have ever eaten snails (or some other food which they would consider exotic); make sure the tenses in the answers are correct.
- Then get students to ask each other more questions using *Have you ever . . . ?*
- You may have to discuss the construction of the Present Perfect, if students are not clear about the difference between past tenses and past participles.
- You may also wish to say a word about the use of *been* as a past participle of *go*, meaning *gone and come back*.

Optional activity: survey
- Exercise 2 can be done as a walk-round survey.
- Ask each student to prepare a question using *Have you ever . . . ?*
- Get everybody to stand up and walk round asking their questions and noting the answers.
- Then get students to report the results of their survey (e.g. *'Seven people out of twelve have had piano lessons'*; *'Nobody has been to Australia'*).

3 Something that not many people have done
- You may need to give students a minute or two to decide what they are going to say and how to say it.

4 Present Perfect or Simple Past
- This can usefully be done by class discussion.
- If the rule involved is not already clear to students, they should come to understand it during the course of the exercise.
- At the end of the exercise, see if students can write down the rule for themselves. Discuss their formulations, and put an agreed version on the blackboard. The rule should cover these facts:
- We often use the Present Perfect to talk about experience, especially when we mention 'time up to the present' (for example *during the last three years*). If *ever* or *often* mean 'up to now', we usually use the Present Perfect with them.
- We do not normally use the Present Perfect when we mention or ask about a finished time (for example *last week*, *when you were a child*, *When . . . ?*).
- Point out to students how a conversation may start with a Present Perfect (*Have you ever . . .*), and then move into past tenses as the speakers talk about the details of time and place (as in the last three questions).

Answers to Exercise 4
1. had   2. have often dreamt   3. have travelled
4. 've never been there   5. didn't like
6. I've spoken   7. made   8. did you ever; ran
9. Have you ever broken; have; did you do
10. Have you ever; have; was it

5 Expressions of finished time
- This may help students to understand more clearly what is meant by finished time adverbials.
- Give students a few minutes to work individually and then let them compare notes in groups.
- Drop the exercise if students are already clear about the point.

6 Preparing an interview
- Divide students into groups of three or four.
- Each group must write at least ten questions, and all the members of the group should write them down.
- Tell them they can use dictionaries; walk round the room to give any help that is needed.

7 Interviewing
- Each student finds a person from another group, and asks all the questions on his or her list.
- Get the students to note the answers (brief notes will do; complete sentences are unnecessary).

8 Writing
- Each student should select a part of the information learnt in the interview and write about it.
- Stress that you do not want a complete picture of the person's life, just six to eight sentences.
- Walk round and help, but don't correct errors (except serious tense mistakes) unless you are asked to. Make sure that students do not write their names or the names of the people they are writing about.

9 Listening and guessing
- When students are ready, collect up all the papers.
- Then read out the paragraphs, while students try to guess who is described in each one.
- Alternatively, you can number the papers and put them on the class notice board for students to read. Tell them to write down the numbers together with the names of the people they think are described.

Optional activity: question-box
- Ask students to prepare at least two questions using *Have you ever . . . ?*
- They must write their questions on separate pieces of paper, fold them up and put them in a box.
- The box is then passed round. Each student draws out a question, opens it, reads it aloud and answers.
- Tell students that they do not have to tell the truth if they don't want to. They can also reject one question, saying *I'd rather not answer* (put this on the board); but they are not allowed to reject two.
- When students have answered their questions, make sure they don't put them back in the box.
- (This activity can also be done after Exercise 3.)

Practice Book exercises
1. Choosing between Present Perfect and Simple Past.
2. Personalisation: sentences using Present Perfect.
3. Contractions and full forms.
4. Vocabulary revision: rooms and furniture.
5. Student's Cassette exercise (Student's Book Exercise 1, answers *b* and *e*). Students listen and try to write down what they hear.
6. Reading for gist.

2 Ask and answer questions beginning *Have you ever eaten / seen / been to / met / climbed / broken* etc. Example:

Have you ever eaten snails?

No, I never have.

Yes, I ate some last summer.

No, but I've eaten snake.

Yes, I've eaten them twice.

Yes, I often eat them.

3 Tell the class something that you have done that not many people have done. Example:

'I've been to Tibet.'

4 Choose the correct tense (Present Perfect or Simple Past). What is the rule?

1. My brother *has had / had* a fight with his neighbour last week.
2. I *have often dreamt / often dreamt* of having a million dollars.
3. During the last three years, I *have travelled / travelled* about 100,000 miles.
4. 'Do you know Canada?' 'No, *I've never been / I never went* there.'
5. I *haven't liked / didn't like* grammar when I was at school, but I'm very interested in it now.
6. *I've spoken / I spoke* to the President several times.
7. When we were small, Mother *has made / made* us delicious ice cream every Sunday.
8. 'When you were a child, *have you ever / did you ever* run away from home?' 'Yes, I *have run / ran* away on my third birthday.'
9. *'Have you ever broken / Did you ever break* your ankle?' 'Yes, I *have / did.*' 'When *have you done / did you do* it?'
10. *'Have you ever / Did you ever* put an advertisement in a newspaper?' 'Yes, I *have / did.*' 'Really? What *has it been / was it* for?'

5 Put some more expressions in this list. What tense is used with these expressions?

last week
when you were a child
when I was at school
in 1985

6 In groups of three or four, make lists of ten or more questions that you can ask about someone's life, interests, work, etc. Examples:

'Where did you live when you were a child?'
'Can you talk about two happy times in your life?'
'Have you ever studied music?'

7 Find a person from another group. Ask the questions that you have prepared (and other questions, too, if you like). Note the answers.

8 Write some sentences (about eight) using some of the information from Exercise 7. Don't use the person's name in your sentences.

9 Pass your sentences to the teacher, who will read them to the class. The class has to guess who the sentences are about.

Present Perfect tense		
I have (I've) seen you have (you've) seen *etc.*	have I seen? have you seen? *etc.*	I have not (haven't) seen you have not (haven't) seen *etc.*

Learn/revise: boat; trip; summer; fight (*noun*); neighbour; million; dollar; grammar; president; ice cream; birthday; ankle; advertisement; newspaper; life (*plural* lives); enjoy; fail; meet (met, met); climb; dream (dreamt, dreamt); travel (travelled); speak to (spoke, spoken); run away (ran, run); study; surprising; last; interested (in); small; delicious; third; several; every; hard; twice; at school; during.

14 Things have changed

Present Perfect; *used to*; *since* and *for*.

1 Complete these sentences and write them out correctly. (You may need to put more than one word in a blank.) To get the information you need, look at the statistics and the background information on Fantasia. Use a dictionary when necessary.

1. The population of Fantasia has *increased / decreased* since 1900.
2. The population of San Fantastico *increased / decreased / has increased / has decreased* since 1950.
3. Fantasia used to be highly industrialised, but now has a mainly agricultural economy. True or false?
4. The percentage of homeless people in Fantasia has *risen / fallen* considerably .... 1900.
5. Unemployment figures .... *improved / got worse* since 1950.
6. The percentage of women in paid employment has *risen / fallen* .... 1950.
7. Fantasia has just .... a .... of Friendship and Protection with Outland.
8. Outland .... to be a Fantasian Colony. It *became / has become* independent in ....
9. The Fantasians .... to have Parliamentary elections every .... years. Since 1980, they *have / had / have had* Parliamentary elections every .... years.
10. Mrs Rask *is / was / has been* President of Fantasia for .... years.
11. President Rask and Mrs Martin *know / knew / have known* each other .... a long time.
12. They *first met / have first met* at the Olympic Games in 19..............., where Mrs Rask *won / has won* a silver medal for the high jump.

FANTASIA AND OUTLAND: SOME BACKGROUND INFORMATION

Since the revolution in 1886, Fantasia has been a parliamentary democracy. There are two Houses of Parliament: elections to both used to be held every seven years, but since the Electoral Reform Act of 1980, elections have been held every four years. The President is elected separately by popular vote; the last presidential election was held three years ago. Mrs Kirsten Rask, the current President, is a distinguished physicist. She is also a former Olympic athlete who won a silver medal for the high jump in the 1960 Games.

Outland was formerly the Fantasian colony of South Wesk, but has been independent since the end of the War of Independence in 1954. Relations between the two countries have become more friendly since Mrs Rask's election, and Fantasia has just signed a 'Treaty of Friendship and Protection' with Outland. President Martin of Outland was at University with the Fantasian President's husband, Dr Erasmus Rask, and Mrs Martin and President Rask have been friends since they met at the 1960 Olympics.

STATISTICS	1900	1950	TODAY
Population	20m	35m	46m
Population of San Fantastico	1m	4m	3m
Average number of children per family	4.5	3.6	2
Working week (hours)	54	49	42
Paid holiday (weeks per year)	0	2	5
Size of army	500,000	200,000	50,000
Homeless	23%	17%	8%
Unemployment	20%	7%	17%
Women in paid employment	18%	23%	79%
Percentage of workforce in agriculture	84%	66%	19%
Contribution of agriculture to Gross National Product	78%	51%	8%
Contribution of industry to Gross National Product	11%	38%	83%
Foreign tourists per year	?	30,000	6m

2 How have you changed since you were a small child? How has your village/town/country changed? Useful structures:

I used to . . . , but now I . . .
People used to . . . , but now they . . .
People didn't use to . . .
There used to be . . .
I have . . .
The government has . . .
They've built . . .
. . . has fallen down.
I don't . . . any more.

Lesson 14

Students practise talking and writing about changes and the duration of current states.
Principal structures: more uses of the Present Perfect; *since* and *for*; *used to*.
Phonology: the letter *e* in stressed and unstressed syllables at the beginnings of words.

Language notes and possible problems

1. Level This lesson is a little harder than what has come before, but it should not be too difficult. In Exercise 1, make it clear that students do not have to understand all the vocabulary in the text; they only have to grasp certain key words in order to complete the task. If some things are not completely clear, this does not matter: the exercise is designed to give students some 'real-life' exposure to natural-sounding language, with all its difficulties. Provided they stay calm and concentrate on the task which they are asked to do, they should be able to complete the exercise successfully.

2. Vocabulary Students are asked to learn a certain number of high-priority words. The lesson contains various other words connected with politics, economics or world affairs; students who wish to do so can be encouraged to learn more (Exercise 6 provides an opportunity for this).

3. Present Perfect Students revise the use of this tense to talk about changes. This use follows the general rule that the Present Perfect is used for past events which have a connection with the present, or some present importance. Remind students that the Present Perfect is not used with adverbs of finished time. There are also examples of the Present Perfect of 'non-progressive' verbs (*have been, have known*) used (with *since* and *for*) to talk about duration up to the present. This use of the Present Perfect, and the use of the Present Perfect Progressive, will be studied more thoroughly in Lesson 16.

4. *Since* and *for* Students may use *since* instead of *for* when talking about duration (in some languages the same word is used for both meanings). Look out for mistakes like *I am here since three days*.

5. *Used to . . .* Make sure students realise that *used to* has no present form. (To talk about present habits and states, we just use the Simple Present tense.) Affirmatives and negatives are introduced here; questions (*Did you use to . . . ?*) will be practised in a later lesson. Note the pronunciation: /ˈjuːstə/; not */ˈjuːzd tə/.

If you are short of time
Leave Exercise 7 for homework.

1 Gathering information

● In this exercise, students focus on several structures (Present Perfect, *since* and *for*, *used to*) as they collect the information they need.

● Explain that students will find the facts they need in the 'background information' text and in the table of statistics.

● Tell them that they can use dictionaries or ask you for the meanings of difficult words if they wish, but discourage them from worrying about the exact meaning of words that they don't actually need to understand.

● Do the first two questions with the class. Show them how the grammar problem in sentence 2 can be solved by looking carefully at the use of tenses in sentence 1.

● Then let them continue, working individually or in groups as you prefer. (If they work in groups they can save time by dividing up the questions between them, but note that earlier questions contain examples of the structures needed to answer later questions.)

● When students have done as much as they can, go over the answers and give whatever grammar explanations you feel are necessary. You will probably want to say something about *used to* (see *Language notes*).

Answers to Exercise 1

1. The population of Fantasia has *increased* since 1900.
2. The population of San Fantastico *has decreased* since 1950.
3. Fantasia *used to* be highly industrialised, but now has a mainly agricultural economy. *False.*
4. The percentage of homeless people in Fantasia has *fallen* considerably *since* 1900.
5. Unemployment figures *have got worse* since 1950.
6. The percentage of women in paid employment has *risen since* 1950.
7. Fantasia has just *signed* a *treaty* of Friendship and Protection with Outland.
8. Outland used to be a Fantasian Colony. It *became* independent in *1954.*
9. The Fantasians *used* to have Parliamentary elections every *seven* years. Since 1980, they *have had* Parliamentary elections every *four* years.
10. Mrs Rask *has been* President of Fantasia for *three* years.
11. President Rask and Mrs Martin *have known* each other *for* a long time.
12. They *first met* at the Olympic Games in *1960*, where Mrs Rask *won* a silver medal for the high jump.

2 Personalisation: How have students changed?

● Give a few examples yourself to start students off.
● You might like them to write one or two of their examples, and then continue the exercise orally round the class.

3 Picture: How has New York changed?

• This can be done in groups. Give students 5–10 minutes to draw up group lists of the ways in which they think New York has changed.

• Leave them free to express their answers as they like, but encourage the use of the Present Perfect and the other structures from Exercise 2.

4 Since and for

• This exercise is for students who confuse *since* and *for*. If your class have no trouble with the distinction, drop the exercise.

• It is best done individually first, with students trying to work out the difference by themselves before moving into groups to discuss their ideas.

• They should all come to see that *since* is used with words which refer to the *beginning* of a period of time, while *for* is used with words that refer to the *whole period*.

• You may need to remind students that English uses the Present Perfect, not the Present, to say how long present states have gone on (as in *President Rask and Mrs Martin **have known** each other for a long time*).

5 Pronunciation: *e* in unstressed prefixes

• When the letter *e* comes in an unstressed syllable at the beginning of a word, it is almost always pronounced /ɪ/.

• Go through the words with the students, helping them with the pronunciation, and getting them to decide how the *e* is pronounced.

• Then tell them to write the words in two groups (or do it yourself on the board), according to the pronunciation of *e*.

• Give students a minute or two to try to see the reason for the difference. Play the recording or say the words while they are thinking about it.

• If they can't work it out, ask them where the stress comes in each word.

• Practise the pronunciation of the words. (Note that the main stress on *revolution* is on the third syllable, although the first is also stressed.)

• Ask if students can think of any more words that could be added to the two groups.

Answers to Exercise 5

/e/ *(first syllable stressed)*
every; medal; President; revolution, secretary; separate; seven

/ɪ/ *(first syllable unstressed)*
become; depend; democracy; economy; election; employment; reform; relations; return

6 Student-directed vocabulary learning

• Ask students to look back at the material in Exercise 1 and choose five or more words that they would like to learn. (These will probably coincide with words in the 'learn-list' at the end of the lesson, but it is important for students to have some say in what they learn.)

• Give any help that students need. When they have made their choices, get them to show each other their lists and try to talk about the reasons for their choices. (Do students choose words because they are useful, common, connected with students' personal or professional interests, or for other reasons?)

• This might be a good occasion to talk about techniques of vocabulary learning. Ask students to say what they do in order to note and memorise words and their meanings. Make suggestions yourself if necessary.

7 Writing

• This should be a reasonably controlled piece of writing, modelled on the text in Exercise 1 (though of course students should feel free to change the structure enough so that they can say what they want to say).

• Encourage students to use plenty of the language they have just learnt.

• If class time is short, it can be done for homework.

Practice Book exercises

1. Past tenses and past participles.
2. Writing about changes in people.
3. *Since* and *for*.
4. Present Perfect in descriptions.
5. Vocabulary revision and extension.
6. Students write sentences about themselves.

Study and memorisation

Even when lessons are motivating, communicative and apparently successful, very few students will remember everything they have learnt unless they do further work. Besides doing the Practice Book exercises, most students will also need to spend some time on formal study of the new language material. They should look over the consolidation lessons, making sure they know the new structures and how they are used. Towards the end of the course, they should also find the Mini-grammar helpful.

For many students, memorisation of vocabulary is useful or necessary. It is worth discussing different possible ways of recording meanings (translation, mother-tongue explanation, English explanation, example in context . . .), and ways of memorising vocabulary. Learning by heart has become unfashionable, but it can be a very useful element in language study.

New York City, 1901

3 Look at the picture. Can you think of some ways in which New York has changed since then?

4 Look back at Exercise 1. In sentences 1, 2, 4, 5, 6 and 9, *since* is used to talk about time. In sentences 10 and 11, *for* is used to talk about time. What is the difference?
Now look at the following expressions and choose between *since* and *for*.

~~for~~ .... a very long time
.... yesterday
.... 9 o'clock this morning
.... three hours
.... my 14th birthday
.... last Tuesday
.... about four years
.... most of my life

5 Pronunciation. These words all have the letter *e* in the first syllable. In some of the words, *e* is pronounced /e/; in others, it is pronounced /ɪ/. Can you divide the words into two groups, according to the pronunciation of *e*? What is the reason for the difference?

become	depend	democracy	economy
election	employment	every	medal
President	reform	relations	return
revolution	secretary	separate	seven

6 Choose five or more words to learn from Exercise 1. Tell another student which words you have chosen, and why.

7 Look again at the text 'Fantasia and Outland'. Write a similar paragraph about the history of your country, or another country you know, or an imaginary country.

> **Used to**
> I **used to** be very shy, but now I'm OK.
> **Did** you **use to** collect stamps?
> People **didn't use to** travel by car.

> **Learn/revise:** agriculture; colony; capital; economy; election; employment; unemployment; figures; government; democracy; parliament; industry; percentage; population; tourist; friendship; war; husband; become (became, become); change; get worse; improve; increase; used to; win (won, won); average; homeless; independent; foreign; a long time; every . . . years; each other; most of.

47

15 What do you say when you . . . ?

Situational language; *some, any, no, too, enough, a little, a few.*

1 What is happening in the pictures?

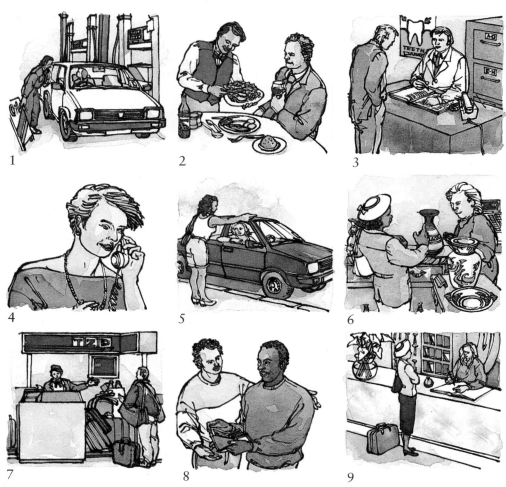

2 Can you match the expressions and the situations? Example:

Can I look round? – Shop

EXPRESSIONS	SITUATIONS
Can I look round?	Shop
I'm afraid you've got the wrong number.	Doctor's surgery
Fill it up with unleaded, please.	Airport
A single for two nights.	Lost property office
Single to Manchester.	Thanking somebody
Check in at 9.30.	Making an appointment
Second on the left.	On the telephone
It was green, with a red handle.	Restaurant
That's very kind of you.	Hotel reception
I'll give you twenty-five for it.	Replying to thanks
Is service included?	Garage / petrol station
Could we make it a bit later?	Hairdresser
It hurts when I bend down.	Borrowing
Not at all.	Giving directions
Not too short, please.	Bargaining
I'll pay you back tomorrow.	Station

Lesson 15

Students revise differences between formal and informal usage, and study the language that is characteristic of various situations.
Principal structures: *a little*; *a few*; revision of other quantifiers.
Phonology: linking.

Language notes and possible problems

1. *A little* and *a few* (Exercise 6)   These have not yet been studied, and will probably need to be explained. Both of them are quite close in meaning to *some*, but tend to suggest a smaller quantity or number. Note that *a little* and *a few* do not mean the same as *little* and *few*, which are more formal equivalents of *not much/many*. Students should easily see that *a little* is used with uncountables and *a few* with plurals.

2. *No* (Exercise 6)   You may need to remind students that *no* is a slightly more emphatic alternative to *not any*.

3. *Enough* (Exercise 6)   Note that *enough* comes before noun phrases (*enough red wine*) but after adjectives alone (*It's hot enough*).

4. Formal and informal language (Exercise 5)   In some cultures the rules governing formal and informal language are very elaborate and rigid, compared with the more flexible European conventions. Students from such cultures may have problems in this area (they may worry unnecessarily, for instance, about exactly how they should speak to a teacher in English). Help them to understand the factors that determine whether we speak formally or informally.

5. Pronunciation: linking (Exercise 3)   In some languages, words tend to be clearly separated in speech one from the next. In English, words are generally run together into phrases. Depending on their mother-tongue, students may have difficulty in linking words **either** when the second begins with a vowel (e.g. *Can I*) **or** when the link involves a cluster of two or more consonants (e.g. *it was*, *red handle*, *that's very*).

If you are short of time
Drop or postpone Exercises 5 and 6. (Note that this is a longer-than-average lesson.)

---

1 Pictures and situations
● Get students to talk about what is happening in the pictures; check that they know key vocabulary relating to the situations (e.g. *petrol station*; *waiter*). Ask if they can guess what the people might be saying.
● You may like to ask students to write down one or two of the answers.

Answers to Exercise 1
1. A woman is buying petrol.
2. A waiter is offering a customer more food.
3. A man is making an appointment at a reception desk.
4. A woman is talking on the phone.
5. A woman is giving directions to a driver.
6. A woman is asking the price of something.
7. A check-in attendant is telling a passenger he has too much baggage.
8. A man is borrowing money from a friend.
9. A woman is booking into a hotel.

2 Situational language
● Give students a few minutes to look through the lists of expressions and situations. Help with vocabulary if necessary.
● Then get them to do the exercise and compare notes.

Answers to Exercise 2
Can I look round? – Shop
I'm afraid you've got the wrong number. – On the telephone
Fill it up . . . – Garage / petrol station
A single for two nights. – Hotel reception
Single to Manchester. – Station
Check in at 9.30. – Airport
Second on the left. – Giving directions
It was green . . . – Lost property office
That's very kind of you. – Thanking somebody
I'll give you twenty-five . . . – Bargaining
Is service included? – Restaurant
Could we make it . . . ? – Making an appointment
It hurts when . . . – Doctor's surgery
Not at all. – Replying to thanks
Not too short, please. – Hairdresser
I'll pay you back tomorrow. – Borrowing

3 Pronunciation: linking

- Practise the examples. (Links which might prove difficult are marked ⌣.)
- Then carry on through the list of expressions, using the recording as a guide if you wish.

4 Listening and matching

- Play each piece of conversation and get the students to discuss which of the pictures in Exercise 1 they think it goes with.

Tapescript and answers to Exercise 4

CONVERSATION 1 – PICTURE 4
'Could I speak to Mrs Holmes, please?'
'Speaking.'
'Oh, hi, June. This is Mary. How's it going?'
'Not too bad, Mary. What can I do for you?'

CONVERSATION 2 – PICTURE 9
'Haven't you got a room at the back?'
'I'm sorry, madam. There are no rooms free at the back. But all our windows are double glazed. I'm sure your room will be quiet enough, madam.'

CONVERSATION 3 – PICTURE 7
'I'm afraid you've got too much baggage, sir. The allowance is 25 kilos, and you have 45. You'll have to pay £55 excess.'
'£55!'

CONVERSATION 4 – PICTURE 3
'How about 9.30? Is that too early?'
'No, that's all right. Do you mind if I bring the children along with me?'
'No, of course not. That's perfectly all right.'

CONVERSATION 5 – PICTURE 5
'Keep straight on for 400 yards and then turn right at the supermarket. You can't miss it.'
'Left at the supermarket. OK, thanks.'

CONVERSATION 6 – PICTURE 1
'Are you all right for oil?'
'Yes. But could you check the tyres for me?'

CONVERSATION 7 – PICTURE 2
'A little more cabbage, sir? And a few peas?'
'No, I've got enough vegetables, thanks. But could I have some mustard?'
'Certainly, sir.'

CONVERSATION 8 – PICTURE 8
'Hey, Joe.'
'Yes?'
'Have you got any money?'
'How much do you need?'
'A fiver. I'll pay you back tomorrow.'
'OK, I suppose so.'
'Thanks a lot.'
'That's OK.'

CONVERSATION 9 – PICTURE 6
'Excuse me. How much is that?'
'£25.'
'Will you take twenty for cash?'
'Yes, all right.'

5 Formal and informal usage

- Students should find this exercise easy. Give them a minute or two to think about the expressions, and then let them compare notes before giving them the answers. Ask if they feel any of the expressions are especially formal or informal.
- Get them to try to think of other very informal expressions.

Answers to Exercise 5
The more formal sentences are:
Hello.   How are you?   Very well, thank you.
Goodbye.   Excuse me.   Could you lend me five pounds?
Thank you very much.   Do you mind if I smoke?
How much is that?

6 Quantifiers

- The exercise can be done orally, in writing, or half-and-half, as you prefer.
- You may need to revise the difference between *some* and *any*, *much* and *many* and/or *too* and *too much*. Problems may also arise with *a little* and *a few*, *no*, and *enough* – see *Language notes*.

Answers to Exercise 6
1. no
2. enough
3. too much
4. too
5. little; few; some; some
6. enough/any
7. How much
8. few
9. too much
10. enough
11. too much
12. How much; too
13. any
14. How many
15. little
16. no
17. some

7 Situational language (continued)

- Now students have to study one situation in detail.
- Tell them to choose the situation they wish to study, and to join up with other students who have chosen the same situation.
- Get them to think of all the things they would typically say in their own language in the situation they have chosen, and to see whether they know how to say these things in English.
- Give them whatever help is necessary.

8 Students' conversations

- When students have drawn up their lists, get them to prepare typical conversations for their situations.
- Let them practise the conversations (with appropriate gestures and movements).
- Then get them to perform their conversations for other groups or for the class.
- You may wish to tape- or video-record the conversations. If so, warn the students beforehand; this will encourage them to aim at a high standard.

Practice Book exercises
1. Quantifiers.
2. Situational language.
3. Situational language.
4. Spelling of -*ly* adverbs.
5. Student's Cassette exercise (Student's Book Exercise 4, first five conversations). Students write down one or more conversations.
6. Recreational reading.

3 Practise the examples. Be careful to join words together, and pay special attention to the links marked ‿. Then practise the other expressions from Exercise 2. Examples:

Can I look round?

Check in at 9.30.

Second on the left.

It was green, with a red handle.

4 📼 Listen to the pieces of conversation. Can you match them to the pictures?

5 Here are some pairs of sentences. In each pair, the two sentences mean the same, but one is more formal and the other is more informal. Can you divide them into more and less formal?

Hello.
Hi.

How's it going?
How are you?

Not too bad.
Very well, thank you.

Goodbye.
See you.

Hey!
Excuse me.

Have you got a fiver?
Could you lend me five pounds?

Thank you very much.
Thanks a lot.

Do you mind if I smoke?
Is it OK if I smoke?

How much is that?
What do you want for that?

6 Put in words from the box.

any	enough	few	how many	how much	little	no
some	too	too much				

1. I'm sorry, madam. There are .... rooms free at the back.
2. I'm sure your room will be quiet ...., madam.
3. I'm afraid you've got .... baggage, sir. The allowance is 25 kilos, and you have 45.
4. How about 9.30? Is that .... early?
5. 'A .... more cabbage, sir? And a .... peas?' 'No, I've got .... vegetables, thanks. But could I have .... mustard?'
6. Have you got .... money?
7. 'Excuse me. .... is that?' '£25.'
8. Could I speak to the manager for a .... minutes?
9. You've given me .... money. It costs £3.50, not £4.50.
10. She's not old .... to drive.
11. There's something wrong with the car – it's using .... oil.
12. '............... is it?' '£65.' 'That's .... expensive. I'll give you £45.'
13. Sorry – we haven't got .... rooms left.
14. .... cigarettes do you smoke a day?
15. Could you cut a .... more off the top?
16. I'm afraid there are .... trains to Flaxborough on Sundays.
17. Give me .... more tea, will you?

7 Work with two or three other students. Make a list of typical expressions for one of the situations from Exercise 2. Your teacher will help you. Useful questions:

'How do you say . . . ?'
'What do you say when . . . ?'
'What's the English for . . . ?'
'How do you pronounce . . . ?'
'How do you spell . . . ?'
'What does . . . mean?'

8 Prepare and practise a conversation for the situation which you studied in Exercise 7.

> **Quantifiers: enough** bread (~~bread enough~~); early **enough** (~~enough early~~); **too** expensive; **too much** oil; **a little** cabbage; **a few** peas; a little/few **more**.

> **Learn/revise:** Choose ten or more expressions from the lesson to learn.

16 Here is the news

Giving news; Present Perfect Progressive; *just* with Present Perfect.

1 📼 The following sentences are taken from a news broadcast. There are mistakes in ten of the sentences. Listen to the broadcast and see how many you can find.

1. President and Mrs Martin of Outland have just arrived in Fantasia for a state visit, which is expected to last three weeks.
2. Dr Rask has known Mrs Martin since their student days at the University of Goroda.
3. Dr Rask has just left for an overseas fact-finding tour.
4. Dr Rask is President of 'Families against Hunger', and for the last six days he has been visiting Third World countries.
5. Demonstrations are continuing against the proposed dam on the Upper Fant river, and demonstrators have been marching through the centre of San Fantastico for several hours.
6. Traffic in Wesk Square has not been able to move since half past eight this morning, and motorists are advised to avoid the city centre.
7. Heavy snow has been falling steadily for the past four weeks.
8. The River Fant has just burst its banks in North Milltown, and most of the town centre is under water.
9. Vegetable prices in San Fantastico have been going up steadily for the last ten days.
10. The Minister for Consumer Affairs has just announced that price controls on vegetables and meat will come into effect next week.
11. The Fantasian grotnik has risen to its highest level against the Outland dollar since last July: the exchange rate is now 1.32 dollars to the grotnik.
12. The fire which has been burning in Grand North Station for the last three days is now under control.
13. Three more firemen have been taken to hospital.

2 Present Perfect Progressive. Look at the examples and then complete the sentences that follow.

For the last six days he **has been visiting** Third World countries.
Demonstrators **have been marching** for several hours.
A fire **has been burning** for three days.
It **has been raining** since Tuesday.
We **have been waiting** for you since 6 o'clock.

1. I .... English for three years. (*learn*)
2. She .... in the same job since 1988. (*work*)
3. It .... for three days. (*snow*)
4. Prices .... very fast for several weeks. (*go up*)
5. How long .... you .... in this hotel? (*stay*)
6. 'What .... you .... all morning?'
   'I .... letters.' (*do; write*)
7. 'You look hot.' 'Yes. I ....' (*run*)

3 Ask other people in the class how long they have been learning English.

4 Non-progressive verbs. Look at the examples.

President Rask and Mrs Martin **have known** each other for a long time.
(... have been knowing ...)
I've **been** in this class since October.
(... 've been being ...)
How long **have you had** that coat?
(... have you been having ...?)

Now ask other people in the class questions beginning *How long have you known/been/had* ...

50

Lesson 16

Students practise talking about news and about the duration of current states and events.
Principal structures: Present Perfect with *just*; Present Perfect Progressive; non-progressive verbs.
Phonology: voiced and unvoiced *th* (/ð/ and /θ/).

1. Present Perfect Students revise the use of this tense to give news (often with *just*). (Like most other uses of the Present Perfect, this involves talking about past events that have present importance or relevance.) Remind students that the Present Perfect is not normally used with adverbs of finished time. *Just* is an exception in British English.
2. Present Perfect Progressive This is used to talk about temporary states and actions which began in the past and have continued up to the present. A common use is to say how long something has been going on (e.g. *Rain has been falling steadily for the past four weeks . . .*). Some students may use present tenses here (e.g. **I learn / am learning English since two years*).
3. Non-progressive verbs *Know, have* and *be* do not have progressive forms in some meanings. Look for mistakes like **How long have you been knowing him?* or **I have been having this car for three months.*

---

1 News broadcast: finding discrepancies

- Let students look briefly through the thirteen sentences. Don't explain too much vocabulary – students do not have to understand every word to do the exercise.
- Play the recording right through once without stopping, and ask students whether they noticed any differences between the spoken and printed versions.
- Then play it again section by section, pausing for students to note the differences.
- Let them compare notes in groups.

Answers to Exercise 1
1. The state visit is expected to last three *days*.
2. Dr Rask has known *President Martin* since their student days.
3. Dr Rask has just *returned* from an overseas fact-finding tour.
4. Dr Rask has been visiting Third World countries for the last six *weeks*.
5. Correct.
6. Traffic in Wesk Square has been *very slow*.
7. *Rain* has been falling.
8. *Parts* of the town centre are under water.
9. Correct.
10. There will be price controls on vegetables and *fruit*.
11. The exchange rate is now *1.23* dollars to the grotnik.
12. The fire is in Grand *South* Station.
13. Correct.

Tapescript for Exercise 1

FBC Radio 2. Here is the news for today, Wednesday 25th April, at eleven a.m.

President and Mrs Martin of Outland have just arrived in Fantasia for a state visit. This is the first official visit by an Outland head of state since the end of the War of Independence in 1954, and it is expected to last three days. The President and her husband were at the airport to welcome President and Mrs Martin, who are old friends of theirs: Mrs Rask and Mrs Martin first met at the 1960 Olympics, in which Mrs Rask won a silver medal for the high jump, and Mrs Martin represented Outland in the 100 metres. Dr Rask has known President Martin since their student days at the University of Goroda.

Dr Rask has just returned from an overseas fact-finding tour. For the last six weeks, he has been visiting Third World countries in his capacity as President of 'Families against Hunger'. Speaking at a press conference shortly after his return, Dr Rask said that increased aid to the Third World was an urgent priority.

Demonstrations are continuing against the proposed dam on the Upper Fant river, and demonstrators have been marching through the centre of San Fantastico for several hours. Traffic in Wesk Square has been very slow since half past eight this morning, and motorists are advised to avoid the city centre.

The heavy rain which has been falling steadily for the past four weeks has caused widespread flooding. The River Fant has just burst its banks in North Milltown, and parts of the town centre are under water. The bad weather has ruined many vegetable crops, and vegetable prices in San Fantastico have been going up steadily for the last ten days. The Minister for Consumer Affairs has just announced that price controls on vegetables and fruit will come into effect next week.

Foreign exchange. The Fantasian grotnik has risen to its highest level against the Outland dollar since last July. The exchange rate is now 1.23 dollars to the grotnik.

The fire which has been burning in Grand South Station for the last three days is now under control. The origin of the fire, which started in the station restaurant on Sunday, is still unknown. Three more firemen were overcome by smoke this morning, and have been taken to hospital.

And now the weather. Heavy rain will continue in most parts of the country, (*fade*).

2 Present Perfect Progressive
- Look through the examples with the students. Discuss the construction of the Present Perfect Progressive (*have been* + past participle) and its use (see *Language notes*).
- Practise pronouncing the examples, paying careful attention to rhythm (*have/has been* are unstressed, and must be pronounced lightly and quickly).
- Get students to write at least two answers, so that you can check on individual problems.

Answers to Exercise 2
1. have ('ve) been learning
2. has ('s) been working
3. has ('s) been snowing
4. have been going up
5. have (you) been staying
6. have (you) been doing; have ('ve) been writing
7. have ('ve) been running

3 Personalisation
- This can be done as a walk-round activity, or students can ask the six or so people nearest to them.
- If it's a silly question (for instance, if all the students have been learning English for the same time), change the question or drop the exercise.
- Here again, pay careful attention to rhythm (*How long have you been learning English?*).

4 Non-progressive verbs
- Students probably know by now that *know, be* and *have* tend not to be used in progressive tenses.
- Discuss the examples with them, and then let them prepare questions and ask each other.

5 Pictures: Present Perfect with *just*

• Look at the first picture, and then get students to study the others in groups, discussing possible answers. They must use the Present Perfect with *just*.

• Point out that *just* is an exception to the rule that adverbs referring to finished time are not used with the Present Perfect.

Possible answers to Exercise 5
(Each answer can of course be expressed in other ways.)
1. A plane has just landed.
2. Somebody has just arrived at a station.
3. A house has just burnt down.
4. A car has just crashed.
5. Somebody has just got up.
6. Somebody has just finished a meal.
7. Two people have just robbed a bank.
8. Somebody has just opened a door.
9. Somebody has just broken a glass.
10. A postman has just delivered letters to a house.
11. Somebody has just had a bath.
12. A motorist has just bought petrol.

6 Pronunciation: /ð/ and /θ/

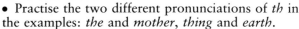

• Practise the two different pronunciations of *th* in the examples: *the* and *mother*, *thing* and *earth*.

• Then tell students to look through the lesson material (including the exercise instructions, but not including the word list in this exercise) to see how many examples of each pronunciation they can find.

• Let them compare notes and discuss the answers with them.

• Then get them to work in groups to divide up the listed words.

• Finally, practise the pronunciation of the various words, using the recording as a model if you wish.

Answers to Exercise 6

Words in the lesson:
/ð/: with; the; there; their; this; that; then; they; other
/θ/: three; third; through; north; think; anything; thing

Word list in Exercise 6:
/ð/: grandmother; rather; those; than; them
/θ/: something; thank; bath; thirsty; thousand; truth; fourth

7 News bulletins

• If there is plenty of time available, each group can prepare a complete news broadcast which they can practise, tape- or video-record, and play to the rest of the class.

• If you don't have time for this, get students to work in groups, preparing one short news item per group. They should of course use the structures (and if possible some of the vocabulary) which they have learnt from the lesson.

• When students are ready, ask a volunteer from each group to read out the group's news item.

Practice Book exercises
1. Present Perfect Progressive.
2. *Since* and *for*.
3. Rhythm and stress in Present Perfect Progressive verb-phrases.
4. Vocabulary revision and extension.
5. Student's Cassette exercise (Student's Book Exercise 1, second half of recording). Students listen for discrepancies between recording and text.
6. Guided writing (text for news broadcast).

Sense of progress
As students learn more, it becomes more difficult for them to get a sense of progress. This is natural: beginners who learn twenty more words have doubled their knowledge, but for intermediate students another twenty words may only represent an improvement of one per cent. It is very important at this level to think about short-term goals. Students need plenty of interesting speaking or writing tasks so that they can do something with their English. Success in such tasks will give them a sense of achievement, and this will counteract the feeling that they have reached a 'plateau' and are not getting anywhere. For this reason, even if time is short, it is important not to drop the longer, more creative speaking and writing exercises in the course. (It is better to leave out some lessons than to rush through everything too fast.) Where time allows, the Optional activities in the Teacher's Book provide extra speaking and writing tasks that may be worth considering.

5 Look at the pictures. What has just happened in each one? Can you think of anything that has just happened in your life, in your country, or in the classroom?

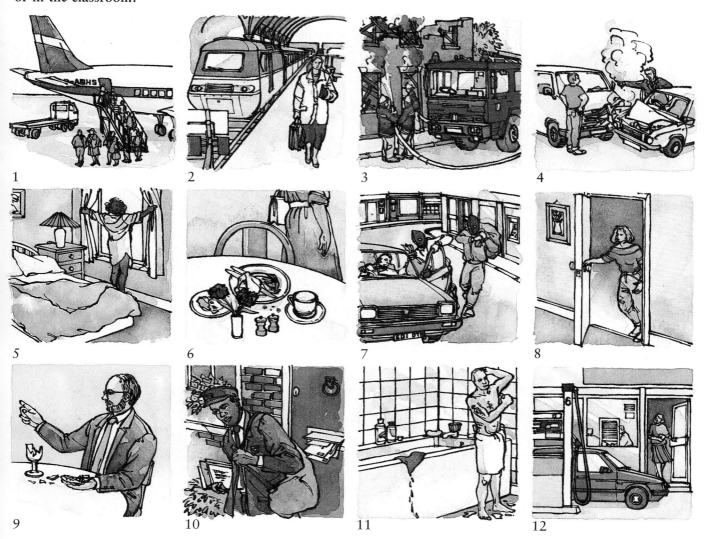

6 Pronunciation. There are two different ways to pronounce *th*: 'voiced' (as in *the* /ðə/, *mother* /'mʌðə(r)/) and 'unvoiced' (as in *thing* /θɪŋ/, *earth* /ɜːθ/). How many words can you find in this lesson that are pronounced with voiced *th*, and how many with unvoiced *th*? And can you divide the following words into two groups according to the pronunciation of *th*?

grandmother   something   rather   thank
bath   thirsty   those   thousand   than
truth   them   fourth

7 Work in groups. Prepare a short news broadcast, with information about things that have been happening and things that have just happened in your country, in the world, in your school or in Fantasia.

Present Perfect Progressive
I have (I've) been working you have (you've) been working *etc.*
have I been working? have you been working? *etc.*
I have not (haven't) been working you have not (haven't) been working *etc.*

Learn/revise: news; visit (*noun and verb*); hunger; river; town; city; student; demonstration; Third World; country; town/city centre; traffic; snow; water; vegetable; meat; price; fire; hospital; grandmother/father/son/daughter; last (*verb*); leave (left, left); continue; move; avoid; burn (burnt, burnt); run (ran, run); stay; heavy; unable; several; through; against; under.

17 USA holiday

NEW YORK, NEW YORK!
Spend two weeks in exciting New York City. Theatre, dance, opera, museums, . . .

WINNER TAKE ALL!
Come to Las Vegas and try your luck. When you're tired of winning at the casino, relax by the pool or go to watch a fabulous show . . .

WHITE WATER MAGIC
If you are a confirmed sportsman or sportswoman, spend an exciting two weeks with us canoeing in the beautiful Rocky Mountains . . .

DO IT YOURSELF
We provide the car or camper van, maps and advice, and you go your own way, discovering the America you want to discover.

ALOHA
You will never forget the warm welcome of Hawaii. Beautiful sunny beaches, friendly people, luscious tropical food . . .

FLOAT ALONG
Enjoy beautiful Texas scenery and wildlife while relaxing on a raft floating down the Rio Grande. A photographer's delight! Comfortable tent accommodation at night . . .

1 Read the travel advertisements; use your dictionary to look up five or more words that you want to remember.

Lesson 17

Students practise talking about holidays; they read and write passages about different sorts of holidays.
Structures: *can*, *will* and *may*.
Phonology: Linking.

Language notes and possible problems

1. *Can* **for possibility**   Some languages have a structure which operates in the same way as *can* in English: to express both ability (*I can type*) and possibility (*If you go on this holiday, you can relax every day*). If your students speak a language that does not have a parallel structure, you may wish to do some extra work with them before doing Exercise 2. You will probably have to remind students that *can* is pronounced /kn/ in affirmative sentences when it is unstressed, and to listen for mistakes with *to* (for example, **You can to relax . . .*).

2. The grammar of possibility is complex. As a rule, *can* is used for 'general' or 'theoretical' possibility (to talk about the sorts of things that happen under various circumstances). To talk about the chances of something actually happening at a particular moment, we prefer to use *may* or *might*. Compare:

People can do stupid things when they're in love.
I'm afraid Mary may do something stupid.

In this lesson, students learn this use of *can* and the use of *may* to mean 'will perhaps'. You may not wish to make the distinction between the two concepts explicit at this stage.

Optional extra materials
Some large sheets of blank paper for making travel posters (Exercise 6).

If you are short of time
Drop the 'walk round and choose' part of Exercise 6.

1   Reading

• Give students a few minutes to look over the advertisements. Tell them that they can use their dictionaries, and that they should choose and write down five or more words from the text to remember.
• Walk round while they are working to give any help that is necessary.
• If there is time, you may want to ask a few students to say which words they have chosen and why (this will help them to remember them).

2 Can, will and may

- First demonstrate the exercise yourself, so students will understand what to do, and to present *may* and the new sense of *can*: choose one of the holidays, and say six sentences, including at least one with *can* and one with *may*. Make sure students understand what these mean.
- Let students vote on which holiday you are talking about.
- Then give them a few minutes to work individually, choosing a holiday from the six listed and writing five sentences from the table.
- Walk round while they are working to give any help that is needed.
- Put them in pairs to read their sentences to each other and try and guess which holidays they have written about.
- Pairs who finish quickly can find new partners and try again.

3 Will or may?

- This exercise reinforces the difference between *will* and *may*, and serves as a check that students have understood.
- Get students to write the answers individually before checking with you.

4 Listening: 'What's America like?'

- Go over the instructions with the students. Get them to read the questions and make sure they understand them.
- Then play the tape, more than once if necessary, while they listen for the answers to the questions.
- Note that the first speaker makes the mistake of using *there are* with a singular; he probably changed his mind in mid-sentence about what he was going to say.

Tapescript and answers to Exercise 4

1. I think that erm, America, in a way rather like Europe except for the language thing, is not just one place. There are a great deal of variety throughout America, and *it's not just like visiting Britain; it's much more like Europe, both in, in styles of living and in personalities of people.* So you'll find a great contrast, I think, throughout, depending on where you go.
2. I think he'll enjoy the people. Erm, I really do. *I think the people are friendlier.* Erm, it, whether it's sincere or not is immaterial.
3. I couldn't wait to get out of New York; *I thought it was an awful place.* I mean I liked an awful lot of America: erm, San Francisco; erm, to some extent New Orleans, which is a bit run down, but it's, it's a, a very interesting place; and lots of places in, in America, particularly in the West; *but, but New York I found dirty, noisy, unpleasant and unfriendly, I must say.*
4. *I think that you find the people are so outgoing, and ready to listen; really interested in what you have to tell them.* Er, it's, it's most impressive. I think that's what you'll find the biggest difference'll be.

5 Pronunciation: linking

- Play the recording or read the sentences yourself, while the students listen especially for the marked linking that occurs when a word beginning with a vowel follows a word ending with a consonant.
- Then ask students to say the sentences, first a line at a time and then without stopping.
- In a small class students can get individual practice. In a larger class you can just do choral practice; or follow choral practice up with group work where students help one another.

6 Writing and speaking: holiday ads

- Put students into groups of three or four. In a multilingual class, try to put people from the same country together.
- If you have brought some large sheets of poster paper, distribute them now; if not, plain pieces of paper will do.
- Each group must make a poster with three or four short advertisements like those in Exercise 1, and draw simple pictures to go with them.
- Walk round while they are working to help if needed, but try to help only if students are really stuck on language points; it's best to leave the creativity to them.
- When they finish, put the posters up on the wall or down on desks where they can easily be seen.
- Each group should choose one member to stay with the poster to answer questions; the others should walk round, look at the other posters and ask questions to choose the holidays they like best. The first one finished should take the place of the person who has stayed with the poster.
- When everyone has had a chance to walk round and choose, hold a vote on the most popular holiday.

Practice Book exercises

1. Completing sentences with *may*.
2. Punctuation practice.
3. *Travel by / on* and equivalent verbs.
4. Word stress.
5. Student's Cassette exercise (Student's Book Exercise 4, third speaker). Students listen and write down all they can understand.
6. Reading skills: relating a text and a map.

2 Choose one of the six holidays, and make five sentences from the table below. Read the sentences to a partner, and see if she or he can guess which holiday you are talking about.

If you go on this holiday,	you can you will you won't you may	go where you like. eat near an open fire. take a lot of evening clothes. see a bear. get very fit. see a good play. get very wet. get a lot of sun. win a million dollars. relax every day. take pictures of wild animals. get an international driving licence. eat a lot of fresh pineapple.

3 *Will* or *may*?

1. If you go to Texas, you .... sleep in a tent.
2. If you go to the Rockies, you .... see some wild deer.
3. If you go to New York, you .... have a big choice of evening activities.
4. If you go to Las Vegas, you .... hear some famous singers and comedians.
5. If you go on a camping holiday, you .... meet some interesting people.
6. If you go to Hawaii, you .... see some beautiful flowers.

4 📟 An Englishman is going to America. We talked to some of his friends who have already been there. Here are some of our questions. Make sure you understand them. Then listen: what do the friends think?

1. Is America more like Britain or more like Europe?
2. Are Americans friendlier or less friendly than people from Britain?
3. Is New York a nice place?
4. Are Americans ready to listen to you?

5 Pronunciation. Listen to the sentences from Exercise 4, paying special attention to the links. Say the sentences yourself.

I think that erm, America,

in a way rather like Europe,

except for the language,

is not just one place.

I mean, I liked an awful lot of America:

San Francisco; erm, to some extent New Orleans,

which is a bit run down,

but it's, it's a, a very interesting place.

6 Work in groups of three or four. Make a poster advertising three or four holidays in your own country/ies, or in countries you know. Write short texts like the ones in Exercise 1, and draw simple pictures. Put your poster where other students can see it. When everyone's posters are finished, take turns to walk round, ask questions, and choose the holiday you like best (leave one person with your poster to answer questions). Vote on the most popular holiday.

Learn/revise: theatre; pool; map; (warm) welcome; advice (*uncountable*); beach; tent; play (*noun*); sun; wild animal; international driving licence; singer; flower; America; Britain; Europe; camping; relax; watch; discover; want; forget (forgot, forgotten); choose (chose, chosen); take pictures (took, taken); sleep (slept, slept); listen (to); won't; may; exciting; tired (of); beautiful; sunny; friendly; comfortable; wet; fresh; famous; at night; near; like.

18 Knife-thrower's assistant wanted

Revision of tenses; integrated skills (reading, writing and speaking).

1 Read the advertisement and the letters. Fill in the numbered gaps with words and expressions from the box. (You can use a dictionary, or ask your teacher about difficult words.)

advertised	age	apply	companies
engineering	experience	faithfully	
look forward	salary	Sales Manager	
several	worked	would like	write

WELL-KNOWN NORTHERN MANUFACTURER REQUIRES

SALES MANAGER

for district between Liverpool and Carlisle.

Very good ......1...... and conditions.
Use of new company car.
......2...... between 25 and 40.
Previous selling ......3...... essential.

......4...... to: Managing Director,
Domestic Engineering Services Ltd,
417 North Way, Whitehaven, Cumbria WN6 4DJ.

---

17 Grove Crescent
Greendale
Cumbria CU6 7LY
24 May 1990

The Managing Director
Domestic Engineering Services Ltd.
417 North Way
Whitehaven
Cumbria WN6 4DJ

Dear Sir/Madam

I ......5...... to apply for the post of ......6...... advertised in the Guardian of 22 May. I am 36 years old and have experience of selling in ......7...... firms. I also have qualifications in ......8......

I look forward to hearing from you.

Yours faithfully

Rosemary Parsons

Rosemary Parsons

---

35 Allendale Road
Carlisle
CA2 4SJ

23 May 1990

Dear Sir or Madam,

I wish to ......9...... for the job of Sales Manager ......10...... in yesterday's Guardian. I have a Higher National Diploma in Business Studies, and have ......11...... as a Sales Manager for two large ......12...... . I am 29.

I ......13...... to hearing from you.

Yours ......14...... ,

Andrew Jardine

54

Lesson 18

Students revise and practise letter-writing conventions in a communicative writing exercise; they conduct simulated job interviews.
Principal structures: *must*; *be able to*; revision of tenses; preview of passive.

Language notes and possible problems

1. Tenses This lesson will require the use of Simple Past and Present Perfect tenses in appropriate situations. You may like to revise the relevant rules at a suitable moment – for instance, before Exercise 4.

2. Passives Past participles are used in this lesson with passive meanings (e.g. *advertised*, *needed*, *wanted*). Make sure students understand the meaning of the structure, but don't give detailed explanations at this stage. Passives will be studied in detail a little later.

3. Letters This is a good opportunity to revise basic letter-writing conventions. Students should note:
– position of the address and salutation
– layout of the letter
– use of *Yours faithfully* in conjunction with *Dear Sir/Madam*, and *Yours sincerely* when the addressee's name is used.

4. Curriculum vitae In real job applications, of course, applicants normally enclose detailed c.v.'s. This is avoided here in order to ensure that information about applicants' supposed experience is exchanged orally during Exercise 4.

5. Formality You may like to draw students' attention to the way different levels of formality can be expressed through choice of vocabulary. Examples in the advertisements: *require/need*; *salary/pay*.

6. Time This lesson is likely to take longer than average (two hours or more).

---

1 Text completion

• The purpose of this exercise is to introduce some of the vocabulary students will need, and to help them revise letter-writing conventions.

• Give students a minute or two to look through the advertisement, and then get them to try to write down the four words that are needed to complete the text.

• Let them use dictionaries or ask you about the words in the box.

• Get them to compare notes in groups before you give them the answers.

• Then work on the two letters in the same way.

• Finally, you may wish to discuss some of the language points and rules for letter-writing (see *Language notes*). Ask students which of the two letters they feel is more 'businesslike', and why. Which applicant do they feel is more likely to get the job?

Answers to Exercise 1
1. salary 2. Age 3. experience 4. Write (or Apply)
5. would like 6. Sales Manager 7. several
8. engineering 9. apply 10. advertised
11. worked 12. companies 13. look forward
14. faithfully

2 Writing a letter

- This exercise can be done individually (with students choosing which letter they want to write), or in groups of four (with each student in a group writing a different letter).
- When students are ready, you can get them to give you the text for each letter while you write it on the board.

Answers to Exercise 2

After the firm's address and the date, and the applicant's address (at the top on the left), the four letters should continue more or less as follows:

Dear Ms Parsons

Thank you for your letter of 24 May.

Please come for an interview on (date) at (time) a.m.

Yours sincerely

(signature)

Dear Mr Jardine

(similar text to previous letter)

Dear Ms Parsons (or Mr Jardine)

Thank you for coming for an interview yesterday. We regret that we are unable to offer you the post.

Yours sincerely

(signature)

Dear Mr Jardine (or Ms Parsons)

Thank you for coming for an interview yesterday. We are pleased to offer you the position of Sales Manager, starting on 1 August, at a salary of £25,000 a year. Please confirm your acceptance as soon as possible.

Yours sincerely

(signature)

---

3 Reading and writing advertisements

- Give students a few minutes to look through the advertisements, either using their dictionaries or asking you for help with difficult words.
- They should note a few useful words and expressions to learn.
- Explain any difficulties. You may want to say something about the use of be able to as the infinitive of can.
- Then get students to write short job advertisements. If they can't think of jobs to advertise, make some suggestions (cleaner, airline pilot, president, gardener, secretary, wine-taster, shop assistant, dress designer etc.).
- When their advertisements are ready, get students to put them on the class notice board, or somewhere else where everybody can see them.

4 Interviews

1. Organising the exercise

- Divide the students into groups of about six.
- In each group, there should be three or so applicants for jobs and three or so interviewers. (Exact numbers are not important.)
- Tell each group to agree on one of the jobs advertised either in the text of Exercise 3 or on the class notice board.
- When students are ready, the three applicants should go and sit separately from the interviewers.

2. Writing letters

- The applicants (working individually) write their letters of application for the job. (Tell them that they can invent as many 'facts' as they like, but that the language they use should be taken largely from the letters in Exercise 1.)

3. Preparing interviews

- Meanwhile, the interviewers in each group work together to prepare suitable questions. The illustration will give them some ideas, but they will need to ask some questions appropriate to the particular job.
- Make sure they don't ask questions which the applicants will be unable to understand.

4. Replies

- When the letters of application are ready, the applicants should deliver them. The interviewers will then write offering interviews.
- Meanwhile, the applicants should start preparing their roles.
- Tell them to decide what jobs they have at present, what experience and qualifications they have, and so on.

5. Interviews

- Applicants go to be interviewed in turn. (The order is determined by the times given in the letters they have received.)
- You may want to put a time-limit on interviews (e.g. five minutes).

6. Offer of job

- When the interviews are finished, the interviewers in each group must decide who they are going to offer the job to.
- They then have to write appropriate letters to all the applicants.
- You will need to give the applicants something to do while they are waiting for their letters.

Practice Book exercises

1. Revision: prepositions and other items.
2. Present and Present Perfect tenses.
3. Making sentences with must.
4. Vocabulary revision.
5. Word stress.
6. Reading (advertisements) and writing (letter of application).

2 Here are some sentences from four letters from Domestic Engineering Services Ltd to Ms Parsons and Mr Jardine. (The sentences are not in order; some of them come in more than one letter.) Two of the letters offer interviews, one offers a job and one rejects an applicant. Can you write one of the letters?

> Dear Mr ....
>
> Dear Ms ....
>
> Yours sincerely
>
> Please come for an interview on .... at .... a.m.
>
> Thank you for your letter of .... May.
>
> Please confirm your acceptance as soon as possible.
>
> Thank you for coming for an interview yesterday.
>
> We regret that we are unable to offer you the post.
>
> We are pleased to offer you the position of Sales Manager,
>   starting on 1 August, at a salary of £25,000 a year.

3 Read the advertisements with a dictionary. Make a list of useful words and expressions. Then write a job advertisement yourself.

4 Job interviews. Work in groups of about six (three interviewers and three applicants).
1. Applicants write letters of application for one of the jobs advertised; interviewers prepare interviews.
2. Applicants are interviewed in turn.
3. Interviewers choose the best applicant and write letters to all three.

Where do you work? How long have you been there? Why do you want to change your job? Where did you go to school? Have you any experience of selling? Can you speak any foreign languages? Have you ever lived abroad? Have you ever been dismissed from a job? What are your interests? Are you married?

What's the salary? What are the hours? Is there a canteen?

Learn/revise: job; advertisement; assistant; education; company; firm; experience; interview; pay (*noun*); qualifications; salary; manager; staff; advertise; apply; age; must; need; sell (sold, sold); swim (swam, swum); able/unable to . . . ; essential; excellent; full-time; part-time; necessary; unnecessary; between; several; Yours faithfully; Yours sincerely; soon; as soon as possible; £25,000 a year; I look forward to hearing from you.

ROSTON TIMES

FULL-TIME DRIVERS WANTED
Clean driving licence. Must be of smart appearance. Aged over 25. Apply: Capes Taxis, 17 Palace Road, Roston.

CABIN STAFF
Southern Airlines require cabin staff for inter-continental flights. Applicants must be between 20 and 33 years old, height 1m60 to 1m75, education to GCSE standard, two languages, must be able to swim. Apply to: Recruitment Officer, Southern Airlines, Heathrow Airport West, HR3 7KK.

TEACHER NEEDED
for private language school. Teaching experience unnecessary. Apply: The Director of Studies, Instant Languages Ltd, 279 Canal Street, Roston.

PART-TIME JOB
Circus has an unexpected vacancy for a knife-thrower's assistant. Excellent pay. Apply in writing to: City Show Office, 13 Rose Lane, Roston.

SECO
Fully
and
requi
spec
ga
Sun
C

c
of

GOOD HOMES REQUIRE
for 5 adorable puppies.

55

Summary C

Simple Present Perfect tense

I have (I've) seen you have (you've) seen *etc.*	have I seen? have you seen? *etc.*	I have not (haven't) seen you have not (haven't) seen *etc.*

Ways of using the Simple Present Perfect

- Talking about experience

  '**Have** you ever **eaten** snails?'
  'Yes, I **have**.'
  'No, I **haven't**.'
  'No, I never **have**.'

- Talking about changes (differences between past and present)

  The population **has increased** since 1950.
  The percentage of homeless people **has fallen**.
  She **has got** much fatter during the last few years.

- Giving news

  Fantasia **has signed** a treaty with Outland.
  The River Fant **has** just **burst** its banks.
  I've lost my keys – could I borrow yours?

Don't use the Present Perfect

- if you talk about a finished time

  Outland **became** independent in 1954.
    (~~Outland has become . . .~~)
  I **saw** Susan yesterday.
    (~~I have seen Susan yesterday.~~)
  What time **did** you **get** home?
  When **did** you last **have** a haircut?

Present Perfect Progressive tense

I have (I've) been working you have (you've) been working *etc.*	have I been working? have you been working? *etc.*	I have not (haven't) been working you have not (haven't) been working *etc.*

Using the Present Perfect Progressive

We use the Present Perfect Progressive to say that something started in the past and is still happening (or has only just finished). We often use the Present Perfect Progressive to say or ask *how long* something has been happening. We do *not* use a present tense to do this.

For the last six days he **has been visiting** Third
  World countries. (~~. . . he is visiting . . .~~)
Demonstrators **have been marching** through the
  centre for several hours.
Heavy rain **has been falling** steadily for the past
  four weeks.
Have you **been waiting** long?
  (~~Are you waiting long?~~)

Non-progressive verbs

With some verbs (for example *know, have, be*), we usually use simple tenses, not progressive tenses.

They **have known** each other for a long time.
  (~~They have been knowing . . .~~)
How long **have** you **had** that coat?
  (~~. . . have you been having . . . ?~~)
I've been in this class since October.

For and *since*

for + period   = *since* + beginning of period

for 24 hours   = since yesterday
for three days   = since Sunday
for ten years   = since we got married
for a long time = since the 15th century

We've lived here **for ten years**.
  (~~We've lived here since ten years.~~)
  (~~We live here for ten years.~~)
I've known her **since 1980**. (~~I know her . . .~~)

This lesson displays most of the more important language points that students should have learnt or revised in the last six lessons. (The functional and situational language learnt in Lesson 15 is not easily summarised, and is not listed here – students should look back over the lesson material and their lesson notes.) Spend a short time going over the material with the students, answering questions and clearing up any difficulties. Students may also need to spend time at home making sure everything is thoroughly learnt.

Practice Book exercises
1. Present Perfect Progressive: putting captions to pictures.
2. Possessive determiners and pronouns.
3. Vocabulary revision: 'odd word out'.
4. Word stress.
5. Translation of material from Lessons 13–18.
6. Recreational reading.

Modal verbs: *can, may, will* and *must*

If you go on this holiday, you **can** relax every day.
you **may** win $1,000,000.
you **will** get very fit.
you **won't** get much sun.
Applicants **must** be between 20 and 33 years old.
must be able to swim.
(~~. . . must can swim.~~)

Used to

I **used to** be very shy, but now I'm OK.
People **didn't use to** travel by car.
Did you **use to** collect stamps when you were
younger?

Quantifiers

Some and *any*
Give me **some** more tea, will you?
I'm sorry, we have**n't** got **any** rooms left.

Enough
Have you got **enough money**?
(~~. . . money enough?~~)
She's not **old enough** to drive.
(~~. . . enough old . . .~~)

A little and *a few*
A little more cabbage, sir? And **a few** more peas?

How much and *how many*
How much is that?
How many cigarettes do you smoke a day?

Too and *too much*
Is that **too early**?
(~~. . . too much early?~~)
You've got **too much baggage**.

No (= *not any*)
I'm sorry. There are **no** rooms free at the back.

Asking about English

How do you say . . . ?
What do you say when . . . ?
What's the English for . . . ?
How do you pronounce . . . ?
How do you spell . . . ?
What does . . . mean?

Formal and informal language

More formal	**Less formal**
Hello.	Hi.
How are you?	How's it going?
Very well, thank you.	Not too bad.
Goodbye.	See you.
Excuse me.	Hey!
Could you lend me . . . ?	Have you got . . . ?
Thank you very much.	Thanks a lot.
Do you mind if . . . ?	Is it OK if . . . ?

Revision C

Look at the exercises, decide which ones are useful to you, and do two or more.

LISTENING

1 Listen to the conversation. Every time you hear the name of a food, write *F*; every time you hear the name of a drink, write *D*. Listen a second time. Try to find and write down an example of each of these: a hard thing, a soft thing, something liquid, something solid, a countable noun, an uncountable noun.

PRONUNCIATION

1 Listen to the conversation. How many times do you hear *there's* and *there are*? Make a note each time.

2 /ə/ is the commonest vowel in English. It comes fourteen times in the following words. Can you find all the examples? Practise pronouncing the words.

Africa   America   Belgium
Brazil   China   Denmark
England   Europe   Germany
India   Israel   Italy   Japan
Morocco   Russia

VOCABULARY

1 Do you know the English names for any other countries besides the ones in Pronunciation Exercise 2? Write down as many as you can think of.

GRAMMAR

1 Close your books and listen to the song. See how much you can remember. Look at the words. Then close your books again, listen once more and try to remember the words that have been left out.

BRIGHTON IN THE RAIN

I've never been to Athens and I've never been to Rome
I've only seen the Pyramids in picture books at home
I've never sailed across the sea or been inside a plane
I've always spent my holidays in Brighton in the rain.

I've never eaten foreign food or drunk in a foreign bar
I've never kissed a foreign girl or driven a foreign car
I've never had to find my way in a country I don't know
I've always known just where I am and where I'll never go.

I've read travel books by writers who have been to Pakistan
I've heard people telling stories of adventures in Iran
I've watched TV documentaries about China and Brazil
But I've never been abroad myself; it's making me feel ill.

I've studied several languages like Hindi and Malay
I've learnt lots of useful sentences I've never been able to say
The furthest place I've ever been was to the Isle of Man
And that was full of tourists from Jamaica and Japan.

I've never been to Athens and I've never been to Rome
I've only seen the Pyramids in picture books at home
I've never sailed across the sea or been inside a plane
I've always spent my holidays in Brighton in the rain.

2 Here are some rules for the use of the Present Perfect (Simple and Progressive). Some of them are good rules; some of them are wrong. Which are the good ones?

1. We can use the Present Perfect when we are talking about things which are still happening now.
2. We cannot use the Present Perfect when we are talking about a finished action.
3. We cannot use the Present Perfect when we give the time of a finished action.
4. We use the Present Perfect for actions which happened recently, and the Simple Past for actions which happened longer ago.
5. We often use the Present Perfect to give news.
6. We often use the Present Perfect to talk about experience.

3 Can you answer these questions?

1. A man says 'I've been in France for six years'. Is he living in France when he says this?
2. A woman says 'I was in Japan for three years'. Is she in Japan when she says this?
3. Somebody says 'I've been working with Eric for 10 years, and I worked with Sally for 6 years'. Which one does he or she still work with?
4. Somebody says 'I did seven years' French at school'. Is he or she still doing French at school?
5. You are in America. Somebody asks 'How long are you here for?' Does the person want to know when your visit started, or when it will end?
6. What does 'How long have you been here for?' mean?

Revision C

Students and teacher choose listening, pronunciation, vocabulary, grammar, speaking, reading and writing exercises.

Note: choice
You may like to ask students which exercises they feel are most useful. If they do not all have the same priorities, groups can work on different exercises.

LISTENING

1 Listening for particular items
- Make sure students understand the task.
- Let them listen once without writing.
- Ask if they noticed any items of food or drink.
- Play it again while students make notes.
- Do the second part of the exercise in the same way.

Answers to Exercise 1
Food: *tomatoes, bread, eggs, butter, steak, chops.*
Drink: *milk, coffee, orange juice, wine.*
Hard things: *tin, eggs, fridge, bottle, matches.*
Soft things: *tomatoes, bread, butter, steak, chops.*
Liquids: *milk, orange juice, wine, washing-up liquid.*
Solids: *tin, tomatoes, bread, coffee, eggs, butter, steak, chops, fridge, bottle, matches.*
Countable nouns: *tin, tomatoes, eggs, pocket, chops, fridge, bottle, matches.*
Uncountable nouns: *milk, bread, coffee, orange juice, butter, steak, wine, washing-up liquid.*

Tapescript for Exercise 1
A: Hello. Did you get everything?
B: Nearly. I forgot the milk, though.
A: It doesn't matter. I'll borrow some from Jenny next door.
B: Here you are, then. A tin of tomatoes, bread, coffee, orange juice and a dozen eggs.
A: What about the butter?
B: Butter, butter. Oh, yes. Here it is in my pocket.
A: And the steak.
B: You didn't ask me to get steak.
A: Yes I did.
B: No you didn't.
A: Well, it doesn't matter. There are some chops in the fridge.
B: I got a bottle of wine.
A: Oh, great!
B: And some matches – we've run out.
A: Clever. Did you get the washing-up liquid?
B: You didn't ask me to get washing-up liquid.
A: Yes I did.
B: No you didn't.
A: Well, it doesn't matter . . .

PRONUNCIATION

1 Perceiving *there's* and *there are*
- Tell students to write THERE'S and THERE ARE.
- Ask how these are usually pronounced; practise the unstressed pronunciations (/ðəz/ and /ðərə/).
- Play the recording; students tick THERE'S or THERE ARE each time they hear it.
- You may need to play the recording more than once.

Tapescript for Exercise 1
Downstairs at the front *there's* a living room and a dining room. At the back *there's* a big kitchen. *There are* three bedrooms on the first floor, and *there are* two small bedrooms on the top floor. *There's* a toilet on each floor, and *there are* bathrooms on the first and second floors. *There's* a big garden, but the garage isn't very big. Come and see the house if you like – we're usually there at weekends.

2 Finding examples of /ə/
- Students may not realise that unstressed *a*, *o* and *u* are usually pronounced /ə/.
- Let them see how many examples they can find. Then say the words or play the recording.
- Discuss the answers and practise the words.

Answers to Exercise 2
(/ə/ comes twice in *America*, and once in all the other words except *Israel* and *Denmark*.)

Africa /ˈæfrɪkə/	Germany /ˈdʒɜːməni/
America /əˈmerɪkə/	India /ˈɪndɪə/
Belgium /ˈbeldʒəm/	Israel /ˈɪzreɪl/
Brazil /brəˈzɪl/	Italy /ˈɪtəli/
China /ˈtʃaɪnə/	Japan /dʒəˈpæn/
Denmark /ˈdenmɑːk/	Morocco /məˈrɒkəʊ/
England /ˈɪŋglənd/	Russia /ˈrʌʃə/
Europe /ˈjʊərəp/	

VOCABULARY

1 Names of countries
- Try to focus on countries that students are likely to be interested in or need to know about. You might also teach the English names of some important cities.

GRAMMAR

1 Song: *Brighton in the Rain*
- The song is recorded complete and with gaps.
- Play the complete version through once, while the students listen with their books closed.
- Ask what they have understood, and write on the board any words and phrases that they can recall.
- Play it again, and see if they can recall any more.
- Then let students open their books and look at the text. Clear up any difficulties.
- Play the gapped version (books closed), while students try to say or sing the missing words.
- If this is too difficult, let students follow the text in their books as they listen.

2 Rules for the Present Perfect
- Make sure students understand what each rule says, and then get them to discuss the rule in groups. They can refer to the Summary for guidance if necessary.
- Ask them to make examples for the correct rules.

Answers to Exercise 2
1. Correct. We often use the Present Perfect to talk about something which is still going on, especially if we say how long it has been going on. Example: *How long have you known her?*
2. Wrong. The Present Perfect is often used to talk about finished actions. Example: *'Have you ever been to China?' 'Yes, I have.'*
3. Correct. The Present Perfect is not normally used with words referring to a finished time. Example: *I saw her yesterday.* (~~*I have seen her yesterday.*~~)
4. Wrong. Both tenses can be used either for recent actions or for actions that happened long ago.
5. Correct. Example: *The President has died.*
6. Correct. Example: *Have you ever been to China?*

Grammar Exercise 3: see page 59

3 Present Perfect and Simple Past

• This exercise studies the use of the Present Perfect to talk about duration up to the present.
• Ask students to think about the first question, write their answers, and compare notes with other students.
• Give them the answer and explain the reason.
• Treat the other questions in the same way.

Answers to Exercise 3
1. Yes. (The Present Perfect is not used with adverbs of finished time, so the 'six years' are not over.)
2. No. (The use of the Simple Past shows that the 'three years' are a finished period.)
3. The Present Perfect shows that the speaker is still working with Eric. (The Simple Present Perfect is also possible: we often use the simple tense when we talk about longer, more permanent states.)
4. No. (The use of the Simple Past shows that the French lessons are finished.)
5. When it will end.
6. 'How long ago did your visit start?'

4 Present, Past and Present Perfect tenses

• This can be done in writing or by class discussion.

Answers to Exercise 4
1. have been writing
2. have you been learning
3. lived
4. have had
5. have you known; were
6. have been
7. I'm going
8. Have you been waiting
9. Have you ever seen
10. Did you ever go
11. did you have
12. has been
13. I've never travelled
14. I've lost
15. I lost

SPEAKING

1 Mime: 'What am I?'

• Give students a minute or two to choose their jobs and work out how to mime them.
• Then let them take turns to perform their mimes.
• Make sure students remember to put *a/an* before the name of the job when they make their guesses.

2 'What are we talking about?'

• Students work in groups of three or pairs.
• Give them fifteen minutes to work out a short and simple conversation in which somebody asks for something or asks somebody else to do something.
• They must write down the text of their conversation.
• When they are ready, one group performs its conversation *without words* for the rest of the class, or for another group. They must show by their actions what they are talking about.
• One or more of the other groups then repeats the first group's mime, trying to add the missing words.
• Finally, the first group repeats its sketch; this time they say the words as well.
• Continue until every group has performed.
• If you have video, this can be used very effectively (record the mime and play it back several times while the class try to decide what the words might be).

3 Descriptions: lost property

• Go over the dialogue practising pronunciation and explaining difficulties.
• Note the use of *leave*, not *forget*, when the place is specified (*I left it on the bus*).
• Give students about a quarter of an hour to make up and practise similar conversations, using as many of the italic words and expressions as possible.
• Then get students to perform their conversations.
• If you are planning to tape- or video-record the performances, tell students in advance – this will give them an incentive to produce good-quality work.

4 Question-box

• This can be a very successful speaking activity.
• Encourage questions which can lead to discussion.
• Before students put their questions in the box, check them for serious mistakes.
• Don't correct the English while students are talking, but note points for attention later if you wish.
• Make sure students don't put their questions back in the box when they have answered them.
• A student can reject a question, saying *'I'm sorry, I'd rather not answer'* (put this on the board), and take another – but only once.
• In a large class, make two or more subgroups.

READING AND WRITING

1 Questionnaire

• There is no scientific basis to the test, and it is not of course to be taken seriously.
• Before starting, ask students to say whether or not they think they are peaceful.
• Tell them to read the text and note their scores.
• Let them use their dictionaries or ask you if they have problems with vocabulary.
• If they disagree with the results, or are critical of the questions, ask if they can suggest improvements.

2 Students' questionnaires

• Put students in groups of three or four.
• Each group should choose one of the subjects and make up a questionnaire with ten or so questions.
• Possible beginnings for questions: *Have you ever . . .* , *Do you ever . . .* or *How often do you . . .*
• You will probably need to help with vocabulary.
• When questionnaires are ready, groups can exchange them and answer the questions.

Practice Book exercises
1. Vocabulary: geographical names.
2. Modal verbs.
3. Irregular verbs.
4. Student's Cassette exercise (Student's Book Grammar Exercise 1, full version of song). Students try to write down the first two verses.
5. Writing a news bulletin.
6. Crossword.

Additional reading
Note that students have now reached a level where they should be able to cope comfortably with the texts in Sections A–C of *Additional reading* in the Practice Book (pages 108 to 111). You can set some of the readings for homework or just suggest that students read any of the texts that interest them when they have the time.

4 Choose the correct form. Look back at Summary C if you have any problems.

1. I *am writing* / *have been writing* / *wrote* letters for the last two hours.
2. 'How long *are you learning* / *have you been learning* English?' 'Since last summer.'
3. When I was a child, we *have been living* / *have lived* / *lived* in a house by a river.
4. I *have had* / *have* this watch since my 18th birthday.
5. 'How long *do you know* / *have you known* Jessica?' 'We *have been* / *were* at school together 40 years ago.'
6. I *am* / *have been* ill for three days now. I think I'd better call the doctor.
7. *I'm going* / *I've been* home on Sunday.
8. Sorry I'm late. *Are you waiting* / *Have you been waiting* long?
9. *Have you ever seen* / *Did you ever see* a boxing match?
10. *Have you ever been* / *Did you ever go* camping when you were a child?
11. Where *have you had* / *did you have* lunch yesterday?
12. Where's the telephone? There *has been* / *was* an accident!
13. *I've never travelled* / *I never travelled* by air.
14. Can you help me? *I've lost* / *I lost* my watch.
15. *I've lost* / *I lost* my glasses the other day.

SPEAKING

1 'What am I?' Choose a job and mime it (act it without speaking) to the other students. They will say what they think you are.

2 'What are we talking about?' Work in groups of three. Prepare a conversation in which somebody asks for something, or asks somebody else to do something. When you are ready, mime your conversation (act it without using the words) for the other students. They will try to find the words.

3 Read the conversation. Then work with a partner and make up a similar conversation about something that has been lost. Try to use the words and expressions in italics.

A: *I've lost* a briefcase.
B: Oh, yes? *What's it like?* Can you describe it?
A: It's brown, *with* a handle on top, and *it's got* a brass lock. *It's about this big.*
B: Anything inside it?
A: Yes. *There are* some books *with* my name *in*, and there's a pen *that* I bought yesterday. And a pint of milk.
B: *Where did you lose it?*
A: I think *I left it* on the bus.
B: Well, *I'll see what I can do* . . .

4 Question-box. Each student writes three questions on separate pieces of paper. One of the questions must begin *Have you ever* . . . , and one must begin *Do you* . . . The questions are folded up and put in a box. Students take turns to draw out questions and answer them.

READING AND WRITING

1 Are you a peaceful person? Answer the questions as honestly as you can and then find out your total score. (But don't take the test too seriously!)

1. If you have ever been in a political demonstration, score 2.
2. If you have lost your temper during the last three days, score 3.
3. If you have ever driven at over 160kph, score 2.
4. If you have ever broken a cup, a glass or plate on purpose, score 1.
5. If you have been in a fight in the last three years, score 3.
6. If you have seen a war film, gangster film, western or other violent film in the last month, score 1.
7. If you have ever been in love with two people at the same time, score 2.
8. If you ever have violent dreams, score 1.
9. If you have ever walked out of a job, score 2.
10. If you have ever watched a boxing-match, score 2.
11. If you like the town better than the country, score 1.

Your score:
 0–9: you are a peaceful person.
10–15: average.
16–20: you are not at all peaceful!

2 Now make up your own questionnaire. Suggestions: find out whether people are energetic, polite, cultured, generous, honest, shy, careful with money, fashion-conscious, interested in sport, interested in politics, or sociable.

Test C

LISTENING

1 Listen to three people talking about past experiences. Copy the table; for each experience put a ✓ if they have had it, and a ✗ if they have not.

	1	2	3
eating snails			
going to America			
spending more than a day in hospital			
running a mile			

Now listen again. Try to pick out these words, and write down the verbs that go with them.

quite often   twice   very often   never
recently   on one occasion   before now

GRAMMAR

1 Choose the right tenses.

New Party Leader
Ted Boot, who *has become / became* leader of the United Aggro Party last month, *has had / had* considerable experience in politics. During his career he *has been / was* a Mafia boss, a Trade Union leader, Conservative MP for Guildford, . . .

Cowboys – Snowboys
The heavy rain which *is falling / has been falling / has fallen / fell* in Texas for the last six weeks *has now turned / now turned* to snow. Questioned on TV yesterday evening about his plans to deal with the disaster, which *has already cost / already cost* the State $450,000,000, President Stabetsi *has said / said* 'It looks like a white Christmas, folks.'

~~~wer~~~
~~~ress~~~ conference this
~~~~servative~~~ MP
~~~~ich~~~

Scots Kids Take Power
8-year-old General Colin McCann, leader of the Scottish Children's Revolutionary Front, *has just returned / just returned* to Edinburgh after talks in London with the British Prime Minister. At a press conference this morning, General McCann *has said / said* that his government . . .

Red Face for Queen
London's night-painters *have done / did* it again. Late last night they *have landed / landed* by helicopter on the roof of Buckingham Palace. When policemen on guard *have woken / woke* up, they found that the whole Royal Family . . .

Lux-Pat War
War *has again broken / again broke* out between Luxembourg and Patagonia. The Patagonians *have invaded / invaded* Luxembourg shortly after 8pm last night, and . . .

~~~d Fake~~~
a Trade Union
~~~Prime~~~ Minister
~~~~ke a~~~

2 Write the past tenses and past participles of these verbs. Example:

go ___went___ ___gone/been___

break   bring   come   drink
drive   eat   get   hear
hold   hope   rain   say   see
speak   stop   tell   think
try   wake   write

3 Put in *may not, won't* or *can't*.

1. The trains are often late on Saturdays, so I .... arrive on time tomorrow.
2. 'Don't forget to say hello to Jane for me.' 'No, I ....'
3. I .... understand anything that she says.
4. I .... be here tomorrow – I've got to go to France.
5. I .... be in the office tomorrow. I'll tell you later, when I'm quite sure.

Test C

Students do a simple revision test.

The purpose of the test

This test covers material from Lessons 13–18. It is not of course necessary to do all of the sections, and teachers should select according to their students' needs. Teachers who do not feel the test will be useful should simply drop it altogether.

If possible, try to make the students feel that they are 'testing themselves', rather than 'being tested'. It is not intended that students should 'pass' or 'fail' the test, and it is not particularly useful to give marks. (If the school or education system requires that this be done, you will need to work out a simple marking scheme.) But students should of course be told whether you feel their performance is satisfactory. In principle, students who have worked systematically through Lessons 13–18 ought to get most answers right.

Administration

The test can be administered in various ways, depending on how strictly you want to control students' performance; whether you want to collect the answers and mark them, or allow the students to correct them in class; and so on.

The second part of the 'speaking' test will need to be done in pairs, with students interrupting their work on the other parts of the test to come and talk to you. You may want to give them time to prepare their conversations just after the listening test.

If you do not collect students' scripts, correction can be done by class discussion when everybody has finished.

Notes, tapescript and answers are given below.

LISTENING

Present Perfect with time adverbials

- Ask students to copy the table.
- Go over any difficult words in the table.
- Play the recording once straight through while they try to complete the table.
- Then play it again, pausing after each speaker for students to check/complete their answers.
- Then get students to copy the time adverbials on their papers, writing them one under the other in the middle of the page.
- When they hear the words, they should write the verbs that go with them.
- Play the recording twice, pausing after each speaker.

Answers and tapescript to Listening Test 1

	1	2	3
eating snails	√	√	√
going to America	√	√	×
spending more than a day in hospital	√	√	√
running a mile	√	×	√

I've quite often *eaten*
I've been . . . twice
I've very often *run*
I've never *run*
I've eaten . . . on one occasion
I have spent . . . before now

1. Yeah, I've quite often eaten snails; I like them with garlic sauce. I've been to America twice. I've, erm, certainly spent more than one day in hospital – I spent ten weeks in hospital once. And I've, I've very often run more than a mile, yeah.
2. I've eaten snails and enjoyed them. I've lived in America for two years. Erm, I spent more than one day in hospital when I had my children. And I've never run more than a mile. (*Laughter*)
3. Well, I've eaten snails on one occasion; quite enjoyed it. I've never been to America. I have spent more than one day in hospital before now. And I have run more than a mile, on, quite, quite often.

GRAMMAR

1 'New Party Leader': became; has had; has been
'Cowboys . . . ': has been falling; has now turned; has already cost; said
'Scots Kids . . . ': has just returned; said
'Red Face . . . ': have done; landed; woke
'Lux-Pat War': has again broken; invaded

2 break – broke – broken
bring – brought – brought
come – came – come
drink – drank – drunk
drive – drove – driven
eat – ate – eaten
get – got – got
hear – heard – heard
hold – held – held
hope – hoped – hoped
rain – rained – rained
say – said – said
see – saw – seen
speak – spoke – spoken
stop – stopped – stopped
tell – told – told
think – thought – thought
try – tried – tried
wake – woke – woken
write – wrote – written

3 1. may not
2. won't
3. can't
4. won't
5. may not

VOCABULARY

1–3 (Various possible answers.)

4 1. wish
2. apply
3. post
4. Manager
5. advertised
6. am
7. old
8. experience
9. several
10. qualification (*or* experience)
11. forward
12. faithfully

LANGUAGE IN USE

1 Possible answers:
1. Can I look round? / I'm just looking.
2. I'm afraid you've got the wrong number.
3. Single to London, please.
4. Excuse me.
5. Not at all. / That's all right.
6. Is service included?
7. Could I use your phone? / Do you mind if I use your phone?
8. What does *spanner* mean?

PRONUNCIATION

1 agriculture (/ˈægrɪkʌltʃə(r)/)
colony (/ˈkɒləni/)
ever (/ˈevə(r)/)
figure (/ˈfɪgə(r)/)
forward (/ˈfɔːwəd/)
government (/ˈgʌvənmənt/)
independent (/ɪndɪˈpendənt/)
industry (/ˈɪndəstri/)
interview (/ˈɪntəvjuː/)
salary (/ˈsæləri/)

2 1. forward
2. essential
3. apply
4. assistant
5. faithfully

SPEAKING

Go over the instructions with the whole class and make sure they understand what they have to do. For Question 2, it is probably best if students prepare their conversations after the listening section, before they start on the rest of the test. Then you can call them out a pair at a time while the others get on with their work. You will need to improvise the part of the Manager, depending on the situation that students have prepared.

If you mark the speaking test, take into account not only correctness but also success in communicating, fluency, breadth of knowledge, appropriacy and variety of language.

WRITING

When correcting this, it is best to judge students mainly on their ability to communicate successfully, using appropriate vocabulary and structures. Excessive emphasis on errors of grammar and spelling can damage students' confidence.

Test Book recordings
A recording for Test 3 in the Test Book follows this lesson on the Class Cassette.

VOCABULARY

1 Write the names of eight or more things that you might find in a kitchen.

2 Write the names of eight or more parts of the body (for example *arm, leg*).

3 Write the names of: a big country; a small country; a country where people speak several different languages; three countries in America; a country in Africa; a country with water all round it.

4 Choose some words from the box.

> Dear Sir/Madam,
>
> I ...1... to ...2... for the ...3... of Sales ...4... ...5... in the Guardian of 22 May. I ...6... 36 years ...7... and have ...8... of selling in ...9... firms. I also have ...10... in marketing. I look ...11... to hearing from you.
>
> Yours ...12...,

advertised	age	am	any	apply
ask	Boss	dear	education	expect
experience	faithfully	forward		have
Manager	need	old	only	post
qualifications	several	sincerely		
understanding	wish	written		
work	your			

LANGUAGE IN USE

1 What do you say when . . .

1. you want to look at things in a shop, but you don't want the assistant to help you?
2. somebody telephones you, but they wanted a different number?
3. you want a train ticket to go to London, but not to come back?
4. you want to say something to somebody who is talking to somebody else?
5. somebody says 'Thank you very much; that's extremely kind of you'?
6. you get the bill in a restaurant and you want to know if you have to pay service too?
7. you want to use somebody else's phone?
8. you want to know what a word (for example *spanner*) means?

PRONUNCIATION

1 The sound /ə/ comes once in the word *mother* (/ˈmʌðə(r)/), twice in the word *America* (/əˈmerɪkə/), and twice in the word *computer* (/kəmˈpjuːtə(r)/). Which of these words are pronounced with /ə/?

agriculture   become   between   colony
ever   figure   forward   government
improve   independent   industry
interview   salary

2 Which word has a different stress? Example:

over   waiting   often   (above)

1. become   between   improve   forward
2. salary   essential   industry   interview
3. figure   ever   apply   happy
4. assistant   holiday   colony   possible
5. faithfully   sincerely   completely   extremely

SPEAKING

1 Tell the teacher about EITHER your last holiday OR an interesting person in your family OR an interesting job that you have done.

2 Work in pairs. One of you is a shop assistant; the other is a customer. Prepare a conversation. During the conversation there is a problem, and one of you calls the Manager. When you are ready, act your conversation for the teacher (he/she will be the Manager).

WRITING

1 Write a few sentences about something interesting that has happened to you this year.

19 Their children will have blue eyes

Talking about the future with *if*, *will* and *may*; reported speech with *said . . . would*.

1 Read the text and answer the questions. Use a dictionary only when it is really necessary.

Why do people look like their parents?

People's appearance (like that of animals and plants) depends on things called *genes*. Genes are found in the cells of people's bodies, and they are passed on from parents to children. A child has some genes from its father and some genes from its mother. The chemistry of genes is very complicated. Here are some facts about eyes.

Many Europeans and Americans can have blue, green or brown eyes. But a brown-eyed person, for example, may also carry genes for another colour in his/her body. So two brown-eyed or green-eyed parents may not have a child with the same colour eyes. If a child's father and mother both have brown eyes, the child will probably also have brown eyes, but this is not certain.

If one parent has got blue eyes and one has got brown eyes, their children may have either blue eyes or brown eyes, but most will probably have brown eyes. (The gene for blue eyes is 'recessive' and the gene for brown eyes is 'dominant'. This means that if a child gets a gene for blue eyes and also a gene for brown eyes from its parents, brown will 'win', and the child's eyes will be brown, not blue.)

People only have blue eyes if their bodies are carrying no genes for other eye colours. So if both parents have got blue eyes, their children cannot have eyes of another colour.

1. If both parents have got blue eyes, their children:
   – will certainly have blue eyes.
   – will probably have blue eyes.
   – may have blue eyes.
2. If both parents have got brown eyes, their children:
   – will certainly have brown eyes.
   – will probably have brown eyes.
   – may have brown eyes.
3. If one parent has got blue eyes and one has got brown eyes, their children:
   – will certainly have blue eyes.
   – will probably have blue eyes.
   – may have either blue eyes or brown eyes.
   – will probably have brown eyes.
   – will certainly have brown eyes.

2 Look at the pictures. Each couple is going to have a baby. What do you think the children will be like? Make sentences using *will probably*, *may* and (*probably/certainly*) *won't*. Example:

'*Carol and Lee's baby may be tall.*'

Lee is a bus driver. He is a very friendly and sociable person. He likes sport, especially ball games. He is interested in science, and he is studying maths at night school. He is not at all musical.

Carol works in a computer firm. She is rather shy. She is not very interested in sport, but she likes playing tennis. She is very musical, and can play several instruments.

Lesson 19

Students practise talking about probability, certainty and the future.
Principal structures: *may* and *will*; simple *if*-clauses; simple reported speech with *would*.
Phonology: /əʊ/.

Language notes and possible problems
1. Modal verbs If necessary, remind students that *may* and *will*, like other modal verbs, are followed by the infinitive without *to*, and that modal verbs have no -*s* in the third-person singular.
2. *Will be able to*; *will have to* Students have met *be able to* and *have to* briefly; you may need to remind them of the meanings before they do Exercise 5.
3. *If* The sentences with *if* in this lesson are unproblematic: normal present and future tenses are used.
4. Reported speech (Exercise 7) In this and the next few lessons, students practise simple reported speech structures. Rather than presenting reported speech all at once as a large complex system, we think it better to introduce it in easy stages, a bit at a time. Here students work on the relationship between direct speech *will* and reported speech *would* in statements. Look out for *She said that I will . . .* instead of *She said that I would . . .*
5. Pronunciation (Exercise 3) Don't be too perfectionist about the pronunciation of /əʊ/ unless students are aiming at a very high standard.

You may like to take this opportunity to focus again on the pronunciation of /ɪ/ (in *if* and *will*).

Optional extra equipment
Packs of cards and bowls for Exercise 6.

If you are short of time
Drop Exercise 3 if pronunciation is not a high priority.

1 Accurate reading
• Give students a reasonable amount of time to read the text. Allow them to use dictionaries, but tell them not to consult them unless they really have to. (You might ask students to see how few words they need to look up in order to do the exercise.)
• When they are ready, get them to decide what they think the answers are (working individually at first, and then comparing notes in groups).
• Finally, discuss the answers. It might also be interesting to talk about how many words it was really necessary to look up in order to understand the text.

Answers to Exercise 1
1. If both parents have got blue eyes, their children will certainly have blue eyes.
2. If both parents have got brown eyes, their children will probably have brown eyes.
3. If one parent has got blue eyes and one has got brown eyes, their children will probably have brown eyes.

2 What will the baby be like?
• This can be done by general class discussion. There are no right answers, of course.
• In a relaxed mixed-sex class, it might be fun to get the students speculating about what kinds of children would result from marriages between various members of the class. ('*If Carlo and Lisa have a child, it will certainly like eating and drinking.*')

3 Pronunciation: /əʊ/

- The standard British /əʊ/ is a difficult sound for most foreigners to make. It may also sound 'funny' to them, so that they may have a psychological resistance to making the sound.
- An easy way to learn to make it is to practise putting together the two sounds /ə/ (as in *father* or *about*) and /uː/ (as in *too*). Get students to say 'er–oo' a few times, and then tell them to put various consonants before the sound: 'ner-oo', 'ger-oo', 'ser–oo'. They should find themselves saying *no*, *go* and *so*.
- Then get them to say the other words and expressions, using the recording as a model if you wish.
- If students find the sound difficult, or are unwilling to make it, tell them that it is not very important for comprehensibility, and that in any case it is not used by many native English speakers except for speakers of standard British English.

4 Personalisation

- Look over the examples. You may wish to practise the pronunciation of *hope*, *don't* and *won't* again before going on.
- Give students a minute or two to think, and then ask for their sentences.
- Younger students may enjoy making insulting predictions about the appearance and/or personality of each other's children, if they have not already done this in Exercise 2.

5 Predicting life in the future

- Look through the example and explain that *be able to* acts as the infinitive of *can*. Remind students what *have to* means if necessary.
- Then put students in groups and give them fifteen minutes or so to think up some ideas and join them into paragraphs. Help with vocabulary if necessary.
- When they are ready, let groups exchange paragraphs, or put all the paragraphs on the class notice board for everybody to read.

6 Fortune telling

- This will need a bit of preparation.
- Get the class to spend a few minutes thinking of things that a fortune-teller might say. Help with vocabulary.
- If anybody in the class actually does fortune-telling, try to get them to demonstrate, using you as a client.
- Then divide the class into 'fortune-tellers' and 'clients'.
- Get the clients to go round to the fortune-tellers finding out about their future. Each client should visit at least three fortune-tellers.
- The exercise can be made livelier if you bring in some props such as packs of cards and bowls (for crystal balls).

7 Reporting

- Look at the example, and clear up any problems.
- Explain that *would* is used as the past of *will* in reported speech.
- Then ask students to say or write some of the things they were told, concentrating on differences between one fortune-teller and another.
- Pay attention to the pronunciation of *said* (/sed/).
- If time allows, get fortune-tellers to become clients, and vice versa, and repeat Exercises 6 and 7.

Practice Book exercises
1. Sentences with *if*: matching beginnings and ends.
2. Predicting with *will*.
3. Predicting with *will certainly/probably* and *may*.
4. Vocabulary revision and extension: containers.
5. Reading and reacting.
6. Recreational reading.

Revision
For successful language learning, regular revision is essential. The course provides a good deal of revision work, both in the lesson material and in the Practice Book exercises. However, you will probably want to do additional informal revision from time to time. One useful approach is to get students to prepare tests for each other on lessons that were done some time ago.

Milton teaches economics at a university. He is very sociable, and likes noisy parties. He plays football and tennis very well. He likes travelling.

Barbara teaches physics at a university. She likes being with people, and hates being alone. She is good at tennis, swimming and dancing. She likes travelling.

3 Pronunciation. Say these words and expressions.

know   so   go   hope   don't   won't
I know   I hope   I won't
I don't know   I hope so   I won't go

4 What will your children be like? (If you already have children, talk about your grandchildren. If you're not going to have children, talk about somebody else's children.) Use *will, won't, may, I (don't) think, I hope*. Examples:

'*I hope my children will be good-looking.*'
'*My sister's children may be musical.*'
'*I don't think Jose's children will be tall.*'
'*My children certainly won't speak English.*'

5 What sort of world will our great-grandchildren live in? Work with other students; write a paragraph using *will be able to* and *will have to*. Example:

Our great-grandchildren will have a wonderful life. They will be able to go to the moon for the weekend. They will only have to work two days a week . . .

6 Half the class are fortune-tellers. The other students go to three or more fortune-tellers, who tell them about their future.

'*You will have a long and interesting life. You will travel to . . .*'

You will meet a rich stranger . . .

7 What did the fortune-tellers say about your future? Use '*. . . said that . . . would . . .*' Example:

'*Maria said that I would never get married, but Mike said that I would get married six times.*'

Reported speech
'You **will** never get married.'
Maria **said** that I **would** never get married.

Learn/revise: future; parent; grandchild (*plural* grandchildren); great-grandchild; eye; colour; body; cell; chemistry; animal; plant; person (*plural* people); fact; the moon; European; American; look like; depend on; carry; say (said, said); tell (told, told); get married; would; complicated; tall; good-looking; wonderful; certain; certainly; probably; the same; like; also; somebody else; half; its; either . . . or; have a baby; I hope (so); What sort of . . . ?; What is . . . like?; What will . . . be like?

20 A matter of life and death

> Talking about the future with *going to*; *should*; agreeing and disagreeing; reported speech.

1 Two explorers are flying across the North African desert. Their plane develops engine trouble. Listen to the recording. Which of these sentences do you hear?

1. The engine's going to break up!
2. We're going to crash!
3. We're going to hit those rocks!
4. The plane's going to turn over!
5. We're both going to die!
6. I don't want to die!
7. Nobody's going to die.
8. You've got to keep calm.
9. I'm going to put the plane down over there.
10. It's going to be a rough landing.
11. I'm going to put my head down!
12. I'm not going to look!

2 How many words do you hear in each sentence? (Contractions like *don't* count as two words.)

3 The plane crashes, but the two explorers are unhurt. The nearest village is 60 miles (100km) away, across waterless desert and mountains. The plane's radio is broken; the only things which were not destroyed in the crash are shown in the picture. Work in pairs and imagine that you are the explorers. What will you take with you? Useful language:

I think we should take . . .
I don't think we should take . . .
We (don't) need . . .
How much does it weigh?
It doesn't weigh much.
It only weighs . . . kg.
No, it's too heavy.
We've got to keep the weight down.
I agree.
I don't agree.
It would be better to take . . .

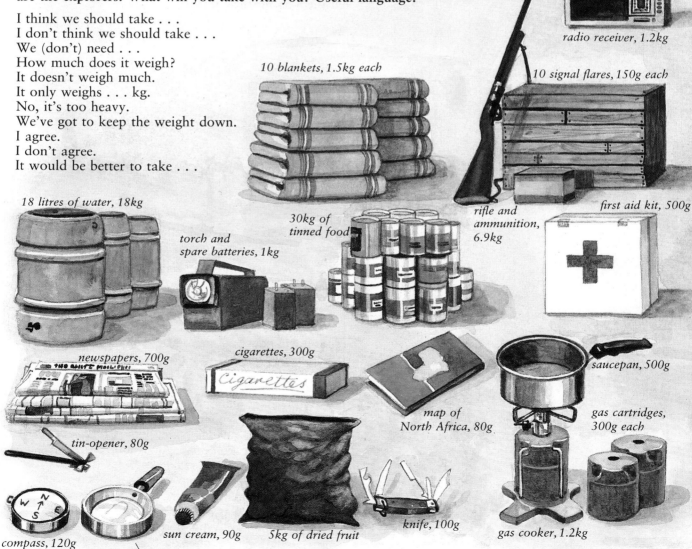

10 metres of rope, 1.3kg

radio receiver, 1.2kg

10 blankets, 1.5kg each

10 signal flares, 150g each

rifle and ammunition, 6.9kg

first aid kit, 500g

18 litres of water, 18kg

torch and spare batteries, 1kg

30kg of tinned food

newspapers, 700g

cigarettes, 300g

map of North Africa, 80g

saucepan, 500g

gas cartridges, 300g each

tin-opener, 80g

compass, 120g

sun cream, 90g

magnifying glass, 40g

5kg of dried fruit

knife, 100g

gas cooker, 1.2kg

Lesson 20

Students **use** discussion to solve a simple problem.
Principal structures: *be going* + infinitive; *should*;
reported speech.
Phonology: decoding rapid speech; conversational
pronunciation of *going to*, *want to* and *got to*.

Language notes and possible problems

1. *Be going* + infinitive Students are probably already
familiar with the *going-to* future. In this lesson they are
reminded of the two main uses: to predict (especially where
one can 'see what is coming'), and to announce intentions.

2. *Should* is used here to talk about what is advisable. If
necessary, explain that *should* is another modal verb, like
can, *may*, *will* and *would*, and that like them it has no *-s* on
the third person and is followed by the infinitive without *to*.
Look out for confusion between *should* and *would* here and
in the next few lessons.

3. Reported speech (Exercise 5) If necessary, point out
that a past verb is necessary after *The first pair said . . .*
Some students may be influenced by their mother tongues
into saying **The first pair said that they are going to . . .*;
others into **The first pair said that they would be going
to . . .*

1 Listening for sentences with *going to*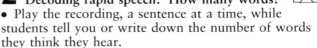

- Go through the list of sentences and clear up any
problems.
- Play the recording once without stopping. Ask
students which of the listed sentences they thought they
heard.
- Play the recording again, while they write down or
tick off the numbers of the sentences that come in the
recording.
- Let them compare notes in groups before you discuss
the answers. (Sentences 2, 3, 5, 6, 7, 8, 10 and 12
occur in the dialogue.)

Tapescript for Exercise 1

A: We're in trouble, Pete. The engine's breaking up.
B: Oh, God! We're going to crash!
A: There goes the engine.
B: We're going to hit those rocks!
A: No, we're not, Pete. We're OK. I'm going to get us down,
   all right?
B: What are you doing? The plane's turning over!
A: Relax, Pete. I know what I'm doing, right?
B: Relax? Relax? What do you mean, relax? We're both going
   to die! I don't want to die! I'm too young to die!
A: Nobody's going to die, Pete. You've got to keep calm.
   Now listen. I'm going to try to put the plane down over
   there.
B: Over where?
A: On that flat patch of hard sand, just ahead. But it's going
   to be a rough landing. So put your head down, and put
   your arms over your head. Landing in ten seconds.
B: Oh, God! We're going to crash! I'm not going to look!
A: Landing now, Pete.
B: (*Screams*)

2 Decoding rapid speech: 'How many words?'

- Play the recording, a sentence at a time, while
students tell you or write down the number of words
they think they hear.
- Play the recording a second time while students try to
decide exactly what the words are.
- Finally, practise the sentences after the recording,
trying to get good rhythm and a natural pronunciation
of weak forms.
- Note the conversational pronunciations of *going to*
('*gonna*'), *want to* ('*wanna*') and *got to* ('*gotta*').

Tapescript and answers to Exercise 2

1. We're going to crash! (5)
2. I don't want to die. (6)
3. You've got to keep calm. (6)
4. I'm not going to look. (6)
5. What are you going to do? (6)
6. Everybody's got to listen to me. (7)
7. Why do you want to go to the station? (9)
8. I don't think this is going to be very interesting. (11)
9. I've got to do a lot of work this morning. (11)
10. We don't want to talk to you. (8)
11. I'm going to go and look for a stamp. (10)
12. What are you going to say to the boss? (9)

3 Discussion: survival problem

- Let the students look at the illustration; make sure
they understand all the words and can pronounce them.
- Ask how much weight they think one person can
carry on a 60-mile march across the desert. (20kg is a
heavy load for a normal person in average walking
conditions.)
- Ask how long they think the march will take.
- Then tell students to begin by drawing up their lists
(for two people) individually.
- Point out that they can split some of the items (they
don't have to take all the blankets or all the food or
water, for instance).
- When students have drawn up their individual lists,
get them to join up into pairs (if you have an odd
number of students, make one group of three).
- Look over the list of 'useful language'.
- Tell students that their task is now to exchange ideas
and draw up one agreed list for each pair.
- Give them a time limit.

4 Reporting

- When students are ready, let each pair report to another pair, a group, or the whole class on what they have decided.
- There is, of course, no one 'right answer' to the problem.

5 Listening: other people's solutions

- Choose a pair of students who have decided to take, say, 4 blankets and demonstrate the use of *each*. Write on the board:

4 blankets = 2 blankets each
6kg of water =
10m of rope =
5kg of dried fruit =

- Get students to give you the answers. (They will need to understand this structure for the listening exercise.)
- Then ask students to take out a piece of paper and write down a list of the names of the things in the illustration (no quantities).
- Play the recording of the first speaker, asking students to note what he and his partner have decided on (either by ticking the thing as he mentions it or by writing the quantity he mentions).
- Do the same for the second speaker.
- Play the recording more than once if students wish.
- Go over the example with the students, pointing out the use of *were going to*.
- Ask them to volunteer other ways in which the two teams differed in their choices.

Answers to Exercise 5

First pair	*Second pair*
10kg each	17.5kg each
2 blankets	4 blankets
1kg dried fruit	5kg dried fruit
6kg water each = 12kg	18kg water
newspapers	a few of the newspapers
compass	–
	sun cream
	map
	magnifying glass
	torch and spare batteries

Tapescript for Exercise 5

1. Well, we've decided that we're going to have ten kilograms each. And we're going to take two blankets, one kilogram of dried fruit, two backpacks and the rope. Erm, we're going to take sic-, we're going to take six kilograms of water each. Erm, we're going to take the matches. We're going to take the knife. We're going to take newspapers in case of erm, sun. We're going to take the first aid kit. We're going to take two pairs of sunglasses. We're going to take a compass and we're going to take two signal flares each.

2. Right. In deciding what we were going to take, we thought we'd have a look at the essential items first and see how much they added up to and then thought whether or not we could carry it. So, looking at the list, we decided we were going to take four blankets and the two backpacks to put all the blankets and all the rest of the stuff in. The ten metres of rope would be useful in the mountains and we're going to take five kilograms of dried fruit and all the water – that's eighteen kilograms. There are a number of small items we thought we'd take as well – the matches, sun cream, map of North Africa, knife, magnifying glass, a few of the newspapers, erm, perhaps to start fires, the first aid kit, two pairs of sunglasses to, would, for the light weight, very useful. We're also going to take the er, torch and spare batteries because we intend to walk at night and four signal flares so we can attract attention. Now, that, I think, means that we're going to leave out the tent. We're not going to take, er, s-, the cooker or the cartridges or the saucepan. We don't smoke, so we don't need the cigarettes, and the radio receiver will be of no use. We're not going to take the rifle and ammunition. So that totalled thirty-five kilograms, which we thought, divided between us, would be all right, 'specially as we're going to consume the food and the water as we go along.

Practice Book exercises

1. Writing sentences using *going to*.
2. Reporting sentences about the future.
3. Contractions.
4. Student's Cassette exercise (Student's Book Exercise 5, first speaker). Students listen to the recording and fill in words that are missing from the text.
5. Reading: students read how two trained soldiers solved the problem from the Student's Book.
6. Writing: students devise 'survival problems'.

Authentic material

At one time, it was considered wrong to give elementary students listening and reading material which had not been very carefully 'graded' by removing unusual words and difficult structures. Clearly tightly graded material can be very useful, but it is also important to expose learners to suitable examples of authentic ungraded language from time to time. This gets them used to the flavour and texture of real-life English, as well as providing valuable 'preview' of words and structures which they will be learning later on. It also trains students to feel comfortable with speech or writing in which they do not understand every word. This is what they will meet when they are exposed to English outside the classroom, and if they have read nothing but simplified texts and heard nothing but the speech of actors in recording studios, 'real-life' English may come as something of a shock.

When working with authentic material, encourage students to listen or read for overall meaning or for specific information; they should not worry if they don't understand every single word and structure.

backpacks, 1.5kg each

tent, 4kg

light clothing

4 Tell the class what you have decided to take with you. Begin *'We're (not) going to take . . .'*

5 [cassette icon] Listen to the recording. You will hear two other pairs of explorers saying what they have decided to take. How many differences do you notice between the two solutions? Example:

'The first pair said that they were going to take two blankets, but the second pair . . .'

Reported speech
'I**'m** going to take . . .'
He **said** that he **was** going to take . . .

Learn/revise: life (*plural* lives); death; desert; engine; landing; mountain; plane; radio; rock; trouble; village; weight; North Africa; head; mile; kilometre; agree; break up (broke, broken); crash; die; fly (flew, flown); hit (hit, hit); keep (kept, kept); put down (put, put); turn over; weigh; need; should; calm; keep calm; heavy; rough; unhurt; broken; nearest; across; both; nobody; only; too.

---

sunglasses, 40g each pair

matches, 20g

21 If you see a black cat, . . .

If and *when*.

1 Superstitions. Do you believe in luck? Put the beginnings and ends together, using expressions from the box. (There are too many expressions.)

If you see ....,
If you spill ....,
If .... is red this evening,
If your first visitor in the New Year has ....,
If .... itches,
If you break ....,

.... will be fine tomorrow.
you'll get .... soon.
you'll have ....
throw .... over your shoulder
    to keep bad luck away.
you'll have .... bad luck.
you'll have good luck ....

a black cat	all year	a mirror	an old shoe	dark hair	four potatoes
good luck	seven years'	some money	some salt	some wine	
the baby	the sky	the weather	your left hand		

2 Say these words and expressions.

will   I'll   you'll   he'll   she'll
I'll tell   I'll think   you'll be
you'll have   You'll have bad luck.
You'll be sorry.   I'll tell you tomorrow.
I'll think about it.   She'll have to go soon.
It'll rain.   Do you think it'll rain tonight?

3 Did you know the superstitions in Exercise 1? Do you know any other superstitions?

4 *If* or *when*? Look at the difference:

When I go to bed tonight, I'll . . .
    (I *will* go to bed.)
If I go to Scotland, I'll . . .
    (I *may* go to Scotland.)

When you are on holiday, think of me.
    (You *will* be on holiday.)
If you are ever in London, come and see us.
    (You *may* be in London.)

Now put in *if* or *when* and choose the correct verb forms.

1. .... I (*get* / *will get*) enough money, I (*travel* / *'ll travel*) round the world.
2. .... it (*rains* / *will rain*) this afternoon, we (*stay* / *'ll stay*) at home.
3. I (*close* / *'ll close*) the curtains .... it (*gets* / *will get*) dark.
4. .... I (*get* / *'ll get*) older, I (*stop* / *'ll stop*) playing rugby.
5. You can't go home now, but you can go .... the game (*'s* / *'ll be*) finished.
6. Get off the bus quickly .... it (*stops* / *'ll stop*).
7. .... you (*say* / *'ll say*) that again, I (*hit* / *'ll hit*) you.
8. .... I (*go* / *'ll go*) to bed tonight, I (*dream* / *'ll dream*) about you.
9. .... you (*are* / *'ll be*) in this country next year, I hope you (*come* / *'ll come*) and see us.

66

Lesson 21

Students practise talking about conditions and probability.
Principal structures: *if*-clauses in open conditions; the distinction between *if* and *when* in subordinate clauses.
Phonology: 'dark *l*'.

Language notes and possible problems

1. *If*-clauses In this lesson, students practise understanding and expressing conditions. The only grammatical problem is the use of a present tense to refer to the future in an *if*-clause (see Exercise 4).

2. Punctuation When an *if*-clause or a *when*-clause begins a sentence, we usually follow the clause with a comma. The comma can be dropped in shorter sentences, but for the moment it might be best to advise students to put a comma in all cases.

3. *If* and *when* (Exercise 4) Speakers of some languages have difficulty in seeing clearly the difference between *if* and *when* in certain contexts. Exercise 4 is designed to help with this.

4. Pronunciation: /ɪ/ This lesson, in which the word *if* comes up repeatedly, is a good opportunity to revise the pronunciation of /ɪ/ once again, if it is still a problem.

If you are short of time

Drop Exercise 2; give Exercise 4 for homework.

1 Superstitions

● Let students do the exercise individually, using dictionaries or asking you about difficult vocabulary.
● Get them to compare notes; discuss the answers.
● Obviously it doesn't matter if they get some of the answers wrong – indeed, they might get a lot of fun out of making absurd combinations.

Answers to Exercise 1

If you see *a black cat*, you'll have *good luck*.
If you spill *some wine*, throw *some salt* over your shoulder to keep bad luck away.
If *the sky* is red this evening, *the weather* will be fine tomorrow.
If your first visitor in the New Year has *dark hair*, you'll have good luck *all year*.
If *your left hand* itches, you'll get *some money* soon.
If you break *a mirror*, you'll have *seven years'* bad luck.

2 Pronunciation: 'dark *l*' 🖵

● 'Dark *l* (the variety of *l* that comes at the end of a word) is difficult for many students.
● An easy way to learn it is to start by saying /ʊ/ (as in *book*), and then to add *l* while continuing to pronounce /ʊ/. *Will, I'll* and *he'll* are almost like 'wi-ull', 'I-ull' and 'he-ull' pronounced rather quickly.
● Get the students to say the words and expressions, using the recording as a model if you wish.
● Students who find this difficult should not worry too much about it: they will be understood even if they use the wrong kind of *l* at the ends of words.

3 Discussion

● Ask students if they knew the superstitions in Exercise 1, and what they think about them. They will probably tell you that they don't believe in them.
● Ask them if they know of any other superstitions; get them to tell the class about them if possible.
● This can be a particularly interesting activity in an international class.
● Watch the pronunciation of *if*.

4 *If* or *when*?

● Go through the examples with the students, and help them see that *when* is used to talk about things that *will* happen, whereas *if* is used to talk about things that *may* or *may not* happen.
● Point out the use of present tenses to refer to the future in the *if*-clauses in the examples. (This happens in most subordinate clauses.)
● Students can do the exercise individually in writing and then discuss their answers in pairs or groups.

Answers to Exercise 4

1. *If* I *get* enough money, *I'll travel* round the world.
2. *If* it *rains* this afternoon, *we'll* stay at home.
3. *I'll close* the curtains *when* it *gets* dark.
4. *When* I *get* older, *I'll stop* playing rugby.
5. You can't go home now, but you can go *when* the game's finished.
6. Get off the bus quickly *when* it *stops*.
7. *If* you *say* that again, *I'll hit* you.
8. *When* I *go* to bed tonight, *I'll* dream about you.
9. *If* you *are* in this country next year, I hope you*'ll come* and see us.

5 Listening: 'What will happen if . . .'

• This is a simple, not very serious dramatised serial story with seven episodes.

• Students listen to each part and then try to guess what will happen next.

• Play each part one or more times, explaining difficulties if necessary, and then ask students to answer the questions in their books.

• Encourage discussion and disagreement.

Tapescript for Exercise 5: see page 127

6 Students' questions

• Give students a few minutes to prepare their questions.

• Help with vocabulary where necessary, but discourage students from using language that the others won't understand.

• When they are ready, get them to walk round asking as many people as time allows.

• Finish by getting them to report back any particularly interesting answers. You will need to help with the reported speech pattern ('*Silvia said that if she **won** a million dollars she **would** . . .* ').

Practice Book exercises

1. Irregular verbs.
2. Distinguishing between *if* and *when*.
3. Tenses in *if*-sentences referring to the future.
4. Vocabulary revision (animals).
5. Student's Cassette exercise (Student's Book Exercise 5). Students listen to the recording and do a comprehension exercise.
6. Developing dictionary skills: students read a text and choose appropriate definitions for some of the difficult words.

'Conditionals'

'Conditional' is a confusing term: it is used both for a verb form (*would* + infinitive) and for a set of sentence-patterns. Textbooks often talk about the 'first', 'second' and 'third' kinds of conditional sentence. This is rather misleading.

A more realistic analysis is as follows:

A Open conditions

In one kind of sentence with *if* (which we can call 'open conditions'), we use the tenses which are normal for the situation, whatever they are. Examples:

*If Mary **came** yesterday, she **won't come** again today.*
*If you **love** me, why **did** you **call** me a fool?*

The only restriction is that it is unusual to have *will* in the *if*-clause; after *if*, a present tense is usually used to express a future idea (as in many other kinds of subordinate clause).

*If you **come** tomorrow, I**'ll see** what I can do.*

B Hypothetical conditions

In the other kind of sentence with *if*, we use special verb-forms to stress that we are talking about something that might not happen, or might not be true. In the *if*-clause we use a past tense to talk about the present or future; in the main clause we use a modal auxiliary (usually *would*). This is the so-called 'second conditional'.

*If I **knew**, I **would tell** you.*
*If you **came** tomorrow, I **might be able** to help.*

To talk about the past (so-called 'third conditional') we use the Past Perfect tense and a 'modal perfect'.

*If you **had been** on time, we **would have** won.*

5 What will happen if . . . ? Listen to the recording and answer the questions. Useful expressions: *I think*; *I'm sure*; *certainly*; *probably*.

6 Write three questions beginning *What will you do if . . .* or *What will happen if . . .* Ask other students your questions.

Learn/revise: good/bad luck; mirror; salt; money; shoulder; sky; cat; weather; wine; baby; back; plate; game; curtain; umbrella; beginning; end; New Year; begin (began, begun); get dark; stop (stopped); play; shut (shut, shut); throw (threw, thrown); keep . . . away (kept, kept); get off; see (saw, seen); use; close; fine; dark; finished; open; quickly; again; this afternoon/evening; on holiday; if; when; about; I'm sure.

22 We don't get on well

Expressing feelings about people you know; expressing interest in what other people have to say; reported speech.

1 Use a dictionary. Read the first text; choose words to complete the second text; and put words in the blanks in the third text.

CHARANJIT
I really like my boss. She's a lovely person, very easy to work for, very fair. She always asks what I think before she changes anything. If there's a problem, we talk about it. She never gets angry. I trust her, and she trusts me. It's a pleasure to work for her.

GEORGE
I get on all right with my boss. He's sometimes a bit *interesting/ difficult* to work for, but he's *never/usually* quite fair, and he trusts me to do my job well. I *hate/like* that. On the other hand, he doesn't always realise how *much/many* time I need for some things, and he *comes/gets* angry when I haven't finished. But on the whole, I don't *know/ think* we get on too badly.

LESLEY
I hate my job, and I can't stand my .... We really don't get .... well at all. He's very .... to talk to, because he just doesn't listen. And he's not fair: he can make mistakes, and that's all right, but when I .... a mistake, he .... angry. He changes his mind about things again and again. I can't leave my job right now, but I am really fed up with that man.

2 Think of one person you know (boss/sister/ uncle *etc.*). Write four sentences about how you get on with that person. Try to use words from Exercise 1. Ask your teacher for help if you need it.

3 Work in groups. Each person reads aloud the sentences from Exercise 2; the others ask as many questions as they can. Some words you can use in your questions:

easy/difficult to talk to	listen	problems
easy/difficult to work for	fair	angry
mistakes trust realise	fed up (with)	

Example:

'Is he difficult to talk to?'

4 Write one sentence to each person in your group. Begin each sentence with one of these expressions.

I was glad to hear (that) . . .
I was interested to hear (that) . . .
I was surprised to hear (that) . . .
I was sorry to hear (that) . . .
I didn't realise (that) . . .

Examples:

'I was glad to hear that you got on well with your uncle.'
'I didn't realise that you didn't like your job.'
'I was sorry to hear that you couldn't stand your boss.'

Lesson 22

Students begin learning to express their feelings about people they know and to express interest in what other people have to say.
Principal structures: reported speech; adjective/noun plus infinitive plus preposition (e.g. *easy to talk to, a pleasure to work for*); *get* plus adjective.
Phonology: signalling a question by intonation; developing students' confidence in pronouncing sounds.

Language notes and possible problems

1. Talking about relationships Some students may be hesitant about discussing any of their relationships in class, even professional or casual ones. For these students you may want to suggest that in Exercises 2 and 3 they have the option of imagining they live or work with a famous person (film star, politician, singer, etc.).

2. Reported speech Exercises 4 and 5 give students practice in the grammar of reported statements. Reported questions are also previewed. Look out for mistakes like **Ian said he doesn't like Mrs Barker; *Ian asked Dave what does/did he think of the new boss.*

3. End-position of preposition Students have already met occasional examples of structures with prepositions at the end (e.g. *Where are you from?*). Not many languages have structures like these, and many students will find them difficult and baffling. This lesson introduces the common 'adjective + infinitive + preposition' structure, as in *She is easy to talk to* (= *It is easy to talk to her*).

4. *Get on (with), fed up (with)* Make sure students notice that *with* is only used with these expressions when there is a direct object. So: *I'm really fed up*, but *I'm really fed up with my boss.*

If you are short of time

Drop Exercise 6 if students' language(s) use(s) the same intonation rules as English. Do Exercise 5 for homework.

1 Presentation: text completion

• Present the new vocabulary, either by teaching it before the students look at the texts; by letting them use their dictionaries while working on the texts; or by getting them to ask you questions as they come up. Students can work alone or in small groups.
• You may want to point out George's use of a negative verb with a 'negative' adjective (*I **don't think** we get on too badly*), used as a weakened affirmative.

Answers to Exercise 1

GEORGE

I get on all right with my boss. He's sometimes a bit *difficult* to work for, but he's *usually* quite fair, and he trusts me to do my job well. I *like* that. On the other hand, he doesn't always realise how *much* time I need for some things, and he *gets* angry when I haven't finished. But on the whole, I don't *think* we get on too badly.

LESLEY

I hate my job, and I can't stand my *boss*. We really don't get *on* well at all. He's very *difficult* to talk to, because he just doesn't listen. And he's not fair: he can make mistakes, and that's all right, but when I *make* a mistake, he *gets* angry. He changes his mind about things again and again. I can't leave my job right now, but I am really fed up with that man.

• When you have finished checking the answers, ask the students if there are any words they would like help in pronouncing.
• A good way of helping the students become more confident about their pronunciation is this: tell them

that you will let *them* decide when they have pronounced a word satisfactorily; say the word, let them say it, and say it again; continue until they are satisfied, and try to avoid letting them know what you think of their pronunciation.

2 Practice

• Get the students each to write four sentences about how they get on with someone they know (or an imaginary person − see *Language note 1*).
• Walk round the room while the students are working to help with any problems.
• Write four sentences yourself.

3 Further practice

• Read your four sentences from the previous exercise to the class.
• Get them to look at the words in Exercise 3 and ask you questions about your relationship.
• Try to be honest; it will be more interesting for the students, and will encourage them to do the same.
• Help out with any pronunciation or grammar problems that occur as they question you.
• Divide the class into small groups and let them read their sentences to one another and ask questions.
• Walk round as the groups are working to give any help that is needed, but try not to correct mistakes that do not impede communication. You can always note down prevalent mistakes for work in a later lesson.

4 Reacting to students' sentences; reported speech

• Using one of the sentences you have overheard while walking round the classroom, say a sentence beginning with one of the four expressions given in the book, for example '*Paolo, I didn't realise that you got on well with your boss.*'
• Then write the original sentence and your sentence on the board, for example:
   I get on well with my boss.
   I didn't realise that you got on well with your boss.
• Circle the two past tenses in the second sentence, and put an arrow from the first to the second (e.g. from *didn't realise* to *got*).
• Explain that when we are talking about something that has been said or thought, if the first verb is in the past, the second one usually is as well.
• Write all five expressions on the board, and ask for a few reactions to what you said in Exercise 3. Make sure students use past tenses.
• When you are sure the students have understood, let them work in their groups once again.
• Each person in the group should write their name at the top of a piece of paper and pass it to the person on their right.
• The person on the right should write at the very bottom of the paper a sentence beginning with one of the five expressions. This should be addressed to the person whose name is at the top of the paper. When the sentence is written, the student should fold the paper up to hide the sentence, and pass it on to the next student on the right. The name will still be visible at the top of the paper.
• Students continue writing and folding until the papers arrive back at their owners, who can then read to themselves what the others had to say.
• Students can choose whether they want to share what has been written or to keep it private.

68

5 Listening

- Point out the pictures of Ian and Dave. Give students a few minutes to read the questions, and then get them to close their books and listen to the recording.
- Let them open their books again and try to find the right name, word or expression for each blank.
- Remind them that they will be using a past tense verb in the second part of each sentence.
- Play the tape again before going over the answers with them.

Tapescript for Exercise 5

DAVE: Hello, Ian. How's it going?

IAN: OK, Dave. Well, what do you think of the new boss?

DAVE: Mrs Barker? She's all right.

IAN: Yeah? I don't like her much.

DAVE: Really? Why?

IAN: Well, I don't know, she doesn't seem to trust us the way Mr Lal did. She's always looking over our shoulders. You know what I mean?

DAVE: Yeah, well, I except that's because she doesn't know us yet.

IAN: Perhaps. But, I mean, why doesn't she talk to us before she changes things? You know our lunch break is twenty minutes shorter now. Look, I'd rather come in early and keep the lunch break the same as before.

DAVE: Well, perhaps we can talk to her about it. She seems like a fair person; perhaps she just doesn't realise there's a problem.

IAN: Yeah, perhaps you're right. We can ask the others what they think.

Answers to Exercise 5

2. *Ian* said he *didn't like* Mrs Barker much.
3. *Ian* said Mrs Barker *didn't / didn't seem to* trust them.
4. *Dave* said it *was* because she *didn't know* them yet.
5. *Ian* asked why Mrs Barker *didn't talk* to them before changing things.
6. *Ian* said the lunch break *was* too short.
7. *Dave* said that Mrs Barker *seemed* like a fair person.
8. *Ian* said that they *could* ask the others what they *thought*.

6 Rising intonation for questions

- Students should already have some feeling for the difference between rising intonation (common in *yes/no* questions) and falling intonation (common in statements).
- Look over the instructions and examples.
- Demonstrate the two different intonations in the example sentences (using the recording if you wish).
- Tell students to write the ten words and expressions on a separate paper.
- Play the recording. Students should write *Q* or *S* after each expression.
- Play the recording again, so that students can change their answers if necessary.
- Let them compare notes before discussing the answers with them.

Answers to Exercise 6

fair *Q*	badly *S*
a problem *S*	fed up *Q*
all right *S*	my job *S*
difficult *Q*	too short *S*
angry *Q*	lunch break *Q*

7 Students' dialogues

- Put students into pairs and explain that they are to write short dialogues of about four lines.
- They can write about any of the things they discussed in Exercises 2 and 3, but they *must* include one short question which is not a sentence – just a word or expression like those in Exercise 6.
- Walk round while they are working to give any help that is needed.
- When students have finished, they should perform their dialogues for another pair, a group, or the whole class.
- Remind them that during their performances their voices must go up on the short question.

Practice Book exercises

1. Putting sentences in order (*easy to work with*, etc.).
2. Using vocabulary from the lesson.
3. Reported speech.
4. Student's Cassette exercise (Student's Book Exercise 6). Students listen and repeat, trying for good intonation.
5. Guided writing.
6. Past tense forms of common verbs.

Use of the mother tongue
Some time ago, language teaching theorists believed that it was quite wrong to use the mother tongue in the classroom. Fortunately, this dogma is now dying out, and most teachers realise that foreign language learning cannot completely bypass the learners' first language, especially in the early stages. Sensible use of the mother tongue, where possible, can speed up class management, and can help to make grammar and vocabulary explanations clearer and more complete. On the other hand, translation-based exercises are generally less effective than English-only exercises, and are probably best used only as quick tests or comprehension checks.

5 Who said what? What did they say? Read the sentences. Then close your books and listen to the dialogue; open your books again and try to complete the sentences. Listen again if you need to.

1. _Ian_ asked _Dave_ what he _thought_ of the new boss.
2. .... said he .... Mrs Barker much.
3. .... said Mrs Barker .... trust them.
4. .... said it .... because she .... them yet.
5. .... asked why Mrs Barker .... to them before changing things.
6. .... said the lunch break .... too short.
7. .... said that Mrs Barker .... like a fair person.
8. .... said that they .... ask the others what they ....

6 🔊 Short questions and statements. Look at these two conversations, and listen to the recording.

1. 'Well, what do you think of the new boss?'
   'Mrs Barker?'

2. 'What's the name of your new boss?'
   'Mrs Barker.'

In the first conversation, *Mrs Barker* is a question. The voice goes up: *Barker?* In the second conversation, *Mrs Barker* is a statement. The voice goes down: *Barker.*

Now listen to the words and expressions on the recording, and decide whether they are questions or statements. Copy the list, and write *Q* or *S* after the words.

fair	badly
a problem	fed up
all right	my job
difficult	too short
angry	lunch break

7 Work with a partner. Use the information from some of your sentences in Exercise 2, and write a four-line dialogue. Include one short question. Say your dialogue for another pair of students. Make sure your voice goes up on the short question!

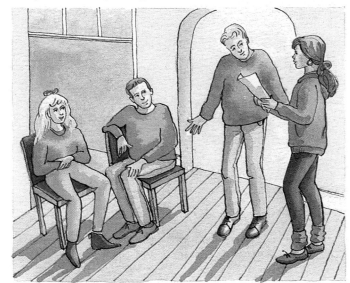

Reported speech
'I **like** my boss.'
She **said** she **liked** her boss.

I **didn't realise** that you **liked** your boss.

Learn/revise: boss; problem; pleasure; mistake; time; uncle; voice; realise; trust; seem; make (made, made); get on (with); can't stand; hate; get angry; talk (about); ask; lovely; fair; glad; surprised; sorry; angry; impossible; fed up (with); usually; sometimes; again and again; easy/interesting/difficult to work for / talk to; right now; a bit; not at all; just; anything; because; change (her) mind; do a job; make a mistake; it's a pleasure to; I was glad/interested/sorry to hear; on the other hand; What do you think of . . . ?

23 If I were you, . . .

1 Match the expressions and the pictures.

up	down	on	off	backwards
forwards	sideways	back to front
inside out	upside down

1

2

3

4

5

6

7

8

9

10

2 🔊 Listen to the dialogue. Are there any differences between the version on the recording and the version in the book?

A: If I were you, I'd turn it upside down.
B: Well, I think I'll try it this way first.
A: I mean, –
C: Hello, I wouldn't do it like that if I were you.
B: Wouldn't you?
C: No, I think you should turn it upside down.
B: Oh, really? I'll think about it.
D: Hi. Why don't you turn it sideways?
B: You think so?
D: Oh, yes, and remember to take the wheels off first.
B: Take the wheels off?
E: Hello. You've got the seat back to front.
A: You should put it up on the table, you know.
B: Well, I –
E: I think it would be much better if he turned it upside down, don't you?

A: That's just what I said.
E: You shouldn't do it with the wheels on.
C: Don't forget to put it on the table.
E: If you moved it backwards a bit, –
D: If you took the wheels off first, –
C: If you turned it upside down, it would be much easier.
A: If I were you, I'd go back to the beginning and start again.
E: I'll help you.
A: I'll help you too.
C: We'll all help him.
B: It's quite all right. I can do it by myself, thank you very much.
E: No, it's no trouble.
A: Come on, everybody.

Lesson 23

Students learn more ways of advising and persuading; they learn to talk about orientation in space.
Principal structures: hypothetical conditions (so-called 'second conditional'); *If I were you, . . .*; *should*; *Why don't you*; *remember* and *forget* + *to*-infinitive.
Phonology: consonant clusters.

Language notes and possible problems

1. 'Conditionals' See Teacher's Book notes to Lesson 21 for a general discussion of sentences with *if*. This lesson introduces 'unreal' or 'hypothetical' conditions, where a past tense is used in the *if*-clause to talk about the present or future, and a modal auxiliary (usually *would*) is used in the main clause. You will probably want to stress that this form suggests 'unreality' – it is used to indicate that something is not the case, or that something is not particularly likely to happen. You will need to make it very clear that the 'past' tense does not refer to past time here.

2. *Should* and *would* Although *should* can be used instead of *would* as a first-person conditional form, it is not introduced here. This is to avoid confusion with the other use of *should* (to advise), which also occurs in this lesson.

3. *If I were you, . . .* You will need to explain that *were* is sometimes used instead of *was* after *if*, especially in this particular expression.

4. *Remember* and *forget* Note that the infinitive is used after these verbs when the meaning is 'remember/forget that one has to do something'.

5. Consonant clusters (Exercise 4) Some languages (like Spanish or Japanese) have few consonant clusters. Students who speak these languages may have great difficulty in pronouncing groups of consonants in English – they are likely to separate the consonants unnaturally, or even put in extra vowels (pronouncing *student* as *'estudent'* or *asked* as *'askid'*, for example).

English consonants often change their pronunciation in clusters. For example, the /d/ in *shouldn't* or *wouldn't* is 'nasally exploded', and sounds quite different from the /d/ in *do*; the /d/ in *I'd turn* or *upside down* is different again (when two /d/'s or /t/'s come together, the first is unfinished or 'unexploded', and sounds more like a hesitation than a consonant); the /t/ in *don't forget* more or less disappears; and so on. Unless students are aiming at a very high standard of pronunciation, they need not worry too much about these refinements. But they should make some attempt to merge consonants together in speech instead of pronouncing them clearly separated; paradoxically, this will probably make them easier to understand.

1 Matching

• Let students do the exercise individually and then compare notes before checking with you.
• Explain the exact meanings of the expressions where necessary, and practise the pronunciation.

Answers to Exercise 1
1. backwards 2. inside out 3. sideways 4. upside down
5. off 6. up 7. back to front 8. on 9. down
10. forwards

2 Dialogue: detecting differences

• Tell students to close their books, if possible before they have a chance to look closely at the printed version of the dialogue.
• Play the recording once without stopping and then ask them what they can remember.
• Tell them to open their books and read the dialogue.
• Ask if they think this is exactly the same as the recorded version, or if there are a few differences, or a lot of differences.
• Ask if they can see any specific differences.
• Tell them to close their books and listen again; see if they can identify some more differences.
• Then let them listen while they follow the text in their books. This time they should be able to pick out virtually all the differences.
• Finally, ask what they think B is doing in the printed version. (Repairing a bicycle?)

Tapescript for Exercise 2
A: If I were you, I'd turn it *inside out*.
B: Well, I think I'll try it this way first.
A: I mean, –
C: Hello. I wouldn't do it like that if I were you.
B: Wouldn't you?
C: No, I think you should turn it *inside out*.
B: Oh, really? I'll think about it.
D: Hi. Why don't you turn it sideways?
B: You think so?
D: Oh, yes, and remember to *put* the wheels *on* first.
B: *Put* the wheels *on*?
E: Hello. You've got the seat *upside down*.
A: You should put it *down* on the *floor*, you know.
B: Well, I –
E: I think it would be much better if he turned it *inside out*, don't you?
A: That's just what I said.
E: You shouldn't do it with the wheels *off*.
C: Don't forget to put it on the *floor*.
E: If you moved it *forwards* a bit, –
D: If you *put* the wheels *on* first, –
C: If you turned it *inside out*, it would be much easier.
A: If I were you, I'd go back to the beginning and start again.
E: I'll help you.
A: I'll help you too.
C: We'll all help him.
B: It's quite all right. I can do it by myself, thank you very much.
E: No, it's no trouble.
A: Come on, everybody.

70

3 Students choose items to learn

• Give students plenty of time to look through the dialogue and ask you questions.
• Leave them free to make their own decisions as to what items they want to learn.
• When students are ready, let them compare notes.
• They may want to add things to their lists after they have seen what other students have chosen.

4 Consonant clusters: fluency practice

• Practise the words and expressions, using the recording as a guide if you wish. Concentrate on getting the students to pronounce the consonant clusters naturally, so that the consonants merge into each other.
• Then ask each student to choose a sentence from the dialogue and say it to you.
• One useful correction technique is to simply repeat the sentences after the students without comment; they should try to hear whether there is any important difference between your version and their own.
• Let students say sentences as many times as they want to (with you repeating them) until they are satisfied.

5 Conditional: practice of forms

• Look at the examples and give whatever explanations are needed. (See *Language notes*.)
• The exercise can be done individually or by class discussion, as you wish, but students should write at least one of the answers individually.

Answers to Exercise 5

1. If John *were* here, he *would know* what to do.
2. Do you think it *would* be a good idea if I *phoned* the police?
3. What *would* you do if you *won* a million pounds?
4. If I *had* more time I *would learn* either karate or judo.
5. What *would* you say if I *asked* you to marry me?
6. If you *changed* your job, what *would* you do?
7. If today *were* Sunday I *would be* in bed.
8. I *would go* and see Jake tomorrow if I *knew* his address.

6 *If-chains*

• Look through the example with the students. Explain any difficulties, and make sure they see how the 'chain' works (the end of one sentence gives the start of the next).
• Students can make up their own chains individually or in groups. One good way to do the exercise is to have the chains go round the class: each student writes the first sentence and then passes his/her paper on to another student, who writes the next sentence and passes it on, and so on.

7 Speeches

• Give students ten minutes or so to collect ideas for their speeches.
• They will probably need help with vocabulary, but they should not use a lot of expressions that the rest of the class will not understand.
• Let them make notes if they want to, but discourage them from writing out complete scripts.
• When they are ready, put them in groups of four or so. Each student in turn should make his or her speech to the group.
• When they have finished, each group should choose the most persuasive speech to be repeated to the whole class.
• Don't make corrections while students are making their speeches, but note mistakes for future treatment if necessary.
• Alternatively, your students may prefer to do this as a one-to-one exercise, with each student walking round and trying to convince as many other individuals as possible.

Optional activity: sketch

• This can be done as an alternative to Exercise 7.
• In groups of four or five, students prepare sketches like the dialogue in Exercise 2.
• One of the students is trying to do something; he/she mimes the actions. The others give advice. The class watch and listen, and have to guess what the first student is doing.
• (Some ideas: washing an elephant; putting up a tent; getting a piano upstairs; dressing a child; getting a big dog into a car.)

Practice Book exercises

1. Past and conditional verbs in *if*-sentences.
2. *Should* or *would*?
3. Vocabulary practice: finding mistakes in a picture.
4. Student's Cassette exercise (Student's Book Exercise 2). Students practise pronunciation, and try to find all the differences between the recorded and printed versions of the dialogue.
5. Vocabulary and grammar: completing a text.
6. Guided writing: using lesson material in a letter.

Creative activities: discussion, role play, etc.
These activities are particularly important both pedagogically and psychologically. Students probably do not assimilate new material very effectively until they are given a chance to use it themselves to express their own ideas. So it is at the 'free use' stage of a lesson that most of the learning is likely to take place. And it is very motivating for students if they can use their English from time to time to say interesting or amusing things – if they can inform, entertain, surprise or move each other by their use of language.

Some students like 'role' communication, and may indeed be more articulate when acting a part than when expressing their own views and feelings. (Shy people are sometimes 'liberated' by this kind of activity.) Other students prefer to be themselves, and do best in exercises where they can say what they really think. It is important to choose exercises that are suitable for both kinds of personality, and to remember that there is not necessarily something wrong if some of one's students are unenthusiastic about role play or if others don't want to talk about themselves.

Correction is generally out of place in creative exercises.

3 Look through the dialogue and write down some useful expressions and structures to learn. Exchange lists with one or more other students and see if you have thought of the same expressions.

4 Fluency practice. Practise the following words and expressions. Then choose a sentence from the dialogue and practise saying it. Try for accurate intonation and rhythm.

turned   don't   don't forget
it's   it's no trouble
that's   that's just   that's just what I said
wouldn't wouldn't do   wouldn't you
shouldn't shouldn't do it
I'd   I'd turn   upside down

5 Look at the examples and then complete the sentences.

If you **turned** it upside down, it **would be** much easier.
If I **were** you, **I'd turn** it upside down.
It **would be** better if he **turned** it back to front.
I **wouldn't do** it like that if I **were** you.

1. If John (*were / would be*) here, he (*knew / would know*) what to do.
2. Do you think it (*were / would be*) a good idea if I (*phoned / would phone*) the police?
3. What (*did / would*) you do if you (*won / would win*) a million pounds?
4. If I (*had / would have*) more time I (*learnt / would learn*) either karate or judo.
5. What (*did / would*) you say if I (*asked / would ask*) you to marry me?
6. If you (*changed / would change*) your job, what (*did / would*) you do?
7. If today (*were / would be*) Sunday I (*were / would be*) in bed.
8. I (*went / would go*) and see Jake tomorrow if I (*knew / would know*) his address.

6 Read the sentences, and then write a similar '*if-chain*' yourself. Start '*If I won a million dollars . . .*'

If I won a million dollars, I would buy a fast car.
If I bought a fast car, I would probably drive it too fast.
If I drove it too fast, perhaps I would have an accident.
If I had an accident, I would go to hospital.
If I went to hospital, perhaps I would meet a beautiful nurse and fall in love with her.
If she fell in love with me, we would get married.
If we got married, we would be very happy at the beginning.
But then, perhaps I would meet somebody else.
If I met somebody else, . . .
etc.

7 Prepare a short speech (maximum two minutes). In your speech, you must try to make other students do something. For example: stop studying English; leave the room; give up smoking; become vegetarians; change their religion; give you a lot of money; buy you a car; change their jobs. Useful expressions:

If I were you, I'd . . .
It would be better if you . . .
Why don't you . . . ?
Don't forget to . . .
Remember to . . .
You (really) should . . .
I think you should either . . . or . . .

IF + PAST,	WOULD + INFINITIVE
If he **knew,**	he **would tell** us.
If I **won** $1,000,000,	I **would buy** a fast car.
If I **were** you,	I **wouldn't do** that.
If today **was/were** Sunday,	I **would be** in bed.

Learn/revise: wheel; accident; hospital; nurse; religion; table; time; address; the police; up; down; on; off; take off (took, taken); start; move; marry; get married; drive (drove, driven); go back; help; fall in love with (fell, fallen); should; everybody; first; by myself; this way; backwards; forwards; sideways; back to front; inside out; upside down; all; either . . . or; I mean; you know; a good idea; It's no trouble; Why don't you . . . ?; I'll think about it; Come on; Remember to . . . ; Don't forget to . . .

24 How about Thursday?

Making appointments; Present Progressive with future meaning; time prepositions.

1 Here are the beginnings and ends of three conversations. Find which beginning goes with which end, and put *in*, *on*, *at* and *until* into the gaps.

1

'Parkhurst 7298.'
'Hello, Paul.'
'Hello. Who's that?'
'This is Audrey. Are you free today?'
'It depends. What time?'

2

'Hello, John. This is Angela. I'm trying to fix the Directors' meeting. Can you tell me what days you're free next week?'
'Well, let me see. Monday morning's OK. Tuesday. Not Wednesday, I'm going to Cardiff .... the morning. Thursday afternoon, I think. Friday's a bit difficult.'
'How about Thursday .... two fifteen?'
'Tuesday two fifteen. Let me look in my diary.'

3

'Hello. I'd like to make an appointment to see Dr Gray.'
'Yes. What name is it, please?'
'Simon Graftey.'
'Yes. Monday .... three o'clock, Mr Graftey?'
'Three o'clock's difficult. I'm working ....
a quarter to three. Could it be later?'

A

'No, Thursday.'
'Oh, I'm sorry, I thought you said Tuesday. Thursday two fifteen. Yes, that's fine.'
'All right. See you then.'
'See you .... Thursday. Bye.'
'Bye.'

B

'............... the afternoon. My mother's coming down, and I'd like you to meet her. About half past four?'
'Half past four's difficult.'
'What about earlier? Say, two?'
'Yes, OK. I'll come round .... two. Your place?'
'My place.'
'OK. See you .... a couple of hours.'
'See you then. Bye.'
'Bye.'

C

'Three thirty?'
'Yes, that's all right. Three thirty .... Monday, then. Thanks very much. Goodbye.'
'Goodbye.'

Lesson 24

Students learn more about making appointments, and revise the conventions for talking on the phone.
Principal structures: use of Present Progressive to refer to the future; revision of time prepositions.
Phonology: stress and rhythm.

Language notes and possible problems
Present Progressive with future meaning   We often use present tenses to talk about future events which are already planned, arranged, or certain to happen. The use of *is going to* has already been revised. Here, students revise the future use of the Present Progressive (as in *My mother's coming down*; *I'm going to Cardiff*). This is particularly common with time expressions, or when it is clear exactly when something is happening. (See the dialogues in Exercise 1 for examples.)

   Note that the Simple Present is rarely used to talk about the future, except in talking about timetables (e.g. *The train leaves at 4.13*).

If you are short of time
Drop Exercise 3 if your students find English stress and rhythm easy; drop Exercise 4.

1   Beginnings and ends of conversations

• This is an easy exercise: the purpose is simply to get students reading the conversations and thinking about what they mean. At the same time, they do some simple revision of time prepositions.
• Get students to do the exercise individually and then compare notes.

Answers to Exercise 1
1B, 2A, 3C
in the morning; *at* two fifteen; *at* three o'clock; *until* a quarter to three; *on* Thursday; *in* the afternoon; *at* two; *in* a couple of hours; *on* Monday

2 Language study

- Play the recording of the conversations.
- Then let students look through the texts for examples of the listed structures.
- Encourage them to think about the use of the structures themselves, asking questions if necessary.
- Then give whatever explanations you feel are needed.
- Next, ask students to choose ten more items from the text to learn.
- When they have done this, let them compare notes and see if they have made the same choices as other students.
- Answer any questions they may have about their chosen items.

3 Stress and rhythm

- This exercise works well in groups of three or four.
- Get students to copy each sentence and mark where they think the main stresses come.
- Then play the sentence and discuss the answer.
- Help students to see what kinds of words are stressed (nouns, verbs, adjectives and adverbs, but not usually pronouns, prepositions, articles or conjunctions, especially when they have one syllable). An auxiliary verb is not usually stressed if it is next to a main verb; in other positions, it may be stressed (e.g. **Could** it be **later?**).
- It is possible to identify several different degrees of stress, and the relationship between stress and intonation is complex. For the sake of simplicity, students are only asked here to identify the most prominent syllables.

Answers to Exercise 3
(Each sentence can of course be stressed in different ways in different contexts. Typical 'neutral' stress patterns are shown here.)
I'd **like** you to **meet** her.
I'm **trying** to **fix** the **Directors'** **meeting**.
Friday's a **bit difficult**.
Let me **look** in my **diary**.
I **thought** you said **Tuesday**.
I'd **like** to **make** an ap**point**ment.
Could it be **later?**

4 Practising the dialogues

- Get students to spend a few minutes practising one or more of the conversations in pairs.
- You may wish to play the recording to provide a model.

5 Diaries

- Get students to copy the diary pages, and to note the times and days when they plan to do their chosen activities.
- They should fill up most of their time (so that they only have three or four hours free).

6 Making arrangements

- Before starting the exercise, you may like to revise the various conventional expressions which we use when telephoning:
  Could I speak to . . . ?
  Speaking
  Who's that?
  This is . . .
  Can I take a message . . . ?
- Remind students that British people tend to answer the phone by giving their number. Note also the use of *that* to refer to the person at the 'other end', and *this* to refer to oneself, as in conversation 1. (Americans use *this* for both.)
- Put students in pairs. The students in each pair should be some distance apart.
- One student in each pair (for instance the one on your left, or the one nearest you) must think of some activity that he or she wants to do with the other student at the weekend.
- Ask a good student to 'telephone' his or her partner and try to arrange something (or demonstrate with a good student yourself).
- When the conversation is finished, ask the class to suggest other expressions that could have been used.
- Then tell the other pairs to improvise in the same way, taking turns. (Or put them back to back and let them work simultaneously.)
- If time allows, get students to try their conversations two or three times, getting in more and more of the expressions listed in the Student's Book.
- If students find it too difficult to do the exercise by improvising, let them prepare their conversations in pairs before you separate them.

Practice Book exercises
1. Revision of lesson material: completing a dialogue.
2. Prepositions of time.
3. *Take* + object + expression of time.
4. Vocabulary revision and extension. Appliances, machines and household objects.
5. Student's Cassette exercise (Student's Book Exercise 2, first conversation). Pronunciation practice.
6. Writing about future plans.

2 🎧 Listen to the conversations. Then look at the text and see how these words and structures are used. Ask your teacher for explanations if necessary.

1. Present Progressive tense with future meaning (e.g. *My mother's coming down*).
2. *How/What about . . . ?* in suggestions.
3. *I'd like to . . .*
4. *I'd like you to . . .*
5. *I'll . . .* (offering or agreeing to do something).

Write down ten more useful words, expressions or structures to learn. Can you find any other students who have chosen the same expressions as you?

3 How many stresses? Where are they? Listen to the recording to check your answers.

I'd like you to meet her.
I'm trying to fix the Directors' meeting.
Friday's a bit difficult.
Let me look in my diary.
I thought you said Tuesday.
I'd like to make an appointment.
Could it be later?

4 Practise one of the conversations with another student.

5 Fill in your diary for Saturday and Sunday. Put in at least eight of the following activities (and any others that you want to add), but leave yourself some free time.

wash your hair   write to your mother   play tennis   buy a sweater
see a film   go to a party   have a drink with a friend
clean the kitchen   mend some clothes   practise the guitar
study English grammar   do your ironing   make a cake   wash the car
go to church   go to see your sister   do some gardening

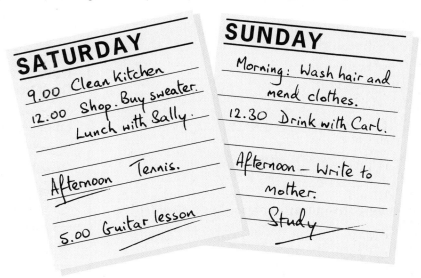

6 'Telephone' another student. Try to arrange to do something together at the weekend. Use some of the following expressions.

Who's that?
This is . . .
Are you free on . . .
It depends.
about . . .
I'm trying to fix . . .
I'd like you to meet . . .
Can you tell me . . . ?

a bit difficult
Let me look in my diary.
I'm . . .ing
Could it be earlier/later?
What/How about . . . ?
I thought you said . . .
See you then.
I'll . . .

Hello, Ann. Are you free on Sunday?

It depends. What time?

About three o'clock?

That's difficult. I'm playing tennis. What about later?

Learn/revise: conversation; meeting; diary; appointment; make an appointment; church; go to church; film; sweater; ironing; gardening; a couple of (hours); my/your place; friend; party; depend; It depends; wash; buy (bought, bought); write to somebody (wrote, written); clean; mend; practise; have a drink; meet (met, met); free; difficult; earlier; later; about; until; which; This is . . . ; Who's that?; Let me see; Let me look; How/What about . . . ?; I'd like you to . . . ; See you then; I thought you said . . . ; make a cake (made, made).

Summary D

Structures used to talk about the future

Will + infinitive without *to*

I will (I'll) arrive
you will (you'll) arrive
he/she/it will (he'll *etc*.) arrive
we will (we'll) arrive
you will (you'll) arrive
they will (they'll) arrive

will I arrive?
will you arrive?
etc.

I will not (won't) arrive
you will not (won't) arrive
etc.

Be going + *to*-infinitive

I am (I'm) going to arrive
you are (you're) going to arrive
etc.

am I going to arrive?
are you going to arrive?
etc.

I am not (I'm not) going to arrive
you are not (you're not / you aren't) going
    to arrive
etc.

Present Progressive tense

I am (I'm) arriving
you are (you're) arriving
etc.

am I arriving?
are you arriving?
etc.

I am not (I'm not) arriving
you are not (you're not / you aren't) arriving
etc.

Talking about the future: predictions with *will*

You **will** have a long and interesting life.
My children certainly **won't** speak English.
I hope my children **will** be good-looking.
I don't think my children **will** be tall.

Will be able + infinitive
Our grandchildren **will be able to go** to the moon for
the weekend. (~~Our grandchildren will can . . .~~)

Talking about the future: *be going to*

Predictions
We're **going to** crash!
It's **going to** rain.

Plans and intentions
We're **going to** take ten litres of water.
I'm **not going to** do any work tomorrow.

Future arrangements: the Present Progressive tense

My mother's **coming** down.
I'm going to Cardiff in the morning.

Predictions with *may*

Carol and Lee's baby **may** be tall.
My children **may** be musical.

'll: agreeing and offering

I'll help you.
OK. I'll come round at two.

If: future possibilities

IF + PRESENT,	WILL + INFINITIVE
If you **are** both tall,	your children **will be** tall.
If you **see** a black cat, (~~If you will see . . .~~)	you'll **have** good luck.
If I **get** rich, (~~If I will get . . .~~)	I'll **travel** round the world.

WILL + INFINITIVE	IF + PRESENT
You **won't find** a job	if you **don't study** now.
I'll **move** to Canada	if I **can** get a visa.

If and *when*

If I get enough money, I'll travel round the world.
    (= I may get enough money.)
When I get older, I'll stop playing rugby.
    (= I will get older.)
When I get tired, I'll go to bed.
    (~~When I will get tired . . .~~)

Summary D

Summary of language taught in Lessons 19–24.

This lesson displays most of the more important language points that students should have learnt or revised in the last six lessons. Spend a short time going over the material with the students, answering questions and clearing up any difficulties. Students may also need to spend time at home making sure everything is thoroughly learnt.

Practice Book exercises
1. Word stress.
2. *When*-clauses.
3. Formation of regular past tenses.
4. Prepositions.
5. Translation of material from Lessons 19–24.
6. Writing about plans with *going to*.

Conditional verb forms

I would (I'd) go you would (you'd) go *etc.*
would I go? would you go? *etc.*
I would not (wouldn't) go you would not (wouldn't) go *etc.*

If: unreal and improbable situations

IF + PAST,	WOULD + INFINITIVE
If he **knew,**	he **would tell** us.
If I **won** $1,000,000,	I **would buy** a fast car.

WOULD + INFINITIVE	IF + PAST
I **wouldn't do** that	**if** I **were** you.
I **would be** in bed	**if** today **was/were** Sunday.

Reported speech

'You **will** never get married.'
Maria **said** (that) I **would** never get married.

'We**'re** going to take ten litres of water.'
They **said** (that) they **were** going to take . . .

'I **like** my boss.'
She **said** (that) she **liked** her boss.

I **didn't** realise (that) you **liked** your boss.

'What do you think of the new boss?'
Ian **asked** Dave what he **thought** of the new boss.

Have (got) + infinitive

You**'ve got to keep** calm.
We**'ve got to keep** the weight down.
Our children **will have to work** two days a week.

either . . . or

Their children may **either** have blue eyes **or** brown eyes.
If I had more time I would learn **either** karate **or** judo.

Adjective + infinitive

I was **glad to hear** that you got on well with your uncle.
I was **sorry to hear** that you couldn't stand your boss.
I was **interested/surprised to hear** . . .

Adjective + infinitive + preposition

She's **easy to work for.**
My boss is **difficult to talk to.**

Nobody

Nobody is going to die.
(Nobody are . . .)

Prepositions of time

I'm going to Cardiff **in** the morning.
The meeting's **on** Thursday **at** 2.15.
I'm working **until** a quarter to three.
See you **in** a couple of hours.

Making appointments

Are you free on . . . ?
It depends.
I'm trying to fix . . .
I'd like to make an appointment.
I'd like you to meet . . .
Let me look in my diary.
Tuesday's a bit difficult.
What/How about Tuesday?
Could it be earlier/later?
See you then.

Discussion: opinions and advice

I think we **should** take a lot of water.
You **shouldn't** do it with the wheels on.
Why don't you turn it sideways?
Don't forget to put it on the table.
Remember to take the wheels off first.
It would be better to turn it upside down.
I agree. (I am agree.)
I don't agree.

Intonation of short questions and statements

– Question

'Well, what do you think of the new boss?'
'Mrs Barker?'

– Statement

'What's the name of your new boss?'
'Mrs Barker.'

Revision D

Look at the exercises, decide which ones are useful to you, and do two or more.

GRAMMAR

1 Here is the beginning of a song. (If you want to hear it, do Listening Exercise 3.) Can you report the singer's words?

It's a rainy Sunday morning and I don't know
  what to do.
If I stay in bed all day, I'll only think about you.
If I try to study, I won't learn anything new,
And if I go for a walk on my own in the park,
I'll probably catch the flu!

*'According to the singer, it was a rainy Sunday
morning and he . . .'*

2 Which sentence-beginning is better?

1. a. If I become President, I will . . .
   b. If I became President, I would . . .
   Answer: *b* (because you probably won't
       become President)
2. a. If I feel tired tomorrow, I'll . . .
   b. If I felt tired tomorrow, I'd . . .
   Answer: *a* (because you may feel tired
       tomorrow)
3. a. If I live to be 120, I'll . . .
   b. If I lived to be 120, I'd . . .
4. a. If I break my leg next week, I'll . . .
   b. If I broke my leg next week, I'd . . .
5. a. If people stop fighting, the world will be . . .
   b. If people stopped fighting, the world would
       be . . .
6. a. If it snows tomorrow, I'll . . .
   b. If it snowed tomorrow, I'd . . .
7. a. If I become rich and famous, will you . . . ?
   b. If I became rich and famous, would you . . . ?
8. a. If I learn to speak English perfectly, I'll . . .
   b. If I learnt to speak English perfectly, I'd . . .
9. a. If I buy a really fast car, I'll . . .
   b. If I bought a really fast car, I'd . . .
10. a. If the world ends tomorrow, I won't . . .
    b. If the world ended tomorrow, I wouldn't . . .

3 Here are the beginning and end of an 'if-chain' like the one in Lesson 23, Exercise 6. Can you fill in the middle? (Make 6–10 sentences.)

If I could do anything I wanted, I would . . .
. . . , I would keep it for ever.

4 The difference between *will* and *going to*. Look at the rules and examples, using a dictionary if necessary. Then do the exercise.

– We use *am/are/is going to* when we can already
   see the future in the present – when future actions
   are beginning to happen, or are already planned.
   Examples:
       Alice **is going to** have a baby.
       It's **going to** rain.
       We're **going to** buy a new car soon.
– We use *will* when we predict future actions by
   thinking, hoping or calculating. Examples:
       Alice's baby **will** have blue eyes, and it **will**
       probably have fair hair.
       She hopes it **will** be a girl.

Will or *going to*?

1. Look out! *We'll / We're going to* crash!
2. I hope one day *I'll / I'm going to* have more free
   time.
3. *Mary'll / Mary's going to* marry an old friend of
   mine in August.
4. I can't talk to you now. *We'll just / We're just
   going to* have lunch.
5. Perhaps in a few hundred years everybody *will / is
   going to* have an easier life.
6. 'What are your plans for this evening?'   'I'll / I'm
   going to* stay at home and watch TV.'
7. 'John's starting university in October.' 'Oh, yes?
   What will he / What's he going to study?'
8. If you and your husband both have green eyes,
   your children *will probably / are probably going
   to* have green eyes too.

LISTENING

1 What will the weather be like? Copy the table. Then listen to Wednesday morning's weather forecast and complete it.

	warm? hot? cooler?	sunshine?	thundery showers or storms?
Wednesday afternoon			20% chance
Wednesday night		–	
Thursday			a few
Friday		?	

76

Revision D

Students and teacher choose grammar, listening, vocabulary, pronunciation, writing and speaking exercises.

Note: choice
Ask students which exercises seem most useful. If necessary, groups can work on different exercises.

Optional extra materials
Cards for the optional grammar activity after Exercise 3.

GRAMMAR

1 Reported speech
- This exercise briefly revises the reported speech structures that students have seen so far.
- It can be done individually or in groups.

Answer to Exercise 1

(Answers can be organised in different ways, but tenses must be right. Past tenses and *would* here indicate reported speech; they do not have the same 'hypothetical' meaning as in Exercises 2 and 3.)

According to the singer, it *was* a rainy Sunday morning and he *did not know* what to do. If he *stayed* in bed all day, he *would* only think about his girlfriend. If he *tried* to study, he *would not learn* anything new. And he felt that if he *went* for a walk on his own in the park, he *would* probably *catch* (the) flu.

2 Open and hypothetical conditionals
- Remind students that 'past' tenses (e.g. *If I became President . . .*) may express unreality, not past time.
- Look over the first two pairs and make sure students understand the reasons for the choice of structure.
- Then continue by class or group discussion.
- Answers will depend on individual circumstances.

3 If-chain
- Look at the 'if-chain' in Lesson 23, Exercise 6.
- In pairs or groups, students should find a plausible way of linking the beginning and the end of the chain.
- Finish by getting students to read out their chains.

Optional activity: beginnings and ends
- Write half-sentences (see below) on cards or slips of paper; give them to students to learn.
- Then get them to walk round saying their half-sentences and looking for their 'other halves'.
- Note that alternative combinations are possible.

Half-sentences
If you heat ice   it changes into water.
If it rains this afternoon   I'm going to stay at home.
If you're going to the shop   could you get some carrots?
If you go to the US   you may need a visa.
If you buy me a drink   I'll buy you one tomorrow.
If anybody telephones   tell them I'm not at home.
If you love me   why did you call me a fool?
If you ever go to Australia   you must go and see my brother in Melbourne.
If you drop this glass   it won't break.
If you make coffee   I'd like some.
If you stayed up late last night   you must be tired.

4 Will and *be going to*
- Explain the rules in the students' language or get them to read the rules with dictionaries.
- Let students do some of the exercise in writing, so that you can pick out anybody who is having trouble.

Answers to Exercise 4
1. We're going to   2. I'll   3. Mary's going to
4. We're just going to   5. will   6. 'I'm going to
7. What's he going to   8. will probably (have)

Optional activity: *going to*
- Students do mimes showing that they are going to do something. The class has to decide what.

Optional activities: *will*
1. Students can predict tomorrow's weather or the results of football matches or other sporting events. In the next lesson, see who was right.
2. Organise an arm-wrestling tournament or some other contest in the class; students predict the winner.

LISTENING

1 The weather
- Go over the table with the students and make sure they understand all the terms.
- They should also understand that they will hear Wednesday morning's forecast.
- Get them to copy the table.
- Play the recording once through while they try to fill in the table.
- Then play it again, pausing at appropriate points, for them to check/complete their answers.
- When you go over the answers with them, you may want to play the recording again.

Answers and tapescript to Exercise 1

	warm? hot? cooler?	sunshine?	thundery showers or storms?
Wednesday afternoon	*hot*	*yes*	*20% chance*
Wednesday night	*warm*	*–*	*20% chance*
Thursday	*hot*	*yes*	*a few*
Friday	*cool*	*?*	*30% chance*

It's gonna be hot and humid this afternoon, spells of hazy sunshine, 20% chance of a thunderstorm during the late afternoon and evening. Temperature high, 27 Celsius, 81 Fahrenheit. Tonight warm and humid, 20% chance of thundery showers, minimum temperature down to 14 Celsius, 57 Fahrenheit. The winds will be light and variable. On Thursday expect a few thundery showers; little change, really, to today. Friday there's going to be a fair bit of change. It'll be a little cooler and cloudier, 30% chance of a thundery shower. Current temperature 21 Celsius, 68 Fahrenheit and rising.

2 If and imperatives
- Students try to obey conditional instructions.
- The instructions get harder as the exercise goes on.

Tapescript for Exercise 2: see page 128

Listening Exercise 2: see page 76

Optional extension
- In groups, students write four or five instructions with *if*, including at least one with *don't*.
- They give their instructions to other groups.

3 Song: *Song For A Rainy Sunday*
- The song is recorded twice, the second time with gaps. (The words are on Student's Book page 124.)
- Play the first version while students listen to it.
- Then ask them to tell you any words they remember; you may want to put these on the board.
- Tell them they will hear the song again with gaps; they must try to remember the missing words.
- Pause at each gap for students to say the word; or play right through once while students write the missing words, and then again while they say them.
- Let them look at the words in their books as you play the complete version a last time.

VOCABULARY

1 **What's wrong with the pictures?**
- Ask students to write their answers to some of the problems; others can be done by discussion.
- Answers can be expressed in various ways, using vocabulary and structures that the students have met. Encourage the use of *should(n't)*.

PRONUNCIATION

1 **Spellings of /ɜː/**
- Students may not realise that words like *bird*, *burn* and *word* have the same vowel; they may also find this vowel difficult to pronounce correctly.
- Give them a few minutes to discuss the question.
- Then pronounce the words (or play the recording), letting them change their answers if they wish.
- Then check whether they have found the right three words (*fire*, *hear* and *heart*).
- Finally, practise the words with /ɜː/.

2 **/eə/, /ɪə/ and /ɜː/**
- Many students find it difficult to distinguish these three vowels.
- The exercise can be done like the last one.

Answers to Exercise 2
/eə/: chair, fair, hair, there, their, they're, where.
/ɪə/: dear, hear, here, we're.
/ɜː/ (weak form /ə/): her, were.

WRITING

1 **Semi-controlled composition**
- Weaker students should stick fairly closely to the model given in Lesson 22. Stronger students can write more freely, but should still be encouraged to use structures and vocabulary from the model.
- Students should produce at least one paragraph.

SPEAKING

1 **The *yes/no* game**
- This game practises short answer forms.
- Students answer as many questions as possible in one minute without saying *yes* or *no*, or nodding or shaking their heads. (Anybody who does is out.)
- Possible answers: *I am, I do, it is, she will*, etc.

- Explain the rules and demonstrate with volunteers. (Suggested example questions are given below.)
- After one or two volunteers have tried it out, get groups to prepare lists of questions.
- A good way to play is to get students from group A to go to group B to be questioned, and vice versa.
- In each group, one student should time each session and one should count the questions answered.
- The winner is the student who answers the most questions.
- Finish by having the whole class question you.
Useful tricks:
1. Ask several questions about the same subject and then throw in a question that looks as if it's 'outside the game' (e.g. *'Am I speaking too fast?'*).
2. Ask a question-word question (e.g. *'How old are you?'*), and reply to the student's answer by repeating it as if asking for confirmation (e.g. *'Twenty-three?'*).
3. Use a question tag (e.g. *'Warm, isn't it?'*).

Demonstration questions

Are you ready?	Are you married?
Do you like speaking English?	Have you got any children?
How old are you?	*How* many?
Did you say twenty?	Four?
Really?	It's cold today, isn't it?
Have you got a watch?	Aren't you cold?
You have?	Can you sing?
Am I speaking too fast?	Sing us a song.
Are you nervous?	Go on.
Do you like driving?	Would you like to?
You haven't got a car, have you?	Are you sure?
	No?
How did you come to school?	Do you smoke?
I beg your pardon – by bus?	Never?
How much did the ticket cost?	How many?
Really?	Twenty?
	This is difficult, isn't it?
Would you like to have a lot of money?	Do you think you can go on for one minute?
It's difficult to answer without saying *yes* and *no*, isn't it?	Look – you see this paper? Can you see this word here?

2 **Sketch**
- Students should be used to this activity by now, and it may be unnecessary to give detailed instructions.
- The sketch may take some time to prepare, particularly if students learn their parts by heart. However, the results should justify the time spent.
- If groups have trouble starting because of the wide choice given, help them make decisions.

Practice Book exercises
1. Tenses in time clauses.
2. *When* and *until*.
3. Vocabulary revision: 'odd word out'.
4. Student's Cassette exercise (Student's Book Listening Exercise 3, full version of song). Students try to write down the first verse.
5. Recreational reading: *Strange but true!*
6. Crossword.

Additional reading
Note that students have now reached a level where they should be able to cope comfortably with the texts in Sections A–D of *Additional reading* in the Practice Book (pages 108 to 111). You can set some of the readings for homework or just suggest that students read any of the texts that interest them when they have the time.

2 Listen to the recording and do what the speakers tell you. (Make sure you know these words: *circle*; *square*; *stamp*; *floor*; *mouth*.)

3 🔊 Listen to the song once. Then listen again and try to remember the words that have been left out. The complete song is on page 124.

VOCABULARY

1 What's wrong with the pictures? Examples:
'The elephant's ears are too small.' OR:
'The elephant's ears should be bigger.'

PRONUNCIATION

1 All except three of these words have the same vowel (/ɜː/). Which three are different?

bird   burn   early   fire   first   hear   heard
heart   hurt   learn   shirt   third   turn
word   world   worst

2 Can you divide these words into three groups according to their pronunciation?

chair   dear   fair   hair   hear   her   here
there   their   they're   were   we're   where

WRITING

1 Read Lesson 22, Exercise 1 again. Then write about how you get on with one of the following: your boss; your teacher; your landlord/landlady; the person who is sitting next to you in class; one of your family; your boyfriend/girlfriend/lover.

SPEAKING

1 The *yes/no* game. Work in groups. One person has to answer questions for one minute; the others ask him or her as many questions as possible. The person who answers must not say *yes* or *no*.

2 Prepare and practise a sketch with two or three other students. In your sketch, you must have:
– a visitor (this can be a person, an animal or a creature from another world);
– a problem (for example somebody is ill; there isn't enough money; something is lost; somebody doesn't understand; somebody is unhappy; something is broken);
– four or more of the following sentences.

That's not my grandfather.
I thought you said 'parrot'.
I'd like to make an appointment.
I can do it by myself, thank you.
Don't forget to give me the keys.
You shouldn't do things like that.
If I were you, I'd go home.
They have all gone to the North Pole.

I hope so.
What's she like?
It's upside down.
I don't agree.
I'm terribly sorry.

Test D

LISTENING

1 Listen to the recording and write what will happen:

1. if you break a mirror.
2. if you put an umbrella up in the house.
3. if you see three magpies (black and white birds).
4. if you see four magpies.
5. if you put a hat on a bed.
6. if you put two teaspoons in a saucer with your cup.
7. if you mention the name Macbeth in a theatre.

a mirror

a magpie

an umbrella

GRAMMAR

1 Put in the right form of the verb.

1. Something very strange .... yesterday while we .... breakfast. (*happen*; *have*)
2. .... you ever .... *Gone with the Wind*? (*see*)
3. I don't want to go for a walk – it .... (*rain*)
4. I'll come and see you if I .... time. (*have*)
5. If I .... you, I would take a holiday. (*be*)
6. I .... English since last May. (*study*)
7. I didn't know you .... a doctor. (*be*)
8. I'm going to London tomorrow .... some shopping. (*do*)
9. Why don't you .... me the truth? (*tell*)
10. Let's .... a party. (*have*)
11. Somebody should .... Mary. (*help*)

2 Choose the correct form.

1. Look out! *We'll / We're going to* crash!
2. 'I'm thirsty.' 'I'll / I'm going to make you some tea if you like.'
3. 'What *will you do / are you doing* this evening?' 'I'll see / I'm seeing Peter and Ann.'
4. *If / When* I ever get rich I'll buy my mother a house.

3 Put the words in the right order.

1. children doing those are what ?
2. my piano very plays sister the well .
3. Europe his are both travelling boss in and my secretary .
4. for is to very good boss my work .
5. Italian badly very speak I .

Test D

The purpose of the test

This test covers material from Lessons 19–24. It is not of course necessary to do all of the sections, and teachers should select according to their students' needs. Teachers who do not feel the test will be useful should simply drop it altogether.

If possible, try to make the students feel that they are 'testing themselves', rather than 'being tested'. It is not intended that students should 'pass' or 'fail' the test, and it is not particularly useful to give marks. (If the school or education system requires that this be done, you will need to work out a simple marking scheme.) But students should of course be told whether you feel their performance is satisfactory. In principle, students who have worked systematically through Lessons 19–24 ought to get most answers right.

Administration

The test can be administered in various ways, depending on how strictly you want to control students' performance; whether you want to collect the answers and mark them, or allow the students to correct them in class; and so on.

For the 'speaking' test, students will need to interrupt their work on the other questions to come and talk to you. Both questions need preparation (which can be done out of class if you wish); the second question can be done individually or in pairs as you prefer.

If you do not collect students' scripts, correction can be done by class discussion when everybody has finished.

Notes, tapescript and answers are given below.

LISTENING

Superstitions

- Get students to look at the illustrations and make sure they understand them.
- Give them a few minutes to read through the questions.
- Then play the recording through once without stopping.
- Play it a second time, pausing after each statement so that they can write their answers.
- Finally, play it straight through a third time so they can check/complete their answers.

Answers and tapescript for Listening Test 1

1. This will bring you seven years' bad luck.
2. Something terrible will happen to you.
3. You will get a letter.
4. You will meet/see a boy.
5. You will have bad luck.
6. You might have a baby.
7. It will bring bad luck.

Superstition that I can remember is erm, never to break a, a mirror, because this will bring you seven years' bad luck, as far as I can remember.

If you put an umbrella up in the house, something'll, terrible'll happen to you.

The birds, the birds, the black and white birds, the magpies, are supposed to be, they can be lucky or unlucky, I think, er, if you see one, one is for sorrow; if you see two, two are for joy; so, 'One for sorrow, two for joy, three for a letter and four for a boy.' I think that is the same superstition; I hope I haven't mixed them up.

It's bad luck to put a hat on a bed.

Don't put two teaspoons in one saucer with your cup; otherwise you might have a baby.

You should never say, say the name Macbeth in a theatre, 'cause it'll bring bad luck.

GRAMMAR

1
1. happened; were having
2. Have (you ever) seen
3. 's/is raining
4. have
5. were (was)
6. have been studying
7. were
8. to do
9. tell
10. have
11. help

2
1. We're going to
2. I'll
3. are you doing; I'm seeing
4. If

3
1. What are those children doing?
2. My sister plays the piano very well.
3. My boss and his secretary are both travelling in Europe.
4. My boss is very good to work for.
5. I speak Italian very badly.

VOCABULARY

1 forwards; well; sell; late; difficult/hard; beginning; slow; off; shut/close(d); forget; finish/stop; that; down.

2 (In some cases, other answers may be possible besides those suggested.)
1. gets/is
2. may/might/should
3. would; came/phoned/*etc.*
4. off
5. don't/can't
6. as
7. sure/certain
8. sorry/surprised
9. earlier/later
10. out

LANGUAGE IN USE

1 (Various answers are possible. Some suggestions:)
1. Tuesday's a bit difficult.
2. See you on Friday.
3. What was the party like?
4. Look out! We're going to crash!
5. Thank you very much.
6. Hello. Cambridge 00672.
7. Can I help you?
8. How much is that?
9. Here you are.
10. What time is it?

PRONUNCIATION

1 b<u>a</u>ckwards; d<u>e</u>sert; <u>e</u>ngine; forg<u>e</u>t; grandf<u>a</u>ther; <u>i</u>nterested; mist<u>a</u>ke; pl<u>ea</u>sure; pr<u>o</u>blem; r<u>ea</u>lise; rem<u>e</u>mber; s<u>i</u>deways; <u>u</u>sually; v<u>i</u>llage.

2
1. soon
2. rough
3. down
4. says
5. said
6. bit
7. draw
8. square
9. lived
10. wash

SPEAKING

Look for appropriate structures in each part of the test. In Question 1, for instance, you can expect conditional structures like *If I were you . . .* or *It would be better if . . .* , and perhaps *should(n't)* and *Why don't you . . . ?* In Question 2, both *will* and *going to* are possible in students' predictions. However, students may be able to carry out the tasks successfully without using the 'expected' structures, and if they manage to do this they should not be penalised. You should in any case take into account not only correctness but also success in communicating, fluency, breadth of knowledge, appropriacy and variety of language.

WRITING

When correcting this, it is best to judge students mainly on their ability to communicate successfully, using appropriate vocabulary and structures (such as the *going-to* construction or the Present Progressive). Excessive emphasis on errors of grammar and spelling can damage students' confidence.

Test Book recordings
A recording for Test 4 in the Test Book follows this lesson on the Class Cassette.

VOCABULARY

1 What are the opposites? Example:

new *old*

backwards   badly   buy   early   easy
end   fast   on   open   remember   start
this   up

2 Put one or more words in each gap.

1. In winter it .... dark before five o'clock.
2. 'What are you doing this evening?' 'I don't know. I .... go and see Pat.'
3. It .... be better if you .... tomorrow.
4. John fell .... a wall and broke his leg.
5. 'People who drive when they've drunk too much should go to prison.' 'No, I .... agree.'
6. Could you tell me as soon .... possible, please?
7. I'm surprised you didn't get my letter – I'm .... I posted it.
8. I was .... to hear that you didn't like your job.
9. Three o'clock's difficult. Could it be ....?
10. Your sweater's inside ....

LANGUAGE IN USE

1 What do you think came before these answers? Example:

Are you free this evening?

'It depends. What time?'

1. 'Then how about Monday?'
2. 'See you then.'
3. 'Terrible.'
4. 'You've got to keep calm.'
5. 'Not at all.'
6. 'This is Peter.'
7. 'I'm looking for some stuff to clean carpets.'
8. 'Five pounds 70.'
9. 'Thank you very much.'
10. 'Half past seven.'

PRONUNCIATION

1 Where are the stresses? Example:

somebody

backwards   desert   engine   forget
grandfather   interested   mistake
pleasure   problem   realise   remember
sideways   usually   village

2 Which word has a different vowel?

1. look   foot   soon   book
2. would   should   took   rough
3. hope   down   throw   flown
4. says   plays   days   raise
5. break   weight   plane   said
6. bit   clean   wheel   leave
7. wash   off   draw   on
8. hurt   circle   square   word
9. lived   buy   wine   fine
10. cash   fact   wash   stamp

SPEAKING

1 You have two minutes to talk to the teacher. You must try to make him/her agree to do one of the following things:
– buy a horse
– give you £1,000
– change his/her job
– go to the North Pole
– learn another language
– buy you an ice cream

2 Talk to another student or the teacher, and tell his or her fortune. You must talk for at least one minute.

WRITING

1 Write about your plans for the next five years.

25 From tree to paper

Talking about processes; Simple Present Passive; no article in 'general' reference.

1 Read the text with a dictionary, and put one of these words into each blank: *paper, wood, trees.* Ask the teacher for help if necessary.

> Excuse me. What does 'invented' mean?

> Excuse me. I don't understand this.

> Excuse me. How do you pronounce this?

> Excuse me. Can you explain this word?

Paper-making centuries ago

Wood fibres magnified

Paper-making today

Future paper

.....1..... was invented by the Chinese in the first century AD. The art of .....2.....-making took seven hundred years to reach the Muslim world and another seven hundred years to get to Britain (via Spain, Southern France and Germany).

Most .....3..... is made from .....4...... When .....5..... are cut down they are transported to paper mills. Here they are cut up and the .....6..... is broken up into fibres which are mixed with water and chemicals. This mixture is then dried and made into .....7......

.....8.....-making is an important British industry, and .....9..... from Britain is exported to Australia,

South Africa and many other countries. Some of the .....10..... used in the British paper-making industry comes from .....11..... grown in Britain, but .....12..... is also imported from other countries such as Norway. One tree is needed for every four hundred copies of a typical forty-page newspaper. If half the adults in Britain each buy one daily .....13....., this uses up over forty thousand .....14..... a day. .....15..... are being cut down faster than they are being replaced, so there may be a serious paper shortage at the beginning of the twenty-first century.

2 🔲 Close your book and listen to the sentences. Are they true or false?

3 The word *America* (/əˈmerɪkə/) has the sound /ə/ twice. Which nine of the following words also contain the sound /ə/?

paper	invented	Chinese
century	southern	Germany
transported	fibre	mixture
exported	Africa	industry
countries	Norway	needed
adults	replaced	serious
shortage		

4 Make some true sentences.

Rice Oil Coal Ships Cars Wheat Wool Oranges Gold Paper Wood *etc.*	is/are (not)	grown produced mined manufactured built	in	Japan. Sweden. Egypt. Brazil. Germany. Britain. the USA. the USSR. Kenya. *etc.*

Lesson 25

Students learn to talk about manufacturing and other processes.
Principal structures: Simple Present Passive; preview of Simple Past and Present Progressive Passives; no article with 'general' reference.
Phonology: perceiving /ə/.

Language notes and possible problems

1. The passive Not all languages contain passive verb forms, and some students may have difficulty in grasping the meaning of the passive at first. But the exercises will give students a feeling for the use of the forms, and by the end of the lesson they should have a reasonable understanding of the point.

You may wish to explain how the 'same' idea can be expressed by active or passive structures, by comparing, for instance, *The Chinese invented paper* and *Paper was invented by the Chinese*. Note, however, that these two sentences don't really have the same meaning. (In the first one we are talking about the Chinese; in the second we are talking about paper.) So active and passive structures should not be presented as exact equivalents.

2. Zero article Students may have difficulty in remembering to omit the article with nouns used in a very general sense (e.g. *paper, wood, paper mills*).

3. Other points The main purpose of this lesson is to give students plenty of experience of passive structures, but it may be worth saying a word about one or two of the following points from the text:
- The difference between *made from* (talking about process) and *made of* (talking about material).
- The use of sequencing and connecting words in the second paragraph (*when, here, and, which, then*).
- The use of *up* to mean 'completely' in *cut up, broken up* and *uses up*.
- Difficult structures which are previewed here include: Present Progressive Passive (*trees are being cut down*); *there may be*; past participle introducing a descriptive phrase (*the wood used in the British paper-making industry*).

4. Phonology Encourage students to improve their pronunciation of /eɪ/ in *paper* and *made*.

5. Vocabulary This lesson contains a large number of new words. Make it clear to students that they do not need to learn them all (see *Learn/revise* list).

---

1 The text
- Tell students to read through the text once without dictionaries, so as to get a general idea.
- Then get them to read it slowly again, looking up words or asking you questions and deciding which of the three words goes in each blank.
- Go round helping where necessary.
- Once the text has been read, you may want to talk about the use of the passive, and other language points arising (see *Language notes*).

Answers to Exercise 1
1. Paper   2. paper   3. paper   4. wood/trees
5. trees   6. wood   7. paper   8. Paper
9. paper   10. wood   11. trees   12. wood
13. paper   14. trees   15. Trees

2 Listening and recall
- Play or read the sentences, and *either* ask students to tell you their answer after each sentence; *or* get them to write the number of each sentence followed by *T* or *F*, and wait till the end to discuss answers.

Answers to Exercise 2
1F   2T   3F   4F   5F   6F   7T   8F   9T

Tapescript for Exercise 2
1. Paper was invented by the Greeks.
2. It was invented in the first century.
3. The British learnt how to make paper in the 18th century.
4. Paper-making is an unimportant industry in Britain.
5. British paper is imported from South Africa.
6. All British paper is made from wood grown in Great Britain.
7. Wood fibres are mixed with chemicals and water, and then dried and made into paper.
8. Four hundred trees are needed to make a typical forty-page newspaper.
9. There may not be enough paper at the beginning of the twenty-first century.

3 Pronunciation (/ə/)
- It is important for students to realise that /ə/ is the commonest vowel in English, and that it is very often pronounced in unstressed syllables where we write *a, e, o* or *u*.
- If students can become sensitive to this point they will find it much easier to understand spoken English (since they will not be confused by hearing /ə/ when they expect a different vowel).
- It is not so important for them to *pronounce* /ə/ in every case where it is required; they can be understood perfectly well without doing this.
- Give students a few minutes to try the exercise individually and compare answers in groups.
- Then play the recording or read the words and help them to correct their answers.

Answers to Exercise 3
The words containing /ə/ are: *paper, century, southern, Germany, fibre, mixture, Africa, industry, serious*.

4 Making sentences
- Start by explaining the vocabulary, or by letting students find out the meanings of the words by using dictionaries or consulting each other.
- Practise the pronunciation of the new vocabulary.
- This activity depends on students having a certain amount of general knowledge. If yours do not, you will need to give prompts (e.g. '*Gold – Russia*').
- You might ask students to write their first sentence before continuing the exercise orally.
- Alternatively, you can turn this into a question-making exercise, with students asking each other, for instance, '*Is rice grown in Britain?*' This provides an opportunity to practise expressions like *I don't know, I think so, I don't think so, I'm not sure.*
- Pay attention to linking (e.g. *rice is*) and to the pronunciation of /ɪ/ in *ships, is, built* and *Britain*.

5 Listening: natural resources

• Before starting the exercise, spend some time going over the map and key with the students, explaining any new words which are not clear.

• Then play the recording or say the sentences and ask students to say or write their answers.

• Encourage them to use full 'short answer' forms like *Yes, it is* and *No, it isn't* rather than just *Yes* and *No*.

• If students are speaking, pay attention to the vowel /ɪ/ in *it is* and *it isn't*.

• You will need to pause for some time after each sentence to give students time to search for the answer and write it down.

Tapescript and answers to Exercise 5

1. True or false? Oil is produced in Texas. (*T*)
2. True or false? Cars are manufactured in Montana. (*F*)
3. True or false? Gold is mined in North Dakota. (*F*)
4. True or false? Maize is grown in Nebraska. (*T*)
5. True or false? Wheat is grown in Kansas. (*T*)
6. True or false? Aircraft are manufactured in Oklahoma. (*F*)
7. Are oranges grown in California? (*Yes, they are.*)
8. Is wheat grown in Arizona? (*No, it isn't.*)
9. Is rice grown in Oregon? (*No, it isn't.*)
10. Are aircraft manufactured in Kansas? (*Yes, they are.*)
11. Is silver mined in Idaho? (*Yes, it is.*)
12. Is paper made in Utah? (*Yes, it is.*)

6 Guessing countries

• Think of a country yourself and say four sentences about it, using verbs from Exercise 4 in three of the sentences.

• As students try to guess, give them clues to help guide them (e.g. *No, it's a bigger country than that*; *No, it's not in Europe*).

• Then divide the class into groups of four or so and let each student take a turn at thinking of a country. (Point out the verbs in Exercise 4.)

• Walk round while they are working to give any help that is needed.

• Do not correct all the errors students make, but try to ensure that they omit the article before words used in a general sense.

Practice Book exercises

1. Putting past participles into passive sentences.
2. Use and omission of *the*.
3. Writing sentences in the Simple Present Passive (saying where certain languages are spoken).
4. Reading a text and completing another one.
5. Student's Cassette exercise (Student's Book Exercise 2, first six sentences). Students listen and write down what they hear.
6. Freer writing about products of the students' country/ies.

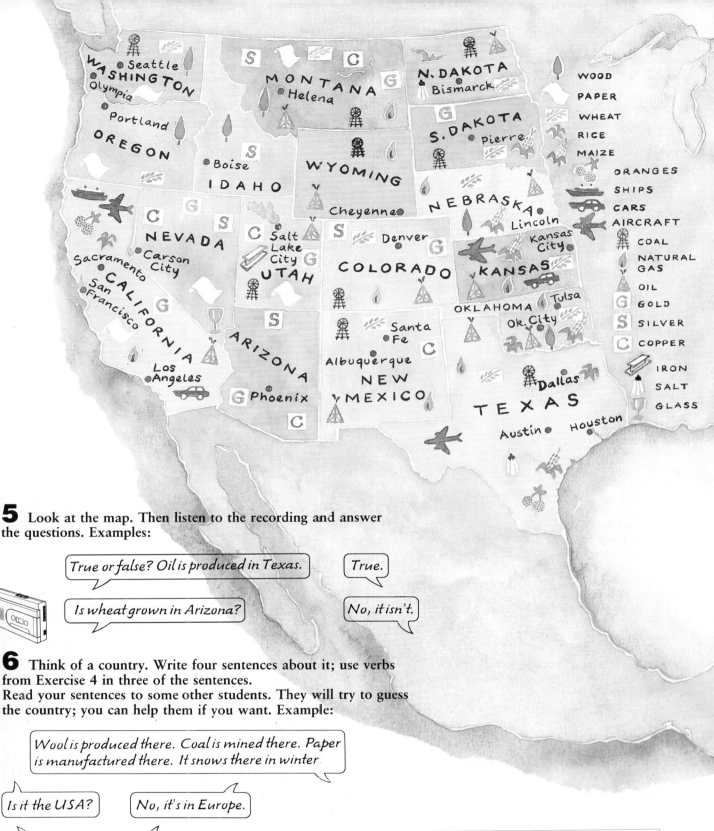

WOOD
PAPER
WHEAT
RICE
MAIZE
ORANGES
SHIPS
CARS
AIRCRAFT
COAL
NATURAL GAS
OIL
G GOLD
S SILVER
C COPPER
IRON
SALT
GLASS

5 Look at the map. Then listen to the recording and answer the questions. Examples:

> *True or false? Oil is produced in Texas.*

> *True.*

> *Is wheat grown in Arizona?*

> *No, it isn't.*

6 Think of a country. Write four sentences about it; use verbs from Exercise 4 in three of the sentences.
Read your sentences to some other students. They will try to guess the country; you can help them if you want. Example:

> *Wool is produced there. Coal is mined there. Paper is manufactured there. It snows there in winter.*

> *Is it the USA?*

> *No, it's in Europe.*

> *Is it Germany?*

> *No.*

> *Britain?*

> *Yes.*

Learn/revise: paper; century; wood; tree; coal; ship; wheat; wool; orange; gold; page; adult; industry; chemical; reach; cut down (cut, cut); cut up; make from (made, made); make into; mix; dry (*verb*); use; grow (grew, grown); produce; mine (*verb*); manufacture; build (built, built); export; import; explain; pronounce; AD; important; Muslim; daily; serious; half; each; other; from . . . to.

Simple Present Passive

SUBJECT	AM/IS/ARE	PAST PARTICIPLE	
Most paper	is	made	from wood.
The wood	is	broken up	into fibres.
Trees	are	transported	to paper mills.

81

26 Who? What? Where? . . .

Talking about past events and their causes; Simple Past Passive; present and past participles.

1 Make some true sentences.

| I think
I'm sure
I know
Perhaps | America   the Taj Mahal
J. F. Kennedy   *Psycho*
The Pastoral Symphony
paper   radium
Hamlet   Kublai Khan
Jane Eyre   TV | was | built
written
directed
discovered
invented
killed
defeated | by | Beethoven   Baird   Columbus
Charlotte Brontë   the Japanese
Pierre and Marie Curie   Oswald
Shakespeare   Shah Jehan
the Chinese   Hitchcock |

in

1963	1808	1898	1281
1600	1847	1923	
1492	the first century		

2 Can you make sentences (like those in Exercise 1) about any of these?

82

Lesson 26

Students practise talking about the causes of past events.
Principal structures: Simple Past Passive; irregular verb forms; present and past participles contrasted.
Phonology: /h/; decoding rapid speech.

Language notes and possible problems

1. Passive verb forms   Students are already reasonably familiar with passives. Exercises 1 to 4 should help to consolidate their understanding of the structure of passive verb forms.

2. 'Past participle'   You may like to point out that this is a confusing name (the form can be used to refer to the past, present or future).

3. Present Progressive and Simple Present Passive
Students tend to confuse forms such as *is breaking* and *is broken*, especially in the early stages of learning English. Exercise 4 will help them discriminate between the two forms.

4. With and by   You will probably want to point out that in passive sentences we use *by* to indicate the *agent* of an action and *with* to indicate the *instrument* which the agent uses to do the action. Compare:

She was killed *by* her lover.
She was killed *with* a knife.

Practice Book Exercise 2 gives work on this point.

Optional extra materials

Pictures of famous achievements and the people responsible for them (see Exercise 2).

If you are short of time

You can leave out Exercise 5 if precise pronunciation is not a high priority for your students; you can leave out Exercise 7.

1 Making past passive sentences

● This exercise requires a certain level of general knowledge, and will be easiest for well-educated students with a European-type cultural background.
● You may want to let the students work in groups first to see how many facts they know or can deduce.
● If you think your students will find the exercise too difficult altogether, you can either give them help (e.g. 'America – Columbus') or replace the exercise with one of your own, containing references that are more familiar to the students.
● Be sure to point out that sentences can end with a name or a date, or both.
● You will probably want to let students work individually at first, writing one or two sentences, and then continue orally.
● If time allows, you might get the students to make up 'true or false' sentences in groups and then try them out on the rest of the class.
● Practice Book Exercise 3 gives more work on forming passive sentences.

Facts from Exercise 1

America was discovered by Columbus in 1492; The Taj Mahal was built by Shah Jehan; J. F. Kennedy was assassinated in 1963 by Oswald; *Psycho* was directed by Hitchcock; *The Pastoral Symphony* was written by Beethoven in 1808; Paper was invented in the first century by the Chinese; Radium was discovered in 1898 by the Curies; *Hamlet* was written by Shakespeare around 1600; Kublai Khan was defeated by the Japanese in 1281; *Jane Eyre* was written by Charlotte Brontë in 1847; TV was invented by Baird in 1923.

2 More practice with past passives

● The same remarks about cultural background apply here as in Exercise 1. If you feel your students will not recognise some of the things and people in the pictures, you may want to collect pictures of your own to use.
● Let students work individually for a few minutes to try and make sentences by pairing up the things and the people in the pictures.
● Then let them compare answers in small groups before checking with you.

Answers to Exercise 2

– Penicillin was discovered by Alexander Fleming.
– Radio was invented by Marconi.
– The North Pole was discovered / first reached by Robert Peary.
– Mount Everest was first climbed by Hillary and Tensing.
– *Gone With the Wind* was written by Margaret Mitchell.
– *St Louis Blues* was first recorded / first played by Louis Armstrong.
– *Don Quixote* was written by Cervantes.
– *The Sunflowers* was painted by Van Gogh.

3 Regular and irregular past participles

- Go over the examples with the students to make sure they understand what the terms *infinitive*, *past tense* and *past participle* mean.
- Then ask them to write the past tenses and past participles of the verbs in the four lists. You may want them to compare answers in groups before checking with you.
- Point out that lists 1 and 2 contain irregular verbs with three and two different forms respectively.
- Lists 3 and 4 are of regular verbs. Note the pronunciation /ɪd/ of the endings in *arrested*, *needed* and *exported*, and the spellings of the endings in list 4.
- Finally, point out that it is the past participle that is used with *am/are/is/was/were* to form the passive, which students met in the last lesson.

Answers to Exercise 3

1. know, knew, known; steal, stole, stolen; go, went, gone/been; drink, drank, drunk
2. find, found, found; build, built, built; think, thought, thought
3. mix, mixed, mixed; question, questioned, questioned; kill, killed, killed; arrest, arrested, arrested; need, needed, needed; export, exported, exported
4. manufacture, manufactured, manufactured; use, used, used; dry, dried, dried

4 Progressive and passive

- Ask students to do at least two or three sentences in writing to make sure that everybody has grasped the point.
- Then continue orally if you like.
- Practice Book Exercise 1 gives more work on this point.

Answers to Exercise 4

1. listening
2. listened
3. built
4. building
5. watching
6. watched
7. blowing, breaking
8. blown, destroyed
9. questioning
10. questioned, killed

5 Pronunciation

- The first part of the exercise can be dropped if students are able to pronounce /h/ without difficulty. Remind students that *h* in *hour* is not pronounced. They will also meet *honest* in Lesson 30.
- Play the recording of the second part of the exercise. The phrases here will appear in the story in Exercise 6, but none of them contains new words. They give students practice in identifying linked words.

Tapescript for Exercise 5

from a dance   anything else   he often said   to kill him
in his car   not as a killer   an old friend
a lot of money   he was at home

6 Information-gap exercise

- This exercise is done in pairs, but you may wish students to do the initial work in small groups.
- Get half the students (for example, the right-hand side of the class) to turn to page 125 in the back of their books; and the other half of the class to turn to page 126.
- Students should read the texts, using their dictionaries or consulting you about new words. They can work in groups.
- Tell students to prepare the questions they are going to ask; give help with word order if needed.
- When everyone is ready, get people from one half of the class to pair off with students from the other half, and let them start asking questions. It does not matter if there is one group of three.
- Students should *not* show one another their books.
- They should make notes of the answers they get.
- When the question-and-answer session is finished, ask students to try to decide who murdered Harrison. This may lead to discussion: help with vocabulary and structures if necessary, but don't correct mistakes at this point unless it is essential.

Answer to Exercise 6

The police arrested Mary Harrison and charged her with Harrison's murder.

They think she came back from the dance some time between 9.30 and 11.30 and shot her husband, leaving a French-English dictionary and a Paris underground ticket by the body to throw suspicion on Cannon. She got her friend Mrs Cannon (who hates Cannon) to give the police false information about Cannon's movements. She took her husband's wallet and threw it away, but gave the money to MacHale, who is her lover.

(*Note:* Your students may think the police are wrong: do let them argue their case if they think it is a better one.)

7 Listening: other people's conclusions

- Students hear English people discussing their conclusions about who killed Harrison; their task is to note down in each case who the people think the killer is.
- Exposure to natural language in a context they are familiar with will help to give them confidence and may aid in unconscious acquisition of language.

Answers to Exercise 7

1. Haynes
2. Haynes (paid by MacHale)
3. Cannon's wife
4. Harrison's wife

Tapescript for Exercise 7

1. Er, well, we think it was Haynes (*laughter*) erm, 'cause erm, we eliminated the times and everything, and we thought that Haynes was the only one who could have done it.
2. Well, PC Anchors and I erm, presume that MacHale plans to run away with Harrison's wife, er, but is not a killer, so is going to pay Haynes to kill Harrison, whom he knows hates him, and this way hopes to avoid any erm, blame falling upon himself.
3. I've been thrown by my partner in crime here, Crimewatch, because she thinks it's Cannon's wife. Erm, so I went along with that because we seem to think that Cannon's wife was having an affair with Harrison.
4. I think the most likely scenario is that erm, Harrison's wife killed him. Erm, she was at a dance; he was talking to a woman in the street; I mean, they obviously didn't a very, have a very happy relationship, erm, and she's very friendly with MacHale, . . . (*fade*)

Practice Book exercises

1. Progressive and passive.
2. *By* and *with* in passive sentences.
3. Guided writing using past passive constructions.
4. Revision of expressions with *have*.
5. Revision of irregular verb forms.
6. Recreational reading: a logic problem.

3 Grammar. Look at the examples.

INFINITIVE:	Could Shakespeare **speak** Latin?
	Shah Jehan decided **to build** the Taj Mahal.
	Marie Curie wanted **to help** young scientists.
PAST TENSE:	Curie **spoke** Polish and French.
	The Chinese **built** early machines for paper-making.
	Queen Isabella **helped** Columbus.
PAST PARTICIPLE:	My sister has **spoken** to her class about *Hamlet*.
	They have **built** a model of Shakespeare's theatre.
	The librarian has **helped** us find out about Baird.
	Latin was **spoken** by many people in Shakespeare's time.
	The sets for *Psycho* were **built** in Hollywood.
	The young Charlotte Brontë was **helped** by her brother.

Now write the past tenses and past participles of these verbs.

1. know   steal   go   drink
2. find   build   think
3. mix   question   kill   arrest   need   export
4. manufacture   use   dry

4 Put the *-ing* form or the past participle.

1. 'What is she doing?'   'She's (*listen*) to the *Pastoral Symphony*.'
2. Beethoven's works are (*listen*) to all over the Western world.
3. When was the Taj Mahal (*build*)?
4. The Royal Shakespeare Company is (*build*) a new theatre.
5. Why are you (*watch*) that film?
6. Kennedy's killing was (*watch*) by millions of people on TV.
7. Storms have been (*blow*) down trees and (*break*) up people's homes in Jamaica.
8. Kublai Khan's ships were (*blow*) away from the Japanese coast by a very big storm, and a lot of them were (*destroy*).
9. The police are (*question*) some people about the damage to the Taj Mahal.
10. Oswald was not (*question*) about killing Kennedy because he was (*kill*) himself soon afterwards.

5 Pronunciation. Pronounce these words.

Hillary   Hitchcock   *Hamlet*   here   home
hated   Harrison   who   how   hand
hungry   happy

Now listen and write what you hear.

6 Find out what the words in the box mean, from your dictionary, your teacher, or other students.

alive	dead	flat	dance	revolver
business	wallet	thief	arrest	sack (*verb*)
suspect	central			

Now turn to the page your teacher tells you. Work with a partner, but DO NOT show your partner your page. Ask each other questions to solve the problem.

7 Listen to people talking about the same problem. Who do they think killed Harrison?

Simple Past Passive

SUBJECT	*WAS/WERE*	PAST PARTICIPLE	
Hamlet	was	written	by Shakespeare in about 1600.
Harrison	was	killed	with a revolver.
All three	were	arrested	the next morning.

Learn/revise: dance (*noun*); body; thief; business; wallet; flat; ticket; cash; world; coast; theatre; film; the police; invent; direct; kill; discover; help; blow (blew, blown); arrest; sack; steal (stole, stolen); hate; owe; search; sure; alive; dead; central; on TV; western; away; soon; afterwards; by.

27 Probability

Expressing probability; *must, can't* and *might*;
reporting past speech.

FRED SMITH

Full Name: Frederick George Smith.
Age: 25
Address: 17 Victoria Terrace, Highbury, London N5.
Profession: Van driver.
Interests: photography, model aeroplanes
Education: Finsbury Park Comprehensive School.
Qualifications: None
Father: Albert Eric Smith, 52, shop assistant.
Mother: Florence Anne Smith, née Henderson, 48, housewife.

1 [cassette] Look at the information about Fred
Smith. Then listen to the recording of a
conversation between Fred and Janet at a party.
What did he say that was not true? Examples:

'Fred said that he lived in Paris and California.'
*'He told Janet that he had been photographing
the President.'*

2 Here are some of the things that Fred said in the conversation.
Do you think they are true? Use one of the expressions in the box.

It must be true.	It could be true.	It's probably not true.
It's probably true.	It might be true.	It can't be true.

1. My friends call me Fred.
2. I photograph famous people.
3. I travel all over the world.
4. I've been photographing the
   President for *Time* magazine.
5. Famous people are all the
   same.
6. I find you interesting.
7. I want to photograph you.
8. I love poetry.

3 Here is a picture of the place where Fred was born.
What can you say about the time and place? Examples:

'It might be morning, because . . .'
'It can't be in Germany, because . . .'
'It must be during the day, because . . .'

LLANDYFRDWY

84

Lesson 27

Students learn more ways of expressing the concept of probability; they practise reporting past conversations.
Principal structures: modal verbs used to express probability and certainty; *say* and *tell*; more practice on reported statements; reported questions.
Phonology: initial consonant clusters beginning with *s*.

Language notes and possible problems

1. Reported statements with *say* and *tell* are revised here. The distinction between these two verbs often causes problems. In Exercise 1, students practise using them with a following *that*-clause. Point out to students that the word *that* can be omitted here. Remind them that *tell* must have a personal object (*He told her that . . .*), while this is unnecessary with *say* (*He said that . . .*). Make sure that they pronounce *said* (/sed/) correctly.

2. Past Perfect Past Perfect forms are previewed here (they occur as reported speech transformations of Present Perfects). No special explanation is necessary at this stage; students simply need to be reminded that *have* changes to *had* after a past reporting verb. The Past Perfect proper is studied in detail in Lesson 32.

3. Modal verbs This lesson practises the use of certain modal verbs (*must, could, might, can't*) to express degrees of probability and certainty. Students should already know the grammar of modal verbs, but you may need to revise the basic facts:
– The verbs have no *-s* in the third-person singular.
– They are followed by the infinitive without *to*.
– Questions and negatives are formed without *do*.

4. *Must* and *can't* Note that the opposite of *must* (when it expresses logical certainty) is *can't*, not *mustn't*. Compare *It must be true* and *It can't be true*. Students may have difficulty with this.

5. Initial consonant clusters with *s* Speakers of certain languages find clusters like *st, sp* very difficult to pronounce at the beginning of a word. Look out for mistakes like **estudent, *espeak*.

6. Reported questions will be a new structure for some students. Point out the basic features of these questions:
– Reported questions do not have the same word-order (auxiliary verb before subject) as most direct questions.
– *Do* is not used.
– There are no question marks.
– Before questions which do not start with a question-word (like *who, where, how*), the word *if* is used.

7. Lying Some of the optional activities here rely on getting students to 'tell lies' for fun. In some cultures, it is not usual to say things which are not true in order to tease or amuse people, and certain students may find the situation slightly shocking.

Optional extra materials

If you are going to do the 'two envelopes' optional activity, you will need two opaque envelopes, one empty and the other containing a picture which students can easily describe.

If you are short of time

Drop Exercise 4 if the pronunciation point is not important for your students; get them to do Exercise 3 for homework.

1 Listening: reporting discrepancies

- Give the students a minute or two to look over the information; help with vocabulary where needed.
- Point out the difference in the way *say* and *tell* are used in the examples.
- You may want to use the tables at the bottom of the Student's Book page to help you.
- Tell students to close their books while you play the recording.

- Then ask if they can remember any of Fred's lies. Encourage them to make sentences beginning *He said that . . .* and *He told her that . . .*; make sure the tenses are all right.
- Play the recording again once or twice until students have understood the main points of the conversation and picked out most of the lies.

Tapescript for Exercise 1: see page 128

2 Degrees of certainty

- Look through the expressions in the box, giving whatever explanations are needed.
- The expressions are arranged in order: see if students can see the basis for this.
- The exercise can be done individually round the class or by group discussion, as you like.

3 Picture: making deductions

- Let students look at the picture for a minute or two.
- Go over the examples with them, and see if they can find ways of completing the sentences.
- Ask them to write one sentence each about the picture, using the same modal verbs as in the last exercise.
- After hearing their sentences, see if they can make some more deductions orally.
- Students might deduce some of the following things. It must be somewhere in the British Isles, because the cars are driving on the left. It must be Sunday, because people are coming out of the church (chapel). It can't be very long ago, because there is a jet in the picture. So the old cars must be taking part in a vintage car rally. It must be late autumn or winter, because there are no leaves on the trees. It must be early in the morning or late in the afternoon, because the sun is low in the sky: but it can't be too early in the morning, because the people are coming out of chapel; so it's probably late afternoon. You may like to finish by telling the class that the scene is in Wales (not England). Mention that Wales has its own language, Welsh, which is quite different from English – the word *Llandyfrdwy* in the picture (pronounced roughly /hlændʌvrduːi/) is a typical Welsh place name.

Optional activity: two envelopes

- Ask for two volunteers, or choose two students who speak quite well.
- Give them each an envelope: one will contain a picture, and the other will be empty, but do not let the class know which is which.
- Tell them to go out of the room for two minutes; the one who has a picture will prepare to describe it to the class; the other will prepare a description of an imaginary picture.
- When the students return, they each give their description, without letting the class know which description is real and which is invented.
- The class ask questions about the pictures.
- Finally, the class decide who was telling the truth.

Optional activity: find the lies

- Tell the students something about yourself; warn them in advance that you are going to include three lies in what you say, and see if they can pick them out.
- Alternatively, ask students to write three sentences about themselves, including at least one lie. Then let them listen to each other's sentences and try to find the lies. (Encourage the use of *must, could, can't* etc.)

Optional activity: 'Alibi'
- Ask for two volunteers.
- Tell them that they are going to be questioned (separately) by the police, who are investigating a crime which was committed yesterday between 4.30 and 5.30.
- The two volunteers must go out of the room for five minutes and prepare a joint alibi for the time of the crime – they must say that they were together, and they must agree on the details of where they were and what they were doing.
- While they are preparing their story, the rest of the class (the police) prepare an interrogation.
- They must try to think of questions which the volunteers will not have foreseen (weather; clothes; who arrived first at the meeting place; . . .).
- Bring in one of the volunteers while the other stays outside out of earshot.
- Let the class ask their questions for a maximum of five minutes. They should note the answers.
- Then bring in the second volunteer and let the class question him/her, trying to break the alibi by finding contradictions between the two stories.
- While this is going on, the first volunteer can listen, but should not be able to signal to the one being questioned.
- When students are used to the game it can be played in groups of six to eight. It gives excellent practice in asking past tense questions.

4 Pronunciation: initial clusters with *s*
- Students who speak Spanish may have difficulty in making *st(r)*, *sp(r)* and *sc(r)* without putting a vowel in front; the same is true of speakers of Arabic, Farsi, and many oriental languages.
- If your students have this problem, get them to practise the words in the exercise after you or the recording until they find it easier, and encourage them to be careful when they come across words of this kind later on.

5 Reported questions
- Give students a few minutes to look at the picture story.
- Go over the examples with them, pointing out the word order in reported questions (no inversions) and the fact that *if* is used to report 'yes/no' questions. You can use the tables at the bottom of the Student's Book page to help you.
- Then get them to work individually filling in the blanks in Janet's letter, by referring to the picture story.
- Let them compare answers in twos or threes before checking with you.
- Go over the answers with them, giving any explanations that are necessary.
- Then divide the class into groups of three or four and ask them to invent the end of Janet's letter.
- They should not stop where the pictures stop: ask them to think of a good ending for the story.
- Walk round while they are working to give any language help that is needed (but encourage them to come up with ideas for their own endings).
- When they have finished, the stories can be posted up round the classroom; or passed from one group to another; or copied for people to read at home; or read aloud to the class.

Answers to the first part of Exercise 5
(Answers to the third paragraph may vary slightly.)
. . . and so we took a taxi. He asked me where I lived, and what my parents were like, and wanted to know if I liked it there. I thought he must be interested in me if he wanted to know about my parents. He asked me (1) *if* I (2) *liked* good food, and asked me what my favourite wine (3) *was*. I'm glad that wine programme was on the telly last week!

Then he asked me (4) *if I could get* some time off work, and I said I thought so. He asked me (5) *when I could phone the shop*, and I said I'd have to wait till the next morning. Well, by this time we were at the studio. It was a wonderful building – all closed as it was so late, of course. He only had Italian money, so he asked (6) *me if I could lend him £5* for the taxi. And then he didn't have a key to the studio, so (7) *he asked me if I had a credit card*, and he used it to open the door! I was a bit surprised, but I thought that artists must live a bit differently from the rest of us.

Well, you'll never guess what happened then! He was showing me the studio when a man walked in and (8) *asked Fred who he was. He asked him if he worked there, and what he was doing there. He asked Fred if he knew those were the man's lights. He asked him how long we had been there.*

Practice Book exercises
1. *Will, might, can't*, or *must*.
2. Expressions of probability.
3. Reported statements.
4. Reported questions.
5. Student's Cassette exercise (Student's Book Exercise 1, up to ' . . . *Time* magazine'). Students listen and try to write down everything they hear.
6. Personalisation: writing true sentences with structures from the lesson.

4 Pronunciation. Say these words.

1. star   stand   studio   start   student
   film stars   don't stand   this student
2. speak   spoke   Spain   spend
   was speaking   the West of Spain   don't spend
3. score   Scotland   Scottish
   right score   in Scotland   she's Scottish
4. spring   spread   strange   street   straight
   screw   scratch   scream

5 Look at part of Janet's letter to a friend. Notice how she writes about the questions that were asked:

'Where do you live?'   'Do you like living there?'
He asked me where I lived.   He asked me if I liked it there.

Now look at the pictures and fill in the blanks in the letter; then imagine what happened next and finish the letter.

. . . and so we took a taxi. He asked me where I lived, and what my parents were like, and wanted to know if I liked it there. I thought he must be interested in me if he wanted to know about my parents. He asked ....1.... I ....2.... good food, and asked me what my favourite wine ....3.... . I'm glad that wine programme was on the telly last week!

Then he asked me ....4.... some time off work, and I said I thought so. He asked me ....5.... and I said I'd have to wait until the next morning. Well, by this time we were at the studio. It was a wonderful building – all closed as it was so late, of course. He only had Italian money, so he asked ....6.... for the taxi. And then he didn't have a key to the studio, so ....7.... and he used it to open the door! I was a bit surprised, but I thought that artists must live a bit differently from the rest of us.

Well, you'll never guess what happened then! He was showing me the studio when a man walked in and . . .

Reported speech

'I **live** in Paris.' He **said** (that) he **lived** in Paris.

'I've been to Rio.' He **told** Janet (that) he **had** been to Rio.

'Where **do** you **live**?' He **asked** me where I **lived**.

'**Do** you **like** living there?' He **asked** me **if** I **liked** living there.

Must and *can't*

It **can't** be in Germany, because they're driving on the left.
It **must** be during the day, because you can see the sun.

Learn/revise: profession; qualifications; education; photographer; information (*uncountable*); taxi; food; programme; building; key; artist; full name; credit card; the rest (of); school; must; can't; might; could; photograph (*verb*); phone (*verb*); pay (paid, paid); wait; love; guess; happen; show (showed, shown); was/were born; true; famous; interested (in); interesting; favourite; glad; wonderful; closed; late; surprised; probably; none; the same; then (= after that); all over the world.

28 Somebody with blue eyes

Describing; comparing; relative clauses with *who*; adjectives like *dark-haired*; *So/Neither . . .* ; *both* and *neither*.

1 Look at pictures 1–6 and the descriptions. Can you put the right name with each picture?

ANN is a dark-haired woman who is rather shy.
LESLEY is a young doctor who plays tennis.
SUSAN is a fair-haired woman who speaks French.
PAT is a company director who eats too much.
KATE is a fair-haired woman who does not smoke.
CAROL is a dark-haired woman who likes animals.

1   2   3

4   5   6

2 Now look at pictures 7–12. Make up names and descriptions for three of the people in them (use *who* in your sentences). Then see if other students can put your names with the right pictures.

7   8   9

10   11   12

3 A person with dark hair is *dark-haired*. Somebody who writes with his or her left hand is *left-handed*. What are the adjectives for these people?

1. a person with brown hair
2. somebody with blue eyes
3. a person who has got broad shoulders
4. people who write with their right hands
5. a person with a thin face
6. somebody with long legs

Now say these in another way.

1. a blue-eyed woman
   'a woman with blue eyes'
2. a brown-haired man
   'a man ....'
3. a left-handed child
   'a child who ....'
4. a fat-faced person
   'somebody who has ....'
5. a dark-eyed girl
   '............'
6. a long-sleeved pullover
   '............ with ....'

4 Pronunciation. Say these sentences. Pay attention to stress, rhythm and linking.

1. **Ann** is a **dark-haired** woman who is **rather shy.**
2. **Pat** is a **company director** who **eats** too **much.**
3. **You** said she was **rather shy** – she **isn't shy at all.**
4. **What** do you **call a woman** with **blue eyes?**
5. **What** do you **call a man** who's got a **thin face?**
6. **Do you mean** that **dark-eyed child?**

Lesson 28

Students practise language used for describing and comparing.
Principal structures: relative clauses with *who*; *both* and *neither* in sentences; *So/Neither* (*am I*, etc.); compound adjectives like *dark-haired*; *do* as pro-verb.
Phonology: stress, rhythm and linking.

Language notes and possible problems
1. Relative clauses with *who* as subject are studied here; other types of relative clauses will be dealt with later.
2. Both Note the word order with *both*, as detailed in the panel on the Student's Book page. Note also the structure *both of us/you/them* etc. (and *neither of us/you/them*).

If you are short of time
Get students to do Exercise 3 for homework; if listening and speaking are not priorities for your students, drop Exercise 4.

1 Relative clauses: matching exercise
• This exercise can be done individually at first. After a few minutes, let students compare notes in groups.
• Point out that the women in pictures 2 and 6 are both reading *Paris Match* (a French magazine).
• Help with vocabulary where necessary, or let students use dictionaries.

Answers to Exercise 1
1. Kate   2. Ann   3. Pat   4. Carol   5. Lesley
6. Susan
(*Note*: 2 could apparently be either Carol or Ann; but 4 can only be Carol – because Ann is shy; so 2 must be Ann.)

2 Relative clauses: practice
• Students should try to make up sets of descriptions like those in Exercise 1. (This activity works well if done in groups of three or four.)
• Get them to write down their descriptions; make sure they use relative clauses with *who*.
• When students are ready, they should exchange papers and try to work out who is who.

3 Compound adjectives with *-ed*
• This is an easy exercise, which can be done in class or for homework as you prefer.

4 Stress, rhythm and linking

• Play or say the sentences, and get the students to imitate them as well as they can.
• Start by making sure they put the stresses in the right places.
• Then work on rhythm, getting the students to say the stressed syllables more slowly than the unstressed syllables.
• Note that many unstressed words and syllables are pronounced with /ə/ (for instance *a*, *do*, *was* and *at*).
• Finally, pay attention to linking words together smoothly, particularly:
– where the second or third word in a phrase begins with a vowel.
– where two vowel sounds come together (*who is*, *who eats* and *blue eyes* almost sound as if there were a /w/ between the two words, and *shy at* as if there were a /j/ between the two words).
• After the first three sentences, get students to try to say the sentences *before* they hear them, and then play the recording so that they can check their pronunciation.

5 Physical descriptions

- Give students a minute or so to look at the pictures.
- Then ask them to work in small groups, choosing one of the people and describing them as completely as they can.
- Most of the students should know most of the vocabulary in the box, but help with unfamiliar words or encourage them to use dictionaries.
- They can use other words that they already know, but should not search their bilingual dictionaries for new words other than the ones in the book.
- Walk round while they are working to give help as needed.
- When they have finished, tell them that they are going to hear five of the people being described; their only task is to decide which person is being described in each case.
- Play the recording once, and let them compare answers in small groups.
- Then play it again so they can check their answers before verifying with you.
- If there are some students who have not got the answers right, ask the others to explain what words helped them to come to their decisions, and play the recording again to give another chance to those who had difficulty.

Tapescript and answers to Exercise 5

a. This woman is short, and rather fat, and has erm, light brown hair and brown eyes and is wearing a green neck-scarf and a purple dress with a red criss-cross pattern on it, and a pair of brown shoes. (*Number 8*)

b. This person is about, a bit above average height, fairly good-looking, erm, male, with light trousers and a dark blue jacket, green tie and a blue shirt. He's got no distinguishing features – no beard or moustache; and a happy, friendly sort of face. (*Number 1*)

c. He's er, quite tall, rather serious-looking, erm, black but with erm, grey or white hair, erm, fairly slim, loose-fitting clothes, quite a big nose. He's erm, he looks quite athletic, he's dancing at the moment. (*Number 5*)

d. This woman is middling in height, rather slim, with red hair and bright blue eyes. Erm, she looks very happy, and is wearing a bligh, a bright blue dress with an orange belt and bright blue shoes. (*Number 4*)

e. We have a plump, youngish, round-faced young gentleman with fair curly hair and a brightly-coloured hooped jumper, casual slacks and brown shoes. He looks fairly at peace with the world, standing with his arms folded. (*Number 2*)

6 Similarities and differences: speaking

- Ask the students to work individually, writing down five facts about themselves. They should include one negative sentence. Make a list yourself.
- Then go over the examples in the book.
- Read your list out sentence by sentence and get volunteers to answer you as in the examples.
- Then ask students to pair up (trying to choose someone they don't know very well) to read out their sentences to each other and reply.

7 Writing about similarities and differences

- Go over the examples in the book, and use the panel at the bottom of the page to teach or revise the use and position of *both*.
- Then ask each pair from Exercise 6 to produce a written record of their similarities and differences as in the example.
- Walk round while they are working to give any help that is needed.
- When they have finished, collect the papers, number them and read them out to the class (or post them around the room).
- Students must listen (or walk round and read), and write down their guesses about which pair wrote each text.
- Check by letting the students tell each other who wrote what.

Optional activity: grouping people

- A volunteer divides the class into groups according to the similarities and differences between students.
- The volunteer does not tell the other students on what basis he or she is dividing them. They have to work out what the people in each group have in common (for instance hair colour, jobs, personality).
- As the volunteer divides the students, he or she should put each group in a different part of the room. This provides an opportunity for revision of prepositions (*Go and stand by the door / under the picture / near the blackboard* etc.).
- When students have managed to guess how they were divided, another volunteer takes a turn.
- Help with vocabulary and structures if necessary.

Practice Book exercises

1. Position of *both*.
2. Regular and irregular plurals.
3. Passives: writing where things are made.
4. Spelling: double and single letters.
5. Past Simple and Past Progressive.
6. Writing descriptions.

5 Choose one of the pictures and describe the person. You can use words and expressions from the box. Then listen to the recording. Which people are being described?

body:	tall/short slim/plump/fat	**face:**	long/round/square/oval
eyes:	blue/brown/green/grey	**nose:**	small/big/long
hair:	long/short/thinning	**general:**	pretty/good-looking/attractive/plain
	straight/curly/wavy		looks calm/cheerful/friendly/
	fair/red/brown/black/grey		worried/depressed/nervous

1   2   3   4   5   6   7   8

6 Work with a student that you don't know very well. Write down five things about yourself and read them out to your partner. Include one negative sentence. Your partner should answer, using *So/ Neither do/am/have I* etc., or *I don't / 'm not / haven't* etc. Examples:

'I've got two sisters and a brother.'
'Really? So have I.'

'I like Beethoven.'
'Oh? I don't, but I like Mozart.'

'I can't play the piano.'
'Neither can I.'

7 Write down the results of Exercise 6. Use *both, neither* and *but*. Example:

We both read the newspaper every day, but we don't read the same newspaper. We have both got good bicycles, and we both go cycling at the weekends. We are both a bit shy. We can both speak a little Russian. One of us likes classical music, but the other doesn't. Neither of us plays the piano, and neither of us has got a cat. Both of us go to church, but we go to different churches.

Now give your paper to the teacher, who will read the papers to the class. Try to guess who has written which paper.

Both	
One-part verbs:	We **both speak** Russian. (~~We speak both . . .~~)
Two-part verbs:	They **have both got** bicycles. (~~They both have got . . .~~)
	Ann and I **can both speak** Russian. (~~We both can . . .~~)
	We **have both been** to Cyprus. (~~We both have been . . .~~)
	They **are both living** in Paris. (~~They both are . . .~~)
Am/are/is/was/were:	My sisters **are both** a bit shy. (~~They both are . . .~~)

Learn/revise: shoulder; face; body; look; dark-haired; fair-haired; left-handed; right-handed; tall; short (= not tall); thin; slim; plump; fat; grey; red (hair); long; short (= not long); straight; curly; round; square; oval; pretty; attractive; plain; good-looking; calm; cheerful; friendly; worried; depressed; nervous; too much; so; neither; both; one (of); the other; the same; different; with.

29 Things

Describing things; relative clauses with and without *that*; position of prepositions.

1 How quickly can you match the words, the pictures and the descriptions? Example:

'Picture A is a gun – a thing that can kill people.'

| arm | calendar | elephant | giraffe | gun | ice | newspaper | pillow |
| platform | purse | shoes | tap | tongue | toothpaste | umbrella | watch |

1. a thing that tells you the time
2. something that tells you the date
3. a thing that can kill people
4. stuff that makes drinks cool
5. a thing (that) you read to find out what has happened in the world
6. something (that) you carry when it rains
7. things (that) you wear on your feet
8. stuff (that) people use when they brush their teeth
9. a thing (that) you talk and taste with
10. something (that) water comes out of
11. a thing (that) you keep money in
12. something (that) you put your head on
13. a place where you wait for a train
14. an animal with a very long nose
15. an animal that has a very long neck
16. a part of your body that joins your hand to your shoulder

In sentences 5–12, the word *that* can be left out. In sentences 1–4, 15 and 16 it can't. Why?

2 Look at sentences 9–12 in Exercise 1, and study the position of the words *with*, *out of*, *in* and *on*. Now complete the following descriptions.

1. A key is something (that) you .... with.
2. A chair is something .... on.
3. A cup is something .... out of.
4. A picture is something .... at.
5. A window is .... out of.
6. A pen is ....
7. A telephone is ....
8. A letter box is ....
9. A fridge is ....
10. Soap is stuff (that) .... with.
11. Shoe polish is ....
12. Money is ....

3 Choose a picture, and write a description of it (like the ones in Exercises 1 and 2). The other students must decide which picture it is.

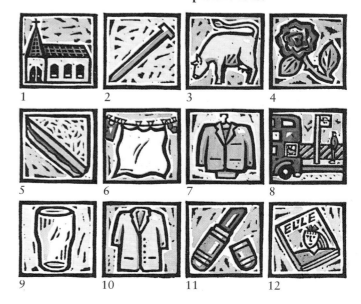

Lesson 29

Students work on the language of descriptions and definitions.
Principal structures: relative clauses with *that*; omission of *that*; end-position of prepositions.

Language notes and possible problems

1. Relatives 'Contact-clauses', in which object relative pronouns are left out (e.g. *something you carry*) are not possible in many languages besides English, so students may find this structure difficult to get used to.

2. End-position of prepositions Students should by now be used to the fact that a preposition may come at the end of a question in English, especially in an informal style (e.g. *Where are you from?*). This lesson practises a more difficult structure: relative clauses ending in prepositions (e.g. *A chair is something you sit on*). This, too, is a structure which does not occur in many other languages.

3. With Note how *with* and *have* can be used to express identical meanings. Compare: *an animal with a very long nose*; *an animal that has a very long neck*.

4. Pronunciation You may wish to focus on the /θ/ and/or the /ɪ/ in *something* (a difficult word for most students).

1 Matching words, pictures and descriptions

● This introduces the structures that are used for defining and describing.

● Let students begin the exercise by working individually; then get them to compare notes in groups before you go over the answers with them and answer questions.

● Finally, see if students can tell you when relative *that* can be left out. (When it is the object of the verb.)

Answers to Exercise 1

Picture A is a gun – a thing that can kill people.
Picture B is a platform – a place where you wait for a train.
Picture C is a tongue – something (that) you talk and taste with.
Picture D is a tap – something (that) water comes out of.
Picture E is an elephant – an animal with a very long nose.
Picture F is an umbrella – something (that) you carry when it rains.
Picture G is a watch – a thing that tells you the time.
Picture H is a pair of shoes – things (that) you wear on your feet.
Picture I is ice – stuff that makes drinks cool.
Picture J is a calendar – something that tells you the date.
Picture K is toothpaste – stuff (that) people use when they brush their teeth.
Picture L is a newspaper – a thing (that) you read to find out what has happened in the world.
Picture M is a purse – a thing (that) you keep money in.
Picture N is a giraffe – an animal that has a very long neck.
Picture O is an arm – a part of your body that joins your hand to your shoulder.
Picture P is a pillow – something (that) you put your head on.

2 End-position of prepositions

● Get students to look over sentences 9–12 from Exercise 1. Tell them that in English prepositions often come at the end of relative clauses.

● Then get them to do the exercise individually or by class discussion, as you prefer.

Answers to Exercise 2

(These are suggestions; other versions are possible.)
1. A key is something (*that*) you *open a door* with.
2. A chair is something (*that*) *you sit* on.
3. A cup is something (*that*) *you drink* out of.
4. A picture is something (*that*) *you look* at.
5. A window is *something* (*that*) *you look out of.*
6. A pen is *a thing* (*that*) *you write with.*
7. A telephone is *something* (*that*) *you talk to people with.*
8. A letter box is *a thing* (*that*) *you put letters in.*
9. A fridge is *something* (*that*) *you keep food in.*
10. Soap is stuff (*that*) *you wash* with.
11. Shoe polish is *stuff* (*that*) *you clean shoes with.*
12. Money is *stuff* (*that*) *you buy things with.*

3 Students' definitions

● Ask students to choose one or more of the pictures and write definitions of them (similar to the ones in Exercises 1 and 2).

● Let them give their definitions and see if other students can decide which pictures they are talking about.

● The exercise can be extended by getting students to write or improvise definitions of other things besides those illustrated.

4 Adjectives: matching opposites

- Students will know most of the words in this exercise.
- Let them work individually; then get them to compare their answers in small groups.
- Check their answers and deal with any problems.
- Then get students to see how many of the adjectives can be applied to things (or people) in the room.

Answers to Exercise 4

heavy – light
light – dark
wide – narrow
big – small
quiet – noisy
tall – short
hard – soft
cold – hot
high – low
loud – quiet
new – old
short – long

5 Materials

- Let students work in groups, pooling their knowledge to see if they can work out the meanings of all the words.
- If there are any words that nobody knows, let students use dictionaries.
- Then see if they can find something in the classroom made of each material.

6 Preparation for 'Twenty questions': information transfer exercise

- Students have to interpret data presented in a table in order to make a choice between seven different things or substances.
- You may like to do this as a competition, asking students to see how fast they can finish.

Answers to Exercise 6

1. a boiled egg   2. a pint of beer   3. a cat   4. a sweater
5. a bicycle   6. a litre of motor oil   7. a pearl

7 'Twenty questions'

- Students may have played this game once or twice earlier in the course. It is excellent for revising interrogative structures.
- Start off yourself; when the students have guessed (or failed to guess) your object, let them continue in groups.

Optional activity: 'Three clues'

- This is rather similar to 'Twenty questions'. Each student should think of something and prepare three things to say about it, including a definition (like those in Exercises 1 and 2), an adjective (see Exercise 4) and the name of a material (see Exercise 5). The rest of the class or group then try to guess what it is in one minute (or not more than six guesses).

Optional activity: 'Blind definitions'

- Get a volunteer to come out in front of the class (preferably somebody with a good vocabulary).
- The student's hands should be behind his or her back, and he or she should face the class.
- Put a small object into the student's hands without letting anybody see it.
- The class have to ask questions to find out what it is.
- The person holding the object can give any information asked for except the name of the object (if he or she knows what it is).
- Carry on until the class have identified the object or until they give up.
- Some things that can be used for this game: key, paper clip, diary, comb, ring, piece of soap, sweet, egg, light bulb, battery, paper tissue, grape, tie, credit card, pocket knife, stamp, toy car.

Practice Book exercises

1. Countable, uncountable and plural nouns.
2. Adjectives with *too* and *enough*.
3. Names of materials.
4. Word stress.
5. Writing descriptive sentences, using structures from the lesson.
6. Reading comprehension practice: identifying the subject matter in a transcribed conversation.

4 Match the opposites. Then look round the classroom for something heavy, something light, something wide *etc.* Can you find examples for all the adjectives?

heavy	light	wide	
big	quiet	tall	hard
cold	high	loud	
new	short		

small	old	light	
short	quiet	low	
dark	narrow	long	
noisy	hot	soft	

5 Do you know all of these words for materials? Can you find things in the classroom that are made of all the materials? Example:

'The lights are made of plastic and glass.'

cotton   glass   leather   metal   paper   plastic   rubber
stone   synthetic fibre   wood   wool

6 Match the numbers and the pictures.

	LIQUID OR SOLID?	ALIVE?	USEFUL?	CAN YOU EAT / DRINK IT?	MANUFACTURED?	CAN YOU WEAR IT?
1	S	No	Yes	Yes	No	No
2	L	No	Yes	Yes	Yes	No
3	S	Yes	Yes	No	No	No
4	S	No	Yes	No	Yes	Yes
5	S	No	Yes	No	Yes	No
6	L	No	Yes	No	Yes	No
7	S	No	No	No	No	Yes

a sweater

a pearl

a litre of motor oil

a pint of beer

a boiled egg

a cat

a bicycle

7 'Twenty questions'. One student thinks of something. The student doesn't tell the others what it is; he/she only tells them that it is 'animal', 'vegetable', 'mineral' or 'abstract'. (For example: a leather handbag is animal, a newspaper is vegetable, a glass is mineral and an idea is abstract.) The other students must find out what the thing is by asking questions (maximum 20); the only answers allowed are *Yes* and *No*. Useful questions:

Can you eat it?
Is it made of wood (metal, glass *etc.*)?
Is it useful?
Can you find it in a house (shop, car *etc.*)?
Is it liquid?
Is it hard (soft, heavy, light *etc.*)?
Have you got one of these?
Is there one in this room (building, street *etc.*)?
Is it manufactured?

Learn/revise: foot (*plural* feet); tooth (*plural* teeth); neck; brush; telephone; stuff; cotton; glass; leather; metal; paper; plastic; rubber; stone; synthetic fibre; wood; wool; part; big; small; cold; hot; dark; light (= not dark); heavy; light (= not heavy); hard; soft; high; low; loud; noisy; quiet; wide; narrow; new; old; liquid; solid; alive; something hard/soft *etc.*; useful; made of.

89

30 Self and others

-*self* and -*selves*; *each other*; *somebody else*; the vocabulary of discussion; *should*.

falling in love
with each other

A woman
looking at herself
in a mirror.

A man looking
at himself
in a mirror.

1 Look at the pictures. Which picture shows two people looking at themselves?

2 Listen to the recording and follow the instructions.

3 You can talk to somebody else or you can talk to yourself. (Do it.) You can marry somebody else but you can't marry yourself. What about these?

draw   fall in love with   feel sorry for   hurt
listen to   look at   photograph   sing to
teach   telephone   think about   visit   wash
write to

4 Work with a partner. Choose one of the following sentences and mime it. The class will decide which sentence you have chosen.

They are talking to themselves.
They are talking to each other.
They are talking to somebody else.
They are talking about somebody else.
They are singing to themselves.
They are singing to each other.
They are singing to somebody else.
They are singing about somebody else.
They are thinking about themselves.
They are thinking about each other.
They are thinking about somebody else.

Lesson 30

Students learn to express the notions of reciprocal and reflexive action, and to contrast self and others; they practise the language of agreement and disagreement in discussion.
Principal structures: reflexive/emphatic pronouns; *each other*; *somebody else*; *do the -ing*; *should*.
Phonology: rhythm and stress.

Language notes and possible problems

1. Reflexive/emphatic pronouns Both meanings of *myself, yourself* etc. are taught here: the reflexive meaning in Exercises 1–4 and the emphatic meaning ('I and nobody else') in Exercise 5.

2. *Each other* In some languages the same pronouns are used to talk about both reflexive and reciprocal actions. This may lead some students to make mistakes like *They've known themselves for about two years.

3. Reflexives and passives In some languages, too, reflexive pronouns are used where English prefers passives (leading to mistakes like *Address writes itself with two d's or Steak tartare eats itself cold).

4. Reflexive pronouns and object pronouns These can have the same form in some languages (leading to mistakes like *I often talk to me when I'm alone).

5. Omission of pronouns Note that reflexive pronouns are normally dropped in a few expressions referring to actions that people most often do to themselves rather than other people. The commonest are *wash* and *dress*.

6. Possessives With more advanced students, you may want to point out that reflexive pronouns have no possessive forms – instead of *myself's, *yourself's etc. we say *my own, your own* etc. Note also that *own* is only used after a possessive – we don't say *an own . . .

7. *Somebody else* Note that the plural equivalent of this is *other people*.

8. *Each other* and *one another* Most people make no distinction between these in modern English.

9. Timing If the discussion (Exercise 7) goes well, this lesson may be a little longer than average.

---

1 Sensitisation: *themselves* and *each other*
- This brief exercise should help students, if necessary, to see that *themselves* does not have the reciprocal meaning of *each other*.
- Let them look at the pictures for a moment. Then get them to think about the question and compare notes with their neighbours. If any students think that the left-hand picture shows 'two people looking at themselves', help them to understand that *themselves* does not have this meaning.
- Finally, look over the table of reflexive pronouns on Student's Book page 91. Practise the pronunciation (making sure students stress the second syllable in each case) and answer any questions.

2 Listening and following instructions
- Make sure students know the meaning of *shake hands* and *touch*. Then play the recording or read the instructions, pausing after each so that students can do the appropriate action.
- Repeat the exercise once or twice if necessary until students can do it easily.

Tapescript for Exercise 2
Look at each other.
Talk to yourselves.
Talk about yourselves.
Talk about each other.
Sing to yourselves.
Sing to each other.
Shake hands with each other.
Shake hands with yourselves.
Touch each other.

3 *Somebody else*
- If necessary, explain that *somebody else* means *another person*.
- Go over the list of actions and make sure students understand all the vocabulary.
- Discuss the examples, and then ask students to write similar sentences for some of the other verbs.

4 *Themselves, each other* and *somebody else*: miming
- Demonstrate first of all with a student. The two of you might, for example, mime 'talking to each other'. Ask the class to say or write the sentence they think you are miming.
- Then put students in pairs and give them a minute or two to choose a sentence and think about how to mime it.
- When they are ready, get pairs to do their mimes in turn.

5 Who does the housework?

- This introduces the emphatic use of *myself* etc.
- Let students work in groups to match up the words and pictures.
- Then practise the pronunciation. Pay attention to *ironing* (/'aɪənɪŋ/) – the *r* is not pronounced in standard British English.
- Tell students whether you do the various things yourself or not. Then ask them for the same information about themselves.
- You can extend the exercise by getting them to talk about other members of their family (e.g. *My father does his ironing himself, but my mother does all the cooking*).

6 Rhythm and stress: agreeing and disagreeing

- Ask each student to draw three columns on a piece of paper, and to try to classify the expressions according to whether they have one, two or three stresses.
- Let them compare notes; then play the recording (or read out the expressions), pausing to give students a chance to change their answers if they want to.
- When you have checked the answers, get the students to say the expressions after you or the recording.
- Then divide the class into groups of three or four and ask them to rank the expressions into a rough order, from those that express strong agreement to those that express strong disagreement.
- There is not, of course, one right answer. See below for one way in which the expressions might be grouped.

Answers to Exercise 6: pronunciation

1	2	3
Of **course**.	**Yes**, I **think** so.	**No**, I don't **agree**.
Per**haps**.	I'm **not** sure.	**No**, I don't **think** so.
I a**gree**.	**Well**, it de**pends**.	**Oh**, I don't **know**.
Probably.	**Yes**, **defi**nitely.	
	Of **course** not.	
	Per**haps** you're **right**.	

(*Note*: In *I (don't) think so*, *so* could also be stressed.)

Answers to Exercise 6: degree of agreement
1. Of course.   Yes, definitely.
2. I agree.
3. Yes, I think so.   Probably.
4. Perhaps.   Perhaps you're right.
5. I'm not sure.   Oh, I don't know.
6. Well, it depends.
7. No, I don't think so.
8. No, I don't agree.
9. Of course not. (*This could also express strong agreement with a negative statement.*)

7 Discussion: reactions to opinions

- In this exercise, responsibility for a fair discussion is shared among members of a group.
- Choose some of the sentences – those you think are most likely to provoke strong reactions. (If you are short of time, just choose four.)
- Make sure all the sentences are clearly understood.
- Then divide the class into groups of four or so. Each person in a group should choose a different sentence.
- Students read out their sentences in turn. The student who has chosen a sentence should make sure that all the others express their opinions on it.
- Walk round while students are working, helping where necessary.
- It is not a good idea to correct mistakes while the discussions are going on. But you may want to note points for later attention.

Practice Book exercises
1. Information transfer: *each other.*
2. *Myself* (emphatic) and *somebody else.*
3. Expressing opinions with *should.*
4. Punctuation and capital letters.
5. Writing a letter of advice.
6. Recreational reading: a poem.

5 Put the words from the box with the right pictures. Do you do these things yourself, or does somebody else do them for you? Examples:

'I do the ironing myself.'
'Somebody else does the decorating.'

| cleaning | cooking | decorating | ironing | mending | shopping | washing | washing up |

1   2   3   4

5   6   7   8

6 One, two or three stresses? Put the expressions from the box into three lists. Example:

1	2	3
Of course.	Yes, I think so.	

Of course.	Perhaps.	Yes, I think so.
No, I don't agree.	I'm not sure.	I agree.
Well, it depends.	Probably.	Yes, definitely.
No, I don't think so.	Of course not.	
Perhaps you're right.	Oh, I don't know.	

Now put the expressions in order, going from strong agreement to strong disagreement.

7 Work in groups. Each student must choose one of the sentences below and find out what the others think about it. Make sure everybody speaks. Use some expressions from Exercise 6 in your discussion.

1. People should cook for themselves at least some of the time.
2. Children should do some of the housework themselves.
3. Children should be free to choose their friends for themselves.
4. At the age of sixteen, children should be free to do what they like.
5. You teach yourself most of the things that you learn.
6. You should never put yourself first.
7. There is something wrong with people who talk to themselves a lot.
8. If you are married and you fall in love with somebody else, you shouldn't tell your wife/husband.
9. People who are in love should tell each other everything.
10. Parents and children should always be honest with each other.

Reflexive/emphatic pronouns	
myself	ourselves
yourself	yourselves
himself	themselves
herself	
itself	

Learn/revise: housework; wife; husband; clean; cook; iron; mend; shop; wash; wash up; do the cleaning/cooking *etc.*; think about (thought, thought); look at; listen to; talk to/about; draw (drew, drawn); sing (sang, sung); write to (wrote, written); feel sorry for (felt, felt); fall in love with (fell, fallen); marry; hurt (hurt, hurt); choose (chose, chosen); teach (taught, taught); learn (learnt, learnt); free; married; honest; somebody else; each other; some of; everything; at least; (I don't) agree; It depends; of course (not); I (don't) think so; I'm (not) sure; definitely; Perhaps you're right; There is something wrong with . . .

91

Summary E

Passives

Simple Present Passive tense

SUBJECT	AM/IS/ARE	PAST PARTICIPLE	
Most paper	is	made	from wood.
Trees	are	transported	to paper mills.

Simple Past Passive tense

SUBJECT	WAS/WERE	PAST PARTICIPLE	
The Taj Mahal	was	built	by Shah Jehan.
Hamlet	was	written	in about 1600.
The trees	were	blown down	by a big storm.

Active and passive
– The Chinese invented paper.
  Paper was invented by the Chinese.
– Shakespeare wrote *Hamlet*.
  Hamlet was written in 1600.

Infinitives, past tenses and past participles

Regular verbs

INFINITIVE	PAST TENSE	PAST PARTICIPLE
watch	watched	watched
clean	cleaned	cleaned

Irregular verbs

INFINITIVE	PAST TENSE	PAST PARTICIPLE
speak	spoke	spoken
build	built	built

Could Shakespeare **speak** Latin?
Curie **spoke** Polish and French.
Have you **spoken** to the boss yet?
Latin was **spoken** by many people in Shakespeare's time.

-ing form and past participle

She is **watching** TV.
That programme is **watched** by 30 million people every week.
When I went to see her she was **writing** letters.
Hamlet was **written** by Shakespeare.

Reported statements

– 'I **live** in Paris.'
  He **said** (that) he **lived** in Paris.
  (He said that he lives in Paris.)
– 'I've **been** to Venice.'
  He **told** Janet (that) he **had** been to Venice.
  (He told Janet that he has been to Venice.)

Say and tell

– Fred **said** that he lived in Paris and California.
  (Fred said Janet that . . .)
– He **told** Janet that he had been photographing the President. (He told that . . .)

Reported questions

– 'Where **do** you **work**?'
  He asked me where I **worked**.
  (He asked me where I work.)
  (He asked me where did I work.)
  (He asked me 'where did I work'.)
  (He asked me where did I work?)
– 'Where **is** your home?'
  He asked me where my home **was**.
  (He asked me where was my home.)
– 'Do you like living there?'
  He asked me **if** I liked living there.

Should

Children **should** do some of the housework themselves.
Do you think people who are in love **should** tell each other everything?

Talking in general: *the* is not used

Oil is produced in Texas.
  (The oil is produced in Texas.)
Trees are being cut down faster than they are being replaced. (The trees . . .)

92

Summary E

Summary of language taught in Lessons 25–30.

This lesson displays most of the more important language points that students should have learnt or revised in the last six lessons. Spend a short time going over the material with the students, answering questions and clearing up any difficulties. Students may also need to spend time at home making sure everything is thoroughly learnt.

Practice Book exercises
1. Materials; *made of*.
2. Personal and reflexive pronouns; *each other* and *somebody else*.
3. Vocabulary revision: adjectives referring to the physical characteristics of things.
4. *By yourself* and *with somebody else*.
5. Translation of material from Lessons 25–30.
6. Recycling vocabulary by writing a story.

So and *neither*

'I've got two brothers and a sister.'   'Really? So
  have I.'
'I can't play the piano.'   'Neither can I.'

Relative clauses: *who, that* and *where*

a young doctor **who** plays tennis
a company director **who** eats too much
a thing **that** tells you the time
a thing **that** you read
a place **where** you wait for a train

Leaving out object relative pronouns
a thing (that) you read
somebody (who) you like

Relative clauses: position of prepositions
a thing (that) you sit **on**
a thing (that) water comes **out of**

Position of *both*

One-part verbs
We **both read** the newspaper every day.
  (We read both . . .)

Two-part verbs
We **have both got** good bicycles.
  (We both have got . . .)
We **will both come** tomorrow.
  (We both will come . . .)

Are/were
We **are both** tall. (We both are tall.)

Neither of . . .

Neither of us has got a cat.
Neither of us plays the piano.

One of us . . . , the other . . .

One of us likes classical music, but **the other** doesn't.

Reflexive/emphatic pronouns

myself	ourselves
yourself	yourselves
himself	themselves
herself	
itself	

She's talking to **herself**.
They always think about **themselves**.
I usually do my ironing **myself**.

Each other

People who love **each other** should try to be honest
  with **each other**.

Somebody else

Do you do the ironing yourself, or does **somebody
  else** do it for you?
My girlfriend has fallen in love with **somebody else**.

Probability and certainty

It must be true.
It's probably true.
It could be true.
It might be true.
It's probably not true.
It can't be true.

It might be morning, because . . .
It can't be evening, because . . .
It must be during the day, because . . .
NOTE: *can't* is the opposite of *must* in this case.

I think . . .
I'm sure . . .
I know . . .
Perhaps . . .

Descriptions: three structures

- a woman **with** dark hair
  a woman **who has** dark hair
  a **dark-haired** woman
- a person **with** a thin face
  a person **who has** a thin face
  a **thin-faced** person

Getting help in class

Excuse me. What does *invented* mean?
I don't understand this.
Can you explain this word?
How do you pronounce this?

Revision E

Look at the exercises, decide which ones are useful to you, and do two or more.

GRAMMAR

1 Choose the correct sentences (passive or reflexive) from these two pairs.

- English is spoken here.
  English speaks itself here.
- Cats are always washed after they eat.
  Cats always wash themselves after they eat.

Now put the correct passive or reflexive forms into these sentences.

1. Most paper _is made_ from wood. (*make*)
2. Most people _talk to themselves_ when nobody is listening. (*talk to*)
3. Stamps .... in post offices. (*sell*)
4. Eggs .... to make cakes. (*use*)
5. Every time I .... in the mirror, I want to cry. (*look at*)
6. We didn't have German lessons at my school, so I bought a book and .... (*teach*)
7. Mercedes cars .... in West Germany. (*manufacture*)
8. 'Petrushka' .... by Stravinsky. (*compose*)
9. Mozart's music .... all over the world. (*listen to*)
10. Selina's a big girl now – she .... this morning. (*dress*)
11. These letters .... by a child. (*write*)
12. 'What are you doing here?' 'I .... by the Managing Director.' (*invite*)

2 Study Practice Book Lesson 26 Exercise 3 for a few minutes. Then prepare a 'guided tour' for a visitor to your school or your home town. Give the talk to a group of other students.

3 Write reported speech sentences as in the examples.

'It's cold.' (She said . . .)
She said that it was cold.

'Am I late?' (He asked her . . .)
He asked her if he was late.

'How much is the diamond ring?' (She wanted to know . . .)
She wanted to know how much the diamond ring was.

1. 'I'm tired.' (She said . . .)
2. 'Are you a doctor?' (He asked her . . .)
3. 'Will the train be late?' (She asked . . .)
4. 'I won't be able to go to the meeting.' (He said . . .)
5. 'Where is my husband?' (She wanted to know . . .)
6. 'What time does the next bus leave?' (He asked . . .)
7. 'You can't have any money.' (I told him . . .)
8. 'Can you swim?' (He asked me . . .)
9. 'Maria doesn't understand English.' (I said . . .)
10. 'Does she know what she's doing?' (I wondered . . .)
11. 'How many people know about the plan?' (She asked . . .)
12. 'It takes about three hours to drive to Cambridge.' (He explained . . .)
13. 'Why do your parents live in Greece?' (She asked me . . .)
14. 'I live a long way away.' (He said . . .)

4 Listen to the recording and then work with other students to produce a report of what was said.

PRONUNCIATION

1 Pronunciations of the letter *u*. Say these words after the recording or after your teacher.

1. hungry   husband   up   unhappy
2. use   Tuesday   true
3. purple   return   Thursday
4. full   put   push
5. until   surprise   nature

Which groups do these words come in? Decide how to pronounce them and then check with your teacher or the recording.

blue   burn   butcher   century   church
continue   curly   cut   difficult   excuse
faithful   figure   hurt   industry   luck
much   must   nurse   picture   pleasure
plump   produce   pull   rubber   shut
stuff   surname   trust   turn   unable
unemployed

Revision E

Students and teacher choose grammar, pronunciation, listening, vocabulary and speaking exercises.

Note: choice
Get students' views about which exercises are most useful before choosing a suitable selection. If necessary, groups can work on different exercises.

Materials needed
Cards for Speaking Exercise 5.

GRAMMAR

1 Passive and reflexive structures
● This exercise revises passive and reflexive structures, and also helps students who tend to confuse the two (see Teacher's Book *Language note 3* to Lesson 30).
● Get students to do at least part of the exercise in writing so that you can check on individuals.

Answers to Exercise 1
English is spoken here.
Cats always wash themselves after they eat.
3. Stamps *are sold* in post offices.
4. Eggs *are used* to make cakes.
5. Every time I *look at myself* in the mirror, I want to cry.
6. We didn't have German lessons at my school, so I bought a book and *taught myself*.
7. Mercedes cars *are manufactured* in West Germany.
8. 'Petrushka' *was composed* by Stravinsky.
9. Mozart's music *is listened to* all over the world.
10. Selina's a big girl now – she *dressed herself* this morning.
11. These letters *were written* by a child.
12. 'What are you doing here?' 'I *was invited* by the Managing Director.'

2 Simple Past Passive: 'guided tour'
● Explain to students that you want them to prepare a short talk about the school, their home town or some public building (real or imaginary), using similar structures to those in the text about Glastrop Cathedral in Practice Book Lesson 26.
● Give them a few minutes to look at the text; then let them prepare their talks individually or in groups as they wish.
● Help with vocabulary, but discourage students from using a lot of 'dictionary words' that the rest of the class won't understand.
● When they are ready, get them to give their talks to the class or to other groups.

3 Revision of reported speech
● This exercise and the next one revise and pull together the different aspects of reported speech that students have already worked on.
● Look over the examples and clear up any problems.
● Then get students to do the exercise individually, in groups or by class discussion, as you prefer.

Answers to Exercise 3
1. She said (that) she was tired.
2. He asked her if she was a doctor.
3. She asked if the train would be late.
4. He said (that) he would not (wouldn't) be able to go to the meeting.
5. She wanted to know where her husband was.
6. He asked what time the next bus left.
7. I told him (that) he could not (couldn't) have any money.
8. He asked me if I could swim.
9. I said (that) Maria did not (didn't) understand English.
10. I wondered if she knew what she was doing.
11. She asked how many people knew about the plan.
12. He explained that it took about three hours to drive to Cambridge.
13. She asked me why my parents lived in Greece.
14. He said (that) he lived a long way away.

4 Reporting a conversation

● Tell students that they are going to hear a conversation, and that their task is to report what was said. Make it clear that they are not expected to produce a word-for-word report, but just to give the main points in their own words (as one does when reporting a conversation in real life).
● Play the conversation twice, and then ask students for very short summaries of what was said. (For example: *'Bill asked Ann if she wanted to go to the mountains, but she said it was difficult because her mother was ill.'*)
● Then get them to fill in some of the details by telling you other things that were said.

Tapescript for Exercise 4: see page 128

PRONUNCIATION

1 Pronunciation of the letter *u*

● The first three groups show the normal stressed pronunciations of the letter *u*:
1. before two consonants, or before one consonant at the end of a word; in the prefix *un-*.
2. in most other cases.
3. before *r*.
The fourth group contains a small number of common words in which *u* is pronounced /ʊ/.
In the fifth group, unstressed *u* is pronounced /ə/.
● Practise the first three groups (using the recording if you wish); let students try to work out the rules.
● Ask what is special about the last two groups.
● Then let students work on the words in the list.

Answers to Exercise 1
1. cut, luck, much, must (*if stressed*), plump, rubber, shut, stuff, trust, unable, unemployed
2. blue, continue, excuse, produce
3. burn, church, curly, hurt, nurse, surname, turn
4. butcher, difficult, faithful, pull (Note that the quality of the *u* in *difficult* is obscure. It could also be regarded as a variety of /ə/, or as being merged with the *l*.)
5. century, figure, industry, must (*if unstressed*), picture, pleasure

LISTENING

1 Listening for gist

- Ask students to turn to Lesson 30, Exercise 7.
- Get them to read the list of discussion topics.
- Then tell them that they are going to hear people discussing some of these topics.
- They need not understand everything the people are saying; their task is merely to decide which of the topics is being discussed in each case.
- Play the recording through once; then play it a second time, pausing after each section.
- When you go over the answers with the students, you may want to play the recording again, pausing to show the points where the topic is mentioned.

Answers to Exercise 1

Recording A: Topic 7	Recording E: Topic 8
Recording B: Topic 9	Recording F: Topic 3
Recording C: Topic 4	Recording G: Topic 1
Recording D: Topic 5	Recording H: Topic 2

Tapescript for Exercise 1: see page 129

2 Song: *My Old Dad*

- Play the recording through once (books closed), and ask the students to tell you any words they remember.
- Let them open their books and read the lyrics.
- Play the song again so that the students can try to hear the missing verbs (mostly irregular past forms).

Tapescript for Exercise 2: see page 129

Answers to Exercise 2

saw; came; sat; read; did; ate
helped; taught; taught; learnt
went; was; loved; sit; watch; was; enjoyed
was; made; was; was

VOCABULARY

1 *Made of*

- Students can do this in groups, using dictionaries.
- Most questions have more than one possible answer. Number 4 is meant to be a credit card, but your students may have another plausible solution.

SPEAKING

1 Half and half dialogues

- Separate the class into halves. One half reads 'Student A' (only) on page 125 of their books; the others read 'Student B' (only) on page 126.
- Tell students to invent the other half of their dialogue, writing out *only* the new half.
- They can work in groups (only with people on their side), but each student must write his/her own copy.
- Help while they are working; speak quietly so that students from the other side will not hear.
- When they are ready, tell them to close their books.
- Put people from opposite sides in pairs, and let them act out the complete new dialogue.
- Most dialogues will make good sense. If one doesn't, help students to see why and to make small changes.
- Students can work with several partners.

2 'Find somebody who . . . '

- Explain vocabulary if necessary.
- Give students five minutes to prepare and ask their questions, and then see who has collected most names.
- The list can be adapted to suit your students.
- (We learnt this exercise from Mario Rinvolucri.)

3 Descriptions

- Students must say as much as possible about somebody in the class before the others guess who it is.
- Let them prepare and then talk in turn.
- Discourage wild guesses from the class.
- After the first few speakers, continue in groups.

4 Watching and recalling

- This practises Simple and Progressive Past tenses.
- Do a number of actions while standing, a number while sitting and a number while walking round.
- Then ask what you did at each stage (e.g. *'You put your hand on your head while you were standing up'*).
- Some suggestions:
  put your hand on your head; put your bag on your head; sing a song; close your eyes for a few moments; open your mouth; scratch your head; turn round; drop something and pick it up; open and close a book; throw something up and catch it; say a sentence in another language; take something out of your pocket or bag; take something off somebody's desk; speak to somebody in the class; laugh; smile; move a chair.
- Get students to do it themselves in groups.

5 Improvisation

- Prepare several cards with one sentence on each of them (see below).
- Ask for six to eight volunteers.
- Get them to sit in two rows facing each other, and tell them that they are strangers on a train. They must start talking and go on for five minutes.
- Give each student a card (tell them not to show the cards to each other).
- They must try to direct the conversation so that they can introduce their sentences naturally.
- Suggested sentences:

My father speaks ten languages.	I prefer dogs to cats.
I think her name's Barbara.	Would you like to go to the moon?
Umbrellas are very expensive.	There are six hotels in my village.
Nobody knows what happened.	It's not easy.
It's very good with cheese.	Singing makes you tired.
I was only seven at the time.	Scotland is full of strange people.
I don't believe it.	I would like a new one.
	I'll kill him if I see him.
	It was under the piano.

Practice Book exercises

1. Writing definitions.
2. The language of physical description.
3. Student's Cassette exercise (Student's Book Listening Exercise 1). Students use the first speaker's statement as a dictation.
4. Reading comprehension.
5. Writing: reporting a telephone conversation.
6. Crossword.

Additional reading

Note that students have now reached a level where they should be able to cope comfortably with the texts in Section A–E of *Additional reading* in the Practice Book (pages 108 to 112). You can set some of the readings for homework or just suggest that students read any of the texts that interest them when they have the time.

LISTENING

1 🔊 Look at Lesson 30, Exercise 7. Then listen to the recording. Which of the ten subjects are the people discussing?

2 🔊 Listen to the song and try to write down the verbs.

MY OLD DAD

We never .... him in the mornings,
And he always .... home late.
Then he .... and .... the paper
And .... the crossword while he ....

He never .... us with our homework,
But he .... me how to swim,
And he .... me to be patient.
I guess I .... a lot from him.

> My old Dad
> He was one of the good guys.
> He was nobody's hero,
> But he was special to me.

Every summer we .... to Blackpool,
Except when he .... unemployed.
He .... to .... and .... the sunset.
That .... one thing we both ....

He .... always very gentle,
Nothing ever .... him mad.
He .... never rich or famous,
But I .... proud of my old Dad.

> My old Dad
> He was one of the good guys.
> He was nobody's hero,
> But he was special to me.

VOCABULARY

1 Work in groups. See which group can finish the questions fastest. Use your dictionaries if you need to. Write the name of:

1. something made of wood that you can play a game with.
2. something made of iron that is found in a house.
3. something made of china.
4. something made of plastic that helps you buy things.
5. something made of glass that helps you see.
6. something made of leather that you can carry things in.
7. something made of wool that people wear on their feet.
8. something in the classroom that is made of steel.
9. something made of cotton that someone in the group is wearing.
10. something made of synthetic fibre that someone in the group is wearing.

SPEAKING

1 Turn to the page your teacher tells you. Invent the other half of the dialogue. Write down ONLY the invented half. Then close your book and find a partner to make a complete dialogue with.

2 Go round the class and see how many of these you can find in five minutes. Write down their names when you find them. Prepare your questions first. Examples:

'Do you like fish?'
'When were you born?'

FIND:
somebody who doesn't like fish.
somebody who was born in June.
somebody who has been to New York.
somebody who likes maths.
somebody who believes in horoscopes.
somebody who can't swim.
somebody who has got a cold.
somebody who hates pop music.
somebody who often has bad dreams.
somebody who has got a headache.
somebody who is very shy.
somebody who is not shy at all.

3 Describe another student. See how long you can talk before the others guess who it is.

4 Watch everything the teacher does. Then work in groups and try to remember everything he/she did: while he/she was standing up; while he/she was sitting down; while he/she was walking round.

5 Work with 5–7 other students. Get a card from the teacher. Imagine that your group are in the same compartment on a long train journey. Start a conversation going. Try to bring in the sentence on your card as naturally as possible.

Test **E**

LISTENING

1 Listen to the conversation. Which of the following expressions do you hear?

1. I'd like some tickets for Monday night.
2. Just a moment.
3. We've got a few at seven pounds.
4. Can I have ten at four pounds?
5. I'll pay by credit card.
6. And your card number?
7. Pick the tickets up at least half an hour before the performance.

2 Listen to the conversation again and write a short report of it. Use reported speech constructions (for example *The man asked if . . .* ; *The woman said that . . .*).

GRAMMAR

1 Put in the right form of the verb.

1. Most paper .... from wood. (*make*)
2. Our house .... in 1660. (*build*)
3. I .... English since last May. (*study*)
4. When I .... home yesterday, the children .... TV. (*get; watch*)
5. I didn't know you .... a doctor. (*be*)
6. Why don't you .... me the truth? (*tell*)
7. Let's .... a party. (*have*)
8. Somebody should .... Mary. (*help*)

2 Give the past tense and past participle of these verbs. Example:

break   *broke*   *broken*

blow   build   choose   cut   dry   fall   feel
grow   happen   hate   learn   make   marry
pay   show   steal   stop   teach   think

3 Put the words in the right places. Example:

Who are you writing? (*to*)
Answer: *Who are you writing to?*

1. Do you know what her name? (*is*)
2. She is at home. (*never*)
3. I go to Wales. (*often*)
4. My wife and I have got blue eyes. (*both*)
5. A chair is not only something that you sit, but also something that you look. (*on; at*)

4 Put in *a, an* or *the* if necessary; or don't put anything.

John Calloway is ...*a*... bank manager. He works in ...*a*... bank in ...*the*... centre of ...*–*... London. Every morning he gets up at seven o'clock, has .... breakfast and .... cup of coffee, and reads .... *Times*. Then he goes to .... work by .... bus. In .... morning he usually makes .... telephone calls, sees .... customers and dictates .... letters. He has .... lunch at .... restaurant near .... bank. In .... afternoon he works until five or five-thirty, and then goes .... home. He doesn't work on .... Saturdays or .... Sundays; he goes to .... cinema or reads. He likes .... novels and .... history. He is not married. He has .... sister in .... Oxford and .... brother in .... London.

5 Put in *may, might, can, could, can't* or *must*. (More than one answer may be possible.)

1. I .... be getting a new job. I don't know yet.
2. 'Here's a letter for you.' 'It's from Greece. It .... be from Sonia – I don't know anybody else in Greece.'
3. 'I'm afraid I've crashed your car.' 'Oh, no! I .... believe it.'
4. .... I look round?
5. John said I .... use his telephone.
6. 'What are you doing this evening?' 'I don't know. I .... go and see Pat, but I'll probably stay in.'

Test E

> **Students do a simple revision test.**

The purpose of the test

This test covers material from Lessons 25–30, as well as revising some points studied earlier in the course. It is not of course necessary to do all of the sections, and teachers should select according to their students' needs. Teachers who do not feel the test will be useful should simply drop it altogether.

If possible, try to make the students feel that they are 'testing themselves', rather than 'being tested'. It is not intended that students should 'pass' or 'fail' the test, and it is not particularly useful to give marks. (If the school or education system requires that this be done, you will need to work out a simple marking scheme.) But students should of course be told whether you feel their performance is satisfactory. In principle, students who have worked systematically through Lessons 25–30 ought to get most answers right.

Administration

The test can be administered in various ways, depending on how strictly you want to control students' performance; whether you want to collect the answers and mark them, or allow the students to correct them in class; and so on.

For the 'speaking' test, students will need to interrupt their work on the other questions to come and talk to you. They will need time for preparation (which can be done out of class if you wish).

Note that dictionaries should be used for the reading section (but not for the other sections). For this reason, you may wish to collect in students' answers to the earlier sections before they start on the reading text.

Notes, tapescript and answers are given below.

LISTENING

1: Listening for detail
Sentences 2, 4, 6 and 7 occur in the conversation.

2: Reporting a conversation
Make it clear to students that they are to produce a rough account of what was said, not to recall and report every sentence. Don't worry too much about small mistakes (but students should use reported speech structures correctly). The following specimen gives an idea of what is wanted, but there are of course hundreds of possible ways of expressing the answer.

Specimen answer to Listening Test 2
A man phoned the theatre and asked if they had any tickets for Monday night. The woman in the office said they had. The man said he wanted four at ten pounds, and asked if he could pay by credit card. The woman said that was all right, and asked the man for his name and address. She told him that he had to pick up the tickets half an hour before the performance.

Tapescript for Listening Tests 1 and 2: see next page (page 97)

GRAMMAR

1
1. is made
2. was built
3. have been studying
4. got; were watching
5. were
6. tell
7. have
8. help

2
blow – blew – blown
build – built – built
choose – chose – chosen
cut – cut – cut
dry – dried – dried
fall – fell – fallen
feel – felt – felt
grow – grew – grown
happen – happened – happened
hate – hated – hated
learn – learnt – learnt
make – made – made
marry – married – married
pay – paid – paid
show – showed – shown
steal – stole – stolen
stop – stopped – stopped
teach – taught – taught
think – thought – thought

3
1. Do you know what her name is?
2. She is never at home.
3. I often go to Wales.
4. My wife and I have both got blue eyes. (OR Both my wife and I have . . .)
5. A chair is not only something that you sit on, but also something that you look at.

4 John Calloway is *a* bank manager. He works in *a* bank in *the* centre of (–) London. Every morning he gets up at seven o'clock, has (–) breakfast and *a* cup of (–) coffee, and reads *The Times*. Then he goes to (–) work by (–) bus. In *the* morning he usually makes (–) telephone calls, sees (–) customers and dictates (–) letters. He has (–) lunch at *a* restaurant near *the* bank. In *the* afternoon he works until five or five-thirty, and then goes (–) home. He doesn't work on (–) Saturdays or (–) Sundays; he goes to *the* cinema or reads. He likes (–) novels and (–) history. He is not married. He has *a* sister in (–) Oxford and *a* brother in (–) London.

5
1. may/might/could
2. must
3. can't
4. Can/Could/May
5. can/could/might
6. might/may

96

VOCABULARY

1 (Alternative answers are possible in a number of cases.)
   1. mean
   2. tell
   3. each other
   4. manufactured/made/produced
   5. imported/brought
   6. needed/used; newspaper/paper
   7. discovered
   8. sure/certain
   9. sacked
   10. owe
   11. favourite
   12. famous/well-known/important

2 1. a pillow
   2. a hat/cap
   3. toothpaste
   4. a newspaper
   5. a platform/station
   6. a tongue

PRONUNCIATION

1 1. (/uː/): blue, use
   2. (/ɜː/): burn, hurt, nurse
   3. (/ʊ/): butcher, push, pull
   4. (/ə/): century, figure
   5. (/ʌ/): cut, luck, shut, unemployed

2 1. women
   2. hour
   3. large
   4. ceiling
   5. turn
   6. nose
   7. listen
   8. school

SPEAKING

This should be acted out, with you playing the part of the police officer. Look for appropriate vocabulary and structures, but don't pay too much attention to small mistakes. You should take into account not only correctness, but also success in communicating, fluency, breadth of knowledge, appropriacy and variety of language. If students are hesitant, help them along with suitable questions (e.g. *'When did you last see her? What was she wearing?'*).

WRITING

Here again, you should take into account not only correctness, but also the other factors that are involved in successful communication.

READING

You may wish to collect in students' answers to the earlier parts of the test before they start on this (so that they can't use their dictionaries to help with the vocabulary and other questions).

Encourage them to read slowly and carefully before they start on the questions.

Make sure they realise that they are supposed to decide whether the sentences express the same ideas as the text or not, not whether the sentences are objectively true.

Answers to Exercise 1
1. D
2. S
3. D
4. S
5. S
6. D
7. D
8. S

Tapescript for Listening Tests 1 and 2
A: Princess Theatre.
B: Have you got any tickets for Monday night?
A: Just a moment. I'll have a look . . . Sorry to keep you waiting. Yes, we've got a few at seven pounds fifty and plenty at ten pounds and fifteen pounds.
B: Can I have four at ten pounds?
A: How do you want to pay?
B: Can I pay by credit card?
A: Yes, of course. Can I have your name and address, please?
B: Michael Buxton, 33 Peace Avenue, Runcorn.
A: And your card number?
B: 4332 7171 2809 7755.
A: Thank you. That's four tickets at ten pounds for Monday the 17th at 8 o'clock. Please call at the theatre and pick the tickets up at least half an hour before the performance.
B: OK. Thanks very much.
A: Thank you. Bye.
B: Bye.

Test Book recordings
A recording for Test 5 in the Test Book follows this lesson on the Class Cassette.

97

VOCABULARY

1 Put a suitable word or expression in each blank.

1. Excuse me. What does this word ....?
2. Could you .... me where I can buy a ticket?
3. They are very deeply in love with ....
4. Cars are .... in Detroit.
5. The wood used for paper-making is ....
   from Norway.
6. One tree is .... for every four hundred
   copies of a typical daily ....
7. Radium was .... by Pierre and Marie Curie.
8. Are you .... that this money is yours?
9. He once worked for our company, but he was
   .... for stealing.
10. Don't forget that you .... me a lot of
    money.
11. 'What's your .... colour?' 'Red.'
12. He's photographed a lot of .... people.

2 What are the following?

1. A thing that you put your head on when you
   sleep.
2. A thing that you put on your head when you
   go out.
3. Stuff that you use when you brush your teeth.
4. A thing that you read to find out what has
   happened in the world.
5. A place where you wait for a train.
6. A thing that you talk and taste with.

PRONUNCIATION

1 Divide these words into five groups, according
to the pronunciation of the letter u.

blue   burn   butcher   century   cut   figure
hurt   luck   nurse   push   pull   shut
unemployed   use

2 In each of these groups, there is a letter that
comes in all four words. But in one of the words it
is pronounced differently. Which is the different
word in each group? Example:

u: cut   shut   stuff   pull
Answer: *pull*. (The letter u is pronounced differently
in *pull* from the way it is pronounced in the other
three words.)

1. o: home   open   don't   women
2. h: horse   hour   hundred   head
3. g: go   large   angry   give
4. c: call   cup   coat   ceiling
5. r: right   turn   fry   hurry
6. s: nose   seen   useful   bus
7. t: after   must   listen   butter
8. ch: child   which   school   catch

SPEAKING

1 Imagine that a friend or relation of yours has
disappeared. You are at the police station, reporting
the disappearance to a policeman or policewoman
(the teacher). Give a description of the person
(clothes, appearance, age, profession, personality),
and say when you last saw him or her.

WRITING

1 Describe one of the people in the room.

READING

1 Read the text. You can use a dictionary.

How much do we know about the world we live in? Some of
us don't know much, it seems. Scientists at Oxford asked
people the following simple questions:
– Does the earth go round the sun?
– Does oxygen come from plants?
– Does sunlight cause skin cancer?
– Is the centre of the earth hot or cold?
– Did the earliest people live before, at the same time as
  or after the dinosaurs?
– If milk is radioactive, can you make it safe by boiling it?

How many of the answers do you know? The Oxford
scientists were surprised to find that many of the men and
women they questioned had no idea of the facts. About 40%
of the people didn't know that the earth went round the sun,
or that oxygen came from plants. While 90% of the people
knew that sunlight could cause skin cancer, and 80% knew
that the centre of the earth was very hot, 54% thought,
wrongly, that the first people lived at the same time as the
dinosaurs. And 35% of people thought that radioactive milk
could be made safe by boiling it.

How important is this? Does it matter if people don't know
whether or not the earth goes round the sun? Perhaps not.
But we do have to make up our minds about many things
which need an understanding of science. Should the
government build more nuclear power stations? Is it a good
thing to spend money on space research? Is it right to carry
out experiments on animals? If we have no basic knowledge
of science, how can we make intelligent democratic
decisions on questions like these?

Now read the following sentences. Write *S* if the
sentence says the same thing as the text, and *D* if
it says something different.

1. Even Oxford scientists don't always know the
   answers to simple questions.
2. Some people don't know much about the world.
3. Only 40% of people thought that the earth
   went round the sun.
4. Oxygen comes from plants.
5. Most people know that sunlight can cause skin
   cancer.
6. More than half of the people questioned thought
   that the first people lived before the dinosaurs.
7. Radioactive milk can only be made safe by
   boiling it.
8. People in a modern democracy need to know
   something about science.

97

31 Before and after

Talking about sequences; time clauses with *as soon as*, *before*, *after*, *until*; *still*, *yet* and *already*; *such* and *so*.

1 Choose one of these questions (or make up a similar question) and ask as many people as possible. Make a note of the answers.

1. Do you get up as soon as you wake up?
2. Do you have breakfast before or after you get dressed?
3. Do you put your left shoe on before your right?
4. Do you make the bed before or after you have breakfast?
5. Do you undress before you brush your teeth at night?
6. Do you put the light out before or after you get into bed?
7. Do you go to bed at a fixed time, or do you wait until you're tired?
8. Before you go to sleep, do you usually read in bed?
9. Do you pay bills as soon as you get them?
10. Before you buy something, do you always ask the price?
11. Do you put salt on food before or after you taste it?
12. Do you read the newspaper before or after you arrive at work?
13. Do you address an envelope before or after you close it up?
14. Do you answer letters as soon as you get them?
15. Do you wait until your hair is too long before you go to the hairdresser?
16. Do you have to translate English sentences before you can understand them?
17. What are you going to do after the lesson has finished?
18. Are you going to study English before you go to bed tonight?
19. Will you study any more languages after you have learnt English?
20. Will you keep on working until you're sixty?

2 Report the answers to the class. Examples:

'Four students out of twelve have breakfast before they get dressed.'
'Sixty per cent of the students read the newspaper after they arrive at work.'
'Most people put their left shoe on before their right.'

3 How do you usually spend the evening? Use this skeleton to help you write a paragraph.

When I ...., I .... Then I .... and .... After that I .... Then I .... until .... Before I ...., I ....

4 Pronunciation. Say these words.

1. possible   on   long   not   stop   want
2. before   more   report   always   saw   course   caught   bought
3. note   go   envelope   close   coat

Now put these words into groups 1, 2 or 3. (One word does not belong in any of the groups.)

no   off   short   got   home   other   fall   thought   draw   lost   horse   open   boat   gone   don't

Can you find any more words to put in the three groups?

5 Look at picture 1 and study the examples. Then put *still*, *yet* or *already* into the other sentences.

1

1. John's still in bed.
   He hasn't got up yet.
   Susan's already dressed.

2

2. The postman has .... been.
   Jane hasn't picked up her letters ....
   They are .... on the mat.

3. Alice's taxi is .... waiting in front of her house.
   Alice isn't ready ....
   She is .... in the bath.

4. 'Have you had lunch ....?'
   'No, I'm .... working. What about you?'
   'I've .... eaten.'

5. Peter and Ann are both nineteen.
   Ann is .... at school.
   Peter is .... married.
   He hasn't got any children ....

6. Jake is nearly forty, but he .... plays football every Saturday.
   His son Andy is not fifteen ...., but he is .... a good footballer, too.

Lesson 31

Students learn more about expressing time relations.
Principal structures: time clauses with *as soon as*, *before*, *after*, *until*; sequencing markers; the use of *still*, *yet* and *already*; *such* and *so* with adjectives.
Phonology: /ɒ/, /ɔː/ and /əʊ/ and their spellings.

Language notes and possible problems

1. Time clauses Students who speak European languages will have little difficulty in understanding or constructing complex sentences containing time clauses. Speakers of other languages may have problems, particularly in cases where the time clause begins the sentence. Practice Book Exercises 1 and 2 provide extra work for those who need it.

2. Tenses You may need to remind students that present tenses are normally used to refer to the future in time clauses (see the last four questions in Exercise 1). Note also the occasional use of a Present Perfect tense to stress the idea of completion (see Exercise 1, questions 17 and 19). For the use of the Past Perfect, see Lesson 32.

3. Yet, still and already These words can cause difficulty: other languages do not always have three separate words with exactly the same range of meaning. Simple rules:
– *Still* expresses continuation. Position: with verb.
– *Yet*: used in questions and negative sentences to talk about something which is expected to happen, but is not known to have happened (or has not happened) so far. Position: at end of clause.
– *Already*: used especially in affirmative sentences to say that something expected has happened (perhaps earlier than expected). Position: with verb or at end of clause.
Another way of looking at it is to consider that these three words show whether something belongs to the past, present or future:
– *Still* says that something belongs to the present, not the past.
– *Not yet* says that something belongs to the future, not to the present; in questions, *yet* asks whether something belongs to the present or the future.
– *Already* says that something belongs to the present or past, not the future.

If you are short of time
Drop Exercise 4 if pronunciation is not a high priority; drop Exercises 7 and 8 or give them for homework.

1 Time clauses: survey
● Tell students to look through the questions, asking you (or using their dictionaries) if they have any difficulty.
● Then tell them each to choose a question (or to make up a question of a similar kind). Try to ensure that students choose different questions as far as possible.
● Get students to walk round (or to talk to as many other students as possible) asking their questions. They should note the number of 'yes' and 'no' answers.

2 Reporting the survey
● Go over the examples and make sure students can use all the structures involved.
● Then get them to report on their findings.
● Make sure they use singular verbs with *nobody* and *everybody* if the occasion arises.

3 Linking sentences into paragraphs
● Here, students practise using conjunctions and simple adverbial markers (*then*, *after that*) to show the sequence of a series of events.
● Some students will find this exercise easy: encourage them to make more complex paragraphs using other sequencing markers (e.g. *as soon as*, *next*, *finally*) if they want to. Other students may need a good deal of help.

4 Pronunciation
● Many students find it difficult to distinguish the three vowels /ɒ/, /ɔː/ and /əʊ/. This exercise should help students to tell them apart and to know which spellings correspond to each vowel. (But note that the analysis applies to British English only — the pronunciation and distribution of these sounds are very different in American English.)
● Get students to try the words in the first group. Then demonstrate them, using the recording as a model if you wish, and get the class to practise them. (A common mistake is to make the vowel without rounding the lips — this makes it sound rather similar to /ʌ/, so that for example *not* and *nut* are confused.)
● Point out that this vowel is usually spelt *o*, but can be spelt with *a* after *w*.
● Try the words in the second group. This vowel is longer; the jaws are further apart, but the lips are more tightly rounded.
● Make sure students notice all the different ways in which /ɔː/ can be spelt: the most common are *or*, *au*, *aw*, and *al*.
● The third vowel (/əʊ/) should be familiar. Students should note the common spellings: final *o*, *o* followed by silent *e*, and *oa*.
● When students can pronounce the sounds well, get them to try the second and third parts of the exercise (preferably before they hear the words pronounced). Let them compare notes in groups before you discuss the answers with them.

Answers to Exercise 4
Group 1 (/ɒ/): off, got, lost, gone.
Group 2 (/ɔː/): short, fall, thought, draw, horse.
Group 3 (/əʊ/): no, home, open, boat, don't.
The word that does not belong is *other* (/'ʌðə(r)/).

5 Still, yet and already
● Let students look at the first illustration and think about the meanings of the three adverbs.
● Then ask them to look at the second illustration and try to fill in the right words.
● If necessary, explain the meanings of the adverbs (see *Language notes*).
● Continue the exercise as an individual or group activity, as you wish.

6 Listening practice: itinerary

- Make sure students understand what they have to do.
- Go over the pronunciation of the place names, to make sure students will recognise them:

Birmingham /ˈbɜːmɪŋəm/
Coventry /ˈkɒvəntri/
Dudley /ˈdʌdli/
Leamington /ˈlemɪŋtən/
Wolverhampton /wʊlvəˈhæmtən/

- Ask the students to copy the place names on a piece of paper.
- Then play the recording and ask students to try to note down the order in which the traveller visits the places.
- Play the recording again once or twice if necessary, but don't stop in the middle or give explanations.
- Let students compare notes in groups before giving them the answer.

Answer to Exercise 6
Dudley, Wolverhampton, Birmingham, Leamington, Coventry.

Tapescript for Exercise 6
SWITCHBOARD: Cooper and Johnson. Can I help you?
COMMERCIAL TRAVELLER: Hello. This is Henry Douglas. Could I speak to Mr Cooper, please?
SWITCHBOARD: One moment. I'll put you through.
BOSS: Arthur Cooper here.
CT: Hello, sir. This is Douglas.
BOSS: Oh, hello, Henry. How's it going? Finished yet?
CT: No, not yet, sir. It's going rather slowly, I'm afraid. The meeting with Fisher and Dennis took half the morning. Those people are so slow!
BOSS: Yes, they are a bit sleepy, aren't they? How were things in Coventry?
CT: I haven't been there yet, sir. I went to Dudley first.
BOSS: I see. So you're going to Coventry next?
CT: No. I want to go to Leamington before I go to Coventry, because Mr Singleton won't be there after three o'clock.
BOSS: Oh, right. And then you'll go on to Wolverhampton, I suppose.
CT: I've already been to Wolverhampton, sir. I went there before I came to Birmingham.
BOSS: Oh, I see. Right. Well, good luck. I hope things go a bit faster now. Give my regards to John Walsh in Coventry, will you?
CT: Yes, of course, sir. See you tomorrow.
BOSS: Right you are. Goodbye.
CT: Goodbye, sir.

7 Story

- Give students a few minutes to read through the story. Explain any difficulties.
- Point out the difference between *such* (used with a noun phrase, as in *such a good dancer*) and *so* (used with an adjective alone, as in *so handsome*). (Practice Book Exercise 5 deals with this point.) You may also like to comment on the use of the Past Perfect, which is previewed here before being studied in detail in Lesson 32.
- Tell students to close their books and see if they can remember some of what happened.

8 Story: students as co-authors

- This story is a collaborative effort: the beginning and end are provided, and students have to make up the middle.
- This is probably best done in groups. Give students ten minutes or so to work out how Alison's life could have changed so dramatically. One person in each group should make notes.
- If you wish, you can then ask students to write out the new chapter (though this will probably take a long time, and might be better done for homework).
- One person from each group should then tell the rest of the class about their plan for Chapter 2.
- Alternatively, get one person from each group to go to another group and pass on their version.

Practice Book exercises
1. Joining sentences with *before*, *after* and *as soon as*.
2. Analysing sentences with *before* and *after*.
3. Choosing *still*, *yet* and *already*.
4. Student's Cassette exercise (Student's Book Exercise 6, up to '*Those people are so slow!*'). Students listen and write down what they hear.
5. *Such* or *so* with adjectives.
6. Recreational reading.

6  Listen to the conversation between a commercial traveller and his boss. The traveller has to visit five places: Birmingham, Coventry, Dudley, Leamington and Wolverhampton (not in that order). Can you list the towns in the order in which he has visited them or will visit them?

7 Read the story.

Alison Bogle

Chapter 1

Alison Bogle lived in Barnstaple and worked in a bookshop. She was 23 – slim and pretty, rather shy and very quiet. She spent most of her spare time reading; at the weekend she went walking on the moors, or drove over to see her parents in Taunton.

Chapter 2

....
....
....

Chapter 3

Alison poured herself another glass of champagne and smiled at Carlos. What a man! He was so handsome. And such a good dancer. And so kind to her. Alison had never met anybody like him. She wondered what he was thinking.

The sun, shining down through the palm trees, made a moving pattern of light and shade on the sand. Carlos smiled back at her and stood up. He took her hand. 'Come on, let's have another swim,' he said.

Alison was quite happy, but sometimes she wished she didn't have such a quiet life. Barnstaple was not really a very exciting place. At half past ten at night, all the lights went out. Nobody ever danced in the streets – at least, Alison had never seen it happen. And it rained all the time. *All* the time.

There were so many things Alison would like to do. So many things she hadn't done. For example, she had never been in an aeroplane.

8 Work with two or three other students. Make up Chapter 2 of the story. Then tell your Chapter 2 to another group.

Learn/revise: bill; price; salt; food; envelope; hairdresser; postman; aeroplane; make a bed (made, made); undress; get up; wake up (woke, woken); get dressed; put on clothes (put, put); brush one's teeth; put out a light; go to bed; go to sleep; taste; understand (understood, understood); address an envelope; answer a letter; translate; study; keep on . . .ing (kept, kept); drive (drove, driven); wonder; smile; tired; per cent; at night; tonight; in front of; as soon as; before; after; until; still; yet; then; already; as much/many as possible; such; so.

32 I hadn't seen her for a long time

Talking about unexpected events; Past Perfect tense.

1 Choose the correct words and expressions to put in the gaps.

I .... down the street one day
Looking at the shops
When someone asked me if I .... the way.
I gave the girl directions
And then saw who it was.
I couldn't .... of anything to say.

I hadn't seen her .... a very long time
Since the day we said goodbye.
She .... changed,
She .... looked young and shy.
I thought perhaps .... changed so much
She didn't .... it was me,
Then I saw the recognition in her eye.

We stood in silence for a while,
Then I .... her to a bar.
I felt as if I was walking with a ghost.
We drank and began to talk
And then her eyes met mine.
Her eyes .... always shown her feelings most.

We .... about the good old days
About family and friends
About the hopes we'd shared .... it all went wrong.
She seemed quite pleased to see me
So I .... two more drinks
But when I got back to the table she .... gone.

I hadn't seen her for a very long time *etc.*

walked / was walking

know / knew

think / to think

since / for

hasn't / hadn't
still / yet
I / I'd
realise / realised

was leading / led

have / had

talked / have talked

before / after

ordered / had ordered
has / had

2 🔊 Listen to the song and check your answers.

3 Pronunciation. Listen to the recording. How many words do you hear in each sentence? What are they? (Contractions like *I'd* count as two words.)

Lesson 32

Students learn more about narrative and the expression of past time relations.
Principal structure: Past Perfect tense.
Phonology: perceiving unstressed syllables.

Language notes and possible problems
Past Perfect tense This may cause problems for students who do not have an equivalent tense in their own language. A simple rule of thumb: the Past Perfect is used when one is already talking about things that happened at some time in the past, and one wants to go back for a moment to an earlier past time. Note the following points:
– The Past Perfect is only used to talk about an earlier past which is not the main focus of attention; if our main interest moves to the earlier period, we start using the Simple Past to talk about it.
– We don't always use the Past Perfect in sentences with conjunctions like *before* or *after*, where the time sequence is already explicit.

1 Song: completing the text
• Give students a few minutes to look at the text and decide which are the correct forms.
• Let them compare notes in groups.

2 Listening to the song
• Play the song, and tell students to check their answers.
• Explain any difficulties.
• See if students can understand the reason for the use of the Past Perfect in the song.
• If students like the idea, play the song again and let them sing along.

Tapescript and answers to Exercise 2

I *was walking* down the street one day
Looking at the shops
When someone asked me if I *knew* the way.
I gave the girl directions
And then saw who it was.
I couldn't *think* of anything to say.

I *hadn't* seen her *for* a very long time
Since the day we said goodbye.
She *hadn't* changed,
She *still* looked young and shy.
I thought perhaps *I'd* changed so much
She didn't *realise* it was me,
Then I saw the recognition in her eye.

We stood in silence for a while,
Then I *led* her to a bar.
I felt as if I was walking with a ghost.
We drank and began to talk
And then her eyes met mine.
Her eyes *had* always shown her feelings most.

We *talked* about the good old days
About family and friends
About the hopes we'd shared *before* it all went wrong.
She seemed quite pleased to see me
So I *ordered* two more drinks
But when I got back to the table she *had* gone.

I hadn't seen her for a very long time *etc.*

3 How many words?
• Play the recording, stopping after each sentence while students try to decide how many words there are, and what they are.
• Play the recording two or three times if necessary.

Tapescript and answers to Exercise 3
1. This all happened about three years ago. (7)
2. I had to go to London. (6)
3. The station's about five miles away. (7)
4. My train was at nine o'clock. (6)
5. By eight-thirty I'd already packed everything. (8)
6. We went out to the car. (6)
7. I got into the car. (5)
8. I realised that I'd forgotten my coat. (8)
9. I drove back home as fast as I could. (9)
10. I arrived at the station just in time. (8)

4 Past Perfect tense

● Look at the examples with the students and make sure they understand the use of the Past Perfect.
● It is probably best to get students to do at least part of the exercise individually in writing, so that you can check that everybody has grasped the point.
● Practice Book Exercises 5 and 6 give further work on the Past Perfect if needed.

Answers to Exercise 4

1. started; had met
2. looked; had tried
3. had remembered
4. examined; had broken
5. had not been
6. had already started; got
7. had learnt
8. brought

5 Listening practice: anecdote

● (This is a true story, which happened to the authors.)
● Look over the pictures first of all. Explain that they are in the wrong order, and that students have to listen to a story and then try to put the pictures in the right order.
● Teach the word *anorak*.
● Play the recording once without stopping.
● Ask students to make a start on the exercise, working individually.
● After a few minutes, play the recording again one or more times.
● When students have done what they can, tell them to continue in groups, trying to agree on a final version.
● Then discuss the answer with them.

Answer to Exercise 5

F, I, D, G, B, H, J, C, A, E
or
F, I, D, G, H, B, J, C, A, E

Exercise 5: summary of story

(The story is too long and rambling to give the complete tapescript. A summary is provided for reference.)

1. Speaker had to go to Zürich for conference. Train from Didcot to Reading, coach Reading to airport. Train at 9.00. By 8.30 had packed and was ready to drive to station (five miles away). Feeling calm and relaxed.
2. Getting into car, hit head on roofrack. Blood started running down forehead. Started driving to station (accompanied by girlfriend, who would take car back home afterwards). Feeling less calm.
3. Halfway to station, realised had forgotten anorak (essential in Zürich in winter). Turned round and raced back to house. Picked up anorak. Drove back to station at enormous speed. Forehead still bleeding. Feeling much less well organised.
4. Kissed girlfriend goodbye and rushed into station. Just managed to jump on to train as it was moving out.
5. Sitting in train (forehead still bleeding) realised had forgotten to give girlfriend car keys. Girlfriend would not be able to take car back home.
6. Saw Oxford through train window instead of Reading. Realised was on wrong train.

6 Conversation

● In a fluent and confident class (especially if numbers are small), you can do this as a whole-class activity.
● Otherwise, put students in groups of four or five.
● Ask if the song, or the story in Exercise 5, reminded them of incidents that have happened to them.
● If so, get them to tell the class or their group about the incident.
● If students are working in groups, finish by asking for one of the stories from each group to be told to the whole class.
● You may have to help with vocabulary, but try not to interrupt students with corrections unless it is absolutely necessary.

Practice Book exercises

1. Vocabulary revision: cardinal and ordinal numbers.
2. Word stress.
3. Months of the year and days of the week.
4. Student's Cassette exercise (Student's Book Exercise 2). Students listen to the song and write down one or more verses.
5. Reading comprehension and practice with the Past Perfect.
6. Guided writing.

4 Past Perfect tense. Look at the examples and then do the exercise.

PAST (THEN):	I **saw** who it was.
EARLIER PAST (BEFORE THEN):	I **hadn't seen** her for a very long time.

PAST:	We **talked** about . . .
EARLIER PAST:	. . . the hopes we**'d shared**.

Put in the correct tense (**Simple Past or Past Perfect**).

1. When we .... talking I realised that we .... before. (*start*; *meet*)
2. When I .... at my suitcase I could see that somebody .... to open it. (*look*; *try*)
3. When we got to the restaurant we found that nobody .... to reserve a table. (*remember*)
4. The doctor .... him, and found that he .... his arm. (*examine*; *break*)
5. Before my eighteenth birthday I .... out of England. (*not be*)
6. We were a few minutes late, so the film .... when we .... to the cinema. (*already start*; *get*)
7. When she got to England, she found that the language was quite different from the English that she .... at school. (*learn*)
8. 'Good afternoon. Can I help you?' 'Yes. I .... my watch to you for repair three weeks ago. Is it ready yet?' (*bring*)

5 Listen to the story and then put the pictures in the right order.

 A

 B

 C

 D E

 F

 G

 H

 I

 J

6 Can you talk about one of these?

1. A day in your life when everything went wrong.
2. A meeting with somebody that you hadn't seen for a very long time.

Past Perfect tense
I had (I'd) seen you had (you'd) seen *etc.*
had I seen? had you seen? *etc.*
I had not (hadn't) seen you had not (hadn't) seen *etc.*

Learn/revise: street; shop; silence; bar; feelings; family; hope; drink; table; suitcase; restaurant; birthday; cinema; language; watch; minute; stand (stood, stood); drink (drank, drunk); give (gave, given); show (showed, shown); share; seem; open; order; realise; sit down (sat, sat); start; bring (brought, brought); remember; go wrong; shy; pleased; late; ready; anything; everything; somebody; nobody; a few; ago; a long time; down.

33 All right, I suppose so

Question tags; reported instructions; weak and strong pronunciations.

1 🔊 Read the dialogue and then listen to the recording. There are six differences between the printed version and the recorded version. Can you find them all?

TONY: Mum, can I have a party next weekend?

MOTHER: Well, I don't know. How many people?

TONY: About twenty, I think. That's OK, isn't it?

MOTHER: I don't know. You're not going to invite that Edwards boy, are you?

TONY: Well –

MOTHER: Because I'm not having him in the house.

TONY: All right, Mum. Well, can I?

MOTHER: You remember what happened last time, don't you?

TONY: Oh, go on, Mum. We'll be very careful. I promise.

MOTHER: Well, all right, I suppose so. But don't invite more than twenty. And you must tell me exactly how many are coming, and you **must** tidy up afterwards.

TONY: OK, Mum. I will.

MOTHER: And you will be careful of the carpet, won't you?

TONY: All right, Mum.

MOTHER: And you **must** get everybody out by midnight.

TONY: Yes, Mum.

MOTHER: And you won't make too much noise, will you?

TONY: No, Mum.

MOTHER: And do put . . .

2 Work in pairs and practise the dialogue.

102

Lesson 33

Students learn more about the language of requests and commands.
Principal structures: negative imperatives, reported questions and instructions; question tags; *do* used for emphasis.
Phonology: strong and weak forms; intonation of question tags.

Language notes and possible problems

1. Reported instructions   Here students use the structure *verb + object + infinitive* to report instructions and requests that somebody should do something (e.g. *She told him to tidy up afterwards*). Make sure students get the right word order in reported negatives (e.g. *She told him **not to invite** the Edwards boy*).

2. Question tags   The meaning of the question-tag structure will probably be easy for students to grasp: many languages have an expression which is added to a sentence in order to invite the hearer's agreement. But students will probably find the complicated structural rules of English question tags difficult to learn, and the intonation is likely to cause problems. See the instructions to Exercise 3 for detailed rules.

3. Must   Students have already met examples of both *must* and *have to*. Note that *must* is generally used to impose or question obligation; *have to* is used more objectively to talk about obligation which already exists.

Timing

This is a longer-than-average lesson. Exercise 6 can be dropped if your students are not aiming at a high standard of pronunciation.

---

1 Dialogue: detecting differences

• Give students a few minutes to read the dialogue and ask questions.

• Then play the recording without stopping. Ask students if they noticed any differences.

• Play it two or three more times and see if they can find all the differences (perhaps combining in groups to share information).

Tapescript and answers to Exercise 1

TONY: Mum, can I have a party next *Saturday*?
MOTHER: Well, I don't know. How many people?
TONY: About *thirty*, I think. That's OK, isn't it?
MOTHER: I don't know. You're not going to invite that Edwards boy, are you?
TONY: Well –
MOTHER: Because I'm not having him in the house.
TONY: All right, Mum. Well, can I?
MOTHER: You *haven't forgotten* what happened last time, *have you*?
TONY: Oh, go on, Mum. We'll be very careful. I promise.
MOTHER: Well, all right, I suppose so. But don't invite more than twenty. And you must tell me exactly how many are coming, and you **must** tidy up afterwards.
TONY: OK, Mum. I will.
MOTHER: And you will be careful of the *furniture*, won't you?
TONY: All right, Mum.
MOTHER: And you **must** get everybody out by midnight.
TONY: Yes, Mum.
MOTHER: And you won't make too much noise, will you?
TONY: No, Mum.
MOTHER: And *don't* put . . .

2 Practising the dialogue

• Get one or two pairs of volunteers to read the dialogue together. Make any essential corrections and then get the class to practise in pairs.

• Go round listening and helping if necessary.

3 Question tags

• Give students time to look at the examples and discuss them. They should find it reasonably easy to work out the basic rules:
- the tag is negative if the sentence is affirmative, and vice versa.
- the tag repeats the auxiliary verb of the sentence; if there is no auxiliary, the tag contains a form of *do*.

• Then get students to do the exercise, either individually or by class discussion as you prefer.

4 Intonation of question tags

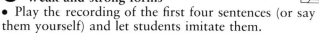

• Play the examples and get students to imitate them.
• Explain how the intonation of the tag depends on the speaker's intention. A rising intonation means that the speaker wants information (it is a real question); a falling intonation means that the speaker is pretty sure of the hearer's agreement.
• Play the sentences one by one and let the class discuss whether they are real questions or not.

Answers to Exercise 4
1. Real question.
2. Asking for agreement.
3. Real question.
4. Asking for agreement.
5. Asking for agreement.
6. Real question.
7. Real question.
8. Asking for agreement.
9. Asking for agreement.
10. Real question.

5 Reported questions and instructions

• Look over the examples. If necessary, revise the rules for reported questions. Then make sure students are clear about how instructions and requests are reported (verb + object + infinitive).
• Go through the exercise. It is probably best to ask students to write some of the answers individually. In Question 1, look out for the mistake *Tony asked his mother to have a party*. Check for correct word order in the negative infinitives (Questions 7 and 8).

Answers to Exercise 5
1. Tony asked his mother if he could have a party.
2. His mother asked him how many people he wanted to invite.
3. She asked him if he remembered what happened last time.
4. She told him to tidy up afterwards.
5. She told him to get everybody out by midnight.
6. She asked him to be careful of the carpet.
7. She told him not to invite more than twenty.
8. She told him not to make too much noise.

6 Weak and strong forms

• Play the recording of the first four sentences (or say them yourself) and let students imitate them.
• Make sure they realise the effect of using the strong form of *must* — it expresses insistence on the importance of the action referred to.
• Then get students to try the next four sentences. Play them or say them yourself so that students can check their pronunciation.
• Let students discuss the meanings of the strong pronunciations in these sentences.
• Finally, see if students can decide how to make the last two sentences emphatic. (Where there is no auxiliary verb, a verb can be made emphatic by adding stressed *do*: *I **do** like your dress*; *He **does** talk a lot*.)

7 Sketches

• Students will probably need twenty minutes or so to prepare and practise their conversations. Encourage them to use expressions from the dialogue in the lesson.
• When they are ready, let them perform them for other groups or the rest of the class.
• You may like to tape- or video-record the performances. If so, let students know in advance: this will motivate them to aim at a high standard.

Practice Book exercises
1. Question tags.
2. Imperatives and negative imperatives (road signs).
3. Word stress.
4. Grammar and vocabulary revision: text completion.
5. Student's Cassette exercise (Student's Book Exercise 1). Students listen to the dialogue and practise pronunciation and intonation.
6. Recreational reading and follow-up writing.

3 Look at the examples and work out the rules. Then complete the sentences.

That's OK, **isn't** it?
You **will** be careful of the carpet, **won't** you?
You **remember** what happened last time, **don't** you?
You**'re not** going to invite that Edwards boy, **are** you?
You **won't** make too much noise, **will** you?

1. Eight o'clock is a good time to start, ... it?
2. You're in London next Saturday night, ... you?
3. You have invited Sally and Bruce, ... you?
4. You will remember to ask Jane, ...?
5. Maria can come on Saturday, ...?
6. You know how many people are coming, ...?
7. We need some more dance music, ...?
8. Joe works on Saturday nights, ...?
9. The room isn't big enough for thirty people, ... it?
10. You're not going to bring Bill, ... you?
11. You haven't forgotten what happened last time, ...?
12. You don't smoke, ...?
13. The party won't go on all night, ...?
14. People won't want food, ...?

4 Listen to the recording. Are the people asking real questions, or just asking for agreement? Examples:

You're Paul Davies, aren't you? (*real question*)

Nice day, isn't it? (*asking for agreement*)

1. You're worried, aren't you?
2. You're tired, aren't you?
3. She's from Greece, isn't she?
4. Lovely car, isn't it?
5. You'll write every day, won't you?
6. You do love me, don't you?
7. Your dog doesn't bite, does he?
8. You don't smoke, do you?
9. You can swim, can't you?
10. The meeting won't go on late, will it?

5 Reported questions and instructions. Can you complete the sentences? Examples:

Tony's mother asked him **if he was going** to invite the Edwards boy.
She **told him to tidy** up afterwards.
She **told him not to** invite the Edwards boy.

1. Tony asked his mother .... have a party.
2. His mother asked him .... people he wanted to invite.
3. She asked him .... remembered what happened last time.
4. She told him .... tidy up afterwards.
5. She told .... everybody out by midnight.
6. She asked him .... careful of the carpet.
7. She told him .... invite more than twenty.
8. She .... make too much noise.

6 Say these sentences in two ways: first with an ordinary pronunciation of *must* (/ms/) and then with an emphatic pronunciation (/mʌst/).

1. You must tell me how many are coming.
2. You must tidy up afterwards.
3. You must get everybody out by midnight.
4. You must be careful of the carpet.

Now say these sentences in two ways.

5. You can have a party.
6. It will stop at midnight.
7. Mary and Peter are coming.
8. She has been to a lot of countries.

How can you make these sentences emphatic?

9. I like your dress.
10. He talks a lot.

7 Work in pairs and prepare a conversation for one of the following situations. Use some of the expressions that you have learnt from the dialogue.

1. A fourteen-year-old wants to go to an all-night party; father or mother doesn't like the idea.
2. A fifteen-year-old asks his or her father or mother for permission to go on a cycling holiday abroad.
3. A student asks his/her father or mother if he/she can borrow the family car for the weekend.
4. A boss asks his or her secretary to do something; the secretary has too much work.
5. A shop assistant asks the manager for a day off.

Question tags

It **is** . . . , **isn't** it?
You **will** . . . , **won't** you?
She **can** . . . , **can't** she?
They **have** . . . , **haven't** they?
You **remember** . . . , **don't** you?
She **likes** . . . , **doesn't** she?

It **isn't** . . . , **is** it?
You **won't** . . . , **will** you?
She **can't** . . . , **can** she?
They **haven't** . . . , **have** they?
You **don't** . . . , **do** you?

Reported instructions
She **told him to tidy up** afterwards.
She **asked him not to make** too much noise.

Learn/revise: carpet; noise; midnight; weekend; boy; idea; cycling; secretary; a day off; manager; invite; promise; bite (bit, bitten); borrow; need; tidy up; must; be careful (of); worried; tired; all right; about; exactly; afterwards; last time; all night; every day; everybody; something; enough; too much; by (midnight); out; have a party; OK; I suppose so; ask for permission.

34 If he had been bad at maths, . . .

Past possibilities; Past Conditional tense.

1 On February 6, 1944, Mark Perkins arrived in Switzerland. But if things had been different . . . Look at the diagram (the path of Mark's life is marked ▬▬▬), and complete the sentences below.

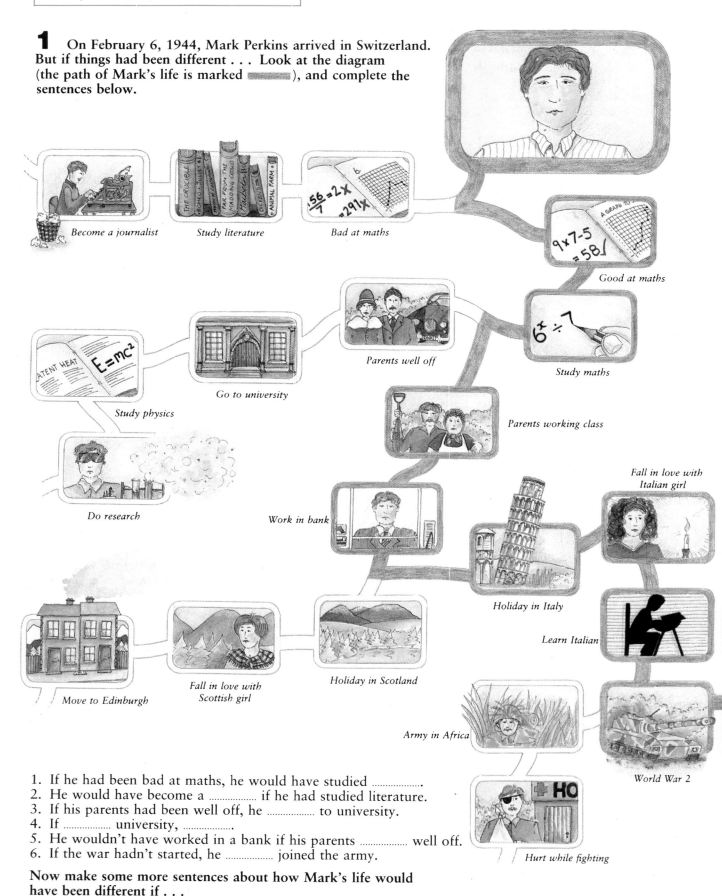

Become a journalist

Study literature

Bad at maths

Good at maths

Study maths

Parents well off

Parents working class

Study physics

Go to university

Do research

Work in bank

Fall in love with Italian girl

Holiday in Italy

Learn Italian

World War 2

Move to Edinburgh

Fall in love with Scottish girl

Holiday in Scotland

Army in Africa

Hurt while fighting

1. If he had been bad at maths, he would have studied ....
2. He would have become a .... if he had studied literature.
3. If his parents had been well off, he .... to university.
4. If .... university, ...
5. He wouldn't have worked in a bank if his parents .... well off.
6. If the war hadn't started, he .... joined the army.

Now make some more sentences about how Mark's life would have been different if . . .

Lesson 34

Students learn to talk about hypothetical situations in the past.
Principal structure: past conditional.
Phonology: stress and rhythm in past conditional sentences, pronunciation of unstressed *a, e, i* and *o* in initial position.

Language notes and possible problems

1. Past conditional: form The concept behind this structure should not be difficult for most students, but the form may present difficulties for students from some language backgrounds. You may have to watch out for mistakes like **If he would have come, I would . . .*

2. Past conditional: pronunciation Sentences containing the past conditional can be difficult to pronounce for many students; practice with the stress and rhythm of the model sentences is important in the initial stages.

If you are short of time

If pronunciation is not a high priority for your students, leave out Exercises 5 and 6.

1 Mark Perkins' life

• Ask students to look at the diagram of Mark Perkins' life. Make sure they understand that the red line is the path his life took, and the uncoloured parts of the line follow possibilities that did not happen.
• Encourage them to use their dictionaries or consult you to find out the meanings of any new words.
• Then ask them to work individually trying to finish the gapped sentences in the book.
• Let them compare notes before checking with you.
• When you go over the sentences with them, work on the stress and rhythm, and on the pronunciation of *would have* (/wʊdəv/) and *wouldn't have* (/'wʊdntəv/).
• Then ask each student to write down at least one other sentence about Mark Perkins' life beginning with *If . . .*
• Point out the fact that the *if*-clause can come at the beginning or the end of the sentence; it should be followed by a comma if it comes at the beginning.
• Point out that both *would* and *had* can be contracted to *'d*.
• Get the students to form groups of three or four to compare sentences and see if they can write any other sentences.
• Walk round while they are working to give any help that is needed.
• When they have finished, ask each group to read out one or more of its sentences. Pay attention to pronunciation, especially stress and rhythm.
• Exercise 4 in the Practice Book revises stress in past conditional sentences.

2 Discussion: *wouldn't have*

- Go over the example with the students; get them to practise the pronunciation of *hadn't* and of *wouldn't have*.
- Put them into pairs to decide which was the most important event in Mark's life.
- Walk round while they are working to give any help that is needed.
- Then each pair should move round finding other pairs, and present and defend their choice of event.
- Alternatively, each pair can present and defend their choice in front of the class; in this case you may want to get the students to vote afterwards for which event was the most important.

3 Contraction *'d: would* or *had*?; Comma or not?

- Remind students that both *would* and *had* can be contracted to *'d*.
- Give them a few minutes, working individually, to look at the five sentences and decide what each *'d* means.
- Then ask them to decide which of the sentences need commas. They can look back at the sentences in Exercise 1 for help.
- They will probably remember the rule better if they can work it out for themselves, so it is best to give them a chance to do so, only helping if they are really stuck.
- When they have finished, check their answers, and ask them what the rule about commas is in these sentences.

Answers to Exercise 3
There are commas after 'Germany' in sentence 1 and after 'be' in sentence 4 (because the *if*-clause is at the beginning in these sentences).

1. had
2. would; had
3. had
4. had; would
5. would; had

4 Personalisation: questions

- Think of two or three important events in your own life and write a sentence about each of them on the board.
- Invite students to ask you questions about them using *'What /Where/How/Who would . . . '* as in the example.
- Help them with the formation of the questions. You may want to point out that *have* sounds like *of* in questions like these, and to help students with linking in *you have* (/ˈjuː əv/), *she have* (/ˈʃiː əv/) and so on.
- Then each student should write one sentence about an important event in their life.
- When they are ready, they should form pairs, reading out their sentences and asking each other questions about them.
- Pairs who finish quickly can find new partners.

5 Unstressed initial vowels

- Get the students to copy the list and then work individually, marking the stresses in the four lists of words.
- Get them to compare answers before checking with you.
- Ask them if they can say anything about the stress in these words; they should be able to see that all the words are stressed on the second syllable.
- Then ask them to mark the unstressed syllables, with a circle around the vowels pronounced /ə/, and a square around the vowels pronounced /ɪ/. Let them compare answers in groups.
- Play the recording or read the lists yourself to give them a chance to modify their answers before checking with you.
- Ask them if they can make any rules about the pronunciation of the first vowel in a word where the second syllable is stressed.
- They should come up with the rule that *a* and *o* in this position are usually pronounced /ə/, and *e* and *i* in this position are usually pronounced /ɪ/.

Answers to Exercise 5
1. ⓐttractive m(a)chine ⓐrrest ⓐlive
2. c(o)mplete c(o)ntraction ph(o)tographer pr(o)fession
3. [e]vent b[e]cause r[e]serve d[e]pressed
4. [i]mportant [I]talian [i]nvent m[i]stake

6 Pronunciation: applying the rules

- Put the students in pairs or small groups. Each student in turn should pronounce a word for the other(s), who will check on them.
- Alternatively, tell the students that they can volunteer to say words and you will say them or play the recording after them, without indicating whether their pronunciation is acceptable or not; they can repeat the word for you to echo until they are satisfied with their own pronunciation.

7 Inventing a story

- Ask the students to look at the Mark Perkins diagram again.
- There are five hypothetical paths that can be continued.
- Put the students into groups of three or four and ask them to choose a path and invent a continuation for it.
- They can follow a straight line or make branching paths, as they like.
- Walk round while they are working to give any help that is needed.
- When they have finished, get each group to present their story to the class, saying what would have happened if things had been different.

Practice Book exercises
1. Writing past conditional sentences.
2. Reading and vocabulary building.
3. Writing sentences with *wouldn't have*.
4. Pronunciation of past conditional sentences.
5. Vocabulary revision and extension (make sure students understand how they are to complete the vocabulary networks).
6. Writing a short life story and saying what would have happened if . . .

2 Work in pairs and decide. What was the most important event in Mark's life? Why? Then discuss with other pairs. Example:

'We think it was going to work in the bank, because if he hadn't worked in the bank he wouldn't have gone to Italy, and . . .'
'Yes, but if he hadn't gone to work in the bank, perhaps he would still have gone to Italy. We think . . .'

3 *Would* or *had*? Comma or no comma?

1. If he'd gone to Germany his Italian wouldn't have helped him.
2. He'd have been a good journalist if he'd tried.
3. Where would he have gone if he'd decided not to go to Italy?
4. If I'd known how important Italian was going to be I'd have studied it much harder.
5. He'd have been sent to Germany if he'd joined the army two weeks earlier.

4 Work in pairs. Write a sentence about an important event or fact in your life. Listen to your partner's sentence and ask *'What/Where/How/Who would . . .'* Example:

'We moved here when I was five.'
'Where would you have gone to school if you hadn't moved here?'

5 Copy this list and mark the stresses in the words like this: a̲bove   ins̲tead

1. attractive   machine   arrest   alive
2. complete   contraction   photographer   profession
3. event   because   reserve   depressed
4. important   Italian   invent   mistake

What can you say about the stress in all of the words? Now put a circle ◯ around the vowels pronounced /ə/ and a square ▢ around the vowels pronounced /ɪ/ (for example, a̲bove i̲nstead). Listen to the tape or your teacher to check the answers. What are the rules?

6 Pronounce these words. They are all stressed on the second syllable.

continue   deliver   abroad   banana   insurance
election   policewoman   repair   intelligence
Olympic   agreement   explain   disgusting

7 Work in groups. Invent the continuation of a path Mark Perkins didn't take. Then tell the rest of the class about it.

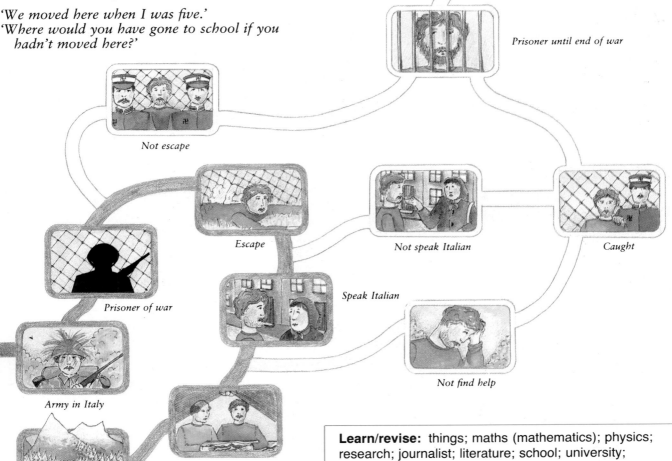

Prisoner until end of war

Not escape

Escape

Not speak Italian

Caught

Prisoner of war

Speak Italian

Army in Italy

Not find help

Find help

Get to Switzerland

> **Learn/revise:** things; maths (mathematics); physics; research; journalist; literature; school; university; bank; parent; world war; army; life; prison; prisoner; Switzerland; Italy; Germany; week; the rest; arrive; help; escape; study; become (became, become); start; join; try; decide; send (sent, sent); move; different; well off; working class; important; hard; early.

Situational language (travel).

1 Match the words and the pictures. (There are too many words.)

accident   bank   check-in
compartment   delay
enquiry   garage
giving directions   holiday
luxury hotel   landing
petrol station   roundabout
speeding   take off   taxi
waiting

A

B

C

D

E

F

G

H

I

J

K

L

M

2 Look at the words and pictures again and listen to the pieces of conversation. Which one goes with which situation? (There is one piece too many.)

3 Listen to one of the pieces of conversation again. Try to remember exactly what was said. Can you write it down?

Lesson 35

Students learn the language appropriate to a number of situations involving travel.
Structures: no new structures.
Phonology: pronunciation of the letter *r*.

If you are short of time
Drop Exercise 4 unless your students are aiming at a very high standard of pronunciation.

1 Matching words and pictures
• Ask students to do this individually first of all; then let them compare notes.
• Go over the answers with them and practise the pronunciation of the new words.

Answers to Exercise 1
A. take off   B. petrol station   C. delay (*or waiting*)
D. holiday   E. compartment   F. waiting   G. taxi
H. garage   I. check-in   J. accident   K. giving directions
L. enquiry   M. speeding   (There are no pictures corresponding to *landing, bank, roundabout* or *luxury hotel*.)

2 Matching conversations and pictures
• Play the recording once without stopping.
• Then play it again while students note their answers.
• Play it a third time as an additional check if necessary.
• Discuss the answers.

Tapescript and answers to Exercise 2
1. . . . or you can have three weeks in Cairo, return air fare, hotel room and full board, and a choice of excursions, for £1,500 inclusive. (*D. travel agent*)
2. What time is the next train to Godalming? (*L. station enquiry office*)
3. First on the right, second on the left. You can't miss it. (*K. giving directions*)
4. How long do you want to leave it for? (*left luggage office*, not illustrated)
5. Do you mind if I open a window? (*E. train compartment*)
6. You go back down the road and stop the traffic. I'll phone for an ambulance. (*J. accident*)
7. 'How often are they supposed to run?'
   'Every ten minutes.'
   'The last one didn't stop, you know. It just went straight on.' (*F. bus stop*)
8. Have you got any hand baggage? (*I. check-in*)
9. 'Do you know how fast you were going, sir?'
   'Er, about 40.'
   'You were doing 55, sir. Have you been drinking?' (*M. stopped by police for speeding*)
10. Fill it up with unleaded, please. And could you check the oil and the tyre pressures? (*B. petrol station*)
11. Hello, darling. I'm going to be a bit late, I'm afraid. There's a traffic jam a mile long. (*C. traffic jam*)
12. We shall shortly be taking off on our flight to Rome. Please observe the no-smoking sign and ensure that your seat belt is fastened and your seat back is in the upright position. (*A. plane taking off*)
13. Could you take me to Victoria, please? (*G. taxi*)
14. It's making a funny noise, and it's very difficult to start from cold. And I think the brakes need checking. And it needs a service. (*H. garage*)

3 Listening for the exact words
• Ask students to choose one of the fragments of conversation that they have just heard. If they can't make up their minds, choose one for them.
• Ask what they can remember of what they heard.
• Play the fragment again and see if they can write down exactly what they hear.
• Play the fragment several times if necessary until they have got as close as they are going to get to the exact words.
• Then write the fragment on the board for them.
• Explain any difficulties.
• If students like the exercise, it can be repeated with another fragment.

4 Pronunciation of the letter *r*

• Most students probably pronounce *r* wherever it is written. This happens in many varieties of English, but not in standard British English, where *r* is only pronounced at the beginning of a syllable (that is to say, before a pronounced vowel). Before a consonant or silence, *r* is not pronounced.

• Get students to discuss the question in groups and try to agree on their answers. When they are ready, play the recording or say the words for them.

• Discuss the answers and practise the pronunciation of the words. See if students can think of any other words in which *r* is not pronounced.

• Point out that a final *r* may be pronounced before a following word that begins with a vowel – compare *car* (/kɑː/) and *the car is . . .* (/ðə kɑːr ɪz/).

• Note that this exercise is only important for students who want a good British-type pronunciation. They will still be understood perfectly well if they pronounce *r* in places where British speakers don't.

Answers to Exercise 4
Words in which r *is pronounced*: enquiry; garage; directions; luxury; petrol; right; roundabout.
Words in which r *is not pronounced*: airport; car; compartment; first; platform; turn.

5 Students' conversations

• Ask students to choose a situation that they would like to study in detail from a language point of view.

• Then get them to join into pairs, according to their first choice of situation as far as possible. (Groups of three are also feasible.)

• Each pair should look over the vocabulary list corresponding to their choice of situation (unless they have chosen one that is not illustrated). Let them ask whatever questions they want to. You will need to go round from group to group while this is going on.

• When students have understood the new words and expressions, they should prepare a simple conversation practising some of what they have learnt.

• Get them to practise their conversations; listen to them and make corrections if necessary (but don't over-correct).

• You may like to tape- or video-record the conversations. If so, warn the students in advance.

Practice Book exercises
1. Expressing purpose with *to* and *because*.
2. Question tags.
3. Indefinite pronouns.
4. Student's Cassette exercise (Student's Book Exercise 2). Students choose some of the fragments of conversation to listen to, and try to write down what they hear.
5. Giving directions.
6. Recreational reading: *Strange but true!*

4 These words all contain the letter *r*, but it is not pronounced (in British English) in all of them. In which words is *r* pronounced? What is the rule?

airport   car   compartment   enquiry   garage   directions
first   luxury   petrol   platform   right   roundabout   turn

5 Work with another student. Prepare and practise a conversation for one of these situations (or a different one if you prefer).

– having a car repaired
– asking/giving directions
– an enquiry about air travel
– a train enquiry
– being stopped by police

Some useful words and expressions:

CAR REPAIRS
steering   brakes   engine   starting   exhaust
silencer   tyres   wipers   wiper motor
check the brakes/steering/plugs . . .
change the plugs/oil
puncture   rust   service

GIVING DIRECTIONS
straight ahead   turn right/left at . . .
take the first/second on the left/right
first right, second left
keep straight on for about 500 metres
crossroads   traffic lights   fork   T-junction
You come to a fork/crossroads/*etc.*

AIRPORT ENQUIRY
flight number   check-in   delay   standby
take off   land   boarding card
smoking/non-smoking   fare   one-way
round trip   baggage   hand baggage
insurance   ticket   make a reservation

TRAIN ENQUIRY
What time . . . ?   the next train for . . .
Which platform for . . . ?   single   return   day return
direct   change   fast train   leave   arrive at
first class   standard class   fare   ticket
seat reservation

STOPPED BY POLICE
How fast were you going?
Is this your vehicle?
overtake   lights   traffic lights   stop sign
speed limit   speeding   driving licence
registration book   certificate of insurance
Have you been drinking?   Blow into this.

Learn/revise: accident; baggage; bank; brake; check-in; compartment; crossroads; directions; driving licence; engine; enquiry; oil; petrol station; platform; police; repair; reservation; roundabout; speed limit; taxi; ticket; single/return; traffic lights; change; check; delay; land; steer; overtake (overtook, overtaken); take off (took, taken); travel; wait; straight ahead; keep straight on (kept, kept); smoking/non-smoking.

36 Shall I open it for you?

Offers and polite replies: phrasal verbs.

1 Match the sentences and the pictures.

1. Shall I open it for you?
2. Shall I carry something for you?
3. Shall I have a look at it?
4. Shall I get it down for you?
5. I'll go, shall I?
6. I'll answer it, shall I?

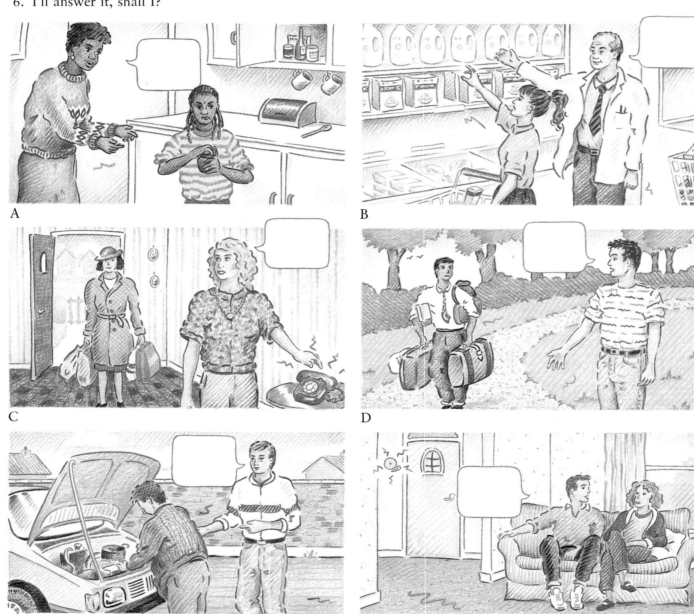

A

B

C

D

E

F

Lesson 36

Students practise making, accepting and rejecting offers.
Structures: *Shall I . . . ?*; use of *'ll* in making decisions and offers; *Would you like me to . . . ?*; *to* as pro-verb in *I'd love to*; phrasal verbs.
Phonology: weak and strong forms of *shall*.

Language notes and possible problems

1. Shall   In modern English, *shall* is not very common except in the first person. Its main functions are as an alternative to *will* when talking about the future, and as a special auxiliary for making suggestions and offers (practised here).

2. 'll   Note the use of *'ll* to announce decisions and firm offers (*I'll go, shall I?*; *I'll keep it on*).

3. Phrasal verbs (verbs with adverb particles)   The grammar of phrasal verbs is introduced here. Help students to see that the adverb particle in a verb such as *sit down* or *switch off* is not a preposition, but the second half of a two-word verb; these particles follow different word-order rules from prepositions (see Exercises 4 and 5). Note, however, that the grammar of phrasal and prepositional verbs is difficult, and the distinctions between the two kinds of complex verb are not always very clear-cut.

Note

Action sequence (Exercise 6)   You will need to prepare a sequence of actions and questions for this exercise.

1 Shall I?

• Give students a minute or two to decide which sentence goes with which picture.
• Let them compare notes and then go over the answers with them.
• Explain any difficulties.
• Note the weak pronunciation (/ʃəl/) in the first four sentences. In the last two, the pronunciation is strong (/ʃæl/): there is no other verb after *shall*, so it carries the stress.

Answers to Exercise 1
1A; 2D; 3E; 4B; 5F; 6C.

2 Accepting and rejecting offers

● Students can do this individually and then compare notes in groups.
● When they are ready, discuss the answers and deal with any difficulties.

Answers to Exercise 2
(Other answers may be possible.)
1. 'Can I hang your *coat/raincoat/overcoat* up for you?'
E. 'No, thanks, I'll keep it on. I'm a bit *cold*.'
2. 'Shall I put the kettle on for a *cup/pot* of tea?'
G. 'I'd prefer coffee, if you've *got* some.'
3. 'Would you like *some* toast?'
H. 'Yes, please, I'd love *some*.'
4. 'Would you like to go and see a *film* this evening?'
F. 'Not *this* evening, thanks. Perhaps *another / some other* time?'
5. '*Would* you like to dance?'
C. '*I'd* love to.'
6. 'Shall I *help* you to carry that?'
A. 'No, thanks. I can do it *myself*.'
7. 'Would you like me to *switch/put/turn* the lights on?'
B. 'That's very kind *of* you.'
8. 'Could you lock up the house and switch off the lights *when/before* you come to bed?'
D. 'Yes, of *course*.'

3 Answering offers

● Go over the questions with students, explaining any difficulties.
● Ask them to decide how they would answer each offer (they can accept it or reject it, as they wish). Check their answers.
● They must use expressions from Exercise 2 for most or all of their answers.
● When students are ready, ask them to close their books and play the recording.
● Stop after each sentence for students to answer; let them speak all together and then pick out individuals to repeat their answers.
● You may like to go through the exercise several times until students are fluent.

4 Phrasal verbs

● Look at the examples, and explain that *pick up* and *look up* are two-part verbs. (It may be interesting to see whether the equivalents in the students' language(s) are one-word verbs.)
● Make sure students understand that adverb particles can go in two different places — before or after the object. (Prepositions cannot go after the object in this kind of structure — we can't say *I'm looking the station for.*)
● Go through the exercise getting students to change the word order.

Answers to Exercise 4
1. She picked her keys up and walked out.
2. Put my handbag down!
3. Could you switch the TV on, please?
4. Why did you switch the light off?
5. It's cold: I think I'll put my overcoat on.
6. I'm going straight to bed: I'm not even going to take my make-up off.
7. Could you lock the house up before you go to bed?
8. Please switch the lights off.
9. I clean the fridge out every Saturday.

5 Phrasal verbs with pronoun objects

● Point out that adverb particles can't go before object pronouns (we can say *I picked it up* but not **I picked up it*).

● See how quickly students can change the sentences.
● As they say the sentences, get them to concentrate on linking the words together (so that the verb, object and particle sound like one word).

Answers to Exercise 5
1. She picked them up and walked out.
2. Put it down!
3. Could you switch it on, please?
4. Why did you switch it off?
5. It's cold: I think I'll put it on.
6. I'm going straight to bed: I'm not even going to take it off.
7. Could you lock it up before you go to bed?
8. Please switch them off.
9. I clean it out every Saturday.

6 Prepositions and phrasal verbs: memorising

● Prepare a series of actions which can be described using prepositions and phrasal verbs. Some possibilities: stand up; sit down; put your hand on your head; put your bag on your head; turn round; pick up somebody's bag/book/pen; throw something up and catch it; take something out of your pocket or bag; switch various things on and off; stand on a chair; look out of the window; put on your coat; take off your sweater or shoe; pick up a dictionary and look up a word.
● Prepare a series of questions to test students' ability to remember what you did. For example: '*What did I do after I stood up?*'; '*What did I do after that?*'; '*Whose handbag did I pick up?*'; '*How many times did I look out of the window?*'. Be careful to include at least one question with *Whose . . . ?*
● Students should not take notes as you do the actions. The questions can be answered orally or in writing, as you prefer.

Optional extension
● Get students to prepare a series of instructions for you (they should ask you to perform a sequence of actions like the ones you have just done). It's best if the whole class do this together, but it can be done in groups if there are too many students. You should leave the room while the class are preparing their instructions.
● They should also prepare questions to test your memory (similar to those you asked in Exercise 6).
● When the class are ready, do your best to do what they tell you to.
● Then get them to ask their questions.
● If you don't feel like being the 'victim' yourself, get a student volunteer to do it.

7 Mime

● Tell students to prepare and write down a short conversation, working in pairs.
● Each conversation should contain an offer and an acceptance or rejection.
● When they are ready, each pair should come to the front and act out their conversation silently, trying to show by mime what the situation is.
● The class must try to guess the exact words that were written down.

Practice Book exercises
1. Prepositions of place.
2. Prepositions and adverb particles.
3. Revision of pronouns.
4. Vocabulary revision and extension.
5. Stress.
6. Writing: giving directions.

2 Complete the sentences, and match the questions and answers. (Some questions can have more than one answer.)

1. Can I hang your .... up for you?
2. Shall I put the kettle on for a .... of tea?
3. Would you like .... toast?
4. Would you like to go and see a .... this evening?
5. .... you like to dance?
6. Shall I .... you to carry that?
7. Would you like me to .... the lights on?
8. Could you lock up the house and switch off the lights .... you come to bed?

A. No thanks. I can do it ....
B. That's very kind .... you.
C. .... love to.
D. Yes, of ....
E. No, thanks. I'll keep it on. I'm a bit ....
F. Not .... evening, thanks. Perhaps .... time?
G. I'd prefer coffee, if you've .... some.
H. Yes, please, I'd love ....

3 Prepare your answers to the following questions. Then close your book, listen to the recording and answer.

Shall I make you a cup of tea?
Would you like some toast?
How would you like a game of tennis?
Would you like to go and see a film this evening?
Shall I switch the TV on?
Would you like a drink?
Would you like to have a rest?
Would you like to see my photos?
Would you like me to help you with your English?
Shall I sing to you?

4 Phrasal verbs. Change the sentences so that the adverb particle comes after the object. Example:

I picked up my dictionary and looked up a word.
'I picked my dictionary up and looked a word up.'

1. She picked up her keys and walked out.
2. Put down my handbag!
3. Could you switch on the TV, please?
4. Why did you switch off the light?
5. It's cold: I think I'll put on my overcoat.
6. I'm going straight to bed: I'm not even going to take off my make-up.
7. Could you lock up the house before you come to bed?
8. Please switch off the lights.
9. I clean out the fridge every Saturday.

5 Now change the sentences in Exercise 4 so that the object is a pronoun (*it* or *them*). The particle must come after the object (e.g. *I picked it up*, not *I picked up it*).

6 Watch the teacher carefully and try to remember everything that he or she does. Then answer the teacher's questions. Examples:

'What did I do after I stood up?'
'You put your jacket on.'
'Whose dictionary did I pick up?'
'Mine.'

7 Prepare a conversation with another student (an offer and an answer). Act the conversation *without speaking*. The other students will try to decide what the words are.

Phrasal verbs: word order
She **picked up** her handbag.
OR: She **picked** her handbag **up**.
She **picked** it **up**. (She picked up it.)

***Like* + object + infinitive**
Would you **like me to switch** the lights on?
(Would you like I switch the lights on?)

Learn/revise: cup of tea/coffee; film; handbag; kettle; key; make-up; offer (*noun and verb*); overcoat; photo; toast; answer (door or phone); carry; clean out; dance; hang up (hung, hung); have a look; have a rest; keep (clothes) on (kept, kept); lock up; look (a word) up; open; pick up; prefer (preferred); put down (put, put); put (a kettle) on; put (clothes) on; take (clothes) off (took, taken); remember; sing (sang, sung); switch on/off; stand up (stood, stood); watch; whose; kind; cold; a bit; carefully; straight; I'd love to; another time.

Summary F

Past Perfect tense

I had (I'd) seen you had (you'd) seen *etc.*	had I seen? had you seen? *etc.*	I had not (hadn't) seen you had not (hadn't) seen *etc.*

When I got back to the table she **had gone**.
I **hadn't seen** her since the day we said goodbye.
I thought perhaps I'**d changed** so much she didn't realise it was me.

Past Conditional

I would (I'd) have gone you would (you'd) have gone *etc.*	would I have gone? would you have gone? *etc.*	I would not (wouldn't) have gone you would not (wouldn't) have gone *etc.*

Talking about the past with *if*

IF + PAST PERFECT,	PAST CONDITIONAL
If his parents **had been** well off, (If his parents would have been . . .)	he **would have gone** to university.
If he **hadn't worked** in the bank,	he **wouldn't have gone** to Italy.

PAST CONDITIONAL	IF + PAST PERFECT
Where **would** he **have gone**	if he'**d decided** not to go to Italy?
He'**d have been** sent to Germany	if he'**d joined** the army earlier.

Question tags

It is . . . , **isn't** it?
You **will** . . . , **won't** you?
She **can** . . . , **can't** she?
They **have** . . . , **haven't** they?
You **remember** . . . , **don't** you?
She **likes** . . . , **doesn't** she?

It **isn't** . . . , **is** it?
You **won't** . . . , **will** you?
She **can't** . . . , **can** she?
They **haven't** . . . , **have** they?
You **don't** . . . , **do** you?

Intonation of question tags

– Real questions

   'You're French, aren't you?' 'No, I'm Swiss.'

– Asking for agreement

   'Nice day, isn't it?' 'Yes, lovely.'

Reported instructions

She **told** him to tidy up afterwards.
She **asked** him not to make so much noise.
   (She asked him to not make . . .)

Phrasal verbs: word order

She **picked up** her handbag.
OR: She **picked** her handbag **up**.
She **picked** it **up**. (She picked up it.)

Like – object + infinitive

Would you **like me to switch** the lights on?
   (Would you like I switch the lights on?)

Sequencing markers

When she . . . , she . . . **Then** she . . . and . . .
After that she . . . **Then** she . . . **until** . . .
Before she . . . , she . . .

110

Summary F

Summary of language taught in Lessons 31–36.

This lesson displays most of the more important language points that students should have learnt or revised in the last six lessons. Spend a short time going over the material with the students, answering questions and clearing up any difficulties. Students may also need to spend time at home making sure everything is thoroughly learnt.

Practice Book exercises
1. Question formation.
2. *Still*, *yet*, *already* and general vocabulary revision.
3. Present Perfect Progressive.
4. Translation of material from Lessons 31–36.
5. Guided composition (picture story).
6. Follow-up writing.

Clauses with *as soon as, before, after, until*

Do you get up **as soon as you wake up**?
Before you buy something, do you always ask the
  price?
What are you going to do **after the lesson has
  finished**? (~~. . . after the lesson will have finished?~~)
Are you going to study English **before you go to bed
  tonight**? (~~. . . before you will go . . .~~)
Will you keep on working **until you're sixty**?
  (~~. . . until you will be sixty?~~)

Still, yet and *already*

John's **still** in bed.
He **hasn't** got up **yet**.
Susan is **already** dressed.

Such and *so*

He's **such a good dancer.**
He's **so good.**
He's **such a handsome man.**
He's **so handsome.**

Offers and replies

Shall I open it for you?
No thanks. I can do it myself.

I'll answer it, **shall I**?
That's very kind of you.

Can I hang your coat up for you?
No thanks. I'll keep it on.

Would you like some toast?
I'd love some.

Would you like some tea?
I'd prefer coffee, if you've got some.

Would you like to dance?
I'd love to.

Would you like to go and see a film this evening?
Not this evening, thanks. Perhaps another time?

Would you like me to carry that for you?
Thank you very much.

Situational language (travel)

(See lists in Lesson 35.)

Revision F

Look at the exercises, decide which ones are useful to you, and do two or more.

GRAMMAR

1 Put in the correct verb forms. (More than one answer may be possible.)

I (*walk*) down the street when I (*see*) this man I thought I knew. I probably wouldn't have recognised him if he (*not smile*) at me, but I'd know that smile anywhere. Chris! I (*not see*) him since I left college. We went and had a drink and (*talk*) about old times and the people we'd known and the things we (*do*) together.

He told me he'd spent the first few years after college working in a hospital in Brazil, and then he (*find*) a job teaching. He said he (*be*) married, but it hadn't worked out, and they (*get*) divorced. It seemed that he (*have*) a pretty bad time, but he said that now things (*start*) to get better. I said I (*often think*) about him, and had wondered what (*happen*) to him.

It's funny. We used to go out together at college, and I thought he was quite serious about me, but he never (*say*) anything. Then he (*go*) off to South America and we lost touch with each other. I sometimes wonder what I (*do*) if he (*ask*) me to marry him. I'd probably have said yes, and then things (*be*) so different for both of us.

Anyway, what's past is past. We said goodbye, and promised to keep in touch, but I don't suppose we (*see*) each other again.

LISTENING

1 Listen to the first conversation and choose the best summary.

1. He said he wanted to go out.
2. He said he was too tired to go out.
3. He said he didn't like going out.

Now listen to the other conversations and write your own summaries.

2 🔲 Listen to the song *You Made Me Love You*. Write down as much as you can, and then check on page 125.

SPEAKING

1 Work in groups. Each group has £1 million. You have 20 minutes to decide how to spend the money so as to do most good to people in the world. When you are ready, tell the rest of the class about your plans.

2 Here are some very informal sentences. Can you make them more formal?

1. Hi!
2. How's things?
3. Kids OK?
4. Hey, got a light?
5. Thanks a lot.
6. Pass the salt.
7. Want a drink?
8. That was a great film.
9. Open the window, would you?
10. This your bag?
11. 'Boss in today?' 'Dunno.'

PRONUNCIATION

1 Do you know how to pronounce these words?

Two syllables, not three: asp(i)rin; bus(i)ness; cam(e)ra; diff(e)rent; ev(e)ning; ev(e)ry; marri(a)ge; med(i)cine.

Three syllables, not four: comf(or)table; secret(a)ry; temp(e)rature; veg(e)table; usu(a)lly.

Silent letters: shou(l)d; cou(l)d; wou(l)d; ca(l)m; wa(l)k; ta(l)k; ha(l)f; i(r)on; i(s)land; lis(t)en; (w)rite; (w)rong; (k)now; (k)nife; (k)nee; (k)nock; (k)nob; dau(gh)ter; hei(gh)t; li(gh)t; mi(gh)t; ri(gh)t; ti(gh)t; strai(gh)t; throu(gh); wei(gh); nei(gh)bour; ou(gh)t; thou(gh)t; g(u)ess; g(u)ide; g(u)itar; (h)our; (h)onest; We(d)n(e)sday; san(d)wich; si(g)n.

Revision F

Students and teacher choose grammar, listening, speaking, pronunciation and vocabulary exercises.

Note: choice
Get students' views about which exercises are most useful before choosing a suitable selection. If necessary, groups can work on different exercises.

GRAMMAR

1 Revision: past verb forms
• This exercise focuses mainly on uses of the Past Perfect. It should help students to see that there is not always a clear 'either/or' choice between tenses — more than one answer is possible to some questions, depending on the meaning or emphasis that is intended.
• The exercise can be done individually, in groups, or by whole-class discussion, as you wish.

Answers to Exercise 1
(Full forms may of course be used instead of contractions.)
I *was walking* down the street when I *saw* this man I thought I knew. I probably wouldn't have recognised him if he *hadn't smiled* at me, but I'd know that smile anywhere. Chris! I *hadn't seen* him since I left college. We went and had a drink and *talked* about old times and the people we'd known and the things we*'d done* together.

He told me he'd spent the first few years after college working in a hospital in Brazil, and then he*'d found* a job teaching. He said he*'d been* married, but it hadn't worked out, and they*'d got* divorced. It seemed that he(*'d*) *had* a pretty bad time, but he said that now things *had started / were starting* to get better. I said I*'d often thought* about him, and had wondered what *had happened / was happening* to him.

It's funny. We used to go out together at college, and I thought he was quite serious about me, but he never *said* anything. Then he *went* off to South America and we lost touch with each other. I sometimes wonder what I*'d have done* if he*'d asked* me to marry him. I'd probably have said yes, and then things *would have been* so different for both of us.

Anyway, what's past is past. We said goodbye, and promised to keep in touch, but I don't suppose we*'ll see* each other again.

LISTENING

1 Reported speech: summarising conversations
• Make it clear that very short (one-sentence) summaries are required. Answers should begin 'He/She said . . . ', or something similar, so as to practise reported speech constructions.
• Play the first conversation, and get students to choose the best summary (2).
• Then play the other conversations one at a time and pause while students write their summaries.
• Let them compare notes before discussing the answers.

Suggested answers to Exercise 1
(The summaries given below are not of course 'right answers' — each conversation can be summarised in many different ways.)

First conversation: *Summary 2*
Second conversation: *He said that Ann had changed her job again and gone to work in a bank.*

Third conversation: *The man said the next day was going to be fine.*
Fourth conversation: *The doctor told the man to stop smoking.*
Fifth conversation: *Ann said she was in love.*

Tapescript for Exercise 1: see page 129

2 Song: *You Made Me Love You*
• Pre-teach *sigh, grand, 'deed = indeed.*
• Play the song once and ask students to tell you anything they understood.
• Play it again, pausing for students to write.
• Don't explain *wanna* and *gimme* in advance, but see if students can work out what they mean.
• When students have done as much as they can, let them turn to page 125 and check their answers.

SPEAKING

1 Discussion
• Before starting, get students to think of useful expressions that they may need (e.g. *I agree*; *I don't agree*; *on the other hand*; *I think we should . . .* ; *What about . . .ing?*; *We could . . .*).
• Each group should appoint a spokesperson who will tell the class about the group's plans.

2 Formal and informal language
• Get students to discuss what makes each sentence informal. Note particularly:
– ellipsis of auxiliary verbs, subject pronouns and articles (*Kids OK?*; *got a light?* etc.)
– vocabulary that is used mainly in informal contexts (*Hi!*; *Hey*; *kids*; *great*; *boss*; *Thanks*; *a lot*)
– informal contractions (*Dunno* for *I don't know*)
– *is* with plural subject in *How's things?*
– imperative requests (*Pass the salt*)

Answers to Exercise 2
(Most of the sentences have more than one formal equivalent. The following are possible answers.)
1. Hello; Good morning/afternoon/*etc.*
2. How are you?
3. Are the children all right?
4. Excuse me, have you got a light?
5. Thank you very much.
6. Could you pass the salt?
7. Would you like a drink?
8. That was a wonderful film.
9. Would you mind opening the window?
10. Is this your bag?
11. 'Is the manager in today?' 'I don't know.'

PRONUNCIATION

1 Misleading spellings
• This exercise gives a few common words with misleading spellings, which students may mispronounce.
• Go through the list section by section, asking students how they think the words are pronounced. Play the recording or demonstrate the pronunciation, and practise words which cause difficulty.

VOCABULARY

1 Treasure hunt

• Make sure students know the words *treasure*, *side*, *over*, *bridge*, *river*, *crossroads*, *along*.

• Explain that students can only find the treasure if they read each clue carefully and do exactly what it says. (The clues are arranged so that it is difficult to find the right place without following them in order, as students will realise if they try to take short cuts.) Note that there are various 'distractors' — for example, there are five number 5s — these will be avoided if students follow the correct route.

• You may want to do the first couple of clues with the class before letting them work by themselves.

• Tell them to be very careful with clues 7 and 9.

• Walk round and help with any problems that come up.

• When students have finished, get them to compare answers with each other before checking with you.

• The treasure is buried at D. The correct route goes via the following sequence of clues: 6, 14, 7, 14, 13, 9, 3, 4, 12, 1, 11, 8, 15, 2, 10, 5, D.

• You may like to offer a small prize to the winner.

2 Reinforcement: writing

• Get students to write down the route they took.

• Check by getting students to write some of their sentences on the board.

3 Students' treasure hunts

• Make sure students understand what they are to do.

• Students who are to 'hunt the treasure' will need to go outside while the clues are being laid.

Practice Book exercises

1. Vocabulary revision and extension (ball games).
2. Tenses of *there is*.
3. Offers and answers.
4. Student's Cassette exercise (Student's Book Listening Exercise 2). Students listen to the song and try to write down the verbs.
5. Recreational reading (a poem).
6. Crossword.

Additional reading

Note that students have now reached a level where they should be able to cope comfortably with the texts in Sections A–F of *Additional reading* in the Practice Book (pages 108 to 114). You can set some of the readings for homework or just suggest that students read any of the texts that interest them when they have the time.

VOCABULARY

1 Treasure hunt. The treasure is buried under one of the trees, at A, B, C, D, E, F, G or H. Follow the clues and find it. Start by reading clue number 6.

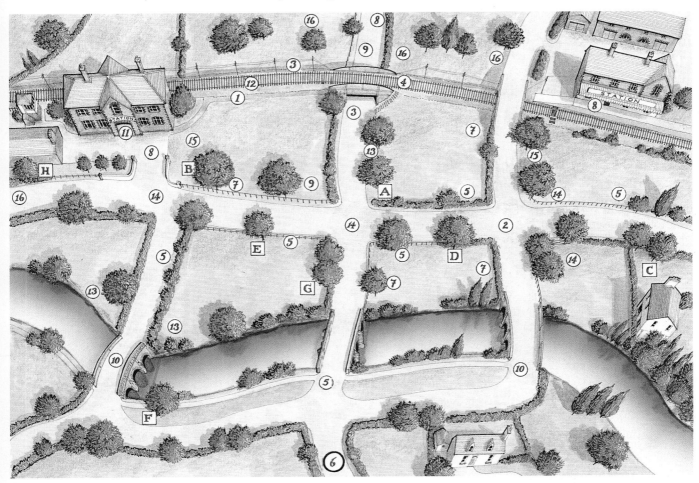

1. Go to the nearest railway station. Go into the station.
2. Keep straight on until you see the next clue.
3. Climb up on to the railway line.
4. Turn left and walk along the railway line until you see the next clue.
5. Turn right. Go to the nearest crossroads and turn right. The treasure is under the second tree on the right.
6. Go straight on over the bridge to the crossroads.
7. Walk back and read the last clue again.
8. Go into the nearest field. The next clue is under the first tree on the right.

9. This clue says the same as number 13.
10. Walk along the river bank to the next bridge.
11. Get on the next train; get off at the other station.
12. There's a train coming. Turn to your left and get off the railway line.
13. Go under the bridge. The next clue is just on the other side.
14. Turn left and go to the second tree on the right.
15. Go straight out of the field and take the shortest way to the river by road. The next clue is at the crossroads.
16. You're lost.

2 Describe how you got to the treasure. Example:

I went straight over the bridge to the crossroads; then I turned left and went to the second tree on the right; . . .

3 Work in groups. Write a treasure hunt with five clues and a treasure. Choose a student outside the group to do the treasure hunt. Example:

1. *Walk across the room and look on the floor.*
2. *Pick up Antonio's book and look under it.*
3. *Turn right/left and walk along to the third desk. Ask the person to stand up and look on the chair.*
4. *The next clue is under a blue notebook.*
5. *Take your watch off and you will win a free cup of coffee after class.*

Test F

LISTENING

1 Listen to the conversation and answer the questions.

1. Is Jill expecting Simon?
2. a. What would Simon like to drink?
   b. What does he get?
3. Did Simon see the report about Joanne in the newspaper?
4. Is Joanne:
   a. an actress?   c. a journalist?
   b. an architect? d. a student?
5. Is Joanne good at her work?
6. Who will be pleased about what has happened to Joanne?
7. How does Joanne feel about Louisa?
   a. She likes her.
   b. She doesn't like her.
   c. We don't know.
8. How does Louisa feel about Joanne?
   a. She likes her.
   b. She doesn't like her.
   c. We don't know.
9. Is Simon:
   a. tired?   d. thirsty?
   b. cold?   e. hungry?
   c. ill?
10. Does Simon take sugar in his tea?
11. What does Simon want to talk to Jill about?
    a. His problems at work.
    b. Joanne and Louisa.
    c. We don't know.

GRAMMAR

1 Put in the right verb forms.

1. 'Have you got a cigarette?' 'Sorry, I ....' (*not smoke*)
2. 'Hurry up, Jeremy, we're late.' 'I ....' (*come*)
3. Aunt Mary .... while we .... supper, as usual. (*arrive; have*)
4. 'What .... you .... for?' 'I .... my glasses. Can you .... me?' (*look; lose; help*)
5. Sorry I'm late. I hope you .... long. (*not wait*)
6. I .... Anna since we .... at school together. (*know; be*)
7. One day last summer, I .... down the street when I .... an old friend of mine. I .... him for over eight years, but I .... him at once. (*walk; see; not see; recognise*)
8. When I was small, I thought that rain .... through holes in the sky. (*come*)
9. If I .... you, I .... a holiday. (*be; take*)
10. She told the boy .... down. (*sit*)
11. Would you like ....? (*dance*)
12. Do you like ....? (*ski*)

SPEAKING

1 Choose four of the pictures (in any order) and four of the words (in any order). Make up a story using the pictures and words, and tell the teacher.

happy	friend	police	cat	mend
soup	garage	shall		

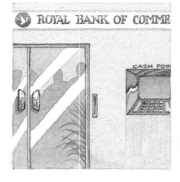

VOCABULARY

1 Choose three of the following subjects and add ten or more words for each.

Food and drink: cheese, plate, waiter, . . .
Travel: ticket, train, fly, . . .
Buildings: hotel, roof, door, . . .
Work: job, boss, engineer, . . .
Study: dictionary, learn, test, . . .
Languages: noun, English, speak, . . .
Sport and games: tennis, play, ball, . . .

Test F

Students do a simple revision test.

The purpose of the test

This test samples material from the whole of the course, and should give you and your students a reasonable idea of how successfully they have worked through Lessons 1–36. It is not of course necessary to do all of the sections, and teachers should select according to their students' needs. Teachers who do not feel the test will be useful should simply drop it altogether.

If possible, try to make the students feel that they are 'testing themselves', rather than 'being tested'. It is not intended that students should 'pass' or 'fail' the test, and it is not particularly useful to give marks. (If the school or education system requires that this be done, you will need to work out a simple marking scheme.) But students should of course be told whether you feel their performance is satisfactory.

Administration

The test can be administered in various ways, depending on how strictly you want to control students' performance; whether you want to collect the answers and mark them, or allow the students to correct them in class; and so on.

For the 'speaking' test, students will need to interrupt their work on the other questions to come and talk to you. They will need time for preparation (which can be done out of class if you wish).

Notes, tapescript and answers are given below.

LISTENING

Listening comprehension

Go through the questions and clear up any difficulties before you start. You will probably want to play the recording twice, pausing after the first time so that students can write their answers.

Tapescript for Listening Test 1

(Doorbell)

JILL: Hi, Simon. What a surprise! Come in.
SIMON: Thanks, Jill. How are you?
JILL: Oh, I'm fine. Come and sit down. Shall I take your coat?
SIMON: No, I'll keep it on, thanks. I'm a bit cold.
JILL: You're not ill, are you?
SIMON: No, just tired, I think.
JILL: What's the matter?
SIMON: Oh, problems at work. Let's not talk about that.
JILL: Well, would you like something to drink? A cup of tea?
SIMON: I'd prefer a beer, if you've got some.
JILL: Not sure. I'll have a look. No, sorry, no beer.
SIMON: Never mind. Tea will be fine.
JILL: Something to eat?
SIMON: No, thanks, I'm not all that hungry.
JILL: Did you see the thing in the paper yesterday?
SIMON: About Joanne? Yes. Isn't it amazing? How did she do it?
JILL: I don't know. I didn't think she was much good, but there she is – Young Actress of the Year.
SIMON: Her mother'll be pleased.
JILL: Perhaps she will. But her sister won't, I can tell you that now.
SIMON: Why not? Don't they get on?

JILL: Oh, Louisa hates Joanne. Always has done.
SIMON: I didn't realise.
JILL: Yes. You see, they're not really sisters. Joanne was adopted.
SIMON: No?
JILL: Yes. When Louisa was four. And of course, Joanne's the pretty one, and she's clever as well, and Louisa hasn't taken it very well. Now, how do you like your tea, Simon?
SIMON: Just milk, please, Jill. Look, I wanted to ask your advice . . .

Answers to Listening Test 1

1. No.
2. a. beer
   b. tea
3. Yes.
4. a.
5. Yes.
6. Her mother.
7. c.
8. b.
9. a, b and perhaps d.
10. No.
11. c.

GRAMMAR

1 (Full and contracted verb forms are both possible in many cases.)

1. 'Have you got a cigarette?'   'Sorry, I *don't smoke.*'
2. 'Hurry up, Jeremy, we're late.'   'I*'m coming.*'
3. Aunt Mary *arrived* while we *were having* supper, as usual.
4. 'What *are* you *looking* for?'   'I*'ve lost* my glasses. Can you *help* me?'
5. Sorry I'm late. I hope you *haven't been waiting* long.
6. I*'ve known* Anna since we *were* at school together.
7. One day last summer, I *was walking* down the street when I *saw* an old friend of mine. I *hadn't seen* him for over eight years, but I *recognised* him at once.
8. When I was small, I thought that rain *came* through holes in the sky.
9. If I *were* you, I*'d take* a holiday.
10. She told the boy *to sit* down.
11. Would you like *to dance*?
12. Do you like *skiing*?

SPEAKING

This is a test of fluency rather than accuracy. Look for confidence, appropriacy and range of language as well as correctness, and don't pay too much attention to small mistakes. The most important thing is success in communicating. One or two students may have difficulty in making up a coherent story, and you may want to keep an alternative test in reserve for anybody who really can't manage it. (For instance, ask them how they spent the weekend.)

VOCABULARY

1 (Various possible answers.)

114

LANGUAGE IN USE

1 (Alternative answers are possible in a number of cases.)
1. Could
2. speak
3. Speaking / This is Ann
4. that
5. This
6. How are
7. thanks
8. you / how are you
9. Listen / Look
10. I've got a
11. need
12. for
13. Could
14. lend
15. Well / I don't know / Perhaps
16. afraid
17. yet
18. ring you later / ring you back
19. course
20. in / at home / here
21. message
22. soon

PRONUNCIATION

1 1. food
2. since
3. brush
4. gone
5. love
6. whose
7. break
8. share
9. catch

WRITING

Like the speaking test, this is partly a test of fluency. Give students credit for breadth of vocabulary, range of structures, clarity and organisation, as well as for grammatical correctness.

READING

This should be done without dictionaries. Encourage students to take their time over the reading before they start on the questions.

1. D	7. S
2. D	8. D
3. S	9. S
4. S	10. D
5. D	11. D
6. S	12. S

Test Book recordings
A recording for Test 6 in the Test Book follows this lesson on the Class Cassette.

LANGUAGE IN USE

1 Put one or more words into each gap.

ANN: Hello. Bristol 816547.
JOE: Hello. ......1...... I ......2...... to Ann, please?
ANN: ......3...... . Who's ......4......?
JOE: Oh, hello, Ann. ......5...... is Joe. ......6...... you?
ANN: Fine, ...7...... . And ......8......?
JOE: I'm OK. ......9......, Ann, ...10...... problem. I ......11...... a video recorder ......12...... a couple of days. ......13...... you possibly ......14...... me yours?
ANN: ......15......, I'll have to ask Phil. I'm ......16...... he's not back from work ......17...... . Can I ......18......?
JOE: Yes, of ......19...... . If I'm not ......20......, you can always leave a ......21...... with Sally.
ANN: OK, Joe. I'll ring you as ......22...... as I've spoken to Phil.
JOE: Thanks a lot, Ann. Bye.
ANN: Bye.

READING

1 Read the text and answer the questions.

FREE TRIP TO AMERICA – NEARLY

Six boys, aged seven to nine, nearly got a free trip to America last Sunday. They got on to the 42,000-ton ship Oriana, one of the world's biggest passenger liners, by saying that their parents had their tickets and passports. As the ship sailed from Southampton on its way to the Caribbean and America, the boys laughed and waved goodbye to policemen standing on the dockside.

Unfortunately for them, the boys were discovered when they asked a sailor the way to the 'café'. The sailor took them to the Captain, who checked up on them and radioed for a police boat to take them back to Southampton. The boys are now in a children's home while police try to trace their parents. Two of the boys are called John, there are two Davids (aged seven and nine), and the others are called Larry and Michael. They say that their surname is Power, and claim to be brothers or cousins. Nine-year-old David said that their parents' caravan was moved on by police from its site near Heathrow Airport on Sunday morning. The boys came back from a swimming trip and found their home gone.

The boys took the Underground to Waterloo, bought platform tickets, and got on the boat train to Southampton. When they arrived there they thought it would be great to go to America, and boarded the Oriana.

Apparently this was not the first time the boys had experimented with foreign travel. They told police that a few weeks ago they went to France on a hovercraft, but were picked up by French police at Amiens and sent home.

Newspaper report

Read the following sentences. For each one, write *S* if the sentence says the same thing as the text, and *D* if the meaning is different.

1. Six boys got a free trip to America.
2. They got on to the ship because their parents had their passports and tickets.
3. As the ship left Southampton, the boys waved goodbye to policemen.
4. The boys were discovered when they were looking for the café.
5. The Captain took them back to Southampton in a police boat.
6. Police are trying to find their parents.
7. If what the boys say is true, they all have the same surname and some of them have the same first names.
8. They are cousins.
9. They say their home is a caravan.
10. After the police moved their home, the boys went to Southampton to try to find their parents.
11. Last time they went to Southampton, they got a boat to France.
12. The French police made them go back home.

PRONUNCIATION

1 One word in each group has a different vowel sound from the others. Write the words that are different.

1. food   look   took   good
2. find   bite   since   drive
3. put   pull   brush   push
4. clothes   gone   drove   ghost
5. wrong   shop   watch   love
6. woke   whose   show   toast
7. break   mean   key   pleased
8. change   taste   straight   share
9. any   many   catch   friend

WRITING

1 Write the story from Speaking Exercise 1.

Vocabulary index

Verbs marked with an asterisk (*) are irregular. There is a complete list of the irregular
verbs in *The New Cambridge English Course* Level 2 at the back of the book.

a bit /ə 'bɪt/ — 2, 22, 36
a couple /ə 'kʌpl/ — 24
a few /ə 'fju:/ — 15, 32
a little /ə 'lɪtl/ — 15
a little/few more /mɔ:(r)/ — 15
a long time /ə 'lɒŋ 'taɪm/ — 14, 32
a lot /ə 'lɒt/ — 10
able /'eɪbl/ — 18
about (= concerning) /ə'baut/ — 21
about: How/What about . . . ?
　/'hau ('wɒt) ə'baut/ — 24
about (= approximately)
　/ə'baut/ — 24, 33
above /ə'bʌv/ — 7
accident /'æksɪdənt/ — 23, 35
across /ə'krɒs/ — 5, 20
actually /'æktʃəli/ — 2
AD /'eɪ'di:/ — 25
address /ə'dres/ — 23
address an envelope /'envələup/ — 31
adult /'ædʌlt/ — 25
advertise /'ædvətaɪz/ — 18
advertisement /əd'vɜ:tɪsmənt/ — 13, 18
advice /əd'vaɪs/ — 17
aeroplane /'eərəpleɪn/ — 31
afraid: I'm afraid I can't
　remember /ə'freɪd/ — 7
afraid: I'm afraid not
　/aɪm ə'freɪd 'nɒt/ — 11
Africa /'æfrɪkə/ — 20
after /'ɑ:ftə(r)/ — 31
afternoon: this afternoon
　/'ɑ:ftə'nu:n/ — 21
afterwards /'ɑ:ftəwədz/ — 7, 26, 33
again /ə'gen/ — 21
again and again /ə'gen ənd ə'gen/ — 22
against /ə'genst/ — 16
age /eɪdʒ/ — 18
ago /ə'gəu/ — 32
agree /ə'gri:/ — 20, 30
agriculture /'ægrɪkʌltʃə(r)/ — 14
ahead: straight ahead
　/'streɪt ə'hed/ — 35
alike /ə'laɪk/ — 9
alive /ə'laɪv/ — 26, 29
all /ɔ:l/ — 23
all: at all /ət 'ɔ:l/ — 22
all night /'ɔ:l 'naɪt/ — 33
all: That's all /'ðæts 'ɔ:l/ — 11
all over the world
　/'ɔ:l 'əuvə ðə 'wɜ:ld/ — 27
all right /'ɔ:l 'raɪt/ — 33
almost /'ɔ:lməust/ — 3
already /ɔ:l'redi/ — 31
also /'ɔ:lsəu/ — 4, 19
always /'ɔ:lweɪz/ — 3
America /ə'merɪkə/ — 17
American /ə'merɪkən/ — 19
angry /'æŋgri/ — 22

animal /'ænɪml/ — 4, 19
animal: wild animal
　/'waɪld 'ænɪml/ — 17
ankle /'æŋkl/ — 13
another time /ə'nʌðə 'taɪm/ — 36
answer /'ɑ:nsə(r)/ — 7
answer a letter /'ɑ:nsər ə 'letə(·)/ — 31
answer a door/phone
　/'ɑ:nsər ə dɔ: (fəun)/ — 36
anybody /'enibɒdi/ — 8
anything /'eniθɪŋ/ — 8, 22, 32
Anything else? /'eniθɪŋ 'els/ — 11
anyway /'eniweɪ/ — 12
apply /ə'plaɪ/ — 18
appointment /ə'pɔɪntmənt/ — 24
army /'ɑ:mi/ — 6, 34
around /ə'raund/ — 4
arrest /ə'rest/ — 26
arrive /ə'raɪv/ — 7, 34
artist /'ɑ:tɪst/ — 27
as (in comparisons) /əz/ — 9
as many as possible
　/əz 'meni əz 'pɒsəbl/ — 31
as much as possible
　/əz 'mʌtʃ əz 'pɒsəbl/ — 1, 31
as soon as /əz 'su:n əz/ — 31
as soon as possible
　/əz 'su:n əz 'pɒsəbl/ — 18
as usual /əz 'ju:ʒuəl/ — 8
ask /ɑ:sk/ — 22
ask for permission /pə'mɪʃən/ — 33
aspirin /'æsprɪn/ — 11
assistant /ə'sɪstənt/ — 18
at all /ət 'ɔ:l/ — 22
at least /ət 'li:st/ — 7, 30
at night /ət 'naɪt/ — 17, 31
at school /ət 'sku:l/ — 13
attractive /ə'træktɪv/ — 28
Australia /ɒs'treɪlɪə/ — 4
average /'ævrɪdʒ/ — 6, 14
avoid /ə'vɔɪd/ — 16
awake /ə'weɪk/ — 3
away /ə'weɪ/ — 3, 11, 13, 21, 26

baby /'beɪbi/ — 19, 21
baby: have* a baby /'hæv ə 'beɪbi/ — 19
back to front /'bæk tə 'frʌnt/ — 23
back (adverb): go* back
　/'gəu 'bæk/ — 23
backwards /'bækwədz/ — 23
bad luck /'bæd 'lʌk/ — 21
bag /bæg/ — 7
baggage /'bægɪdʒ/ — 35
baker('s) /'beɪkə(z)/ — 11
banana /bə'nɑ:nə/ — 6
bank /bæŋk/ — 34, 35
bar /bɑ:(r)/ — 32
bath /bɑ:θ/ — 3
be* born /bi: 'bɔ:n/ — 27

be* careful (of) /'bi: 'keəfl (əv)/ — 33
beach /bi:tʃ/ — 17
beard /bɪəd/ — 9
beautiful /'bju:tɪfl/ — 17
because /bɪ'kɒz/ — 22
become* /bɪ'kʌm/ — 14, 34
bed /bed/ — 3, 31
bed: go* to bed /'gəu tə 'bed/ — 31
bed: in bed /ɪn 'bed/ — 3
bed: make* a bed /'meɪk ə 'bed/ — 31
before /bɪ'fɔ:(r)/ — 31
believe /bɪ'li:v/ — 5
better /'betə(r)/ — 6
better: had better /həd 'betə(r)/ — 12
between /bɪ'twi:n/ — 3, 18
bicycle /'baɪsɪkl/ — 10
big /bɪg/ — 29
bill /bɪl/ — 31
bird /bɜ:d/ — 4, 10
birthday /'bɜ:θdeɪ/ — 13, 32
bit /bɪt/ — 2, 22, 36
bite* /baɪt/ — 33
blow* /bləu/ — 26
boat /bəut/ — 13
body /'bɒdi/ — 19, 28
body (= dead body) /'bɒdi/ — 26
bookshop /'bukʃɒp/ — 11
boring /'bɔ:rɪŋ/ — 8
born /bɔ:n/ — 27
borrow /'bɒrəu/ — 12, 33
boss /bɒs/ — 22
both /bəuθ/ — 9, 20, 28
bottle /'bɒtl/ — 11
boy /bɔɪ/ — 33
brake /breɪk/ — 35
Brazil /brə'zɪl/ — 4
bread /bred/ — 4
break* /breɪk/ — 7
break* up /'breɪk 'ʌp/ — 20
bring* /brɪŋ/ — 3, 32
Britain /'brɪtn/ — 17
broken /'brəukn/ — 20
brush (noun) /brʌʃ/ — 29
brush one's teeth /'brʌʃ wʌnz 'ti:θ/ — 31
build* /bɪld/ — 25
building /'bɪldɪŋ/ — 27
burn* /bɜ:n/ — 16
bus /bʌs/ — 10
business /'bɪznɪs/ — 3, 26
but /bət, bʌt/ — 9
butcher('s) /'butʃə(z)/ — 11
buy* /baɪ/ — 24
by (time) /baɪ/ — 33
by (in passives) /baɪ/ — 26
by myself /baɪ maɪ'self/ — 23

cake: make* a cake /'meɪk ə 'keɪk/ — 24
call: What do you call . . . ?
　/'wɒt də jə 'kɔ:l/ — 11

calm /kɑːm/ 20, 28
camera /ˈkæmrə/ 11
camping /ˈkæmpɪŋ/ 17
can* /k(ə)n, kæn/ 12
Can I look round?
/kən aɪ ˈlʊk ˈraʊnd/ 11
Can you tell me the way to . . . ? 12
can't /kɑːnt/ 27
can't stand /ˈkɑːnt ˈstænd/ 22
capital /ˈkæpɪtl/ 14
car /kɑː(r)/ 10
careful: be* careful (of)
/ˈbiː ˈkeəfl (əv)/ 33
carefully /ˈkeəfli/ 36
carpet /ˈkɑːpɪt/ 33
carry /ˈkæri/ 10, 19, 36
cash /kæʃ/ 26
cat /kæt/ 10, 21
catch*: I didn't catch your name
/kætʃ/ 1
cell /sel/ 19
central /ˈsentrəl/ 26
centre: city/town centre
/ˈsɪti (ˈtaʊn) ˈsentə(r)/ 16
century /ˈsentʃəri/ 9, 25
certain /ˈsɜːtn/ 19
certainly /ˈsɜːtnli/ 19
change (for £1) /tʃeɪndʒ/ 12
change (verb) /tʃeɪndʒ/ 6, 14, 35
change one's mind
/ˈtʃeɪndʒ wʌnz ˈmaɪnd/ 22
cheap /tʃiːp/ 6
check /tʃek/ 35
check-in /ˈtʃekɪn/ 35
cheerful /ˈtʃɪəfl/ 28
chemical /ˈkemɪkl/ 25
chemistry /ˈkemɪstri/ 19
chemist('s) /ˈkemɪst(s)/ 11
chicken /ˈtʃɪkɪn/ 6
Chinese /tʃaɪˈniːz/ 9
choose* /tʃuːz/ 17, 30
Christmas /ˈkrɪsməs/ 7
Christmas Eve /ˈkrɪsməs ˈiːv/ 7
church /tʃɜːtʃ/ 24
cinema /ˈsɪnəmə/ 32
city /ˈsɪti/ 16
city centre /ˈsɪti ˈsentə(r)/ 16
class: working class
/ˈwɜːkɪŋ ˈklɑːs/ 34
clean (verb) /kliːn/ 11, 24, 30
clean out /ˈkliːn ˈaʊt/ 36
cleaning: do the cleaning
/ˈduː ðə ˈkliːnɪŋ/ 30
clear /klɪə(r)/ 6
climb /klaɪm/ 13
close (verb) /kləʊz/ 21
closed /kləʊzd/ 27
clothes /kləʊðz/ 4
clothes shop /ˈkləʊðz ˈʃɒp/ 11
coal /kəʊl/ 25
coast /kəʊst/ 26
coffee /ˈkɒfi/ 36
cold /kəʊld/ 29, 36
colony /ˈkɒləni/ 14
colour /ˈkʌlə(r)/ 19

come* home /ˈkʌm ˈhəʊm/ 8
Come on /ˈkʌm ˈɒn/ 23
comfortable /ˈkʌmftəbl/ 17
company /ˈkʌmpəni/ 18
compare /kəmˈpeə(r)/ 9
compartment /kəmˈpɑːtmənt/ 35
complicated /ˈkɒmplɪkeɪtɪd/ 19
continue /kənˈtɪnjuː/ 16
conversation /kɒnvəˈseɪʃn/ 24
cook /kʊk/ 30
cooking: do* the cooking
/ˈduː ðə ˈkʊkɪŋ/ 30
corner: round the corner
/ˈraʊnd ðə ˈkɔːnə(r)/ 8
correct /kəˈrekt/ 1
cost* /kɒst/ 10
cotton /ˈkɒtn/ 29
could /kəd, kʊd/ 12, 27
Could you say that again? 7
country /ˈkʌntri/ 6, 16
couple: a couple /ə ˈkʌpl/ 24
course: of course /əv ˈkɔːs/ 8, 12
crash /kræʃ/ 7, 20
creature /ˈkriːtʃə(r)/ 5
credit card /ˈkredɪt ˈkɑːd/ 27
crossroads /ˈkrɒsrəʊdz/ 35
cup of tea/coffee
/ˈkʌp əv ˈtiː (ˈkɒfi)/ 36
curly /ˈkɜːli/ 28
curtain /ˈkɜːtn/ 21
cut* /kʌt/ 11
cut* down /ˈkʌt ˈdaʊn/ 25
cut* up /ˈkʌt ˈʌp/ 25
cycling /ˈsaɪklɪŋ/ 33

daily /ˈdeɪli/ 25
dance (noun) /dɑːns/ 26
dance (verb) /dɑːns/ 36
dangerous /ˈdeɪndʒərəs/ 6
dark /dɑːk/ 21, 29
dark-haired /ˈdɑːkˈheəd/ 28
darling /ˈdɑːlɪŋ/ 8
day: every day /ˈevri ˈdeɪ/ 33
day: one of these days
/ˈwʌn əv ˈðiːz ˈdeɪz/ 12
day off /ˈdeɪ ˈɒf/ 33
dead /ded/ 7, 26
death /deθ/ 20
decide /dɪˈsaɪd/ 7, 34
deep /diːp/ 7
definitely /ˈdefənətli/ 30
delay /dɪˈleɪ/ 35
delicious /dɪˈlɪʃəs/ 13
democracy /dɪˈmɒkrəsi/ 14
demonstration /demənˈstreɪʃn/ 16
dentist /ˈdentɪst/ 3
depend (on) /dɪˈpend (ɒn)/ 19, 24
depend: it depends
/ɪt dɪˈpendz/ 24, 30
depressed /dɪˈprest/ 28
desert /ˈdezət/ 4, 20
diary /ˈdaɪəri/ 24
die /daɪ/ 7, 20
difference /ˈdɪfrəns/ 5
different (from) /ˈdɪfrənt (frəm)/ 9, 28, 34

difficult /ˈdɪfɪkʊlt/ 24
difficult to work for etc.
/ˈdɪfɪkʊlt tə ˈwɜːk ˈfɔː/ 22
direct /dəˈrekt/ 26
directions /dəˈrekʃənz/ 35
discover /dɪsˈkʌvə(r)/ 17, 26
do*: How do you do?
/ˈhaʊ də jə ˈduː/ 1
do* a job /ˈduː ə ˈdʒɒb/ 22
do* the cleaning/cooking etc.
/ˈduː ðə ˈkliːnɪŋ (ˈkʊkɪŋ)/ 30
dog /dɒg/ 10
dollar /ˈdɒlə(r)/ 13
Don't forget to . . .
/ˈdəʊnt fəˈget tə/ 23
door /dɔː(r)/ 5
door: answer a door
/ˈɑːnsər ə ˈdɔː(r)/ 36
down /daʊn/ 6, 23, 32
draw* /drɔː/ 30
dream* (verb) /driːm/ 5, 13
dress (noun) /dres/ 7, 12
dressed: get* dressed
/ˈget ˈdrest/ 3, 31
drink (noun) /drɪŋk/ 24, 32
drink: have* a drink
/ˈhæv ə ˈdrɪŋk/ 24
drink* (verb) /drɪŋk/ 32
drive* /draɪv/ 23, 31
driving licence
/ˈdraɪvɪŋ ˈlaɪsəns/ 17, 35
dry (adj) /draɪ/ 4
dry (verb) /draɪ/ 25
during /ˈdjuːrɪŋ/ 3, 13

each /iːtʃ/ 4, 25
each other /ˈiːtʃ ˈʌðə(r)/ 14, 30
earlier /ˈɜːlɪə(r)/ 24
early /ˈɜːli/ 3, 34
ear-ring /ˈɪərɪŋ/ 9
Earth /ɜːθ/ 5
easy to work for etc.
/ˈiːzi tə ˈwɜːk fɔː/ 22
eat* /iːt/ 4
economy /ɪˈkɒnəmi/ 14
education /edjuːˈkeɪʃn/ 18, 27
either . . . or
/ˈaɪðə(r) . . . ˈɔː(r)/ 19, 23
either: not . . . either
/ˈnɒt . . . ˈaɪðə(r)/ 2
election /ɪˈlekʃən/ 14
else: anything else /ˈeniθɪŋ ˈels/ 11
else: somebody else
/ˈsʌmbədi ˈels/ 19, 30
employment /ɪmˈplɔɪmənt/ 14
engine /ˈendʒən/ 20, 35
English: What's the English
for . . . ? /ˈwɒts ðiː ˈɪŋglɪʃ fə(r)/ 1
enjoy /ɪnˈdʒɔɪ/ 13
enough /ɪˈnʌf/ 15, 33
enquiry /ɪŋˈkwaɪri/ 35
envelope /ˈenvələʊp/ 31
escape /ɪˈskeɪp/ 34
essential /ɪˈsenʃʊl/ 18

Europe /ˈjʊərəp/ 17
European /jʊərəˈpɪən/ 19
even /ˈiːvən/ 2
evening: this evening /ðɪs ˈiːvnɪŋ/ 21
ever: hardly ever /ˈhɑːdli ˈevə(r)/ 3
every /ˈevri/ 13
every day /ˈevri ˈdeɪ/ 33
every . . . years /ˈevri . . . ˈjɪəz/ 14
everybody /ˈevribɒdi/ 5, 23, 33
everything /ˈevriθɪŋ/ 30, 32
exactly /ɪgˈzæktli/ 33
example: for example
  /fər ɪgˈzɑːmpl/ 7
excellent /ˈeksələnt/ 18
except /ɪkˈsept/ 7
exciting /ɪkˈsaɪtɪŋ/ 17
expensive /ɪkˈspensɪv/ 9
experience /ɪkˈspɪərɪəns/ 18
explain /ɪkˈspleɪn/ 25
export /ɪksˈpɔːt/ 25
eye /aɪ/ 19

face /feɪs/ 28
fact /fækt/ 19
fail /feɪl/ 13
fair (= not dark) /feə(r)/ 9
fair (= not unfair) /feə(r)/ 22
fair-haired /ˈfeəˈheəd/ 28
fairly /ˈfeəli/ 3
faithfully: Yours faithfully
  /ˈjɔːz ˈfeɪθfuli/ 18
fall* /fɔːl/ 6
fall* in love (with)
  /ˈfɔːl ɪn ˈlʌv (wɪð)/ 23, 30
false /fɔːls/ 10
family /ˈfæməli/ 4, 32
famous /ˈfeɪməs/ 17, 27
far (with comparatives) /fɑː(r)/ 10
fast (adjective) /fɑːst/ 10
fast (adverb) /fɑːst/ 6
fat /fæt/ 28
favourite /ˈfeɪvrɪt/ 27
fed up (with) /ˈfed ˈʌp (wɪð)/ 22
feel* /fiːl/ 12
feel* sorry for /ˈfiːl ˈsɒri fə(r)/ 30
feelings /ˈfiːlɪŋz/ 32
few: a few /ə ˈfjuː/ 15, 32
fewest /ˈfjuːɪst/ 10
fibre: synthetic fibre
  /sɪnˈθetɪk ˈfaɪbə(r)/ 29
field /fiːld/ 5
fight (noun) /faɪt/ 13
figures /ˈfɪgəz/ 14
film (for a camera) /fɪlm/ 11
film (= movie) /fɪlm/ 24, 26, 36
find* /faɪnd/ 4
fine /faɪn/ 21
finish /ˈfɪnɪʃ/ 8
finished /ˈfɪnɪʃt/ 21
fire /ˈfaɪə(r)/ 16
firm (noun) /fɜːm/ 18
first /fɜːst/ 2, 23
fish /fɪʃ/ 4
flat (noun) /flæt/ 10, 26
flower /ˈflaʊə(r)/ 17

fly* /flaɪ/ 20
food /fuːd/ 4, 27, 31
foot /fʊt/ 12, 29
foot: on foot /ɒn ˈfʊt/ 4
for example /fər ɪgˈzɑːmpl/ 7
foreign /ˈfɒrən/ 14
forget* /fəˈget/ 17, 23
forward: look forward to
  /ˈlʊk ˈfɔːwəd tə/ 18
forwards /ˈfɔːwədz/ 23
fourth /fɔːθ/ 2
free /friː/ 24, 30
free time /ˈfriː ˈtaɪm/ 10
fresh /freʃ/ 17
friend /frend/ 24
friendly /ˈfrendli/ 17, 28
friendship /ˈfrendʃɪp/ 14
from . . . to /frəm . . . tə/ 25
front: back to front
  /ˈbæk tə ˈfrʌnt/ 23
front: in front of /ɪn ˈfrʌnt əv/ 31
fruit /fruːt/ 4
full name /ˈfʊl ˈneɪm/ 27
full-time /ˈfʊlˈtaɪm/ 18
future /ˈfjuːtʃə(r)/ 19

game /geɪm/ 21
gardening /ˈgɑːdnɪŋ/ 3, 24
Germany /ˈdʒɜːməni/ 34
get* (= become) /get/ 6
get* angry /ˈget ˈæŋgri/ 22
get* dark /ˈget ˈdɑːk/ 21
get* dressed /ˈget ˈdrest/ 3, 31
get* off /ˈget ˈɒf/ 21
get* married /ˈget ˈmærɪd/ 19, 23
get* on (well) together
  /ˈget ˈɒn (ˈwel) təˈgeðə(r)/ 2
get* on with /ˈget ˈɒn wɪð/ 22
get* out /ˈget ˈaʊt/ 5
get* ready /ˈget ˈredi/ 8
get* up /ˈget ˈʌp/ 3, 31
get* worse /ˈget ˈwɜːs/ 14
give* /gɪv/ 32
glad /glæd/ 22, 27
glad: I'm glad to meet you 1
glad: I was glad to hear 22
glass (uncountable) /glɑːs/ 29
glasses /ˈglɑːsɪz/ 7
go* back /ˈgəʊ ˈbæk/ 23
go* down /ˈgəʊ ˈdaʊn/ 6
go* home /ˈgəʊ ˈhəʊm/ 8
go* on . . .ing /ˈgəʊ ˈɒn/ 2, 5
go* out with somebody
  /ˈgəʊ ˈaʊt wɪð ˈsʌmbədi/ 12
go* shopping /ˈgəʊ ˈʃɒpɪŋ/ 3
go* to bed /ˈgəʊ tə ˈbed/ 31
go* to church /ˈgəʊ tə ˈtʃɜːtʃ/ 24
go* to sleep /ˈgəʊ tə ˈsliːp/ 31
go* up /ˈgəʊ ˈʌp/ 6
go* wrong /ˈgəʊ ˈrɒŋ/ 32
gold /gəʊld/ 25
good idea /ˈgʊd aɪˈdɪə/ 23
good-looking /ˈgʊdˈlʊkɪŋ/ 19, 28
good luck /ˈgʊd ˈlʌk/ 21
government /ˈgʌvənmənt/ 14

grammar /ˈgræmə(r)/ 13
grandchild /ˈgræntʃaɪld/ 19
grandmother/father/son/daughter
  /ˈgrænmʌðə(r)/ 16
great: look great /ˈlʊk ˈgreɪt/ 12
great-grandchild /ˈgreɪtˈgræntʃaɪld/ 19
greengrocer('s) /ˈgriːngrəʊsə(z)/ 11
grey /greɪ/ 28
grocer('s) /ˈgrəʊsə(z)/ 11
grow* /grəʊ/ 25
guess /ges/ 27
guitar /gɪˈtɑː(r)/ 10
gun /gʌn/ 5

had better /həd ˈbetə(r)/ 12
hair: dark/fair-haired
  /(ˈdɑːk) ˈfeəˈheəd/ 28
hair: red hair /ˈred ˈheə(r)/ 28
hairdresser /ˈheədresə(r)/ 3, 31
half /hɑːf/ 19, 25
half an hour /ˈhɑːf ən ˈaʊə(r)/ 12
hand: on the other hand
  /ɒn ði ˈʌðə ˈhænd/ 2, 9, 22
hand: left/right-handed
  /(ˈleft) ˈraɪthændɪd/ 28
handbag /ˈhændbæg/ 36
handle /ˈhændl/ 11
hang* up /ˈhæŋ ˈʌp/ 36
happen /ˈhæpn/ 5, 27
happy /ˈhæpi/ 9
hard (adj) /hɑːd/ 13, 29
hard (adverb) /hɑːd/ 34
hardly ever /ˈhɑːdli ˈevə(r)/ 3
hate /heɪt/ 22, 26
have* a baby /ˈhæv ə ˈbeɪbi/ 19
have* a drink /ˈhæv ə ˈdrɪŋk/ 24
have* a look /ˈhæv ə ˈlʊk/ 12, 36
have* a party /ˈhæv ə ˈpɑːti/ 33
have* a rest /ˈhæv ə ˈrest/ 36
Have you got a light? 12
Have you got the time? 12
head /hed/ 20
hear* /hɪə(r)/ 5
hear* from /ˈhɪə frəm/ 18
heavy /ˈhevi/ 3, 16, 20, 29
height /haɪt/ 6
helicopter /ˈhelɪkɒptə(r)/ 7
help /help/ 23, 26, 34
hers /hɜːz/ 12
herself /həˈself/ 30
high /haɪ/ 29
himself /hɪmˈself/ 30
his /hɪz/ 12
hit* /hɪt/ 7, 20
hold* /həʊld/ 5
hole /həʊl/ 11
holiday /ˈhɒlədi/ 6
holiday: on holiday /ɒn ˈhɒlədi/ 21
home: come*/go* home
  /ˈkʌm (ˈgəʊ) həʊm/ 8
homeless /ˈhəʊmləs/ 14
honest /ˈɒnɪst/ 30
hope /həʊp/ 32
hope: I hope (so) /aɪ ˈhəʊp (ˈsəʊ)/ 19
horse /hɔːs/ 10

hospital /'hɒspɪtl/ 16, 23
hot /hɒt/ 4, 29
hour: a couple of hours
 /ə 'kʌpl əv 'auəz/ 24
hour: half an hour
 /'hɑ:f ən 'auə(r)/ 12
housework /'hauswɜ:k/ 3, 30
How about . . . ? /'hau ə'baut/ 24
How do you do? /'hau də jə 'du:/ 1
How do you spell . . . ?
 /'hau də jə 'spel/ 1
how many /'hau 'meni/ 5
hunger /'hʌngə(r)/ 16
hungry /'hʌngri/ 6
hurry: in a hurry /ɪn ə 'hʌri/ 12
hurt* /hɜ:t/ 7, 30
husband /'hʌzbənd/ 14, 30

I (don't) agree /aɪ ('dəunt) ə'gri:/ 30
I didn't catch your name 1
I don't think so
 /aɪ 'dəunt 'θɪŋk 'səu/ 30
I had (I'd) better
 /aɪ həd (aɪd) 'betə(r)/ 12
I hope (so) /aɪ 'həup ('səu)/ 19
I look forward to hearing
 from you 18
I mean /aɪ 'mi:n/ 23
I see /aɪ 'si:/ 8
I suppose so /aɪ sə'pəuz 'səu/ 33
I think so /aɪ 'θɪŋk 'səu/ 12, 30
I thought you said . . .
 /aɪ 'θɔ:t ju: 'sed/ 24
I was glad/interested/sorry
 to hear 22
ice cream /'aɪs 'kri:m/ 13
I'd like to introduce . . .
 /aɪd 'laɪk tu: 'ɪntrə'dju:s/ 1
I'd like you to . . . /aɪd 'laɪk jə tə/ 24
I'd love to /aɪd 'lʌv tu:/ 12, 36
idea /aɪ'dɪə/ 33
idea: a good idea /ə 'gud aɪ'dɪə/ 23
if /ɪf/ 21
if you don't mind
 /ɪf ju: 'dəunt 'maɪnd/ 12
I'll think about it
 /aɪl 'θɪŋk ə'baut ɪt/ 23
I'm a stranger here myself 12
I'm afraid I can't remember 7
I'm afraid not /aɪm ə'freɪd 'nɒt/ 11
I'm being served /aɪm 'bi:ɪŋ 'sɜ:vd/ 11
I'm glad to meet you 1
I'm looking for . . .
 /aɪm 'lukɪŋ fə(r)/ 11
I'm not sure /aɪm 'nɒt 'ʃɔ:(r)/ 30
I'm sorry, I don't understand 7
I'm sure /aɪm 'ʃɔ:(r)/ 21, 30
import /ɪm'pɔ:t/ 25
important /ɪm'pɔ:tənt/ 25, 34
impossible /ɪm'pɒsəbl/ 22
improve /ɪm'pru:v/ 14
in a hurry /ɪn ə 'hʌri/ 12
in bed /ɪn 'bed/ 3
in front of /ɪn 'frʌnt əv/ 31
in love /ɪn 'lʌv/ 23

in some ways /ɪn 'sʌm 'weɪz/ 9
in the sky /ɪn ðə 'skaɪ/ 5
increase /ɪŋ'kri:s/ 14
independent /ɪndɪ'pendənt/ 14
industry /'ɪndəstri/ 14, 25
information /'ɪnfə'meɪʃn/ 27
inside /ɪn'saɪd/ 5
inside out /'ɪnsaɪd 'aut/ 23
intelligence /ɪn'telɪdʒəns/ 10
interested (in) /'ɪntrəstɪd (ɪn)/ 13, 27
interested: I was interested to
 hear 22
interesting /'ɪntrəstɪŋ/ 8, 27
interesting to work for/talk
 to etc. 22
international driving licence
 /'ɪntə'næʃənl 'draɪvɪŋ 'laɪsəns/ 17
interview /'ɪntəvju:/ 18
into /'ɪntə, 'ɪntu:/ 8
introduce /'ɪntrə'dju:s/ 1
introduce: I'd like to introduce . . .
 /aɪd 'laɪk tu: 'ɪntrə'dju:s/ 1
invent /ɪn'vent/ 26
invite /ɪn'vaɪt/ 33
iron (verb) /aɪən/ 30
ironing /'aɪənɪŋ/ 3, 24
It depends /ɪt dɪ'pendz/ 30
Italy /'ɪtəli/ 34
It's a pleasure to
 /ɪts ə 'pleʒə tə/ 22
its /ɪts/ 19
itself /ɪt'self/ 30
It's no trouble /ɪts 'nəu 'trʌbl/ 23

jacket /'dʒækɪt/ 12
job /dʒɒb/ 18
job: do* a job /'du: ə 'dʒɒb/ 22
join /dʒɔɪn/ 34
journalist /'dʒɜ:nəlɪst/ 34
journey /'dʒɜ:ni/ 3
juice /dʒu:s/ 1
just /dʒəst, dʒʌst/ 2, 22
just when /'dʒʌst 'wen/ 8

keep* /ki:p/ 20
keep* . . . away /'ki:p . . . ə'weɪ/ 21
keep* calm /'ki:p 'kɑ:m/ 20
keep* (clothes) on /'ki:p 'ɒn/ 36
keep* on . . . ing /'ki:p 'ɒn/ 31
keep* straight on /'ki:p 'streɪt 'ɒn/ 35
kettle /'ketl/ 36
key /ki:/ 27, 36
kill /kɪl/ 7, 26
kilo /'ki:ləu/ 10
kilometre /'kɪləmi:tə(r), kɪ'lɒmɪtə(r)/ 20
kind /kaɪnd/ 12, 36
kind: That's very kind of you 12
king /kɪŋ/ 9
knee /ni:/ 7
know*: Sorry, I don't know 7
know*: you know /ju: 'nəu/ 23
kph (= kilometres per hour)
 /keɪ pi: 'eɪtʃ/ 10

land (verb) /lænd/ 5, 35

landing /'lændɪŋ/ 20
language /'læŋgwɪdʒ/ 32
large /lɑ:dʒ/ 6
last (adj) /lɑ:st/ 13
last (verb) /lɑ:st/ 16
last time /'lɑ:st 'taɪm/ 33
late /leɪt/ 27, 32
later /'leɪtə(r)/ 24
laugh /lɑ:f/ 9
lazy /'leɪzi/ 6
leaf /li:f/ 4
learn* /lɜ:n/ 7, 30
least: at least /ət 'li:st/ 7, 30
leather /'leðə(r)/ 29
leave* /li:v/ 7, 16
left-handed /'left'hændɪd/ 28
lend* /lend/ 12
length /leŋθ/ 6
less /les/ 9
Let me look /'let mi: 'luk/ 24
Let me see /'let mi: 'si:/ 24
letter: answer a letter
 /'ɑ:nsər ə 'letə(r)/ 31
lie* /laɪ/ 3
life /laɪf/ 13, 20, 34
light (= not dark) /laɪt/ 29
light (= not heavy) /laɪt/ 10, 29
light (noun) /laɪt/ 5
light: Have you got a light? 12
light: put* out a light
 /'put 'aut ə 'laɪt/ 31
like (prep) /laɪk/ 17, 19
like: look like /'luk 'laɪk/ 12, 19
like: sound like /'saund 'laɪk/ 8
like: What is . . . like?
 /'wɒt ɪz . . . 'laɪk/ 19
like (verb): I'd like you to . . .
 /aɪd 'laɪk ju: tə/ 24
liquid /'lɪkwɪd/ 11, 29
listen (to) /'lɪsən (tə)/ 17, 30
literature /'lɪtrətʃə(r)/ 34
little: a little /ə 'lɪtl/ 15
lock up /'lɒk 'ʌp/ 36
long /lɒŋ/ 9, 28
long: a long time /ə 'lɒŋ 'taɪm/ 14, 32
look (at) /luk (ət)/ 2, 9, 28, 30
look: Can I look round?
 /kən aɪ 'luk 'raund/ 11
look: look great etc. /'luk 'greɪt/ 12
look: have* a look
 /'hæv ə 'luk/ 12, 36
look: I look forward to hearing
 from you 18
look: I'm looking for
 /aɪm 'lukɪŋ fə(r)/ 11
look: Let me look /'let mi: 'luk/ 24
look for /'luk fə(r)/ 7
look forward to /'luk 'fɔ:wəd/ 18
look like /'luk 'laɪk/ 12, 19
look (a word) up /'luk 'ʌp/ 36
lorry /'lɒri/ 10
lose* /lu:z/ 8
lot: a lot /ə 'lɒt/ 10
loud /laud/ 29
love /lʌv/ 27

love: fall* in love with
/'fɔ:l ɪn 'lʌv 'wɪð/ 23, 30
love: I'd love to /aɪd 'lʌv tu:/ 12, 36
lovely /'lʌvli/ 12, 22
low /ləʊ/ 29
luck /lʌk/ 21

machine /mə'ʃi:n/ 5
made of /'meɪd əv/ 4, 29
make (noun) /meɪk/ 11
make* a bed /'meɪk ə 'bed/ 31
make* a cake /'meɪk ə 'keɪk/ 24
make* a mistake
/'meɪk ə mɪs'teɪk/ 22
make* an appointment
/'meɪk ən ə'pɔɪntmənt/ 24
make* from /'meɪk frəm/ 25
make* into /'meɪk ɪntə/ 25
make-up /'meɪkʌp/ 36
manager /'mænədʒə(r)/ 18, 33
manufacture /'mænju:'fæktʃə(r)/ 25
many: as many as possible
/əz 'meni əz 'pɒsəbl/ 31
many: how many /'haʊ 'meni/ 5
map /mæp/ 17
married /'mærɪd/ 1, 30
married: get* married
/'get 'mærɪd/ 19, 23
marry /'mæri/ 23, 30
material /mə'tɪərɪʊl/ 11
maths (mathematics) /mæθs/ 34
matter: What's the matter?
/'wɒts ðə 'mætə(r)/ 12
may /meɪ/ 17
May I introduce myself?
/'meɪ aɪ ɪntrə'dju:s maɪ'self/ 1
maybe /'meɪbi/ 2
meal /mi:l/ 3
mean* /mi:n/ 1
mean: I mean /aɪ 'mi:n/ 23
mean: What do you mean?
/'wɒt də jə 'mi:n/ 7
mean: What does . . . mean?
/'wɒt dəz . . . 'mi:n/ 1
meat /mi:t/ 4, 16
medium /'mi:dɪəm/ 11
meet* /mi:t/ 13, 24
meet: I'm glad to meet you 1
meeting /'mi:tɪŋ/ 8, 24
mend /mend/ 24, 30
message /'mesɪdʒ/ 5
metal /'metl/ 29
midnight /'mɪdnaɪt/ 33
might /maɪt/ 27
mile /maɪl/ 20
milk /mɪlk/ 11
million /'mɪlɪən/ 13
mind: change one's mind
/'tʃeɪndʒ wʌnz 'maɪnd/ 22
mind: if you don't mind
/ɪf ju: 'dəʊnt 'maɪnd/ 12
mine (verb) /maɪn/ 25
mine (possessive) /maɪn/ 12
minute /'mɪnɪt/ 32
mirror /'mɪrə(r)/ 21

mistake /mɪs'teɪk/ 22
mix /mɪks/ 25
money /'mʌni/ 21
month /mʌnθ/ 4
moon /mu:n/ 19
more /mɔ:(r)/ 9
more: a little/few more
/ə 'lɪtl ('fju:) 'mɔ:(r)/ 15
morning: this morning
/ðɪs 'mɔ:nɪŋ/ 8
most /məʊst/ 10
most of /'məʊst əv/ 14
most of the time
/'məʊst əv ðə 'taɪm/ 2
motorbike /'məʊtəbaɪk/ 10
mountain /'maʊntɪn/ 20
mountain: the mountains
/ðə 'maʊntɪnz/ 10
move /mu:v/ 16, 23, 34
much (with comparatives) /mʌtʃ/ 10
much: as much as possible
/əz 'mʌtʃ əz 'pɒsəbl/ 1, 31
much: so much /'səʊ 'mʌtʃ/ 1
much: too much
/'tu: 'mʌtʃ/ 15, 28, 33
Muslim /'mʌzlɪm/ 25
must* /məst, mʌst/ 18, 27, 33
myself /maɪ'self/ 30
myself: by myself /baɪ maɪ'self/ 23
myself: I'm a stranger here
myself 12
myself: May I introduce myself?
/'meɪ aɪ ɪntrə'dju:s maɪ'self/ 1

name: full name /'fʊl 'neɪm/ 27
name: I didn't catch your name 1
narrow /'nærəʊ/ 29
nationality /'næʃə'næləti/ 1
near /nɪə(r)/ 17
nearest /'nɪərɪst/ 20
nearly /'nɪəli/ 10
necessary /'nesəsri/ 3, 18
neck /nek/ 29
need /ni:d/ 12, 18, 20, 33
neighbour /'neɪbə(r)/ 13
neither /'naɪðə(r)/ 9, 28
nervous /'nɜ:vəs/ 28
never /'nevə(r)/ 3
new /nju:/ 29
New Year /'nju: 'jɪə(r)/ 21
news /nju:z/ 16
newsagent('s) /'nju:zeɪdʒənt(s)/ 11
newspaper /'nju:speɪpə(r)/ 3, 13
next /nekst/ 7
Nice to see you again /naɪs/ 1
night: all night /'ɔ:l 'naɪt/ 33
night: at night /ət 'naɪt/ 17, 31
nobody /'nəʊbədi/ 7, 20, 32
noise /nɔɪz/ 33
noisy /'nɔɪzi/ 29
none /nʌn/ 27
non-smoking /'nɒn'sməʊkɪŋ/ 35
normally /'nɔ:məli/ 3
North Africa /'nɔ:θ 'æfrɪkə/ 20
nose /nəʊz/ 9

not at all /'nɒt ət 'ɔ:l/ 22
not . . . either /'nɒt . . . 'aɪðə(r)/ 2
not really /'nɒt 'rɪəli/ 8
now: right now /'raɪt 'naʊ/ 22
number /'nʌmbə(r)/ 6
nurse /nɜ:s/ 23

occasionally /ə'keɪʒənli/ 3
of course /əv 'kɔ:s/ 8, 12, 30
of course not /əv 'kɔ:s 'nɒt/ 30
off /ɒf/ 23
offer /'ɒfə(r)/ 36
office /'ɒfɪs/ 8
often /'ɒfən/ 3
Oh dear /'əʊ 'dɪə(r)/ 12
oil /ɔɪl/ 35
OK /'əʊ'keɪ/ 33
old /əʊld/ 29
on /ɒn/ 23
on foot /ɒn 'fʊt/ 4
on holiday /ɒn 'hɒlədi/ 21
on the other hand
/'ɒn ðɪ ʌðə 'hænd/ 2, 9, 22
on TV /ɒn 'ti:'vi:/ 26
one (of) /'wʌn (əv)/ 28
one of these days
/'wʌn əv 'ði:z 'deɪz/ 12
only /'əʊnli/ 20
onto /'ɒntə/ 8
orange /'ɒrɪndʒ/ 25
orange juice /'ɒrɪndʒ 'dʒu:s/ 1
order /'ɔ:də(r)/ 32
other /'ʌðə(r)/ 25, 28
other: each other /'i:tʃ 'ʌðə(r)/ 14, 30
other: on the other hand
/'ɒn ðɪ ʌðə 'hænd/ 2, 9, 22
ours /'aʊəz/ 12
ourselves /aʊə'selvz/ 30
out /aʊt/ 33
out of /'aʊt əv/ 7
oval /'əʊvl/ 28
over /'əʊvə(r)/ 5
over: all over the world
/'ɔ:l 'əʊvə ðə 'wɜ:ld/ 27
overcoat /'əʊvəkəʊt/ 36
overtake /'əʊvə'teɪk/ 35
owe /əʊ/ 26

page /peɪdʒ/ 25
paper /'peɪpə(r)/ 25, 29
paper: writing paper
/'raɪtɪŋ 'peɪpə(r)/ 11
parent /'peərənt/ 19, 34
parliament /'pɑ:lɪmənt/ 14
part /pɑ:t/ 29
part-time /'pɑ:t'taɪm/ 18
party /'pɑ:ti/ 24
party: have* a party
/'hæv ə 'pɑ:ti/ 33
pay* (verb) /peɪ/ 27
pay (noun) /peɪ/ 18
per cent /pə 'sent/ 31
percentage /pə'sentɪdʒ/ 6, 14
perhaps /pə'hæps/ 30
Perhaps you're right

/pə'hæps jɔː 'raɪt/ 30

permission: ask for permission
/'ɑːsk fə pə'mɪʃn/ 33

person /'pɜːsn/ 19

petrol /'petrʊl/ 11

petrol station /'petrʊl 'steɪʃn/ 11, 35

phone (verb) /fəʊn/ 27

phone: answer a phone
/'ɑːnsər ə 'fəʊn/ 36

phone call /'fəʊn kɔːl/ 8

photo /'fəʊtəʊ/ 36

photograph (verb) /'fəʊtəgrɑːf/ 27

photographer /fə'tɒgrəfə(r)/ 27

physics /'fɪzɪks/ 34

piano /pi'ænəʊ/ 1

pick up /'pɪk 'ʌp/ 8, 36

picture /'pɪktʃə(r)/ 2

picture: take* pictures
/'teɪk 'pɪktʃəz/ 17

piece /piːs/ 11

place /pleɪs/ 4

place: my/your place
/'maɪ ('jɔː) 'pleɪs/ 24

plain /pleɪn/ 28

plane /pleɪn/ 7, 10, 20

plant /plɑːnt/ 19

plastic /'plæstɪk/ 29

plate /pleɪt/ 21

platform /'plætfɔːm/ 35

play (verb) /pleɪ/ 21

play (noun) /pleɪ/ 17

pleased /pliːzd/ 32

pleasure /'pleʒə(r)/ 22

plump /plʌmp/ 28

police /pə'liːs/ 23, 26, 35

pool /puːl/ 17

population /pɒpju:'leɪʃn/ 6, 14

possible: as many as possible
/əz 'meni əz 'pɒsəbl/ 31

possible: as much as possible
/əz 'mʌtʃ əz 'pɒsəbl/ 1, 31

possible: as soon as possible
/əz 'suːn əz 'pɒsəbl/ 18

post /pəʊst/ 6

postman /'pəʊstmən/ 31

post office /'pəʊst 'ɒfɪs/ 11

potato /pə'teɪtəʊ/ 5

pound /paʊnd/ 10

powder /'paʊdə(r)/ 11

practise /'præktɪs/ 24

pram /præm/ 10

prefer /prɪ'fɜː(r)/ 36

president /'prezɪdənt/ 13

pretty /'prɪti/ 2, 28

price /praɪs/ 6, 16, 31

prison /'prɪzn/ 34

prisoner /'prɪzənə(r)/ 34

probably /'prɒbəbli/ 9, 19, 27

problem /'prɒbləm/ 6, 22

produce /prə'djuːs/ 25

profession /prə'feʃn/ 27

programme /'prəʊgræm/ 27

promise /'prɒmɪs/ 33

pronounce /prə'naʊns/ 25

pub /pʌb/ 8

put* /pʊt/ 11

put* (a kettle) on /'pʊt 'ɒn/ 36

put* down /'pʊt 'daʊn/ 20, 36

put* on clothes
/'pʊt 'ɒn 'kləʊðz/ 31, 36

put* out a light /'pʊt 'aʊt ə 'laɪt/ 31

qualifications
/kwɒlɪfɪ'keɪʃənz/ 18, 27

quickly /'kwɪkli/ 21

quiet /kwaɪət/ 29

quite different (from)
/'kwaɪt 'dɪfrənt (frəm)/ 9

quite often /'kwaɪt 'ɒfən/ 3

radio /'reɪdiəʊ/ 20

rather /'rɑːðə(r)/ 8

reach /riːtʃ/ 25

ready /'redi/ 32

ready: get* ready /'get 'redi/ 8

realise /'rɪəlaɪz/ 22, 32

really: not really /'nɒt 'rɪəli/ 8

recognise /'rekəgnaɪz/ 7

red hair /'red 'heə(r)/ 28

relax /rɪ'læks/ 17

religion /rɪ'lɪdʒən/ 23

remember /rɪ'membə(r)/ 23, 32, 36

remember to . . . /rɪ'membə tə/ 23

remember: I'm afraid I can't
remember 7

repair /rɪ'peə(r)/ 35

research /rɪ'sɜːtʃ/ 34

reservation /rezə'veɪʃn/ 35

rest: have* a rest /'hæv ə 'rest/ 36

rest: the rest /ðə 'rest/ 4, 27, 34

restaurant /'restrɒnt/ 32

return (ticket) /rɪ'tɜːn/ 35

rich /rɪtʃ/ 6

right: Perhaps you're right
/pə'hæps jɔː 'raɪt/ 30

right now /'raɪt 'naʊ/ 22

right-handed /'raɪt'hændɪd/ 28

ring* (verb) /rɪŋ/ 8

rise* /raɪz/ 6

river /'rɪvə(r)/ 7, 16

rock /rɒk/ 20

roof /ruːf/ 4

room /ruːm/ 9

rough /rʌf/ 20

round (adj) /'aʊnd/ 5, 28

round the corner
/'raʊnd ðə 'kɔːnə(r)/ 8

round: Can I look round?
/kən aɪ 'lʊk 'raʊnd/ 11

roundabout /'raʊndəbaʊt/ 35

rubber /'rʌbə(r)/ 29

run* /rʌn/ 16

run* away /'rʌn ə'weɪ/ 13

sack /sæk/ 26

salary /'sæləri/ 18

salt /sɔːlt, sɒlt/ 21, 31

same /seɪm/ 2, 9, 19, 27, 28

say* /seɪ/ 19

say: Could you say that again? 7

school /skuːl/ 27, 34

school: at school /ət 'skuːl/ 13

sea /siː/ 10

search /sɜːtʃ/ 26

second: Wait a second
/'weɪt ə 'sekənd/ 12

second (adj) /'sekənd/ 2

secretary /'sekrətri/ 33

see* /siː/ 21

see: I see /aɪ 'siː/ 8

see: Let me see /'let mi: 'siː/ 24

see: Nice to see you again 1

See you then /'siː ju: 'ðen/ 24

seem /siːm/ 22, 32

self-confident /'self'kɒnfɪdənt/ 1

sell* /sel/ 18

send* /send/ 5, 34

serious /'sɪəriəs/ 25

serve: I'm being served
/aɪm 'biːɪŋ 'sɜːvd/ 11

several /'sevrʊl/ 4, 9, 13, 16, 18

shall /ʃəl, ʃæl/ 12

Shall I . . . ? /'ʃæl aɪ/ 12

share /ʃeə(r)/ 32

ship /ʃɪp/ 10, 25

shoe shop /'ʃuː ʃɒp/ 11

shop /ʃɒp/ 30, 32

shop: clothes/shoe shop
/'kləʊðz ('ʃuː) ʃɒp/ 11

shopping: go shopping
/'gəʊ 'ʃɒpɪŋ/ 3

short /ʃɔːt/ 3, 28

should /ʃəd, ʃʊd/ 12, 20, 23

shoulder /'ʃəʊldə(r)/ 21, 28

short /ʃɔːt/ 28

show* /ʃəʊ/ 27, 32

shower /ʃaʊə(r)/ 3

shut* /ʃʌt/ 3, 21

shy /ʃaɪ/ 1, 32

side /saɪd/ 5

sideways /'saɪdweɪz/ 23

silence /'saɪləns/ 32

sincerely: Yours sincerely
/'jɔːz sɪn'sɪəli/ 18

sing* /sɪŋ/ 30, 36

singer /'sɪŋə(r)/ 17

single (ticket) /sɪŋgl/ 35

sit* down /'sɪt 'daʊn/ 32

size /saɪz/ 6

sky /skaɪ/ 5, 21

sky: in the sky /ɪn ðə 'skaɪ/ 5

sleep* /sliːp/ 3, 17

sleep: go* to sleep /'gəʊ tə 'sliːp/ 31

sleepy /'sliːpi/ 6

slim /slɪm/ 28

slowly /'sləʊli/ 6

slowly: Please speak more slowly
/'pliːz 'spiːk 'mɔː 'sləʊli/ 7

small /smɔːl/ 13, 29

smile /smaɪl/ 31

smoking /'sməʊkɪŋ/ 35

snow /snəʊ/ 16

so (so am I etc.) /səʊ/ 28

so (so handsome, so much etc.) 31
/səʊ/

121

so: I don't think so
/aɪ dəʊnt 'θɪŋk 'səʊ/ 30
so: I hope so /aɪ həʊp 'səʊ/ 19
so: I suppose so /aɪ sə'pəʊz 'səʊ/ 33
so: I think so /aɪ 'θɪŋk 'səʊ/ 12, 30
so much /'səʊ 'mʌtʃ/ 1
So what? /'səʊ 'wɒt/ 2
soap /səʊp/ 11
soft /sɒft/ 29
solid /'sɒlɪd/ 29
some of /'sʌm əv/ 30
somebody /'sʌmbədi/ 32
somebody else /'sʌmbədi 'els/ 19, 30
something /'sʌmθɪŋ/ 8, 33
something hard/soft etc.
/'sʌmθɪŋ 'hɑːd ('sɒft)/ 29
something: There is something
wrong with . . . 30
sometimes /'sʌmtaɪmz/ 3, 22
somewhere /'sʌmweə(r)/ 8
soon /suːn/ 18, 26
soon: as soon as /əz 'suːn əz/ 31
soon: as soon as possible
/əz 'suːn əz 'pɒsəbl/ 18
sorry /'sɒri/ 22
Sorry, could you say that again? 7
Sorry, I don't know
/'sɒri aɪ dəʊnt 'nəʊ/ 7
sorry: feel* sorry for
/'fiːl 'sɒri fə(r)/ 30
sorry: I'm sorry, I don't
understand 7
sorry: I was sorry to hear 22
sort /sɔːt/ 8
sort: What sort of . . . ?
/'wɒt 'sɔːt əv/ 19
sound like /'saʊnd 'laɪk/ 8
spare time /'speə 'taɪm/ 1
speak* (to) /spiːk (tə)/ 13
speak* (languages) /spiːk/ 9
speak: Please speak more slowly
/'pliːz 'spiːk 'mɔː 'sləʊli/ 7
speed: top speed /'tɒp 'spiːd/ 10
speed limit /'spiːd 'lɪmɪt/ 35
spell*: How do you spell . . . ?
/'haʊ də jə 'spel/ 1
spend* /spend/ 7
square /skweə(r)/ 5, 28
staff /stɑːf/ 18
stamp /stæmp/ 11
stand* /stænd/ 32
stand: can't stand
/'kɑːnt 'stænd/ 22
stand* up /stænd 'ʌp/ 36
start /stɑːt/ 23, 32, 34
stationer('s) /'steɪʃənə(z)/ 11
stay /steɪ/ 3, 16
steal* /stiːl/ 26
steer /stɪə(r)/ 35
still /stɪl/ 2, 31
stone /stəʊn/ 29
stop /stɒp/ 21
story: tell* a story /'tel ə 'stɔːri/ 4
straight /streɪt/ 28, 36
straight: keep* straight on

/'kiːp 'streɪt 'ɒn/ 35
straight ahead /'streɪt ə'hed/ 35
strange /streɪndʒ/ 5
stranger: I'm a stranger here
myself 12
street /striːt/ 32
student /'stjuːdənt/ 16
study /'stʌdi/ 13, 31, 34
stuff /stʌf/ 11, 29
such /sətʃ, sʌtʃ/ 31
sugar /'ʃʊɡə(r)/ 6
suit (noun) /suːt/ 5
suitcase /'suːtkeɪs/ 32
summer /'sʌmə(r)/ 13
sun /sʌn/ 17
sunny /'sʌni/ 17
supermarket /'suːpəmɑːkɪt/ 11
suppose: I suppose so
/aɪ sə'pəʊz 'səʊ/ 33
sure /ʃɔː(r)/ 26
sure: I'm (not) sure
/aɪm ('nɒt) 'ʃɔː(r)/ 21, 30
surprised /sə'praɪzd/ 22, 27
surprising /sə'praɪzɪŋ/ 13
sweater /'swetə(r)/ 24
swim* /swɪm/ 7, 18
switch on/off /'swɪtʃ 'ɒn ('ɒf)/ 36
Switzerland /'swɪtsələnd/ 34
synthetic fibre /sɪn'θetɪk 'faɪbə(r)/ 29

table /teɪbl/ 23, 32
take* /teɪk/ 3
take* off /'teɪk 'ɒf/ 23
take* off (aeroplane) /'teɪk 'ɒf/ 35
take* clothes off /'teɪk 'ɒf/ 36
take* pictures /'teɪk 'pɪktʃəz/ 17
talk (noun) /tɔːk/ 8
talk: easy/interesting/difficult
to talk to /tɔːk/ 22
talk about /'tɔːk ə'baʊt/ 22, 30
talk to /'tɔːk tə/ 30
tall /tɔːl/ 9, 19, 28
taste /teɪst/ 31
taxi /'tæksi/ 27, 35
tea: cup of tea /'kʌp əv 'tiː/ 36
teach* /tiːtʃ/ 30
tear* (verb) /teə(r)/ 7
teeth: brush one's teeth
/'brʌʃ wʌnz 'tiːθ/ 31
telephone (noun) /'telɪfəʊn/ 29
tell* /tel/ 19
tell: Can you tell me the way
to . . . ? 12
tell* a story /'tel ə 'stɔːri/ 4
temperature /'temprɪtʃə(r)/ 6
tent /tent/ 17
than /ðən, ðæn/ 9
that: Who's that? /'huːz 'ðæt/ 24
That's all /'ðæts 'ɔːl/ 11
That's very kind of you 12
theatre /'θɪətə(r)/ 17, 26
theirs /ðeəz/ 12
themselves /ðəm'selvz/ 30
then /ðen/ 27, 31
There is something wrong

with . . . 30
thief /θiːf/ 26
thin /θɪn/ 28
thing /θɪŋ/ 5
things /θɪŋz/ 34
I think*: I don't think so
/aɪ 'dəʊnt 'θɪŋk 'səʊ/ 30
think*: I think so
/aɪ 'θɪŋk 'səʊ/ 12, 30
think*: What do you think
of . . . ? 22
think* about /'θɪŋk ə'baʊt/ 30
think* about: I'll think about it
/aɪl 'θɪŋk ə'baʊt ɪt/ 23
third /θɜːd/ 2, 13
Third World /'θɜːd 'wɜːld/ 16
this afternoon/evening
/ðɪs 'ɑːftə'nuːn ('iːvnɪŋ)/ 21
This is . . . /'ðɪs ɪz/ 24
this morning /ðɪs 'mɔːnɪŋ/ 8
this way /'ðɪs 'weɪ/ 23
though /ðəʊ/ 2
through /θruː/ 16
throw* /θrəʊ/ 21
ticket /'tɪkɪt/ 26, 35
tidy up /'taɪdi 'ʌp/ 33
time /taɪm/ 22, 23
time: a long time /ə 'lɒŋ 'taɪm/ 14, 32
time: another time /ə'nʌðə 'taɪm/ 36
time: free time /'friː 'taɪm/ 10
time: full-time /'fʊl'taɪm/ 18
time: Have you got the time? 12
time: last time /'lɑːst 'taɪm/ 33
time: most of the time
/'məʊst əv ðə 'taɪm/ 2
time: spare time /'speə 'taɪm/ 1
tired /'taɪəd/ 31, 33
tired of /'taɪəd əv/ 17
toast /təʊst/ 36
together /tə'ɡeðə(r)/ 8
together: get* on (well) together
/'get 'ɒn ('wel) tə'ɡeðə(r)/ 2
tonight /tə'naɪt/ 31
too /tuː/ 2, 15, 20
too much /'tuː 'mʌtʃ/ 15, 28, 33
tool /tuːl/ 11
tooth /tuːθ/ 29
top /tɒp/ 5
top speed /'tɒp 'spiːd/ 10
tourist /'tʊərɪst/ 14
town /taʊn/ 7, 16
town centre /'taʊn 'sentə(r)/ 16
traffic /'træfɪk/ 16
traffic lights /'træfɪk 'laɪts/ 35
train /treɪn/ 10
translate /trænz'leɪt/ 31
travel /'trævl/ 3, 13, 35
tree /triː/ 4, 25
trip /trɪp/ 13
trouble /'trʌbl/ 20
trouble: It's no trouble
/ɪts 'nəʊ 'trʌbl/ 23
true /truː/ 7, 10, 27
trust /trʌst/ 22
try /traɪ/ 8, 12, 34

turn over /'tɜːn 'əʊvə(r)/   20
turn up /'tɜːn 'ʌp/   8
TV: on TV /ɒn 'tiː'viː/   26
twice /twaɪs/   13

umbrella /ʌm'brelə/   21
unable /ʌn'eɪbl/   16, 18
uncle /'ʌŋkl/   22
under /'ʌndə(r)/   16
understand* /'ʌndə'stænd/   31
understand: I'm sorry, I don't
   understand   7
undress /ʌn'dres/   31
unemployed /ʌnɪm'plɔɪd/   6
unemployment /ʌnɪm'plɔɪmənt/   6, 14
unhappy /ʌn'hæpi/   9
unhurt /ʌn'hɜːt/   20
university /'juːnɪ'vɜːsəti/   34
unnecessary /ʌn'nesəsri/   18
until /ən'tɪl/   24, 31
up /ʌp/   6, 23
upside down /'ʌpsaɪd 'daʊn/   23
use /juːz/   25
used to /'juːst tə/   14
useful /'juːsfʊl/   29
usual /'juːʒuːʊl/   8
usual: as usual /əz 'juːʒuːʊl/   8
usually /'juːʒəli/   3, 22

vegetable /'vedʒtəbl/   4, 16
village /'vɪlɪdʒ/   4, 20
visit /'vɪzɪt/   16
visitor /'vɪzɪtə(r)/   5
voice /vɔɪs/   22

wait /weɪt/   27, 35
Wait a second /'weɪt ə 'sekənd/   12
wake* up /'weɪk 'ʌp/   31
wallet /'wɒlɪt/   26
want /wɒnt/   17
war /wɔː(r)/   14
war: world war /'wɜːld 'wɔː(r)/   34
warm welcome /'wɔːm 'welkəm/   17
wash /wɒʃ/   24, 30
wash up /'wɒʃ 'ʌp/   30
watch (noun) /wɒtʃ/   32
watch (verb) /wɒtʃ/   17, 36
water /'wɔːtə(r)/   16
way /weɪ/   9
way: Can you tell me the way
   to . . . ?   12
way: in some ways /ɪn 'sʌm 'weɪz/   9
way: this way /'ðɪs 'weɪ/   23
wear* /weə(r)/   4
weather /'weðə(r)/   3, 21
week /wiːk/   34
weekend /'wiːk'end/   33
weigh /weɪ/   20
weight /weɪt/   10, 20
welcome /'welkəm/   17
well /wel/   2
well off /'wel 'ɒf/   34
western /'westən/   26
wet /wet/   4, 17
What about . . . ?

/'wɒt ə'baʊt/   12, 24
What does . . . mean?
   /'wɒt dəz . . . 'miːn/   1
What do you call . . . ?
   /'wɒt də jə 'kɔːl/   11
What do you mean?
   /'wɒt də jə 'miːn/   7
What do you think of . . . ?
   /'wɒt də jə 'θɪŋk əv/   22
What is . . . like?
   /'wɒt ɪz . . . laɪk/   19
What sort of . . . ? /'wɒt 'sɔːt əv/   19
What's the English for . . . ?
   /'wɒts ðiː 'ɪŋglɪʃ fə(r)/   1
What's the matter?
   /'wɒts ðə 'mætə(r)/   12
wheat /wiːt/   25
wheel /wiːl/   10, 23
when /wen/   21
when: just when /'dʒʌst 'wen/   8
whereabouts /'weərə'baʊts/   1
which /wɪtʃ/   24
Who's that? /'huːz 'ðæt/   24
whose /huːz/   36
Why don't you . . . ?
   /'waɪ 'dəʊnt juː/   23
wide /waɪd/   29
wife /waɪf/   30
wild animal /'waɪld 'ænɪml/   17
will* /wɪl/   12
win* /wɪn/   14
wine /waɪn/   21
with /wɪð/   28
without /wɪð'aʊt/   6
wonder /'wʌndə(r)/   31
wonderful /'wʌndəfl/   19, 27
won't /wəʊnt/   17
wood /wʊd/   4, 25, 29
wool /wʊl/   25, 29
work: easy/interesting/difficult to
   work for /wɜːk/   22
working class /'wɜːkɪŋ 'klɑːs/   34
world /wɜːld/   26
world: all over the world
   /'ɔːl 'əʊvə ðə 'wɜːld/   27
world: Third World /'θɜːd 'wɜːld/   16
world war /'wɜːld 'wɔː(r)/   34
worried /'wʌrɪd/   9, 28, 33
worse /wɜːs/   6
worse: get* worse /'get 'wɜːs/   14
would /wʊd/   12, 19
write to /'raɪt tə/   24, 30
writing paper /'raɪtɪŋ 'peɪpə(r)/   11
wrong: go* wrong /'gəʊ 'rɒŋ/   32
wrong: There is something
   wrong with . . .   30

year /jɪə(r)/   4
year: every . . . years
   /'evri . . . 'jɪəz/   14
year: New Year /'njuː 'jɪə(r)/   21
year: £25,000 a year   18
yet /jet/   31
you know /ju: 'nəʊ/   23
yours /jɔːz/   12

Yours faithfully /'jɔːz 'feɪθfʊli/   18
Yours sincerely /'jɔːz sɪn'sɪəli/   18
yourself /jɔː'self/   30
yourselves /jɔː'selvz/   30

Additional material

Lesson 1, Exercise 6, Student A

A: ....
B: Yes, I am.
A: ....
B: Oh, yes, hello, Mr Benjamin. I'm very glad to meet you. Your sister is a fine doctor.
A: ....
B: Yes, please. I'll have an orange juice, please.

Revision Lesson A, Listening Exercise 3

YOU'RE PERFECT

You *smile* and I *see* a gap in your teeth.
It *makes* me *laugh* inside.
You *may not be* perfection,
But you*'re* always on my mind.
And when you *dance* you*'ve got* two left feet.
You*'ll* never *be* a Broadway star.
You *may not be* perfection,
But I *love* you just the way that you *are*.

And sometimes when the sun *goes* down,
We*'re* alone, nobody else around,
I *have got* to *face* the truth:
You*'re* perfect.
You*'re* perfect.
You*'re* perfect, to me.

Out on the town you always *lose* your way:
Better if you *stayed* at home.
You *may not be* perfection,
But I just *can't leave* you alone.
You *look* such a mess when you*'re dressing* up.
Nothing ever *looks* quite right.
You *may not be* perfection,
But *will* you *be* mine tonight?

'Cause darling when the sun *goes* down,
We*'re* alone, nobody else around,
I *know* that I *can face* the truth:
You*'re* perfect.
You*'re* perfect.
You*'re* perfect, to me.
Perfect to me.

(Steve Hall)

Lesson 9, Exercise 4, Student A

Jeanne of Aragon

Revision Lesson D, Listening Exercise 3

SONG FOR A RAINY SUNDAY

It's a rainy Sunday morning and I don't know what to do
If I stay in bed all day, I'll only think about you
If I try to study, I won't learn anything new
And if I go for a walk on my own in the park,
I'll probably catch the flu!

I just don't know (He doesn't know)
What to do (What to do)
I just don't know (He doesn't know)
What to do (What to do)

If I stay in bed all day, I'll only think about you
If I try to study, I won't learn anything new
And if I go for a walk on my own in the park,
I'll probably catch the flu – atchoo!

It's nearly Sunday lunchtime and I don't know where to eat
If I walk to the fish and chip shop, I'll only get wet feet
If I stay at home for lunch, I'll have to eat last week's meat
And if I get in my car and drive to the pub, I probably won't get a seat

I just don't know (He doesn't know)
Where to eat (Where to eat)
I just don't know (He doesn't know)
Where to eat (Where to eat)

If I walk to the fish and chip shop, I'll only get wet
    feet
If I stay at home for lunch, I'll have to eat last week's
    meat
And if I get in my car and drive to the pub, I
    probably won't get a seat

The rain has stopped and I'd like to go out
But I don't know where to go
If I invite you out for a drink, you'll probably say no
If I go to the theatre alone, I won't enjoy the show
And if I stay here at home on my own, I'll be bored
    and miserable, so

I just don't know (He doesn't know)
Where to go (Where to go)
I just don't know (He doesn't know)
Where to go (Where to go)

If I invite you out for a drink, you'll probably say no
If I go to the theatre alone, I won't enjoy the show
And if I stay here at home on my own, I'll be bored
    and miserable, so

I'm going to the theatre but I don't know what to
    wear
I know if I look through my socks, I'll never find a
    pair
If I put on my new green boots, people will probably
    stare
And if my tie isn't straight and they complain 'cause
    I'm late,
I'll say, 'Listen mate: I don't care!'

I just don't care (He doesn't care)
What I wear (Life isn't fair)
I just don't care (He doesn't care)
What I wear (Life isn't fair)

I know if I look through my socks, I'll never find a
    pair
If I put on my new green boots, people will probably
    stare
And if my tie isn't straight and they complain 'cause
    I'm late,
I'll say, 'Listen, mate: I don't care!'

(Jonathan Dykes – lyrics   Robert Campbell – music)

Lesson 26, Exercise 6, Student A

- HARRISON was last seen alive at 9.30 p.m.
  (*Where?*)
- He was found dead in his flat by his wife Mary
  when she came home from a dance. (*What time?*)
- He was killed with a revolver. A small French-
  English dictionary was found by his body.
  (*Anything else? Was anything stolen?*)
- The police suspect Haynes, MacHale and Cannon.
  All three were arrested the next morning.

- HAYNES once worked for Harrison, but was
  sacked. (*Why?*)
- He has often said he hates Harrison, and would
  like to kill him. He was seen by three witnesses at
  10.30. (*Where?*)
- When he was arrested, a revolver was found in his
  car. (*Where were his fingerprints found?*)

- MacHALE is known to the police as a thief, but not
  as a killer. (*Where is he from?*)
- He is an old friend of Harrison's. (*Does he know
  Mrs Harrison?*)
- When he was arrested, £2,000 in cash was found
  in his wallet. (*Anything else?*)

- CANNON works in an import-export business.
  (*Where?*)
- Harrison owed him a lot of money. When he was
  questioned, he said that he was at his hotel from
  9.30 to 11.30. (*What did his wife say?*)
- He was seen earlier coming out of Harrison's flat.
  (*What time?*)
- Cannon's wife is an old friend of Mary Harrison's.

WHO DO YOU THINK KILLED HARRISON?

Revision Lesson E, Speaking Exercise 1, Student A

MOTHER: ....
DAUGHTER: Sure, Mum, what's the problem?
MOTHER: ....
DAUGHTER: But Mum, I was in by twelve o'clock!
MOTHER: ....
DAUGHTER: Well, I don't think so. All the other kids
                      stay out late.
MOTHER: ....
DAUGHTER: Yeah, some of them do, I suppose.
MOTHER: ....
DAUGHTER: But last night was special. It was the
                      disco at the club.
MOTHER: ....
DAUGHTER: All right, Mum. Perhaps you're right. I'll
                      talk to you about it next time.
MOTHER: ....

Revision Lesson F, Listening Exercise 2

YOU MADE ME LOVE YOU

You made me love you
I didn't wanna do it
I didn't wanna do it
You made me love you
And all the time you knew it
I guess you always knew it.
You made me happy, sometimes
You made me glad
But there were times when
You made me feel so sad.

You made me sigh, 'cause
I didn't wanna tell you
I didn't wanna tell you.
I think you're grand, that's true,
Yes I do, 'deed I do, you know I do.
Gimme, gimme, gimme, gimme
What I cry for
You know you've got the kind of kisses
That I'd die for
You know you made me love you.

(Monaco and McCarthy)

Lesson 1, Exercise 6, Student B

A: Excuse me, are you Dr Coates?

B: ....

A: Oh, hello, Dr Coates, I'm Peter Benjamin. My sister works with you.

B: ....

A: Oh, thank you. I think she's wonderful, but she is my sister. Can I get you a drink?

B: ....

Lesson 9, Exercise 4, Student B

Elizabeth I as Princess

Lesson 26, Exercise 6, Student B

— HARRISON was last seen alive talking to a woman in the street outside his flat in central London. (*What time?*)

— He was found dead by his wife (*Name?*) when she came home from a dance at 11.30. (*How was he killed?*)

— A Paris underground ticket was found by his body. (*Anything else?*)

— His wallet had been stolen.

— The police suspect Haynes, MacHale and Cannon. All three were arrested the next morning.

— HAYNES once worked for Harrison, but was sacked for stealing. He has often said he hates Harrison, and would like to kill him. He was seen by three witnesses 50km from Harrison's home. (*What time?*)

— His fingerprints were found in Harrison's flat. When he was arrested, his car was searched by the police. (*Was anything found?*)

— MacHALE is from Scotland. He is a very old friend of Mrs Harrison's. (*Did he know Mr Harrison?*)

— When he was arrested, a love letter (signed 'Mary') was found in his pocket. (*Anything else? Find out if MacHale is known to the police.*)

— CANNON works in Paris. (*What does he do? Find out if he owed Harrison money.*)

— He was seen coming out of Harrison's flat at 9.15. When his wife was questioned, she said that he was out of his hotel all evening. (*What did he say? Find out if Cannon's wife knows Mary Harrison.*)

WHO DO YOU THINK KILLED HARRISON?

Revision Lesson E, Speaking Exercise 1, Student B

MOTHER: Can I speak to you for a minute, Em?

DAUGHTER: ....

MOTHER: Well, I'm very upset about how late you were out last night.

DAUGHTER: ....

MOTHER: I still think that's too late for a fifteen-year-old girl who has to go to school the next day.

DAUGHTER: ....

MOTHER: Well, you're not all the other kids. And I'm sure some of them have to be in early.

DAUGHTER: ....

MOTHER: Especially on school nights. I don't want you in after ten when you've got school the next day.

DAUGHTER: ....

MOTHER: Well, if there's a special night we can talk about it before you go. I'm sure we can agree if we talk about it.

DAUGHTER: ....

MOTHER: Thanks, darling.

Tapescripts

Lesson 3, Exercise 1

ADELE:

My mornings usually start fairly late, particularly at the weekends. I might stay in bed with the newspaper until possibly nine or half past nine. My husband usually brings the morning cup of tea up. Very often we have house guests over the weekend, which entails a lot of cooking, and seeing to everybody's comfort, which makes it a very busy weekend. But when there isn't an activity like that, I tend to do housework if I feel like it, washing and ironing. If it's very good weather, I might do some gardening. We don't have a lot of cooked meals. So there isn't much cooking to be done. I might take the dog for a walk. As I am heavily involved with the local youth club, I do occasionally take a group of members to the ice skating rink in Oxford, or recently I took eight of the members to an assault course at Bicester Garrison. I sit and read the newspapers at some time during the weekend. I watch television in the evening; possibly make several telephone calls to the family; maybe visit my elderly mother in Newbury; and mostly do exactly what I feel like doing.

RUFUS:

Erm, if I have business, er, then I get into my office, which is not far from the bedroom, at any time after six o'clock in the morning, and then I work there for as long as is necessary. Take er my wife up a cup of tea, followed by a cup of coffee a bit later. Er, we don't usually have breakfast, sh-, occasionally we have Saturday lunch, but not very often, and usually a light meal in the evening. Erm, when I'll have finished er, office work, then I normally sit down with the Saturday newspaper and do the crossword puzzle. On Sunday mornings, I usually sleep in – not sleep in, but lie in, oh, possibly until midday. I get up and ge-, usually and get some tea and then some coffee and erm, let the dog out into the garden when he feels, wants to go there. In the afternoon will depend upon whether we go out in the car or er, whether I just er, sit d-, quietly with the papers.

Revision Lesson A, Listening Exercise 1

1. I know he loves me. But he says he loves Janet too. Can you really love two people at the same time?

2. 'Mother.'
   'Yes, darling?'
   'I'm in love.'
   'Not again, dear. Who with this time?'
   'Eric, of course. He's the most wonderful man in the world. But I don't know if he loves me.'

3. I really like her. I mean, she's a very nice person. But it's not love.

4. 'What do you think of Eric?'
   'Don't like him much.'
   'No, I don't like him either.'
   'I think he fancies you, you know.'

Revision Lesson A, Listening Exercise 2

You are walking along a beach, by the sea. It's a hot day. The sun is burning down on your head. You're hot and tired. You're walking slowly . . . more and more slowly . . . you stop. You sit down on the sand. You look at the sea. You pick up some small stones from the beach, and you throw them into the sea. One . . . two . . . three . . . four . . . five . . . You stand up slowly, and you take off your shoes. You walk forward, and stand with your feet in the water. That feels good. It's very good; very, very good.

Suddenly you see something in the water. A long way away. You look very hard, but you can't see just what it is. It comes nearer, nearer. It's a person. A man. He walks towards you out of the sea. An old man, with white hair, and a beautiful face. He stops. There he is, standing in front of you. He smiles

at you – a wonderful warm smile. You smile back at him. You close your eyes for a moment. You open them again: he's gone. He isn't there any more. Where is he? You look round – you look everywhere. Nothing to be seen. Was it a dream?

You start walking again. Now the sun has gone. It's cold. Very, very cold. You walk faster, to get warm. Faster and faster. There are stones under your feet – hard, sharp stones. Your feet hurt. You feel unhappy. Suddenly you see a small house in front of you. You walk up to the door. You open the door and walk in. There he is, smiling at you – the old man. You close the door and walk towards him.

You wake up.

Lesson 21, Exercise 5

Episode 1
John is having lunch in a restaurant. Suddenly he sees a beautiful girl at the next table. She is *very* beautiful. He wonders whether to speak to her. She smiles at him.
JOHN: Shall I speak to her?

What will happen if John speaks to the girl?

Episode 2
JOHN: Excuse me.
GIRL: Yes?
JOHN: May I join you?
GIRL: Of course.
JOHN: What's your name?
GIRL: Olga. Let's have some champagne. Lots of champagne.

What will happen if John drinks lots of champagne?

Episode 3
JOHN: Waiter! A bottle of champagne, please!
WAITER: Certainly, sir.

JOHN: Waiter! A bottle of champagne, please!
WAITER: Certainly, sir.

JOHN: Waiter! A bottle of champagne, please!
WAITER: *Another* bottle, sir?

OLGA: Darling.
JOHN: Yesh?
OLGA: Let's go to the zoo.
JOHN: The zoo? But I've got to go to work.
OLGA: Work? How boring. We're going to the zoo. I want to see the snakes.

What will happen if John goes to the zoo?

Episode 4
OLGA: Look at those lovely snakes.
JOHN: Be careful. Don't lean over!
OLGA: Oh! I've dropped my bag!
JOHN: Where is it?
OLGA: Down there. By that green snake. Get it for me, darling.
JOHN: What?
OLGA: Do you love me?
JOHN: Er, yes.
OLGA: Then get my bag.

What will happen if John tries to get Olga's bag?

Episode 5
JOHN: All right. I'll get it with my umbrella. Just a moment. Here you are, darling. I've got it. Darling! Where are you? Where's she gone? That's funny. She's gone. And I don't know where she lives, or anything . . . Perhaps her address is in her bag – I'll have a look. My God! What's this? A revolver! What shall I do? Perhaps I should go to the police.

What will happen if John goes to the police?

Episode 6

John doesn't go to the police. He goes back to his office.

JOHN: Good afternoon, sir.

BOSS: Good evening, Mr Armitage. Do you know what time it is? It's five o'clock.

JOHN: Yes, sir. Well, I met this girl and we went to the zoo and she dropped her bag in the snake-pit and I got it out with my umbrella and she wasn't there any more and there was a revolver in her bag.

BOSS: Girl . . . zoo . . . bag . . . snakes . . . revolver . . . That's it! You've gone too far! I'm sorry, Mr Armitage, but you'll have to go.

JOHN: You can't do this to me!

BOSS: Oh yes I can! Get out!

JOHN: Oh no you can't. I've got a revolver!

BOSS: Hey! What are you doing! No! Don't shoot!

What will happen if John shoots his boss?

Episode 7

John shoots his boss. He takes £20,000 out of the office safe, leaves the office and takes a taxi to the airport.

JOHN: First class to San Francisco, please.

CLERK: One way or round trip?

JOHN: One way. What time is the flight?

CLERK: Six-thirty, sir.

JOHN: Good. Time for a drink.

JOHN: A large whisky, please.

John sits down with his whisky. Suddenly he sees a beautiful girl at the next table. She is *very* beautiful. He wonders whether to speak to her. She smiles at him.

What will happen if John speaks to the girl?

Revision Lesson D, Listening Exercise 2

1. If you can understand this sentence, write your name.
2. If today is Tuesday, write the number 12. If not, don't write anything.
3. If your arms are longer than your hair, draw a circle. If not, draw a square.
4. If you can see the sun, stand up.
5. If it's raining, look at your feet. If not, look at another person – but don't look at the teacher.
6. If Edinburgh is in the north of England, shut your eyes for ten seconds.
7. If you can't buy stamps in a bank, don't say hello to another student.
8. If there are more than fifteen students in your class, put your pen on the floor. If not, put it in your mouth.
9. If your eyes are blue, put up your right hand. If they are brown, put up your left hand. If they are neither blue nor brown, don't put a hand up.

Lesson 27, Exercise 1

'Hello, then. What's your name?'

'Oh, er, Janet. Janet Parker.'

'Oh, yes? I'm Frederick. Frederick Getty Onassis. But my friends call me Fred.'

'Oh. What do you do, er, Fred?'

'Oh, I'm a photographer. I photograph famous people: film stars, pop singers, people like that.'

'Oh, yes? Where do you work, then? Are you based in London?'

'Oh, no. I live in Paris. Paris and California. But I travel all over the world.'

'Oh, yes?'

'I've just got back from Washington. I've been photographing the President for *Time* magazine.'

'Oh, have you?'

'Before that, I was in Venice for the film festival. In a few days, I'll be in Tokyo for a fashion show. It's a busy life, you know. A busy life.'

'It must be terribly interesting. All that travelling. All those famous people.'

'Oh, no. Famous people – they're all the same, really. I was

saying to Paul McCartney only last week – I get so tired of famous people. Sometimes I just want to be with ordinary simple people. Ordinary people have more character. More real beauty. Now you, Janet. I find you interesting. You have a very unusual face.'

'Oh, yes? Have I really?'

'Yes, Janet. You have wonderful eyes. Wonderful. Very expressive. Tell me, what do you do? Are you an actress? A model?'

'Oh, no. I work in a shop.'

'Really? In a shop! You surprise me. Janet, I want to photograph you. I'll put your face on the covers of the world's fashion magazines. We'll do some pictures in my London studio first of all. And then probably I'll take you to Paris – or perhaps to California: the light is better in California. Yes. We'll go to California in my Boeing 747.'

'Oh! You've got a Boeing 747?'

'Well, it's really my father's. He's quite a rich man.'

'What does he do?'

'Oh, oil, diamonds, gold, ship-building – boring things like that. I'm not interested in business myself. I'm more the artistic type. Like my mother. She's a Shakespearean actress, you know. I'm like her. I love nature, poetry, ideas, beauty.'

'Oh, yes. So do I. So do I.'

'Janet. This isn't a very interesting party. We'll go to my studio now . . . '

Revision Lesson E, Grammar Exercise 4

BILL: Hello, Ann.

ANN: Hi, Bill. How's it going?

BILL: OK. What about you?

ANN: Oh, not too bad. What are you doing at the weekend? Anything exciting?

BILL: Yes, actually. Going to the mountains with some friends.

ANN: Yeah? Who?

BILL: Oh, Pete and Rosie. Karen. And a couple of friends of Pete's from Coventry.

ANN: Where are you staying?

BILL: Don't know yet. We're camping.

ANN: Oh, that sounds nice.

BILL: Well, why don't you come with us? Do you want to?

ANN: Oh, dear. Yes, I do want to. But –

BILL: Well, what's the trouble?

ANN: It's my mother. She's ill, and she can't do much for herself. I have to stay at home and look after her at the weekends.

BILL: Well, can't you get somebody else to help?

ANN: Perhaps I can. When are you leaving?

BILL: Friday afternoon, just after lunch. We're driving up in two cars, so there's plenty of room.

ANN: Friday's a bit difficult. I don't know. Look, I'll ask my sister. Maybe she can stay with Mum for the weekend. I'll phone you tomorrow, OK?

BILL: OK. Hope you can make it.

ANN: Yeah, I hope so too. See you.

BILL: Bye.

Revision Lesson E, Listening Exercise 1

A. (*Richard*) I hope not, 'cause I talk to myself all the time, and er, I'm aware of it. 'Specially when I was in London, I used to talk to myself all the time, and you see a lot of people talking to themselves a lot. No, I don't think there's any-, anything wrong. Sometimes I think you, you rationalise things out for yourself by talking to yourself. You sort things out for yourself. (*Susan*: Mm.) Erm, other times, it's erm, it's a problem not having somebody to talk to.

B. (*Rufus*) In my opinion it is not necessarily a good thing to tell one's partner everything that has happened in one's past life. (*Adele*: That's true.) And er, I'm si, yes, (*Adele*: Yes, because it upsets a lot of people.) (*Richard*: Isn't it a good thing?) (*Adele*: Mm. Mm.) My wife agrees with me.
(*Richard*) Really?
(*Rufus*) Oh yes. She has told me a lot, I think I've told her a lot, but certain things that I'm sure that she would think would upset me she has not told me, and I have not asked for them. I would not ask for them.
(*Richard*) Oh dear, I think I've made a big mistake then, 'cause I've told my partner everything.

C. (*Susan*) Erm, in this day and age, I would prefer – sixteen is quite young – and I'd prefer, erm, with the unemployment, I would prefer . . . If he said to me 'I'm leaving school. I'm not doing any exams. I can't be bothered, I'm just leaving', I would try and talk him out of, out of that, of that, erm, view. I would try and talk him round. I would try and do the best I could to erm, make him see, 'cause I mean, I, I know fr-, I mean I'm little more than a child myself, and I know that erm, a child does not listen, really, as much as they should.

D. (*Rufus*) I have learned many things in, in, in my life, but the things that have, have really helped me have been what I have been taught properly. I'm still learning an awful lot. Every day I'm studying something or other. But it's taking me, as with you, so much longer and so less effectively, to study oneself rather than to be taught properly.

E. (*June*) You could imagine that either you've got a strong feeling for your husband, and you've been with him for a long time. But because you've been with him for a long time, and then another strong feeling comes along. Because you've really still got a strong feeling for him, would you feel you've got to be honest?
(*Ellen*) No, I think it would be wrapped up in whether or not you're going to stay together as a couple.

F. (*June*) Er, more or less, yes. But, erm, I think if you're obviously aware that your children are getting in bad company, then you've sort of erm, got to diplomatically, er, tell your children that you don't approve of their friends, really. But very diplomatically: you can't really just say, 'No, you can't play or be friends with these', but er, try and sort of get them to drop those friends. (*Laughs*)

G. (*Ellen*) Having said I would never marry anybody who didn't know how to cook and been proven wrong: yes, I think people should cook for themselves some of the time. A, to give people who do the cooking most of the time a break, and also because er, you know, it's (*Daniel*: Because why?) it can be fun.

H. (*Ellen*) Do you, is that a rule in your house, Kara?
(*Kara*) Yeah, I agree. Yeah. I erm, often help with housework. And I find that when I go round to friends' house, their mother does everything for them, and y-, you know, they don't have, they don't know a lot, they aren't very independent. Er, they'll say, 'Mum, can you do this; Mum, can you do that', and their mum will go and do it. But as they get older they're going to need to learn it all anyway, so it's best if you know it.

Revision Lesson E, Listening Exercise 2

MY OLD DAD

We never saw him in the mornings,
And he always came home late.
Then he sat and read the paper
And did the crossword while he ate.

He never helped us with our homework,
But he taught me how to swim,
And he taught me to be patient.
I guess I learnt a lot from him.

> My old Dad
> He was one of the good guys.
> He was nobody's hero,
> But he was special to me.

Every summer we went to Blackpool,
Except when he was unemployed.
He loved to sit and watch the sunset.
That was one thing we both enjoyed.

He was always very gentle,
Nothing ever made him mad.
He was never rich or famous,
But I was proud of my old Dad.

> My old Dad
> He was one of the good guys.
> He was nobody's hero,
> But he was special to me.

(Dykes and Campbell)

Revision Lesson F, Listening Exercise 1

'Going out tonight?' 'Oh, I don't think so. I've been out three times this week, and I've got a long day tomorrow. Anyway, I'm really tired. No, I reckon I'll stay in. Get an early night for once.'

'Heard anything from Ann?' 'Yes, she rang up yesterday. I'm a bit worried about her, to tell the truth. She's changed her job again – typical Ann, she can't stay in one place for more than five minutes – and now she's working in a bank down in Exeter.' 'Stupid girl. Why can't she stick to one thing and try to make something of it?'

'So what's the weather going to do, John?' 'Well, Sue, the general picture tomorrow is fine weather over almost the whole country, much warmer than today, maybe getting up to 19 or 20 degrees Celsius in the south, possibly some patches of cloud in hilly areas, but basically it looks like being a good day to get out the picnic baskets.' 'Thanks, John. I don't know what we've done with ours but I'll start looking.'

'Well, doctor, what should I do?' 'Well, the main thing is to think about your smoking. It's obviously doing you harm – your blood pressure's high, you're getting dizzy spells, you've got a cough the whole time, you're pretty unfit.' 'You think I should cut it down a bit?' 'Cut it down? My advice to you is, if you want to live to see your grandchildren, cut it out altogether. Stop smoking today. Give it up.'

'You're very dreamy these days, Ann.' 'Am I? Yes, I suppose I am.' 'Is anything the matter?' 'No, not really. I mean, yes, in a way, I suppose. I told you about this boy I met in Greece, didn't I?' 'Stavros?' 'Yes, Stavros, that's right. Well, I keep thinking about him. I mean, at first I thought it was just sort of a, you know, holiday romance kind of thing, but I don't know, I can't get him out of my mind.' 'Has he written to you?' 'Yes, I've had a couple of letters from him.' 'Well, what did he say?' 'Well, you know, his English isn't very good, but I think he meant to say . . .'

Index of structures, notions and functional/situational language

Ability	2, 18, 19, 28
A few	15
A little	15
A lot with comparatives	10
Able	18, 19
Adjective + infinitive	22
Adjectives: comparison	6, 9, 10
Adjectives like *left-handed*	28
Adverb particles	23, 36
Adverb position	3
Adverbs and adverbials of frequency	3
Advising	23
After (conjunction)	31
Agreeing and disagreeing	2, 20
Airport	15, 35
Already, still and *yet*	31
Any, some and *no*	15
Anything to . . .	12
Applications	18
Appointments	15, 24
Arrangements	24
Articles: *the* not used in generalisations	25
As . . . as	9, 10
As and *than*	9
As much/many as . . .	10
As soon as	31
Asking about English	1, 15, 25
Asking for clarification	7
Asking for things	12
Asking for things when you don't know the words	11
At with places	11
Bargaining	15
Be	2
Be (non-progressive verb)	14, 16
Be able	18, 19
Before (conjunction)	31
Borrowing and lending	12, 15
Both	9, 28
By and *with* in passives	26
Can	2, 12, 17, 27, 36
Causes and origins	26
Certainty and possibility	17, 19, 27
Change	6, 14
Commas in *if-* and *when*-clauses	21, 34
Commentaries	5
Comparative adjectives	6, 9, 10
Comparison	6, 9, 10, 28
Compound adjectives (e.g. *left-handed*)	28
Conditions	19, 21, 23, Rev D, 34
Conditions: past conditions	34
Connecting expressions	2, 31
Conversation management	7, 8
Could	12, 27
Demonstratives (telephone)	24
Describing people	2, Rev A, 9, 22, 28
Describing things	Rev A, 10, 11, 29
Differences and similarities	9, 10
Directions	15, 35
Discourse markers	2
Discussion	20, 30
Do as pro-verb	9, 28
Do used for emphasis	33
Doctor's surgery	15
Duration of present states	14

Each other	14, 30
Ellipsis	8
Else	30
Enough	15
Emotions	22
Enquiries	15, 35
Ever with Present Perfect	13
Experience	13
Far with comparatives	10
Feelings	22
Few: *a few*	15
Fewest	10
Fillers	2
For and *since*	14
Forget to . . .	23
Formal and informal language	15, 18, Rev F
Formal letters	18
Frequency adverbs and adverbials	3
Future	19, 20, 21, 24, Rev D
Garage	15, 35
Generalisations: *the* not used	25
Get + adjective	22
Get with comparatives	6
Giving directions	15
Going to	20
Going to and *will*	Rev D
Greetings	1, 15
Habits	3, 4
Had better	12
Hairdresser	15
Have (non-progressive verb)	14, 16
Have got	2, 12
Have (got) to	19, 20
Hope + clause	19
Hotel reception	15
How about . . . ?	24
How much/many	15, 20
I hope + clause	19
I (don't) think + clause	19
If (conditions)	19, 21, 23, Rev D, 34
If in reported speech	27
If and *when*	21
If I were you . . .	23
I'll (offers, agreement)	12, 24, 36
Imperatives	33
Indirect questions	22, 27
Indirect speech	19, 20, 22, 27
Infinitive after adjective	22
Infinitives with and without *to*	12
Informal and formal language	15, 18, Rev F
-ing form or past participle	26
-ing forms: spelling	5
Intentions	20, 24
Interrogative structures with *who*	Rev A
Introductions	1
Inviting	24
Irregular verbs	7, 26
Just with Present Perfect	16
Keeping a conversation going	8
Know (non-progressive verb)	14, 16
Leaving out words in speech	8
Lending and borrowing	12, 15
Less than	9, 10
Letters	18
Likes and dislikes	22
Like: would like to . . .	12, 24, 36
Like: would like + object + infinitive	24, 36

131

Linking expressions	2, 31
Little: *a little*	15
'll (offers)	12
Look forward to . . .ing	18
Lost property	15
Made from/of	25
Make + object + infinitive	12
Making appointments	15, 24
May	17, 19
Might	27
Modal verbs	12, 17, 19
Modification of comparatives	10
More (quantifier)	10
Most (quantifier)	10
Much	10, 15, 20
Much with comparatives	10
Must	18, 27, 33
Narrating	7, 31, 32
Neither	28
Neither am/do I, etc.	9, 28
Necessity	33
News	16
No (= *not any*)	15
Non-progressive verbs (Present Perfect)	14, 16
Noun complementation	11
Object pronouns: position with phrasal verbs	36
Obligation	12, 19, 20, 23, 30, 33
Offers	12, 36
Opinions	20
Passive	18, 25, 26
Passive and reflexive structures	Rev E
Past conditions	34
Past participles	13, 26
Past Perfect	32, 34
Past Progressive	8, Rev B
Past Simple	7
Past Simple Passive	25, 26
Past Simple and Past Perfect	32
Past Simple and Progressive	8
Personal information	1, 3
Personal pronouns: position with phrasal verbs	36
Personal relationships	22
Petrol station	15
Phrasal verbs	36
Place relations	Rev F
Plans	20, 24
Polite refusals	12, 15
Possessive pronouns	12
Possibility and certainty	17, 19
Predicting	19, 20, 21
Prepositions: end-position after infinitive	22
Prepositions: end-position in relative clauses	29
Prepositions referring to place	11, Rev F
Prepositions referring to time	24
Present and past participles	26
Present participles: spelling	5
Present Perfect and Present	14, 16, Rev C
Present Perfect and Simple Past	13, 18, Rev C
Present Perfect Progressive	16, Rev C
Present Perfect Simple	13, 14, Rev C
Present Progressive	5, 6, Rev A, 24
Present Progressive with future reference	24
Present Progressive Passive	25
Present Simple	3, 4, Rev A
Present Simple Passive	25
Present tense with future reference	21, 24
Probability	19, 21, 27
Processes	25
Punctuation: commas in *if-* and *when*-clauses	21

Quantifiers	10, 15, 28
Question tags	33
Question-word as subject and object	Rev A
Railway station	15, 35
Reacting to information	7
Reflexive and emphatic pronouns	30
Reflexive and passive structures	Rev E
Refusals	12, 15
Relationships	22
Relative pronouns and clauses	28, 29
Remember to . . .	23
Reported speech (instructions)	33
Reported speech (questions)	22, 27
Reported speech (statements)	19, 20, 22, 27
Requests	12
Restaurant	15
Routines	3, 4, 8
Same: *the same as*	9
Say and *tell*	27
-self	30
Sequencing markers	31
Shall (offers)	12, 36
Shopping	11, 15
Should	12, 20, 23, 30
Similarities and differences	9, 10, 28
Simple Past	7
Simple Past and Past Perfect	32
Simple Past and Past Progressive	8, Rev B
Simple Past and Present Perfect	13
Simple Past forms: spelling	Sum B
Simple Past Passive	25, 26
Simple Present	3, 4, Rev A
Simple Present Passive	25
Simple Present Perfect	13, 14
Since and *for*	14
So and *such*	31
So am/do I, etc.	9, 28
Some, *any* and *no*	15
Somebody else	30
Something to . . .	12
Spelling of *-ing* forms	5
Spelling of third-person singular forms	Sum A
Spelling of Simple Past forms	Sum B
Station	15, 35
Still, *yet* and *already*	31
Story-telling	7, 31, 32
Such and *so*	31
Suggestions	12, 24
Superlative adjectives	6, 10
Tag questions	33
Telephoning	15, 24
Tell and *say*	27
Telling stories	7, 31, 32
Than and *as*	9
Thanks	15
That and *this* (telephone)	24
That (relative)	29
The: not used in generalisations	25
The same as	9
Think + clause	19, 20
Third-person singular forms: spelling	Sum A
This and *that* (telephone)	24
Time clauses	8, 21, 31
To as pro-verb used for whole infinitive	12, 36
Too (quantifier)	15
Travel	15, 17, 35
Until	31
Used to	14

What about . . . ?	12, 24
When and *if*	21
When-clauses	8, 21
While-clauses	8
Who? as subject and object	Rev A
Who (relative)	28
Why don't you . . . ?	12, 23
Will	17, 19, 21
Will and *going to*	Rev D
Will (offers)	12
Wishes	11
With and *by* in passives	26
With in descriptions	28
Word order: *both*	28
Word order: end-position of prepositions	22, 29
Word order: frequency adverbs	3
Word order: phrasal verbs	36
Working relationships	22
Would (conditional)	12, 23, 34
Would have . . .	34
Would in reported speech	19
Would like to . . .	12, 24, 36
Would like + object + infinitive	24, 36
Yet, still and *already*	31
Zero article	25

Acknowledgements

The authors and publishers are grateful to the following copyright owners for permission to reproduce photographs, illustrations, texts and music. Every endeavour has been made to contact copyright owners and apologies are expressed for any omissions.

page 30: *l* Self-portrait by Dürer, copyright © Prado Museum, Madrid. All rights reserved. Total or partial reproduction prohibited. Reproduced by kind permission of the Prado. *r* Portrait of François I, King of France, by Clouet reproduced by kind permission of the Musées Nationaux, Paris. Copyright © Photo R.M.N. pages 30 and 31: Background map courtesy of the British Map Library (Ortelius, Map of Europe, 1588). page 90: *l* Hannah Hooper of Chilton County Primary School, Chilton, Oxon; *r* Sarah Turner of John Ball Primary School, Blackheath, London.

page 14: *t* and *c* Robert Harding Picture Library. page 34: Leighton Gibbins ARPS. page 47: Hulton-Deutsch Collection. page 50: Courtesy of TVS. page 80: *l* Mary Evans Picture Library. page 80: *cl*, *cr* and *r* The Image Bank.

Revision Lesson F, Listening Exercise 2, page 112: *You Made Me Love You* by Joe McCarthy (lyrics) and James V. Monaco (music). Reproduced by permission of EMI Music Publishing, International Music Publications and the Mechanical Copyright Protection Society.

The authors and publishers are grateful to the following:

Young Artists: Amy Burch, pages 36, 86, 87; Pat Fogarty, pages 8 and 9, 64 and 65, 72, 73, 82; Sarah John, pages 10, 28; Ashley Pearce, pages 124 and 125.

Maggie Mundy: Hemesh Alles, pages 14 *b*, 15, 23, 26 and 27, 77, 114; Sharon Pallent, pages 48, 51, 91, 106 and 107.

Artists Partners: Derek Brazell, pages 42, 43, 70, 71, 108, 109; Katherine Dickinson, pages 66, 67; Bill Gregory, pages 32 and 33; Angus McKie, page 85; Tony Richards, pages 16, 17.

The Inkshed: Julia Bigg, pages 81 and 84; Tony Watson, page 18 *tl*.

Nancy Anderson, pages 88, 89; Stephen Conlin, page 113; Richard Deverell, pages 18 *b* and 19 *b*; Tony Richards, pages 34 and 35; Liz Roberts, pages 52, 62, 63, 98, 99; Gillian Sharpe, pages 52 and 53 (flag), 104 and 105; Michela Stewart, pages 12, 68, 69, 100, 101, 102; Tony Watson, pages 44, 78, 79.

Steve Hall for *You're Perfect* (Revision Lesson A, Listening Exercise 3, page 23).

Jonathan Dykes (lyrics) and Robert Campbell (music) for *A Bigger Heart* (Revision Lesson B, Listening Exercise 2, page 40), *Brighton in the Rain* (Revision Lesson C, Grammar Exercise 1, page 58), *Song for a Rainy Sunday* (Revision Lesson D, Listening Exercise 3, page 77), *My Old Dad* (Revision Lesson E, Listening Exercise 2, page 95), *Another Street Incident* (Lesson 32, Exercise 2, page 100).

t = top   *b* = bottom   *c* = centre   *r* = right   *l* = left

Phonetic symbols

Vowels

symbol	example
/iː/	eat /iːt/
/i/	happy /'hæpi/
/ɪ/	it /ɪt/
/e/	when /wen/
/æ/	cat /kæt/
/ɑː/	hard /hɑːd/
/ɒ/	not /nɒt/
/ɔː/	sort /sɔːt/; all /ɔːl/
/ʊ/	look /lʊk/
/uː/	too /tuː/
/ʌ/	cup /kʌp/
/ɜː/	first /fɜːst/; burn /bɜːn/
/ə/	about /ə'baʊt/; mother /'mʌðə(r)/
/eɪ/	day /deɪ/
/aɪ/	my /maɪ/
/ɔɪ/	boy /bɔɪ/
/aʊ/	now /naʊ/
/əʊ/	go /gəʊ/
/ɪə/	here /hɪə(r)/
/eə/	chair /tʃeə(r)/
/ʊə/	tourist /'tʊərɪst/

Consonants

symbol	example
/p/	pen /pen/
/b/	big /bɪg/
/t/	two /tuː/
/d/	day /deɪ/
/k/	keep /kiːp/; cup /kʌp/
/g/	get /get/
/tʃ/	choose /tʃuːz/
/dʒ/	job /dʒɒb/; average /'ævrɪdʒ/
/f/	fall /fɔːl/
/v/	very /'veri/
/θ/	think /θɪŋk/
/ð/	then /ðen/
/s/	see /siː/
/z/	zoo /zuː/; is /ɪz/
/ʃ/	shop /ʃɒp/; directions /də'rekʃənz/
/ʒ/	pleasure /'pleʒə(r)/; occasionally /ə'keɪʒənli/
/h/	who /huː/; how /haʊ/
/m/	meet /miːt/
/n/	no /nəʊ/
/ŋ/	sing /sɪŋ/; drink /drɪŋk/
/l/	long /lɒŋ/
/r/	right /raɪt/
/j/	yes /jes/
/w/	will /wɪl/

Stress

Stress is shown by a mark (') in front of the stressed syllable.

mother /'mʌðə(r)/   **average** /'ævrɪdʒ/
about /ə'baʊt/   **tonight** /tə'naɪt/

Irregular verbs

Infinitive	Simple Past	Participle
be /biː/	was /wəz, wɒz/, were /wə(r), wɜː(r)/	been /bɪn, biːn/
become /bɪ'kʌm/	became /bɪ'keɪm/	become /bɪ'kʌm/
begin /bɪ'gɪn/	began /bɪ'gæn/	begun /bɪ'gʌn/
bite /baɪt/	bit /bɪt/	bitten /'bɪtn/
blow /bləʊ/	blew /bluː/	blown /bləʊn/
break /breɪk/	broke /brəʊk/	broken /'brəʊkn/
bring /brɪŋ/	brought /brɔːt/	brought /brɔːt/
build /bɪld/	built /bɪlt/	built /bɪlt/
burn /bɜːn/	burnt /bɜːnt/	burnt /bɜːnt/
buy /baɪ/	bought /bɔːt/	bought /bɔːt/
can /k(ə)n, kæn/	could /kʊd/	been able /bɪn 'eɪbl/
catch /kætʃ/	caught /kɔːt/	caught /kɔːt/
choose /tʃuːz/	chose /tʃəʊz/	chosen /'tʃəʊzn/
come /kʌm/	came /keɪm/	come /kʌm/
cost /kɒst/	cost /kɒst/	cost /kɒst/
cut /kʌt/	cut /kʌt/	cut /kʌt/
do /dʊ, də, duː/	did /dɪd/	done /dʌn/
draw /drɔː/	drew /druː/	drawn /drɔːn/
dream /driːm/	dreamt /dremt/	dreamt /dremt/
drink /drɪŋk/	drank /dræŋk/	drunk /drʌŋk/
drive /draɪv/	drove /drəʊv/	driven /'drɪvn/
eat /iːt/	ate /et/	eaten /'iːtn/
fall /fɔːl/	fell /fel/	fallen /'fɔːlən/
feel /fiːl/	felt /felt/	felt /felt/
find /faɪnd/	found /faʊnd/	found /faʊnd/
fly /flaɪ/	flew /fluː/	flown /fləʊn/
forget /fə'get/	forgot /fə'gɒt/	forgotten /fə'gɒtn/
get /get/	got /gɒt/	got /gɒt/
give /gɪv/	gave /geɪv/	given /'gɪvn/
go /gəʊ/	went /went/	gone /gɒn/, been /bɪn, biːn/
grow /grəʊ/	grew /gruː/	grown /grəʊn/
hang up /'hæŋ 'ʌp/	hung up /'hʌŋ 'ʌp/	hung up /'hʌŋ 'ʌp/
have /(h)əv, hæv/	had /(h)əd, hæd/	had /hæd/
hear /hɪə(r)/	heard /hɜːd/	heard /hɜːd/
hit /hɪt/	hit /hɪt/	hit /hɪt/
hold /həʊld/	held /held/	held /held/
hurt /hɜːt/	hurt /hɜːt/	hurt /hɜːt/
keep /kiːp/	kept /kept/	kept /kept/
know /nəʊ/	knew /njuː/	known /nəʊn/
lead /liːd/	led /led/	led /led/